5/13/72

Music Reviewed
1940–1954

Music Reviewed

1940-1954

by **VIRGIL THOMSON**

VINTAGE BOOKS

A Division of Random House • *New York*

PREFACE

Once in the dear dead days beyond recall I worked for a newspaper. It was called The New York *Herald Tribune,* and its owner-editor was Ogden Reid. Its editorial page was liberal Republican, its readership reasonably cultured and well-to-do. With a circulation of only 450,000 (the weekly book section went to 750,000), it was in no sense a mass medium. On the contrary, it sought direct political influence, largely through family acquaintances, and aspired to intellectual distinction, the latter chiefly through its columnists—including in my day Walter Lippmann, Dorothy Thompson, Joseph Alsop—and its critical writers—Percy Hammond and Richard Watts for drama (later Walter Kerr), Royal Cortissoz (later Emily Genauer), for art, and my predecessors for music Henry Edward Krehbiel and Lawrence Gilman.

On that paper a writer's distinction was judged less by his leadership of public taste—high, low, or middlebrow—than by his skill in handling words, sentences, and paragraphs. Neither Ogden Reid nor Geoffrey Parsons, his chief aide in matters cultural, could be shocked by radical opinions on art, nor by the reactionary. Their attitude was that any informed statement *could* be published if it observed the amenities and was expressed in clear English.

My engagement as music critic of the *Herald Tribune,* which took place in October, 1940, was determined less, I think, by my musical accomplishments, though these were known, than by my particular way of writing about music (at once sassy and classy), which had earlier come to notice through *Vanity Fair* and the quarterly *Modern Music,* and just the year before in my book *The State of Music.* For

v

only such an assumption can explain why a musician so little schooled in daily journalism, a composer so committed to the modern, and a polemicist so contemptuous as myself of music's power structure should have been offered a post of that prestige. Still more, why the paper kept me on for fourteen years. No other would have done so, I am sure. My editors, during the first two stormy seasons, I know were not wholly happy about their choice. But after that they relaxed and began to purr. My column carried professional prestige; it even, they believed, sold papers.

The present assemblage of reviews and Sunday articles from that column paints a picture of music during World War II as reviewed from New York and points west, of music during the succeeding decade as observed from Europe as well. Many of the pieces in this omnibus volume have already appeared in books now out of print. Those written after 1950 are from the files. A chronological arrangement of them all has been adopted for narrative interest. And the publisher has encouraged me to cover the period copiously.

How wholly of the past that period can seem today only young people know. For them the world did not begin till 1950, or at whatever date around that time television became universal and obligatory. They still read books, I know; they certainly buy them. But there is little time for talking with their elders any more and small way except through reading to imagine what people's lives could possibly have been like before theirs began. This personal account of a prehistoric time—World War II and the ten years that followed—is offered therefore not only as information, but also for whatever shiver of strangeness it may provoke. And should some be surprised at what I got away with on a serious and responsible paper, if only in terms of uncustomary views and coverages, that very fact may help to bring the 1940s back as a golden time. Which they were, of course, as all decades tend in memory to become.

New York, 1966

Contents

vii

1942

1943

1944

Contents

1947

1948

Contents

1949

Music Reviewed
1940–1954

1940

AGE WITHOUT HONOR

¶ The Philharmonic-Symphony Society of New York opened its ninety-ninth season last evening in Carnegie Hall with John Barbirolli conducting. There was little that could be called festive about the occasion. The menu was routine, the playing ditto.

Beethoven's Overture to *Egmont* is a classic hors d'œuvre. Nobody's digestion was ever spoiled by it and no late comer has ever lost much by missing it. It was preceded, as is the custom nowadays, by our national anthem, gulped down standing, like a cocktail. I seem to remember that in 1917 and 1918 a sonorous arrangement of *The Star-Spangled Banner* by Walter Damrosch was current at these concerts. After so long a time I couldn't be sure whether that was the orchestration used last night. I rather think not. Last night's version seemed to have more weight than brilliance. It had the somber and spiritless sonority of the German military bands one hears in France these days. That somberness is due, I think, to an attempt to express authority through mere blowing and sawing in the middle ranges of the various instruments, rather than by the more classical method of placing every instrument in its most brilliant and grateful register in order to achieve the maximum of carrying power. I may be wrong about the reasons for it, but I think I am right about the general effect, unless my seat was in an acoustical dead spot of the hall, which I do not think it was. The anthem, to me, sounded logy and coarse; it lacked the buoyancy and the sweep that are its finest musical qualities.

Elgar's "Enigma" Variations are an academic effort not at all lacking in musical charm. I call them academic be-

3

cause I think the composer's interest in the musical devices
he was employing was greater than his effort toward a
direct and forceful expression of anything in particular. Like
most English composers, Elgar orchestrates accurately and
competently. Now, when a man can do anything accurately and competently he is always on the lookout for occasions to do that thing. In the Continental tradition of music-
writing orchestration is always incidental to expression,
to construction, to rhetoric. Many of the greatest composers—Chopin and Schumann, for instance—never bothered to become skillful at it in any major way. Others,
like Beethoven and Brahms, always kept its fanciness down
to the strict minimum of what expression needs. I've an
idea the Elgar Variations are mostly a pretext for orchestration, a pretty pretext and a graceful one, not without charm
and a modicum of sincerity, but a pretext for fancywork all
the same, for that massively frivolous patchwork in pastel
shades of which one sees such quantities in any intellectual British suburban dwelling.

Twenty years' residence on the European continent has
largely spared me Sibelius. Last night's Second Symphony
was my first in quite some years. I found it vulgar, self-indulgent, and provincial beyond all description. I realize that
there are sincere Sibelius-lovers in the world, though I must
say I've never met one among educated professional musicians. I realize also that this work has a kind of popular
power unusual in symphonic literature. Even Wagner
scarcely goes over so big on the radio. That populace-pleas-
ing power is not unlike the power of a Hollywood class-A
picture. Sibelius is in no sense a naïf; he is merely provincial.
Let me leave it at that for the present. Perhaps, if I have to
hear much more of him, I'll sit down one day with the
scores and really find out what is in them. Last night's
experience of one was not much of a temptation, however,
to read or sit through many more.

The concert as a whole, in fact, both as to program and
as to playing, was anything but a memorable experience. The
music itself was soggy, the playing dull and brutal. As a
friend remarked who had never been to one of these concerts before, "I understand now why the Philharmonic is
not a part of New York's intellectual life."

October 11, 1940

SONOROUS SPLENDORS

¶ And so, in cerulean sunshine and through indescribable splendors of autumnal leafage, to Boston—the Hub of the Universe, the Home of the Bean and the Cod. The home, as well, of the Boston Symphony Orchestra, the finest by all-around criteria of our resident instrumental foundations.

The sixtieth season of its concerts opened this afternoon with Vaughan Williams's *London Symphony*. I remember hearing the work nearly twenty years ago in that same Symphony Hall, Pierre Monteux conducting. It is the same piece it was then, too, in spite of some cuts operated by the composer. The first two movements are long, episodic, disjointed. The third is short, delicate, neatly sequential, compact, efficacious, charming. The finale is rich and varied. Its musical material is of high quality, its instrumental organization ample and solid. Also it is not without expressive power. Perhaps one is accustomed to the lengthiness and the slow reflective atmosphere of the symphony by the time one gets to this movement. The improvement in melodic material that manifests itself as the work progresses helps too. In any case, the last two of the symphony's four movements are anything but dull, which the first two are, and more than a little.

Making a program out of only that and Beethoven, out of one live Englishman and one dead German, classic and great though he be, is an obvious reference to current events and sympathies. The reference might have turned out in its effect to be not nearly so gracious as in its intention had those last two movements of the *London Symphony* not been in themselves so impressive, the finale so moving and deeply somber. It was written in 1913, I believe. It might have been written last month, so actual is its expressive content.

The Vaughan Williams symphony served also as a vehicle

for a display of orchestral virtuosity on the part of Dr. Koussevitzky and his men such as few orchestras are capable of offering their subscribers. Not that the piece itself is of any great difficulty; it is only reasonably hard to play, I imagine. But the Boston organization is in such fine fettle after its Berkshire season that every passage, any passage, no matter what, serves as a pretext for those constant miracles of precision and of exact equilibrium that a first-class modern orchestra is capable of.

Musically considered, these refinements are more of a delight in themselves than a help of any kind to the work played. They rather tend, especially in the fine molding and rounding off of phrases, to interrupt the music's continuity, to give it an exaggerated emphasis all over that obliterates any real emphasis or meaning that the score may imply. Only the toughest of the classics and the most glittery of the moderns can satisfactorily resist that kind of polish in execution.

The Beethoven Fifth Symphony resists it quite satisfactorily indeed. Dr. Koussevitzky, be it said to his credit, doesn't try to get away with too much careful modeling, either. Rather he puts his effort into a rhythmic exactitude that adds to Beethoven's dynamism a kind of monumental weight that is appropriate and good. When he tries to achieve more of that weight by forcing the strings beyond their optimum sonority, the result is not so good. The sound that comes out is less loud and less weighty than that which would have come out if the point of maximum resonance had not been surpassed.

All instrumentalists know this; and conductors, of course, know it too when they are calm enough to remember it. But at the back of every conductor's mind is a desire to make his orchestra produce a louder noise than anyone else's orchestra can produce, a really majestic noise, a Niagara Falls of sound. At some time in the course of nearly every concert this desire overpowers him. You can tell when it is coming on by the way he goes into a brief convulsion at that point. The convulsion is useful to the conductor, because it prevents his hearing what the orchestra really sounds like while his fit is on. But if you watch carefully from the house you will usually find that the sound provoked out of a group of exacerbated musicians by any

gesture of the convulsive type is less accurate in pitch and
less sonorous in decibels than a more objectively conducted
fortissimo.

It may seem graceless on my part to mention here a fault
almost no conductor is free of and to imply by so doing
that there is something particularly regrettable about Dr.
Koussevitzky's sharing it. I do mean to imply exactly that,
however, because somewhere, some time, some conductor
must get around to doing some serious work on the orchestral fortissimo comparable to the work that has already produced from our orchestras such delights of delicacy. And I
think it not unfair to suggest that perhaps our finest instrumental ensembles might be just the groups to profit most
by such an effort, that maybe it is even their duty to do
something about correcting the inefficiency that comes
from being overstrenuous.

October 12, 1940

VELVET PAWS

¶ There is a whispering campaign around New
York which would pretend that the Philadelphia Orchestra has gone off too, and seriously. Do not believe it. The
Philadelphia ensemble is as fine a group of orchestral players as exists anywhere, and the sounds that emerge from
their instruments are in every way worthy of the superb
musicians who play these instruments. Certainly last night's
performance showed no evidence, to my ear, of carelessness,
of indifference, or of sabotage.

Nowhere else is there such a string choir; one would like
to stroke its tone, as if the suavity of it were a visual and a
tactile thing, like pale pinky-brown velvet. If memory does
not trick, that luxurious and justly celebrated string-tone is
less forced, less hoarse and throaty than it was in the days
of the all too Slavic ex-King Leopold, now of Hollywood.

There are conductors more highly paid than Eugene

Ormandy, in all probability. There are certainly some more highly advertised. Very few musicians anywhere in the world, however, conduct an orchestra with such straightforwardness, such lively understanding, such dependable architectonics. No lackadaisical daisy he, and no Holy Roller either. His every gesture is civilized, sane, effective. The resultant musical performance is in consequence civilized, sane, and effective beyond all comparison with that of his more showily temperamental colleagues.

Last night's program opened with Mr. Ormandy's own reorchestration of a Handel piece here entitled Concerto for Orchestra in D major. For once let us praise a man for tampering with the classics. The score is as brilliant and gay and Handelian as one could wish. I found it no end jolly.

I also sat through another Sibelius symphony, No. 1, listening attentively. The melodic material was everywhere of inferior quality; the harmonic substructure was at its best unobtrusive, at its worst corny. The scoring seemed accurate and sure-fire. [It later came to my knowledge that Mr. Ormandy, like many another conductor, does not hesitate to alter a composer's scoring if he considers this to require improvement.]

The formal structure, such as there was, was a smooth piecing together of oddments, not unlike what is known to the film world as "cutting." As in a well-cut film, occasions for compensating the essential jerkiness of the flow were exploited whenever they could be found; at those moments something took place not unlike the "plugging" of a theme song.

There is not space here, nor time tonight, to go into the Sibelius matter any further than this. Suffice it to say that for the present I stick to my opinion of last Friday, which was that I found his music "vulgar, self-indulgent, and provincial." Respighi's brilliant but meretricious *Feste Romane* sounded last night like good clean musical fun in comparison.

October 16, 1940

GREAT MUSIC

¶ It is not easy to define what we mean by great music, but it is very easy to agree that the nineteenth century produced lots of it. It is also easy for musicians to agree that Frédéric Chopin was one of the great composers of that century, quite possibly the very greatest of them all. Last night a whole fistful of Chopin's greatest works were played in Carnegie Hall by one of our greatest living pianists, Artur Rubinstein.

Mr. Rubinstein is a delight to watch as well as to hear. Though he is as fastidious as one could wish in his musical execution, his platform manner is straightforward, well bred, businesslike. His delicacy is delicate, his forte powerful, his melodic tone rich and deep. He can play loud and soft and fast and slow without interrupting the music's rhythmic progress. He is a master of his instrument and of the music he plays, and he finds no reason for attracting undue attention to anything else. He is authoritative, direct, and courteous, like the captain of a transatlantic liner.

His pianism is of the close-to-the-key school. Hence the good marksmanship. Hence, also, its lack of any bright, pearly brilliance. His arms and torso are of stocky build. Hence the power of his climaxes, the evenness of his pianissimo. He is Polish by birth, if I mistake not. Hence his complete at-homeness in Chopin's music, like a host in his father's house.

He is most at home in straightforward pieces, like the études, and in long, massive works like the sonatas, the ballades, the scherzos, works that call to action his mastery of dramatic line, of architectural sweep. He plays the tricky mazurkas and nocturnes with less ease. They don't give him enough room to move around in, and so he rather streamlines them than builds them.

His rubato is of the Paderewski tradition. I do not know

how that tradition got started, but I do not think it comes from Chopin. It sounds Viennese to me.

Chopin's prescription for rubato-playing, which is almost word for word Mozart's prescription for playing an accompanied melody, is that the right hand should take liberties with the time values, while the left hand remains rhythmically unaltered. This is exactly the effect you get when a good blues singer is accompanied by a good swing band. It is known to the modern world as *le style hot.* The Paderewski tradition of Chopin-playing is more like the Viennese waltz style, in which the liberties in the melody line are followed exactly in the accompaniment, the two elements keeping always together and performing at the same time a flexible distortion of strict rhythm that manages by its very flexibility to keep the procedure from seeming arbitrary or the continuity from collapsing. Mr. Rubinstein is skillful with this kind of rubato. He keeps the music surging. But I don't believe for a moment it resembles anything Frédéric Chopin ever did or had in mind.

On more than this count does Rubinstein make one think of Paderewski. Among his encores (he played the C-sharp minor Waltz and the Étude for the Little Finger also) he did such a rendition of the A-flat Grande Polonaise as it has not been my pleasure to hear in many a day. Such speed, such power, such fury, such truly magnificent transcending both of the pianoforte's limitations and of his own customary accuracy were the very substance of Paderewski's greatness. They were Mr. Rubinstein's last night, a final jewel in his already laureate crown.

October 26, 1940

SILK-UNDERWEAR MUSIC

¶ Robert Russell Bennett's *Hexapoda,* musical sketches of the jitterbug world, are pretty music. Also they are evocative of swing music without being themselves swing music or any imitation of swing music. They manage with skill and integrity to use swing formulas as a décor for the musical depiction of those nerve reflexes and soul states that swing-lovers commonly manifest when exposed to swing music. They are, in addition, expertly written for the violin. They come off, as the phrase has it, like a million dollars.

Jascha Heifetz's whole recital rather reminded one of large sums of money like that. If ever I heard luxury expressed in music it was there. His famous silken tone, his equally famous double-stops, his well-known way of hitting the true pitch squarely in the middle, his justly remunerated mastery of the musical marshmallow, were like so many cushions of damask and down to the musical ear.

He is like Sarah Bernhardt, with her famous "small voice of purest gold" and her mastery of the wow-technique. First-class plays got in her way; she seldom appeared in one after thirty. Heifetz is at his best in short encore pieces (the Bennetts are beautifully that) and in lengthy chestnuts like Spohr's *Gesangscene*, where every device of recitative style, of melodic phrase turning, and of brilliant passage work is laid out, like the best evening clothes and the best jewelry, for Monsieur to put his elegant person into. No destination, no musical or emotional significance, is implied.

The Richard Strauss Sonata, a work of the author's early manhood, lacks none of that composer's characteristic style. The themes could only be his (albeit one was practically straight out of *Carmen*), bombastic, second-rate (I except the one that starts the last movement, which is bombastic and first-rate), inflated, expressing nothing but the composer's fantastic facility, his jubilant gusto at writing music. Mr. Heifetz's execution of this was almost embarrassingly refined.

Of his Mozart, the less said the better. It is of the school that makes a diminuendo on every feminine phrase-ending, that never plays any phrase through with the same weight, that thinks Mozart's whole aim was to charm, that tries so hard to make out of the greatest musician the world has ever known (those are Joseph Haydn's words) something between a sentimental Pierrot and a Dresden china clock that his music ends by sounding affected, frivolous, and picayune. If that is Mozart, I'll buy a hat and eat it.

I realize that my liking or not liking what Mr. Heifetz plays and how he plays it is a matter of no import to the stellar spaces in which he moves. But it happens that I did go to the concert last night and that I did observe pretty carefully his virtuosity. It was admirable and occasionally very, very beautiful. The fellow can fiddle. But he sacrifices everything to polish. He does it knowingly. He is justly admired and handsomely paid for it. To ask anything else of him is like asking tenderness of the ocelot.

Four-starred super-luxury hotels are a legitimate commerce. The fact remains, however, that there is about their machine-tooled finish and empty elegance something more than just a trifle vulgar.

October 31, 1940

CORRECT AND BEAUTIFUL

¶ Straightforwardness on the concert platform is something rarely encountered except on the part of children and of the very greatest artists. Straightforwardness in musical execution is met with practically only on the part of great artists. Kirsten Flagstad is straightforward in her platform manner and in her musical interpretations.

She is not, for that, an unsubtle musician. Nor is her majestic voice an unsubtle instrument. All the shading is there that one might wish and all the refinement of expression that lieder repertory requires, which is much. But such an assured mistress is she of her voice, and so clear is her comprehension of the songs she sings, that she is not constrained to seek to please her listeners by any trick of willful charm or cuteness or feigned emotion.

In consequence, she can afford the highest luxury of the concert stage, which is to sing the songs of Brahms and Grieg and Hugo Wolf and of our American song-writers as simply and as candidly as Miss Helen Hayes, say, might read Shakespeare's sonnets. No intonation is false, no word un-

clear, no sentiment either under- or overstated. By eschewing exploitation of her personality, she warms all hearts to
that personality. By not feeling obliged to give her operatic all to every tender melody, she offers us each song as if
it were a living thing in our hands, like a bird.

Our century has known great mistresses of vocalism
and many intelligent interpreters of songs. I doubt if there
has existed within the memory of living musicians another
singer so gifted as to voice, so satisfying as to taste, and
withal such mistress of her vocal instrument as Miss Flagstad. Some singers sing by nature, others take lessons for
years. It is scarcely more than once or twice in a century
that any vocalist ever masters his voice with the kind of
mastery that pianists have of the pianoforte, masters it seriously and completely, while he is still in command of all his
vocal resources. Mostly they sing by ear and learn to use
the voice correctly only after its best notes are worn out
and gone. Miss Flagstad has a great voice now which she
handles as if it were a race horse she had bred and trained.

She can sing loud and she can sing soft. She can sing fast
and she can sing slow. She can sing high, low, in strict
time, in free time, with clear words, on pitch, swelling or
diminishing in volume. This, plus a clear comprehension
of the human significance of the music one wishes to sing,
is the whole art of singing.

Her voice must not have been an easy one to train,
either. Her high, low, and middle registers are noticeably
different in timbre. Her scale is as smooth as that of a flute
or trumpet; but her ranges, heard separately, are as sharply
differentiated as the ranges are of any other wind instrument. One of the most satisfying qualities of her singing
is the way her chest-voice sounds like chest-voice, her head-
voice like head-voice, and her middle-voice like ordinary
speech, while at the same time the transition from one
range to another is so even as to be virtually imperceptible
excepting when there is a skip in the melodic line.

Edwin McArthur accompanied from memory. He gave
support, allowed flexibility, was in general straightforward
and highly pleasant to hear. He was more like a partner
in a duet than like the more usual obsequious accompanist.

November 9, 1940

COMPLETE AUTHORITY

¶ Josef Lhevinne seems to have replaced the late Leopold Godowsky as the acknowledged master of pianoforte mastery. A full house paid him homage last night at Carnegie Hall as he, in turn, paid his audience the honor of executing a distinguished program of the piano's masterworks with authority and no playing down to anybody.

A more satisfactory academicism can scarcely be imagined. Mr. Lhevinne's performance, especially of the Schumann Toccata and the Chopin Études, was both a lesson and an inspiration. He made no effort to charm or to seduce or to preach or to impress. He played as if he were expounding to a graduate seminar: "This is the music, and this is the way to play it."

Any authoritative execution derives as much of its excellence from what the artist does not do as from what he does. If he doesn't do anything off color at all, he is correctly said to have taste. Mr. Lhevinne's taste is as authoritative as his technical method. Not one sectarian interpretation, not one personal fancy, not one stroke below the belt, not a sliver of ham, mars the universal acceptability of his readings. Everything he does is right and clear and complete. Everything he doesn't do is the whole list of all the things that mar the musical executions of lesser men.

This is not to say that tenderness and poetry and personal warmth and fire are faults of musical style, though they frequently do excuse a faulty technique. I am saying that Mr. Lhevinne does not need them. They would mar his style; hence he eschews them. He eschews them because his concept of piano music is an impersonal one. It is norm-centered; it is for all musical men. Any intrusion of the executant's private soul would limit its appeal, diminish its authority.

Thus it is that Mr. Lhevinne's performance is worthy of the honorable word *academic*. And if he seems to some a

little distant, let us remind ourselves that remoteness is,
after all, inevitable to those who inhabit Olympus.

November 18, 1940

MUSIC FROM CHICAGO

¶ The Chicago Symphony Orchestra sounds like a
French orchestra. Its fiddle tone, thin as a wedge, espouses
by resemblance that of oboe and trumpet, absorbs nothing,
stands clear in the orchestral bouquet. All the instrumental
sounds stand clear and separate. Their harmony is one of
juxtaposition, not of absorptive domination. As in an eighteenth-century flower picture, all is distinct, nothing
crushed.

Brahms's Third is the best built, the most continuous of
his symphonies; and it contains, on the whole, the strongest
melodic material of the four. With no weakness of structure
to conceal and no gracelessness in its musical content to dis-
turb the clarity of its message, it offered to Frederick Stock
occasion for one of those rare and blessed readings in
which the music seems to play itself. Especially the end
movements, the first and the last, floated on a Viennese lilt,
pastoral, poetic, and effortlessly convincing. The passage
in the finale was particularly happy where the winds play
sustained harmonic progressions which the violins caress
with almost inaudible tendrils of sound, little wiggly figures
that dart like silent goldfish around a rock.

Roy Harris's *American Creed* invites kidding, as all of
his programistically prefaced works do. If we take his
music as he offers it, however, we risk refusing a quite
good thing. No composer in the world, not even in Italy
or Germany, makes such shameless use of patriotic feelings
to advertise his product. One would think, to read his
prefaces, that he had been awarded by God, or at least by
popular vote, a monopolistic privilege of expressing our
nation's deepest ideals and highest aspirations. And when

the piece so advertised turns out to be mostly not very
clearly orchestrated schoolish counterpoint and a quite
skimpy double fugue (neither of which has any American
connotation whatsoever), one is tempted to put the whole
thing down as insincere and a bad joke.

The truth, however, is other. Mr. Harris, though the
bearer of no exceptional melodic gifts and the possessor of
no really thorough musical schooling, has an unquench-
able passion to know and to use all the procedures of musical composition. He has pondered over the medieval
French melodic line and over the problem of continuous
(non-repeating) melodic development, and he has come
by this road to understand where the crucial problem lies
in America's musical coming-of-age. That problem would
seem to be how shall we absorb all of European musical
culture rather than merely that current in Vienna between
the years 1790 and 1890. Harris has learned by meditation
and hard work that if we expect to produce music worthy
to rank with that of the Viennese masters we must go
through a selective evolution comparable to that which
took place in Europe for at least three centuries before the
miracle of Vienna occurred.

He knows that musical material, even folklore material,
is as international as musical form and syntax, that local-
ism is no more than one man's colorful accent. He knows
this so well that he avoids, as though it were of the devil,
any colorful accent whatsoever. He puts his musical effort
on serious problems of material and of form. He does not
always get anywhere in his music; but it is serious music,
much more serious music than his blurbs would lead one to
believe.

He is monotonous in his material and in his form. (All
his pieces begin alike.) But every now and then something
really happens. It happened last night in the closing pages
of both movements of his *Creed*. It was unexpected, original (in spite of the Stravinsky allusion), and beautiful. And
it had exactly as much to do with America as mountains or
mosquitoes or childbirth have, none of which is anybody's
property and none of which has any ethnic significance
whatsoever.

November 21, 1940

THEATER AND RELIGION

¶ Managers refer to him as The Maestro. Orchestral players call him The Old Man in much the same spirit of reverence and fear with which persons resident on the banks of the Mississippi never use any other name for that mighty stream than simply The River. This department had anticipated employing the polite but noncommittal form, Mr. Toscanini. After last Saturday night's rendition of the Verdi Te Deum and Requiem, we feel more like shouting to the city: "The Old Man is back!"

No better piece could he have chosen than the Verdi Requiem to make us appreciate his qualities as a master of musical theater. Gaudy, surprising, sumptuous, melodramatic, and grand is Verdi's homage to Italy's poet and his own dear friend, Manzoni. No religious musical work of the last century is more sincerely or more completely what it is. Theatrical religion or religious theater? Let him answer who could tell us the same of nineteenth-century Neapolitan church architecture. Nowhere as in Naples does the eye find such constant verification of what the ear tells us when we listen to Palestrina, to Bach, to Mozart—namely, that to the sincerely religious there is no difference between sacred and secular style.

Verdi, though not a particularly pious man, was a sincere Catholic; he was also a man of the theater and an Italian. His Requiem is as sincere a piece of theatrical Italian Catholicism as has ever been written. Sincere Protestants often find it shocking. Sincere nonbelievers are likely to find it comic. But so might any one find the Dies Iræ itself who had no stomach for horror.

The only sound aesthetic standard I know of that covers all works and epochs is that anything is all right if it is enough so. That is to say that extremism in art, when it really is extreme, and middle-of-the-road normality, when it is really clear and comprehensible to all men, carry in their very extremism and universality the hallmarks of their authenticity. The Verdi Requiem has never raised any eyebrows in Naples (with which city, the seat of Verdi's greatest operatic successes, I like to identify it spiritually) or even in Milan (where it was first performed, in 1874). The question of its acceptance into the musical tradition of Protestant America is still, on account of its extreme theatricality, undecided.

As music that is not only very beautiful in itself, but that is also really "enough so," I give it my vote. I have not always been of that mind; I have long considered it an oddity of which the intrinsic worth scarcely justified the difficulties of a proper execution. After Saturday's performance I have no reserves.

The Maestro conducted it as if it were no more complicated than the "Miserere" from *Il Trovatore* and no less splendidly compelling than *Otello* or *La Traviata*. The Westminster Choir, handsomely gowned in white satin and violet velvet of ecclesiastical cut, sang perfectly. But perfectly. The soloists, Zinka Milanov, Bruna Castagna, Jussi Bjoerling, and Nicola Moscona, sang like stars from some celestial opera house. The two ladies merit each a mark of 99 per cent for their rendition of the impossible Agnus Dei passage in parallel octaves unaccompanied. The kettle-drummer, whose name I do not know, merits mention in heaven for his two-stick, unison explosions in the Dies Iræ and for the evenness of his Verdian *ppppp* rolls elsewhere.

Worthy of mention, too, is the implied homage to a regretted musician in the choice of this particular program by Mr. Toscanini to raise money for the Alma Gluck Zimbalist Memorial of the Roosevelt Hospital Development Fund. Just as the great expatriate Italian could have chosen no work more advantageous for himself to conduct, I can think of no more appropriate piece of music with which to honor the memory of a much-loved opera singer than Verdi's sincerely and superbly operatic Requiem.

November 25, 1940

PIPE-ORGAN OBSESSION

¶ It becomes increasingly clear to this listener that Leopold Stokowski's concept of orchestral music is derived from organ-playing. He cares nothing for the spontaneous collaboration that is the joy of ensemble players, the kind of perfect concord that swingsters call being "in the groove" and that French instrumentalists refer to as "the little blue flame." He treats his men as if they were 110 stops of a concert organ, each complete with swell-box, all voiced for solo use and mutually adjusted for producing balanced chords of any timbre at any degree of loudness or softness.

His latest seating arrangement is an adaptation to orchestral uses of pipe-organ antiphony. He long ago did away with the classical symphonic antiphony of first violins on one side against seconds on the other, through both of which pierce succeeding layers of supporting woodwind, brass, and percussion. He has his musicians arranged now with all the strings massed at back center as if these were a single homogeneous body of foundation tone, like Great Organ diapasons, with woodwinds out in front, like a Choir Organ or *positif,* and with the brasses at the right and left downstage corners, like the heavy solo reeds of a French organ, the horns playing antiphonally on one side against the trumpets and trombones on the other.

This massive acoustico-architectural layout established, he proceeds to play on the whole thing with his bare fingers as if it were a solo instrument. Nothing is left to the musicians' personal taste or feeling. He even went so far last night as to mold William Kincaid's flute passages by hand, an insulting procedure toward an artist of Mr. Kincaid's stature, but a necessary procedure for producing the kind of one-man musical performance that Mr. Stokowski has in mind.

He carries his pipe-organ obsession to the extent of imitating organ rhythm, even. Now the organ, a mechanical wind instrument, knows no lilt or swing. It executes an even scale and an evenly progressive crescendo or diminuendo. It can play *sforzando* and *fortepiano,* but its accent knows no beat. Its rhythm is entirely quantitative, a question of long and short note-values, never of beat-stresses varied within the measure.

To have made Brahms's Haydn Variations, with their Viennese lilt and only occasional passage of non-accentual music that sets off by contrast their otherwise steadily swinging rhythm, into something that sounded like nothing so much as a skillful organ transcription of these same Variations is a triumph of will power as well as of conductorial skill. The thoroughness and clarity of the technical procedures by which this deformation was operated make any questioning of its aesthetic value seem like quibbling, since, as always with Stokowski, the means employed, no matter what aesthetic end is achieved by them, are a contribution to orchestral technique.

It is just as well that he chose for his technical exhibition last night music that could take it. Beethoven's *Leonora* No. 3, Brahms's Haydn Variations, and Siegfried's Death Music from *Die Götterdämmerung* are all foolproof and virtuoso-proof. No matter how you play them, they sound.

Shostakovich's Sixth Symphony, like all the later works of that gifted and facile composer, is pretty hard to conceal, too. It is clear, obvious, effective, old-fashioned. It is not, perhaps, as successfully pulled off as his First and Fifth. Its allegiance seems to be divided between a romanticized, and hence attenuated, neo-classicism and a full-blooded Muscovite orientalism à la Borodin. Each movement begins with a gesture of goodwill toward the lately reputable International Style and goes off as quickly as possible into the atmospheric market-place-and-landscape painting that Russians have always loved. It is a pleasant piece and not without a certain concentration. If it were signed by an American composer, say Harl McDonald or Walter Piston, it would be classifiable as good salable academicism.

December 4, 1940

THE VERDI CASE

¶ Hearing Verdi's *The Masked Ball* at the Metropolitan Opera House has led me to wonder why that work, so satisfying orchestrally and so brilliant in its vocal writing, has never moved much the layman's heart and why, even among musicians, it is more admired than deeply loved.

It is easy enough to pick flaws in the book, for these are many and grave. The heroine has no character. The hero has little more, not enough to make him interesting. An opera can get away with a vague tenor (Mozart's *Don Giovanni* does) if the heroine is a live woman and the villain sufficiently wicked. It is hard to interest an audience in two lovers whose personalities are so imprecise and whose passion is so trivial.

The lovers are further thrown into shadow by the lady's husband, Renato. This future regicide is an extremely interesting person. He is kind, loyal, and passionate. All one's sympathy goes out to him. It seems a pity that such a tactful and forbearing spouse, once he had got his silly wife home from a midnight expedition where she had gone to gather a magic herb some fortune-teller had told her about and where she had ended by compromising her husband in front of his political enemies, it seems really too bad that after their long walk home in the snow he didn't sit down with her and quietly, by some straight-from-the-shoulder questioning, find out what really had or hadn't been going on and then decide on some sensible course of action. I was sorry to see a good man's home broken up so uselessly.

Oscar, the king's frivolous page, whose indiscretions betray his master's interests every time he opens his mouth, was a favorite of Verdi himself among his dramatic creations. Musically this preference is understandable, be-

cause rarely has a composer expressed so well frivolity and
empty-headedness as they are in Oscar's staccato coloratura airs. The trouble with this role nowadays is the necessity of its being sung by a woman. Italian stage conventions are more precise than ours about femininity and mas-
culinity. Consequently travesty is easier to get away with
in Italy than here. It is virtually impossible on the Anglo-
Saxon stage for a woman to represent an effeminate youth
without seeming merely to be playing a male role ineffec-
tually.

The opera's libretto is not its only fault. Its very musical strength is its weakness. The expressive nature of the
orchestral accompaniments, the appropriateness of the contrapuntal writing, the sustained characterization of individual parts in the concerted numbers, the thematic unity of
the whole work, are justly celebrated. Neither Meyerbeer
nor Rossini ever etched a theatrical design more deeply.
Richard Wagner himself, though a more sumptuous painter
of psychological traits, was less accurate in his timing.
Verdi did an A-1 professional job on *The Masked Ball*.

But music never lives by its professional quality. It lives
by its tunes. And the tunes in *The Masked Ball* are every
one of them tricky. Let us except the baritone aria "Eri
tu," Oscar's "Saper vorreste," and just possibly the Laugh-
ing Chorus. All the others fall somewhere between broad
simplicity and full, complex expression.

La Traviata and *Il Trovatore* are full of simple melodies
that depict character and feeling in elementary but universally acceptable music. Wagner, at his best, and Mozart
wrote melodies that express the same broad values but that
comment more profoundly on the drama at the same time.

The orchestral accompaniment of *The Masked Ball* is a
more elaborate picture of the play than is the orchestral
accompaniment of any opera Verdi has written. It sounds
like the best French contemporary work, bearing little resemblance to the previously current Italian style that Wagner described as "making the orchestra sound like a big guitar." The trios, quartets, and other ensemble pieces are
equally fine. The melodic material all these are made out
of is simply not good enough. The tunes are pretty—little
more. They lack the grand and elementary plainness of
those in the earlier works. And they lack the penetrating

accuracy of great stage music. They are affected and soft, like the libretto.

One could put the blame for the whole trouble on the libretto if one didn't know that Verdi's career was always dominated by the same problem. In *Aïda* he went back to broad writing. But he was obsessed by the desire to make Italian operas that would be as penetrating psychologically as French operas and as sumptuous musically as the German. He mastered psychological penetration instrumentally and wrote, in *Otello* and *Falstaff*, two of the most sumptuous musical works of the century. He could write big simple melodies and magnificent vocal bravura passages. He never learned how to build a melodic line that would be at the same time monumental and penetratingly expressive of the text. This inability to interpret character delicately is what gives to *Otello* and *Falstaff* a certain air, in spite of their instrumental delights, of banality. The same inability gives to *La Traviata* its rough grandeur.

The lack of really delicate delicacy in Verdi's melodic contours, compensated though it be by pungent orchestration and the soundest dramatic building, makes the whole body of his work seem just a bit commercial. One is more often tempted, in fact, to take off one's hat to his triumphs of pure musical theater than one is to bare one's head before any revelations of the subtleties of human sentiment or the depths of the human heart.

December 8, 1940

CONFUSION ORDERED

¶ Much has been said about the stupidity and the useless complexity of *The Magic Flute*'s libretto. It has certainly never made much sense to this reviewer. Last night's performance at the Juilliard School made it seem as simple as a Sunday-school pageant. And when all is said and done, that is about what *The Magic Flute* is. It is an al-

legorical fairy tale in praise of Freemasonry and the broth-
erhood of man.

The locale of the action and the identity of the characters have usually been represented as fanciful. Tamino,
being a Japanese prince, has been put into every imaginable
kind of Oriental armor. Zoroaster is classically got up Per-
sian. Pamina is likely to be vague in style. And the scenery
is normally Biedermeier Egyptian. Is it any wonder we
don't quite get the plot?

Frederick Kiesler, the present production's designer, has
taken for granted that calling the high priest Zoroaster and
at the same time having him pray to Isis and Osiris was not
necessarily an anachronism on the part of the authors, but
was rather simply the routine language of the Masonic
Lodges, which pretended to trace their origin to Egypt and
which certainly welcomed into their fold believers from all
religions. The prince's Japanese birth he takes to be a literary masquerade, since it is highly probable that he represents the Emperor Joseph II, recently inducted to the
Lodge, as the Queen of the Night represents Joseph's
mother, Maria Theresa, who never approved of Freemasonry.

Kiesler has taken everybody out of masquerade except
the Queen, though Mr. Kiesler informs me that his original
project required that the Queen of the Night be dressed to
represent Maria Theresa. Tamino, Pamina, and the Priests
are represented as eighteenth-century gentlefolk. The Bird-
Man and Bird-Woman he has left in their feathers, as indeed they were left by the plot to live out their simple lives
without the enlightenment of Masonic initiation.

He has used a permanent stage-set, indicating changes
of locale by changing painted pictures that are framed in a
sort of late eighteenth-century pavilion, upstage center, and
indicating changes of weather by projecting clouds, flames,
and other atmospheric effects on a cyclorama at the back.
As a result we know not only that we are dealing with real
people in the chief characters, but that these are living
through a series of adventures and trials that take place in
various real sites and climatic conditions, rather than
merely going through a series of pretexts for singing on a
stage a diversified series of songs in fancy dress.

It has long been a conviction of this reviewer that the

best theatrical results are rarely obtained from professional stage designers, but rather from artists who practice professionally the more basic plastic techniques. To be specific, from oil painters, sculptors, and architects. The only real renovations of staging that have taken place in the last thirty years have been due to the collaboration of constructivist sculptors, cubist and post-cubist painters with opera and ballet. Kiesler has approached *The Magic Flute* as an architect. He has made the decorations clear and functional, and he has given them an unbelievable architectural solidity and a high seriousness of expression. Their lack of meretriciousness is astounding.

There is no malice in my spending my space today on the visual aspects of last night's *The Magic Flute*. The singing was excellent, the orchestra excellent, the whole auditory presentation an honor to the school and a pleasure to it hearers (and hearing *The Magic Flute* is no mean pleasure). But it does seem to me that there is more news value in Kiesler's having made the opera make sense than there could be in anybody's having sung it no matter how well.

December 12, 1940

MOZART'S LEFTISM

¶ Persons of humanitarian, libertarian, and politically liberal orientation have for a century used Beethoven as their musical standard-bearer. I employ the word *use* deliberately. Because it is hard to find much in Beethoven's life or music—beyond the legend of his having torn up the dedication of his "Heroic" Symphony to Napoleon when that defender of the French Revolution allowed himself to be crowned Emperor—to justify the adoration in which he has always been held by political liberals.

Wagner, yes. Wagner was full of political theory; and he got himself exiled from Germany (losing also his conducting post at the Dresden Opera) for participating in the unsuccessful revolutionary uprising of 1848 beside his friend, the philosopher of anarchy, Mikhail Bakunin. If he had not gone pseudo-Christian and jingo at the end of his life, he would probably be venerated by members of the Third and Fourth Internationals in the same way that Beethoven is worshipped (rather than really listened to) by adherents of the Second.

Mozart, both his life and his works inform us, was more continuously occupied than either of these other composers with what we nowadays call "leftism" (not to be confused with "left wing," Communist Party euphemism meaning the Communist Party).

Mozart was not, like Wagner, a political revolutionary. Nor was he, like Beethoven, an old fraud who just talked about human rights and dignity but who was really an irascible, intolerant, and scheming careerist, who allowed himself the liberty, when he felt like it, of being unjust toward the poor, lickspittle toward the rich, dishonest in business, unjust and unforgiving toward the members of his own family.

As a touring child prodigy Mozart was pampered by royalty, though he worked hard all the time. But after the age of twelve he was mostly pushed around by the great, beginning with Hieronymus Colloredo, Archbishop of Salzburg, going on through Grimm and Madame d'Epinay in Paris, and ending with the Emperor Francis I of Austria. He took it like a little man, too. Few musical lives bear witness to a more complete integrity of character in sickness and in health, in riches and in poverty, such little riches as he knew.

Mozart was not embittered by illness and adversity; he was tempered by them. Furthermore, he was acquainted with French libertarian ideas, having been fully exposed to these in Paris, where he spent his twenty-third year. But he was never at any time a revolter. He was an absorber and a builder. He never tried to throw out of the window his Catholic faith or his allegiance to his Emperor, in spite of much unpleasant treatment from both Church and State. He merely added to them his belief in human rights and the practice of Masonic fellowship as he had learned these in Paris and in Vienna.

The three great theater-pieces of his maturity, *Die Zauberflöte*, *Le Nozze di Figaro*, and *Don Giovanni,* are all of them celebrations of this faith and fellowship, of what we should call liberalism or "leftism" and what the eighteenth century called Enlightenment.

Die Zauberflöte, in spite of its obscure libretto, is the easiest of these to grasp. Mozart, like practically all other self-respecting men in those days, like the French King and his own Emperor Josef II, and, like our own George Washington and Benjamin Franklin, was a Freemason. Freemasonry was not the anti-Catholic secret society it became in nineteenth-century America, and it was far from being the conspiracy of job-holding that it developed into under France's Third Republic. It was more like Rotary. Something between that, perhaps, and organized Marxism. It softened the manners and broadened the viewpoint of all classes in society. Even in Austria, the most retarded country in Europe politically, its fellowship was practiced, at least after Maria Theresa's death, without interference or suppression.

On account of changes that were operated upon the libretto of *Die Zauberflöte* during its composition and mounting, the fairy-story allegory it tells has always been considered obscure. Obscure it is in its details, if you like, in its mixing up of Zoroaster with Egypt and Japan. But surely its main moral is clear, that married happiness and dignity are to be won only by renouncing pride and snobbery and by conducting oneself as an ethical being. And certainly its textual references to liberty, equality, and fraternity are unmistakable.

If this were Mozart's only work with ideas of the kind in it, we could discount its humanitarian content as we discount the stilted verses of *Idomeneo*. But it is not. *Figaro,* to Beaumarchais's satirical play, was revolutionary in its egalitarianism; and *Don Giovanni* is the most humane and tolerant piece about sacred and profane love that anybody has ever written.

In Lorenzo da Ponte, who made the libretti for *Figaro* and *Don Giovanni*, Mozart had a collaborator ideal to his taste. They worked together so closely that the libretti seem almost to have been made to fit the music, the music to come spontaneously out of the libretti. With a da Ponte text he was able to do completely what he was able later to do only partially with Schikaneder's fairy tale *Die Zauberflöte*—namely, to transform the whole thing into an expression of his own ideas.

The reason why the "meaning" of the two more naturalistic works is less easy to grasp than that of the fairy tale is that the humanitarianism of the fairy tale is its only easily comprehensible element. In the others practically everything is stated directly *but* the composer's attitude toward his characters.

Beaumarchais's *The Marriage of Figaro* is straight social satire, a poking fun at the nobility for not being noble enough. It is closer to pamphlet journalism than it is to humane letters. It is what we might call a snappy and sophisticated little number. Mozart and da Ponte changed all the accents, made everybody human, gave to all the characters, to masters and servants alike, the human dignity of their faults and of their virtues. They produced out of a piece of propaganda that was scarcely literature one of the most touching pictures of eighteenth-century life that exists.

Don Giovanni is a tragicomedy about sacred and profane love. Its dramatic tone is of the most daring. It begins with a dirty comic song, goes on to a murder, a series of seductions, a sort of detective-story pursuit of the murderer in which one of the previously seduced ladies plays always a high comedy role; a party, a ballet, a supper scene with music on the stage, a supernatural punishment of the villain, and a good-humored finale in which everybody reappears but the villain.

The villain is charming; the ladies are charming; everybody in the play is charming. Everybody has passion and character; everybody acts according to his passion and his character. Nobody is seriously blamed (except by the other characters) for being what he is or for acting the way he acts. The play implies a complete fatalism about love and about revenge. *Don Giovanni* gets away with everything, Donna Elvira with nothing. Donna Anna never succeeds in avenging her father's unjust murder. Punishment of this is left to supernatural agencies. Love is not punished at all. Its sacred (or at least its honorable) manifestations and its profane (or libertine) practice are shown as equally

successful and satisfactory. The only unsatisfied person in
the play is Donna Elvira, who is not at all displeased with
herself for having sinned. She is merely chagrined at having been abandoned.

Mozart is kind to these people and pokes fun at every
one of them. The balance between sympathy and observation is so neat as to be almost miraculous. *Don Giovanni*
is one of the funniest shows in the world and one of the
most terrifying. It is all about love, and it kids love to a
fare-ye-well. It is the world's greatest opera and the world's
greatest parody of opera. It is a moral entertainment so
movingly human that the morality gets lost before the play
is scarcely started.

Why do I call it leftist? I don't. I say the nearest thing
we know to eighteenth-century Enlightenment is called today liberalism or leftism. But there is not a liberal or leftist
alive who could have conceived, much less written, that
opera. It is the work of a Christian man who knew all
about the new doctrinaire ideas and respected them, who
practiced many of the new precepts proudly, and who belonged to a humanitarian secret society; but who had also
suffered as few men suffer in this world. He saw life clearly,
profoundly, amusingly, and partook of it kindly. He expressed no bitterness, offered no panacea to its ills. His life
was the most unspeakable slavery; he wrote as a free man.
He was not a liberal; he was liberated. And his acquaintance, through doctrine and practice, with all the most advanced ideas of his day in politics, in ethics, in music, was not
for nothing in the achievement of that liberation.

December 15, 1940

BACH GOES TO CHURCH

¶ The closer the performing conditions for Sebastian Bach's concerted music are approximated to those of
early eighteenth-century provincial Germany the more

that music sounds like twentieth-century American swing. The exactitude with which a minimum time unit is kept un-altered at all times, the persistence of this unit as one of exactly measured length rather than of pulsation, the omni-presence of the harpsichord's ping, like a brush on a cym-bal, the constant employment of wiggly counterpoint and staccato bass, all make it a matter of preference between anachronisms whether one puts it that Bach has gone to town or that some of the more scholarly jitterbugs of the town have wandered into a church.

Last night's performance at All Souls Church of the *Christmas Oratorio* was full of swing and gusto. The solo-ists, particularly the ladies, sang their arias to the accompa-niment of solo woodwinds as neatly and enthusiastically as if they were playing instrumental duets with Benny Good-man. The gentlemen sang the magnificently dramatic rec-itatives with clarity and dispatch. The chorus came in on the big numbers as if these were the gayest of contrapuntal merry-go-rounds, which indeed they are; the high trum-pets played out of tune, as they must have in Leipzig at Bach's own Thomaskirche; and the inexorable rhythm of Mr. Ralph Kirkpatrick's harpsichord sustained the whole with vigor and brightness.

It was the conductor Arthur Mendel's intention to repro-duce as closely as possible the sonorities of what may be called the world premieres of the work, for the six Can-tatas that it comprises were never executed under Bach in any one day, as these took place under the composer's di-rection more than two hundred years ago. Instrumentally the revival was highly credible, except that the Thomas-kirche organ, still playable, is more frankly bright in sound than any modern instrument. The chorus of thirty-two voices, a number somewhat larger than Bach had available, sang with good rhythm and surprisingly clear German diction. But the fuzzy, fluty quality of Anglo-Saxon vocalization bears little resemblance to the harsh and sono-rous brilliance of a Continental chorus. And when we re-member that in Bach's choir the treble parts were all sung by boys, whose voices are more penetrating, even, than those of women, it is terrifying to imagine the piercing noises that must have filled that stone-pillared and stone-walled auditorium with rejoicing.

Even without the resonance that must have been literally an earful for St. Thomas's congregation, the final chorus with three high trumpets tootling for dear life in the neighborhood of high D was as jolly a bit of Christmas cheer as has come your reviewer's way this Nativity. God rest you merry, gentlemen! Let nothing you dismay!

December 31, 1940

1941

FRENCH MUSIC HERE

¶ Darius Milhaud has communicated to me the catalogue of an exhibit held recently at Mills College, Oakland, California, of Erik Satie's manuscripts. These manuscripts, the property of Milhaud, were brought by him last summer from France at some inconvenience, since the traveling facilities available at that time did not always include transportation of unlimited personal impedimenta. That Monsieur Milhaud should have made room for these at the cost of leaving behind manuscripts and orchestral material of his own for which he might have need during his stay here is evidence of the esteem in which he holds the unpublished works of the late Sage of Arceuil.

The collection, as one can see from the above brief digest, is an extensive one. Its importance depends on what one thinks of Erik Satie as a musical figure. This writer is in agreement with Darius Milhaud and with some of the other contemporary French composers in placing Satie's work among the major musical values of our century. He has even gone so far in print, nearly twenty years ago, as to parallel the three German B's—Bach, Beethoven, and Brahms—with the three S's of modern music—in descending order of significance, Satie, Schönberg, and Stravinsky.

French and other Parisian music of the 1930's has been but little performed in America. (That is an old quarrel of mine with the League of Composers.) Such of it as has been performed here is usually considered to be mildly pleasant but on the whole not very impressive. This estimate is justified only on the part of persons initiated to its aesthetic. And its aesthetic, as was that of Debussy, is derived directly from the words and from the works of Satie, whose firmest conviction was that the only healthy thing music can do in our century is to stop trying to be impressive.

The Satie musical aesthetic is the only twentieth-century musical aesthetic in the Western world. Schönberg and his school are Romantics; and their twelve-tone syntax, however intriguing one may find it intellectually, is the purest Romantic chromaticism. Hindemith, however gifted, is a neo-classicist, like Brahms, with ears glued firmly to the past. The same is true of the later Stravinsky and of his satellites. Even *Petrushka* and *The Rite of Spring* are the Wagnerian theater symphony and the nineteenth-century cult of nationalistic folklore applied to ballet.

Of all the influential composers of our time, and influence even his detractors cannot deny him, Satie is the only one whose works can be enjoyed and appreciated without any knowledge of the history of music. These lack the prestige of traditional modernism, as they lack the prestige of the Romantic tradition itself, a tradition of constant Revolution. They are as simple, as straightforward, as devastating as the remarks of a child.

To the uninitiated they sound trifling. To those who love them they are fresh and beautiful and firmly right. And that freshness and rightness have long dominated the musical thought of France. Any attempt to penetrate that musical thought without first penetrating that of Erik Satie is fruitless. Even Debussy is growing less and less comprehensible these days to those who never knew Satie.

When Satie used to be performed here occasionally, the works were found difficult to understand. French music in all centuries has been rather special, not quite like anything else. In our century it has become esoteric to a degree not currently admitted even in France. It has eschewed the impressive, the heroic, the oratorical, everything that is aimed at moving mass audiences. Like modern French poetry and painting, it has directed its communication to the individual.

It has valued, in consequence, quietude, precision, acuteness of auditory observation, gentleness, sincerity and directness of statement. Persons who admire these qualities in private life are not infrequently embarrassed when they encounter them in public places. It is this embarrassment that gives to all French music, and to the work of Satie and his neophytes in particular, an air of superficiality, as if it were salon music written for the drawing rooms of some snobbish set.

To suppose this true is to be ignorant of the poverty and the high devotion to art that marked the life of Erik Satie to its very end in a public hospital. And to ignore all art that is not heroic or at least intensely emotional is to commit the greatest of snobberies. For, by a reversal of values that constitutes one of the most surprising phenomena of a century that has so far been occupied almost exclusively with reversing values, the only thing really hermetic and difficult to understand about the music of Erik Satie is the fact that there is nothing hermetic about it at all.

It wears no priestly robes; it mumbles no incantations; it is not painted up by Max Factor to terrify elderly ladies or to give little girls a thrill. Neither is it designed to impress orchestral conductors or to get anybody a job teaching school. It has literally no devious motivation. It is as simple as a friendly conversation and in its better moments exactly as poetic and as profound.

These thoughts occurred to me the other evening at a League of Composers concert of recent works by Milhaud. Not a piece on the program had a climax or a loud ending. Nothing was pretentious or apocalyptical or messianic or overdramatized. The composer's effort at all times was to be clear and true. And when I saw the catalogue of the Satie manuscripts and learned how Milhaud had brought them to America at the cost of not bringing all his own, when I remembered also the brilliant and theatrically effective works of Milhaud's youth, *Le Bœuf sur le toit* and *Le Train bleu* and *La Création du monde,* I realized that after Satie's death he had been led, how unconsciously I cannot say, to assume the mantle of Satie's leadership and to eschew all musical vanity. That, at any rate, is my explanation of how one of the most facile and turbulent talents of our time has become one of the most completely calm of modern masters; and how, by adding thus depth and penetration and simple humanity to his gamut, he has become the first composer of his country and a leader in that musical tradition which of all living musical traditions is the least moribund.

January 5, 1941

THE HINDEMITH CASE

¶ Paul Hindemith's music is both mountainous and mouselike. The volume of it is enormous; its expressive content is minute and not easy to catch. His output is voluminous; that implies a certain facility. His tonal grammar and syntax are perfectly clear; that is evidence of care taken. His work has style also; and that is proof of its artistic integrity, of an integration between what its author feels and what his listener hears.

There is nevertheless a good deal that is obscure about it. How often has one sat through pieces by Hindemith that seem to make sense musically but little or no sense emotionally! Even so ingratiating a piece as the Third String Quartet sounds more like the work of a composer who had nothing better to do one morning than like something that had got itself born out of inner necessity. His work could hardly be called hermetic, because hermetism is usually pretty compact. I should say that the obscurity one encounters in it is due rather to the diffuseness of its thought than to any especial concentration of meaning or any rigidly novel technique.

It is not, properly speaking, academic music. It is too loosely put together for that. It is cleanly written down but not much polished, and it meanders more than is considered good "form" in academic circles. Also, its instrumentation, though completely sure-handed, is rarely brilliant or "effective" in the way that the work of celebrated pedagogues is likely to be. He does not seem to be interested in stylistic or cultural showing off any more than he is in emotional expansiveness or emotional concentration.

His music exerts a great fascination, however, over

music students; and it is not without a certain impressiveness for the music public in general. It is obviously both competent and serious. It is dogmatic and forceful and honest and completely without charm. It is as German as anything could be and farther removed from the Viennese spirit than any music could possibly be that wasn't the work of a German from the Lutheran North. It has no warmth, no psychological understanding, no gentleness, no *Gemütlichkeit,* and no sex appeal. It hasn't even the smooth surface tension of systematic atonality. It is neither humane nor stylish, though it does have a kind of style, a style rather like that of some ponderously monumental and not wholly incommodious railway station.

Having reflected in this vein for some years about Hindemith's non-programmatic music, it was with the hope of maybe finding I was all wrong that I went to hear the National Orchestra from Washington play symphonic excerpts from *Mathis der Maler* last Tuesday evening. I wanted to see what the least picturesque composer alive would do with the most picturesque subject imaginable. I remembered his having tried his hand some years ago at a picturesque subject drawn from modern life in an opera called *Neues vom Tage*, and I remembered having been amused at the way he had managed to write music for that work that was ponderous and cute at the same time.

Mathis der Maler turned out to be more of same, only more serious in tone, on account of its subject matter, which has to do with three religious pictures by Mathias Grünewald—a *Descent of Angels*, an *Entombment*, and a *Temptation of Saint Anthony*. The subject is an ambitious one and presents a problem of musical method for which there is no precedent in musical tradition.

There are several classic procedures for representing visual images by means of music. There is the ancient and simple one employed by Rameau and Handel and Sebastian Bach, which is to imitate in the melodic contours either the silhouette or the characteristic motion of the thing one wishes to describe, valleys being exalted, for instance, the crooked being made straight and the rough places plain, Adam falling out of paradise, troupes of angels tripping down the major scale, and gentlemen attempting from love's sickness to fly-y-y-y-y-y-y-y-y in vain. There is also the Romantic procedure of adding to this auditive and kinetic vocabulary of visual suggestion a subjective description of the emotional effect of it all on some sensitive observer or participant. Bacchanalian routs, debauches in Venusberg, Swiss mountain weather, graveyard ballets, and visits to hell on Walpurgisnacht are common in nineteenth-century music.

Mendelssohn's contribution to landscape technique consisted in making the observer always the same man, himself. In Scotland, in Italy, in fairyland, he is always Mendelssohn, sympathetic and sensitive and strictly non-participant. The modern French technique of musical landscape painting, of which Debussy was the most skillful practitioner, is essentially Mendelssohnian, though the expressive range and psychological intensity of Debussy's work are greater than those of Mendelssohn's because it is not bound to the German conception of thorough bass or to the idea of "developing" the thematic material. It conceives any melodic line as a self-sufficient expressive unit, counterpoint as a plurality of such units, harmony and rhythm as coloristic ornamentation to melody. "Form" in the German sense of harmonic progress is something to be avoided, since it implies that the author is either going somewhere or trying to make a point, instead of receiving and transmitting a series of related impressions from some point of view where he is supposed to remain motionless, his will immobilized by the intensity of the visual-auditive photographic process. Musical landscape painting does not need "form" in the sense of progress. It needs, on the contrary, a static musical unity based on sequential statement of all the things that need to be said in order to make the piece a proper description of its subject.

All these procedures exist as known ways of translating sight into sound. There is no known way of translating into sound visual pictures that have already been translated into so stylized a medium as painting. A composer's version of a painter's version of the Church's version of scenes from sacred history is what *Mathis der Maler* purports to be. As such it is naturally not very successful. It couldn't be. When one considers, in addition, that Hindemith has never properly liberated himself from the German bass, that his rhythm is constrained and unimaginative, that whenever

he can't think what to do next he writes imitative counterpoint, that his melodic contours, though dignified enough,
are inexpressive, that his creative concentration is too diffuse to allow him to write effectively either visual music or
subjective emotional music, it is surprising that the *Mathis*
tryptich should come off at all.

It comes off, just as all his music does, in spite of everything, by good intentions and by being playably orchestrated. The *Entombment* has a certain directly expressive
quality, though the influence of Grünewald would seem to
be present more as private stimulus to the composer's invention than as anything a listener need take cognizance
of. The *Descent of the Angels* and the *Temptation of Saint
Anthony* are not handled as convincingly, on the whole,
as the Romantic masters handled similar subjects. Saint
Anthony's victory over temptation, for instance, is represented by a routine Lutheran chorale harmonized for brass
in a routine manner that might just as well represent Mr.
Hindemith's satisfaction at getting to the end of his piece as
a saint's triumph over his lower nature.

Mathis der Maler is typical of North Germany at its best
and of modern scholastic facility at its worst. It is complex,
ineffective, unpolished, lacking in both grace and expressive power. All the same, it has a moral elevation and a
straightforward, if clumsy, honesty that make it at all times
unquestionably "good" music.

February 9, 1941

REVUELTAS

¶ Europe has often produced composers like the
late Silvestre Revueltas, the Americas rarely. Our music
writers are most likely to do the light touch with a heavy
hand. Revueltas's music reminds one of Erik Satie's and of
Emmanuel Chabrier's. It is both racy and distinguished. Familiar in style and full of references to Hispanic musical
formulas, it seeks not to impress folklorists nor to please

audiences by salting up a work with nationalist material. Neither does it make any pretense of going native. He wrote Mexican music that sounds like Spanish Mexico, and he wrote it in the best Parisian syntax. No Indians around and no illiteracy.

The model is a familiar one of the nationalist composer whose compositional procedures are conservative and unoriginal but whose musical material consists of all the rarest and most beautiful melodies that grow in his land. Villa-Lobos is like that and Percy Grainger; so was Dvořák. The contraries of that model are Josef Haydn and Satie and a little bit Georges Auric, certainly Darius Milhaud. These writers use the vernacular for its expressivity. But their musical structure and syntax are of the most elegant. Their music, in consequence, has an international carrying power among all who love truly imaginative musical construction.

Revueltas's music could never be mistaken for French music. It is none the less made with French post-Impressionist technique, amplified and adapted to his own clime. It is static harmonically, generously flowing melodically, piquant and dainty in instrumentation, daring as to rhythm. He loves ostinato accompanying figures and carries them on longer than a more timid writer would. He orchestrates à la Satie, without doubling. He fears neither unexpected rhythmic contrasts nor familiar melodic turns. His music has grace, grandeur, delicacy, charm, and enormous distinction.

March 4, 1941

SACRED SWING

¶ Last Sunday I went to Newark to attend the evening services of a Negro congregation known as The Church of God in Christ, where Brother Utah Smith, a traveling evangelist of that denomination, was closing his engagement. Brother Smith is a stocky gentleman in the mid-forties, neither old nor young, whose musical accomplishments had been signaled to me by swing experts. He is known in religious circles as The One-Man Band, was so introduced, in fact, by the local pastor. His whole musical equipment is an electric guitar, his only vestment an ordinary sack suit of dark blue, with a pair of white wings made of feathered paper attached to his shoulders like a knapsack by crossed bands of white tape.

His religious message is delivered more by music and dancing than by preaching. Only after the preliminary prayers, solos and congregational hymns are over does he take charge of the meeting. Then an open space is cleared between the chancel rail and the first congregational seats. These last are allowed to be wholly occupied, no mourners' bench being reserved at all, since the nature of the service is one rather of general rejoicing than of personal penitence. The Brother makes a few remarks to the congregation and then, without any formal address or other preface, goes straight into his number, if I may so refer without irreverence to his music-making.

He plays the guitar with a high pick-up that fills the auditorium with a rich and booming sonority. He does not sing. He only plays and, like all swingsters, pats his foot. His musical fancy is of the highest order. I have rarely heard such intricate and interesting swing. From time to time he shouts: "I've got wings! Dust my feet!" Persons in the congregation reply with: "Dust my feet!" with "Praise the Lord!" and similar ceremonial phrases, as is customary among many colored religious groups. Practically everybody claps his hands in time to the music, claps on the offbeat, as is also customary in swing circles.

The music goes on for quite a long time, the Brother swinging chorus after chorus with ever increasing fantasy and insistence. Various persons of the congregation who feel so inclined first edge timidly toward the edge of the open space and then one by one start dancing. Each dances alone, some with raised and some with lowered head, all with eyes closed. Some jerk a little; others do rapid and complex footwork. The floor sways with their impact as if about to collapse. When the music stops, the dancers come out of their trancelike absorption and regain their seats as calmly as persons leaving any ballroom floor.

At no time during my stay did I observe any licentious behavior or other evidence that the ceremony was not a bona fide religious manifestation. Brother Smith himself, though full of humor and jollity, and not without a certain naïve showmanship, impressed me as sincere. And if I was not conscious during my one brief visit to his services of any extraordinary or commanding inspiration in them, neither was I aware of anything that might make me think them phony.

In any case, his musical gift is real and his musical imagination abundant. I am, consequently, taking occasion this Easter Sunday to make reference to what struck me as an interesting musical manifestation and to point an example from contemporary life of the truism that in those societies or groups where religion is most vigorous there is no difference whatever between the sacred and the secular musical styles, the consideration of what is sacred and what is profane in music applying only to the moral prestige in society of the ceremonies that it accompanies. As a swing artist Brother Utah Smith is worthy to rank among the best. As a stimulator of choric transports he incites the faithful to movements and behavior not very different from those of any true jitterbug. Myself, I found it distinctly pleasant to hear good swing and to observe its effects in surroundings imbued with the white magic of Protestant Christianity, rather than among alcoholic stupidities and even more somber diabolisms of the nightclub world.

April 13, 1941

FA SOL LA FA SOL LA MI FA

¶ These are the syllables used by oldsters in rural regions of the South to intone the major scale, exactly as they were used in the British Isles long before Shakespeare. Indeed, the Elizabethan fa la la is no more than a conventional reference to the habit of singing any part-song first with the tonal syllables, so that melodies may be learned before words are attempted. So, still, is the custom in all those parts of America where *The Sacred Harp* and *Southern Harmony* are used as singing books.

The former is common in Georgia, the Carolinas, Kentucky, Tennessee, Alabama, Arkansas, Louisiana, and Texas. It has been reissued four times since its first appearance in 1844 and has sold upward of five million copies.

Southern Harmony, published in 1835, sold a half-million copies before the Civil War, then was out of print till the Federal Writers' Project of Kentucky, under the sponsorship of the Young Men's Progress Club of Benton, Marshall County, reprinted it in facsimile in 1939.

By far the most celebrated in musicology circles of all the American song books, since Dr. George Pullen Jackson, of Vanderbilt University, revealed it to the learned world in *White Spirituals in the Southern Uplands*, its usage among the folk is confined today to a very small region in southwest Kentucky. William ("Singing Billy") Walker, its author, considered it so highly that he ever after signed himself, even on his tombstone, A. S. H., meaning "Author of *Southern Harmony*." Today it is used by about forty old people, who meet every year at the County Court House of Benton and sing from nine till four.

I went to hear the *Southern Harmony* singing this year, lest it cease to exist before another, though most of the ancients looked healthy enough, I must say, and sang with a husky buzz; and a handful of youngsters of forty or more seemed active in perpetuating the style and repertory of it all.

The style is that of all back-country vocalism: a rather nasal intonation, a strict observance of rhythm and note (plus certain traditional ornaments and off tones), and no shadings of an expressive nature at all. Each song is sung first with the Fa Sol La syllables and then with its words. Various persons take turns at leading. The effect of the syllable singing is rather that of a Mozart quintet for oboes; the effect of the verbal singing rather that of a fourteenth- or fifteenth-century motet.

The repertory is all the grand and ancient melodies that our Protestant ancestors brought to America in the seventeenth and eighteenth centuries. Most are pentatonic and hexatonic, many of them Dorian or Phrygian in mode. The part-writing is French fifteenth-century. There are usually three parts: a bass, a tenor (the melody), and a treble. Both of the latter are doubled at the octave by women and men, making of the whole a five-part piece. Since chords of the open fifth are the rule and parallel fifths common, the addition to these of constant octaves gives to the whole an effect at once of antiquity and of the most rigorous modernism. Each part is a free melody, constantly crossing above or below the others; no mere harmonic filling attenuates the contrapuntal democracy. There is something of the bagpipe, too, in the sound of it all, as well as in the configuration of many of the tunes.

Though the words are always sacred words (often of high poetic quality), neither the *Southern Harmony* nor *Sacred Harp* singings are, strictly speaking, religious manifestations. The proof of that is the fact that they have never become involved in the sectarian disputes that are the life of religion. Religion is rather the protective dignity under which a purely musical rite is celebrated. That rite is the repetition year after year of a repertory that is older than America itself, that is the musical basis of almost everything we make, of Negro spirituals, of cowboy songs, of popular ballads, of blues, of hymns, of doggerel ditties, of all our operas and symphonies. It contains our basic conceptions of melody, of rhythm, and of poetic prosody. It contains in addition the conception of freedom in part-writing that has made of our jazz and swing the richest popular instrumental music in the world.

To persons traveling southward I do not recommend the *Southern Harmony* singing as the best introduction to this richness of style and repertory. The ancients are too few in number and too note-bound, and the singing is far too slow for nervous city tastes. Easier to find on any summer Sunday and more lively in tone and rhythm are the devotees of the *Sacred Harp*. The style and repertory are similar, but the vigor of the rendition is greater. If possible, buy a book and learn to sing yourself from the square and triangular notes. It is more fun that way.

May 26, 1941

PARIS FOREVER

¶ In the French version of *La Vie Parisienne* a
Swedish family is the protagonist of that love affair with
Paris that seems to come once into the lives of so many people from so many lands. In the A. P. Herbert version it is
an English household. Messieurs Felix Brentano and Louis
Verneuil have for the present adaptation brought their vis-
itors from Chicago, which is appropriate and charming of
them. The real subject of the piece, however, is the homage
that Offenbach himself, a German from the Rhineland,
was offering to the city which he loved and which loved
him.

Paris has always been good for foreign musicians and
sometimes good to them. To none was ever it more generous than to Jacques Offenbach, né Levy, from Offenbach-
am-Main. And no musician, foreign or French, not even
the Gustave Charpentier of *Louise*, ever placed at the
feet of his mistress a fresher or a lovelier tribute than *La
Vie Parisienne*. It is a crown of waltzes picked out with
polkas and quadrilles and interwoven with melodies that
distill the tender sentiment, the whole tied up with a great
big lacy ribbon in the form of a cancan. And the melodies
are as fresh as the day they were picked; the rhythm pops
like champagne. Every company that acts that operetta
communicates its effervescence. This production is certain
to sell lots of fizz-water for the tonier bistros of the town.
And to leave happy memories with all. The grand quadrille
and cancan that end the third scene are a very ocean of
lace and of legs. As Jean Cocteau, himself no mean lover
of the Lutetian strand, once said of such an occasion,
"Venus herself, nascent, could not have kicked up more
foam."

One has one's reserves about any transformation of a
text one loves. I regret the omission, on silly moralistic
grounds presumably, of the flirtatious wife. I regret the
omission of the traditional gesture with which the nym-

phomaniac widow ends her number, "Es-tu content, mon
colonel?" which is a lifting high of the hoopskirt to expose
black panties worn in memory of the departed mate. I
regret the omission of the patter song, "Repeuplons les
salons du Faubourg Saint-Germain," and of the father's
chop-licking, "Je veux m'en fourrer jusque-là." Also the virtual omission of the theme song: "Je serai votre guide dans
ce ville splendide." Nevertheless, this version is a good one.
The spoken text is less ingenious than Marion Farquhar's
rhymed lyrics, which are tiptop. All in all, it is difficult to
imagine a better adaptation and translation of a musical
play, or to remember one.

From the specially hand-painted curtain in the Chéret
manner to the last detail of gloves and footwear, the stage-
sets and the costumes are sumptuous and witty, rich in
material, designed and combined with both taste and brilliance. So are the dancing and the stage movements. As a
musical show *La Vie Parisienne* makes the rest of Broadway both look and sound silly; and this applies to the
Thirty-ninth Street crematorium as well, whenever that
ancient and honorable institution tries to do light opera. I
do hope the New Opera Company can keep the show running. Or possibly sell it to a producer. It would not surprise
me if there should turn out to be gold in those trills. If the
Paris of Offenbach, which is, after all, about as near to the
eternal Paris as any, not excepting that of the late Third
Republic, can sell bubbly in the bars and put other operas
at the Forty-fourth Street over the spring, she will have
made a pretty return for the love that New Yorkers have
long borne her.

November 6, 1941

HAYDN, BEETHOVEN, AND MOZART

¶ Lately I have been reading and rereading the
Haydn piano sonatas. Like all of Haydn's music they represent a gold mine of melody and of instrumental imagina-

tion. There is scarcely one that does not contain some passage familiar to us all, familiar, I may add, more often than
not because of Beethoven's unacknowledged quotation of
it in sonata or symphony. They also represent, as do
equally the piano sonatas of Mozart and of Beethoven, the
counterpart to the symphonies of these masters. If one
wants to understand the latter, one must study the former;
and vice versa.

What strikes me most about Haydn is that of the three
great Viennese masters he is by far the most melodious.
His thematic invention is the most varied of them all and
his thematic development the most tuneful. His whole musical concept is lyrical. For this reason he is at his best in
the non-lyrical movements. The first movement and the
minuet are commonly his richest. The development of his
first-movement themes through a cycle of sonata-form
modulations gives symmetry and weight to what might be
merely graceful if no such formal layout were employed.
Similarly, the minuet's quality of dance music enforces a
certain objectivity upon his process of composition that
adds to Haydn's abundance of personal fancy the welcome
solidity of a straightforward and easily understood human
significance. The rondo, Haydn's most frequently observed
last-movement scheme, gives too much play to his musical
imagination, obliges him too little to expression. The same
is true of his slow movements, which are melodious and
full of incidental invention, but which do not say much.

The truth is that Haydn wrote music like an old bachelor (which, for all practical purposes, he was). A self-con-
tained and self-sufficient lyricism is its dominant characteristic, an avuncular generosity its chief means of contact
with the listener. Of humane objectivity it has virtually
none save in the jolly and waltzlike dance movements,
where he remembers his peasant upbringing. The encounter
of his native lyrical abundance with sonata-form formali-
ties, however, as that takes place in his first movements,
produces a kind of three-dimensional grandeur that is acceptable in terms of its sheer musical magnificence, without regard to what its expressive intention may be. In this
respect Haydn's instrumental music looks backward to that
of Domenico Scarlatti and the Bach family, just as his oratorios resemble strongly those of Handel. His technical proce-

dures are those of Romanticism; but his thought is neither
expansive, like Beethoven's, nor dramatic, like that of Mozart. It is a lyrical fountain forever overflowing and constantly inundating everybody with melody.

Beethoven really was an old bachelor. But he never
liked it. All his music is cataclysmic, as if he were constantly
trying to break out of his solitude. His first movements state
the problem squarely. His slow movements are less interesting, because they try unsuccessfully to avoid it; they
tread water. His minuets and scherzos reopen the problem
and announce the hope of a solution. The finales, often the
finest and certainly the most characteristic movements in
Beethoven, are the solution that the whole piece has been
working up to. That solution is usually of a religious nature.
It represents redemption, the victory of soul over flesh.
It varies from calm serenity to active triumph, but joy is
its thesis. In the Ninth Symphony a German ode on that
subject is inserted to clinch the matter. The bonds of solitude are broken because they are imagined as being
broken. That breaking is of a purely mystical nature, a temporary identification of the self with God or with all humanity. The form of the musical expression is free and infinitely varied. The finales show Beethoven at his most
personal and most masterful. They are grand, terribly
serious, and, for the most part, inspiring.

Solitude was unknown to Mozart. Except for a short
time in Paris, just after his mother died there, he was probably never in all his life alone for so much as half a day.
His music, likewise, is full of dramatic animation. His
themes are like people, his developments a working out of
their contrasting natures. His first movements, in spite of
the beauty of their material, are little more than a first act
or prelude to the drama of the rest. The slow movements
are always the crux of the matter, the freest, grandest, and
most fanciful part of any Mozart sonata or symphony.
They are impossible to interpret unless one considers them
as theater, as a dramatization of real characters, a conflict among other people's emotions. The minuet which follows (in the quartets it more commonly precedes) is pure
ballet. It has nothing to do with Haydn's peasant gambols.
It is slow and stately and complex. It, too, shows a conflict
of sentiments, as if the dramatic struggles of the preceding

movement were here resolved, or at least appeased, through observance of the social amenities. It is a tense and static little affair.

The finales are not dramatic at all. They are mostly fast and always furious. Nothing in music, excepting maybe five or six of the Bach organ fugues, have that kind of power and insistence, as of an element unchained. They do not have to be played at breakneck speed. Those for piano solo definitely profit by moderation in this regard. But rhythmic tension they must have and dynamic contrast. They are the moral of the piece. They show, as Mozart was always trying to show in his operas, how marvelously vigorous life can be when people make up their minds to put their petty differences on the shelf and to collaborate in full good will at being human beings together. Their whole effect can be spoiled unless the preceding movement, whether that is an adagio or the more usual minuet, is presented at a contrasting tempo. Any speed that suggests the scherzo in rendering a Mozart minuet not only falsifies the significance of the minuet itself but steals, as well, the fire of the movement that follows.

December 21, 1941

1942

UNDERSTANDING MODERN MUSIC

¶ Common belief has it that new music is difficult to understand, while older and more familiar music presents comparatively few problems of comprehension. I do not think this is true. It is certain that in the epochs of rapid aesthetic advance there is always some time lag between the understanding of new work on the part of persons connected with the movement that produces it and the understanding or acceptance of that same work by the general public of music-lovers. Professional musicians and pedagogues, if they happen not to be part of the inner circle where such work is being produced, are sometimes more uncomprehending than the general public, even.

But this age is not one of rapid advance in music. It is one rather of recession. The great frontal attack on musical conservatism that is still known as Modern Music took place between 1885 and 1914. Its salient victories include the works of Richard Strauss, of Debussy, of Ravel, of Schönberg, Stravinsky, and Erik Satie. No composer has made since 1914, if we except the works that some of these same men wrote after that date, any impression on his time comparable to that made by these composers during the great revolutionary years before the other World War.

We have since witnessed the triumphal progress of careers laid down before that war, and we have assisted at the test flights of two minor musical movements. The first of these, characteristic of the 1920's, was known to its adepts as Contemporary Music and included two branches, the Twelve-tone School (seated in Vienna with an outpost in Berlin) and the Neo-Classicists, or School of Paris. A second movement (also seated in Paris) was the characteristic musical movement of the 1930's and is called Neo-Romanticism. It is exactly contemporaneous with the painting movement of the same name.

I call the last two decades and their characteristic movements minor, because they were occupied chiefly with the exploitation of technical devices invented by a previous generation. I may be underestimating the Neo-Romantics. Indeed, I hope I am, because I am one of their founding fathers. But the possibility that the progress of the movement may have been only interrupted by the present war rather than terminated by it cannot obscure the fact that the Neo-Romantics, like the Neo-Classicists before them, represent for the most part a novel usage of syntactical devices perfected long before rather than any notable discoveries in musical technique.

The gamut of musical device that was correctly called Modern, or Revolutionary, before 1914 is now taught in most of our schools and colleges. In any case, it is available to educated composers; and the whole musical public has been exposed to it for twenty-five or more years. Many of the works that exemplify it have enjoyed, indeed, a world-wide success. There is no reason why anybody in the music world, professional or layman, should find himself in the position of not understanding a piece of twentieth-century music, if he is willing to give himself a little trouble.

It is probably the fact that today's music is at least partially comprehensible to all that makes it so amazing to some. The habit of merely enjoying music without attempting to understand it literally is a comfortable one. And it is far easier to indulge that habit in listening to the music of another age and century than it is when music made in our own time is being played. Because, in spite of the worst will in the world, no listener can fail to penetrate, at least partially, a contemporary work.

The art music of the past, most of all that eighteenth- and nineteenth-century repertory known as "classical" music, is, on the other hand, about as incomprehensible as anything could be. Its idiom is familiar. But its significant content is as impenetrable as that of the artwork of the Middle Ages. It was made by men whose modes of thought and attitudes of passion were as different from ours as those of Voltaire and Goethe and Rousseau and

Casanova and Heine and Lamartine and Victor Hugo were
different from those of Bernard Shaw and Marcel Proust
and Ronald Firbank and E. E. Cummings and Gertrude
Stein and Mickey Mouse and William Saroyan. Not that
these writers are always of the utmost limpidity. On the contrary, they are mostly either deceptively lucid or deceptively obscure, as is the custom of our century. But it is difficult not to find in ourselves, as twentieth-century men
and women, some spontaneous identification with the
world that they depict. Whereas the travels of Lord Byron,
the private lives of John Keats and of Emily Dickinson,
are as far from anything we have ever known as is the
demise of Richard Wagner's Isolde, who, having nothing
organically wrong with her, stands in the middle of a stage
and falls dead merely because her lover has just died
of real wounds gotten in a fight.

These reflections occurred to me one evening apropos
of a gathering that I had attended to hear some musical
compositions by Stefan Wolpe. Mr. Wolpe is a skilled composer whose works have so far been little performed here,
on account of what passes in professional circles for their
extreme difficulty both of execution and of interpretation.
In one corner four musicians were gathered together to
glance at the scores of the music played and to discuss
its nature and merits. That they all understood it both as
to technique and as to substance is proved by the fact that
they found themselves in perfect agreement about these.
Four musicians who agree on practically nothing else
in music not only thought that Mr. Volpe's work was interesting and excellent (that would have been easy), but
thought so for the same reasons.

Those same four musicians are irreconcilably divided
about Mozart and about Sibelius. None of them would be
capable of explaining in any reasonable manner at all a
sonata by Haydn, much less of convincing the others that
his explanation was correct. Their divers comprehensions
of Schumann's piano music, of the Beethoven quartets, of
Schubert, and of Chopin, though they might agree on the
excellence of all these, have nothing in common. On con-
troversial figures like Brahms and Berlioz and Wagner they
could almost come to blows.

And so I got to thinking about what is called "difficult

new music," and I concluded that there is no such thing any more. There used to be, I presume. It certainly must have taken more than goodwill and a mild effort of the mind for persons hitherto unacquainted with Debussy's work to accept and understand *Pelléas et Mélisande* in 1902. In 1941 there is no longer any really novel music. There is only live music and dead music, the music of our time and the music of other times.

Dead music is very beautiful sometimes and always pretty noble, even when it has been painted up and preened by the undertakers who play or conduct it with such solemnity at our concerts. Live music is never quite that beautiful. Neither that beautiful nor that dumb. Because live music speaks to us all. We may not like what it says, but it does speak. Dead music, that whole Baroque, Rococo, and Romantic repertory we call "classical," is as comfortable and as solacing to mental inactivity as a lullaby heard on a pillow made from the down of a defunct swan.

I am not proposing its abolishment from our lives or from our concerts. No sensible person would wish to be without access to the history of culture. I am merely saying to those persons who think the music of today is accessible to the comprehension of only a limited group that it is, on the contrary, much easier to understand than the music of the past. Very few people have any real comprehension at all of the art of preceding generations, of what it is all about and of how the men felt who made it. Those who do have an inkling or two about it, who have made up for their own use a certain way of envisaging the relics of times past by applying to their interpretation facts and principles they have learned from modern life, are, of course, always persons who have a pretty comprehensive acquaintance with the music of the modern world. All modernists are not necessarily musicologists. I have known people who understood Stravinsky or Schönberg pretty thoroughly but whose knowledge of Bach and Beethoven was conventional and unreflected. I have never, however, known a person with any original or penetrating knowlelge about the musical past who had not arrived at that understanding by first mastering the elements of the divers musical procedures that lay about him.

January 4, 1942

CONDUCTING MODERN MUSIC

¶ The prime consideration in interpreting new musical works is to avoid doing anything that might possibly make these appear to be emulating the music of the past. Such emulation may or may not have been a part of the composer's intention, but playing it up in presentation produces a false relation between a work and its own time that is fatal to the comprehension of the work by its own time. Dressing and directing *Hamlet* as if it were a modern play is a piquant procedure. Treating a modern play as if it were Shakespeare's *Hamlet* can only make for pretentiousness and obscurity.

There is a prestige attached to any art work that has survived the death of its author that no work by a living hand can enjoy. This fact of survival is correctly called immortality, and that immortality surrounds the surviving work with a white light. In that radiance all becomes beautiful. Obscurities disappear, too; or at least they cease to bother. When I refer, as not infrequently I do, to live music and dead music, I mean that there is the same difference between the two that there is between live persons and dead ones. The spirit and influence of the dead are often far more powerful than those of the living. But they are not the same thing, because you can only argue *about* them, never *with*. The dead have glory and a magnificent weight. The living have nothing but life.

The glorification of the dead is a perfectly good thing. Indeed, the greater civilizations have always done it more than the lesser. But a clear separation of the dead from the living is also a mark of the higher cultures. That is the fecundating drama between tradition and spontaneity that keeps peoples and empires alive. Consequently no good is accomplished by pretending, or seeming to pretend, that a work by Igor Stravinsky or Aaron Copland or myself is a museum piece, because it isn't and won't be till we're dead, if then. And framing such a work among museum pieces in such a way that it appears to be subsidiary to them invariably makes the living work seem deader than a doornail. Its lack of white-light immortality makes it appear gravely inferior to the works on the same program that have such an aura and glamour.

The moral of this explanation is that new works must be played alone, in company with other new works, or surrounded by old ones carefully chosen, if one wishes to bring out their resemblances to the traditional past as well as their essential differences from that past. A new work may not be the most important piece on the program; but unless it is the determining item in the choice of the whole program, it will always sound like second-rate music, because it is pretty certain to be placed in unfair glamour competition with the classics of repertory. Modern music indiscriminately programmed, no matter what kind of music it is, is framed to flop.

Neither can it be interpreted in the same style as older music. Insufficient rehearsal often works to a new piece's advantage. When there isn't time to do much but read the notes and observe the author's tempos, it gets a neutral reading that is at least better than a false interpretation. If the conductor has time to work it up into an imitation of all his favorite war-horses or to streamline it into a faint reminder of Beethoven and Tchaikovsky, it is very difficult for the listener to hear anything in it but a memory of these authors, or at most a feeble attempt to dethrone them by being arbitrarily different.

The best international style for playing the classics is one that reduces them to a common denominator of clarity and elegance. That was always Toscanini's force as a conductor of standard repertory. He was never very effective as a conductor of modern music (and he avoided it whenever possible, for that reason, I imagine), because he knew no other way of conducting anything. Characteristic national differences, which are of minor importance in standard repertory but which are the very essence of modern stylistic comprehension, seem to have escaped him. And being a musician of too high temperament to be satisfied with a mere neutral reading of anything, he wisely refrained from taking on a job in which neither he nor the living composer was likely to do much shining.

The conductors who do best by the music of our century are seldom equally good at interpreting all the kinds of it. Koussevitzky does well by anything Russian and fair by the English and the Americans, provided these last are not too local in flavor. He is not bad with German music, adds to it a Slavic elegance that is sometimes advantageous. French music escapes him utterly, in spite of his many years' residence in Paris. Mitropoulos is at his best with the central-European styles. Beecham is fine for English music, for all Slavic, for some German, for anything that has lyric afflatus or rhythmic punch. The Germans are rather messy when they play German music—always were, as Richard Wagner pointed out. Some are excellent with French music, however, Furtwängler, for instance, and Stock, of Chicago. Italians do not always do their best by Italian works, especially those of strong French influence, though they do beautifully by anything Germanic, even Brahms. Only the French (and a few Germans) make sense with French music. Nobody, literally nobody, who has not passed his formative adolescent years in this country ever conducts American music with complete intelligibility.

The basis of American musical thought is a special approach to rhythm. Underneath everything is a continuity of short quantities all equal in length and in percussive articulation. These are not always articulated, but they must always be understood. If for any expressive reason one alters the flow of them temporarily, they must start up again exactly as before, once the expressive alteration is terminated. In order to make the whole thing clear, all instruments, string and wind, must play with a clean, slightly percussive attack. This attack must never be sacrificed for the sake of a beautiful tone or even for pitch accuracy, because it is more important than either. Besides, once a steady rhythm is established, the music plays itself; pitch and sonorities adjust themselves automatically; as in a good jazz band the whole takes on an air of completeness.

French music is the nearest thing in Europe to our music, because French rhythm, like ours, is less accentual than quantitative. Keeping downbeats out of a Debussy rendition, for instance, is virtually impossible to anybody but a Frenchman. Steady quantities, a little longer than ours and requiring no percussive definition at all, are its rhythmic foundation. Definition is achieved by a leisurely breathing between phrases and an almost imperceptible waiting before attacking, with no added force, what in any other music would be played as a downbeat. As with American music, a proper rhythm is cardinal and must be achieved before the pitch and the tone-production can be polished up.

Modern German music is not very interesting rhythmically. It needs no exact quantities, only a thwacking downbeat. Even that can be advanced or held back, as is the Viennese custom, to express sentiment. What is most important is to get the harmony right, for pitch is all-important to the German mind. Get the harmony right and don't go *too* sentimental. Nothing else counts, provided care for the harmony includes a clear plotting out of the key-relations in the whole piece. This means being sure there is always plenty of bass at the piece's joints.

Russian music is an alternation of very free rhythms with rigid and insistent ones. The latter are easy to render. But few conductors ever take enough liberties with the sentimental passages. English formulas are always closely related to the Russian (*vide* the English novel and the English Church). In music, both peoples conceive of rhythm as either nonexistent or quite inflexible. Both observe beat-rhythms, too, not quantities. And both alternate speech inflections with footwork, as in a song-and-dance. The chief difference between them is that the Russian mind dramatizes itself with a grandiloquent simplicity, whereas the English tradition values a more intimate and personal kind of forthrightness in the expression of tender thought. The grander passages of both repertories may be rendered with the utmost of pomp and of panache.

Matters like these seem to me more important to restate than international aesthetic principles. All conductors know nowadays what the Neo-Classic style is all about. Also the Neo-Romantic style and the twelve-tone syntax. And certainly the survivals of late Romanticism are not difficult to decipher. But these are the stylistic elements that underlie all modern music; they have been written about *ad infinitum* and *ad nauseam*. What I am pointing out is that underneath these international tendencies and observances there are ethnic differences that must be taken account of. Also to remind my readers that these ethnic differences preclude the possibility that conductors of foreign upbringing now resident among us will play a leading role in our present musical expansion. They render great service by their constant acts of goodwill toward homemade music. But they have only the vaguest idea of what it's all about. And so has that part of our musical public that hears it only through their well-intentioned but unconvincing renditions.

January 25, 1942

RHYTHMIC GRANDEURS

¶ I am not going to review Bach's "Goldberg" Variations, which are one of the monuments of musical art, except to note that, as Wanda Landowska played them, there were no dull moments, though the concert lasted little less than two hours. I should like rather to cast an analytic eye on the work of this extraordinary performer, whose execution, no matter what she plays, is one of the richest experiences available to lovers of the tonal art. That she should play for two hours without striking a false note is admirable, of course; that she should play thirty pieces varying greatly in volume without ever allowing us to hear any thumping down of the keys proves a mastery of the harpsichord that is, to my knowledge, unique. That she should phrase and register the "Goldberg" Variations with such clarity and freedom that they all sound like new pieces is evidence of some quality at work besides mere musicianship, though the musicianship does run high in this case.

A performance so complete, so wholly integrated, so

prepared, is rarely to be encountered. Most artists, by the time they have worked out that much detail, are heartily sick of any piece and either walk through it half asleep or ham it up. It is part of the harpsichord's curious power that the more one is finicky about detail, the livelier the whole effect becomes.

All musicianly and expert qualities are observable at their highest in Landowska's harpsichord-playing. But so are they in the work of many another virtuoso. Her especial and unique grandeur is her rhythm. It is modern quantitative scansion at its purest. Benny Goodman himself can do no better. And it is Bach's rhythm, as that must have been. Writing constantly for instruments of no tonic accent, like the harpsichord and the organ, all Bach's music is made up out of length values. If you want to realize how difficult it is to express a clear rhythm without the aid of stresses, or down-beats, just try it on an electric buzzer. And if you want to realize what elaborate rhythmic complications the eighteenth-century performers did manage to make clear (else these would not have been written) on accentless instruments, just take a look at Bach's music for organ and that for harpsichord, particularly the "Goldberg" Variations.

The introduction of the pianoforte at the end of the eighteenth century changed the nature of music radically, substituting pulse for measure and punch for complexity. Only in our day, through the dissemination of American and South American popular music, which differs from European in being more dependent on quantitative patterns than on strong pulsations, has a correct understanding of Bach's rhythm been possible and a technique reinvented for rendering it. (Highly dramatic accents can be obtained with no added force, for instance, by delaying ever so slightly the attack on the note it is desired to accent. Also, expressive liberties of rhythm take on their full expression as liberties when they are taken upon some previously established rhythmic exactitude.)

Of all these matters Landowska is mistress. The pungency and high relief of her playing are the result of such a mastery's being placed at the service of a penetrating intelligence and a passionate Polish temperament. The final achievement is a musical experience that clarifies the past by revealing it to us through the present, through something we all take for granted nowadays, as Bach's century took it for granted, but that for a hundred and fifty years has been neglected, out of style, forgotten. That is the cultivation of rhythmic complexity by an elimination from musical thought of all dependence on rhythmic beat.

February 22, 1942

MASTER OF DISTORTION AND
EXAGGERATION

¶ If one had never heard before the works Vladimir Horowitz played last night in Carnegie Hall, or known others by the same authors, one might easily have been convinced that Sebastian Bach was a musician of the Leopold Stokowski type, that Brahms was a sort of flippant Gershwin who had worked in a high-class night club, and that Chopin was a gypsy violinist. One might very well conclude also that Liszt's greatest musical pleasure was to write vehicles for just such pianists as Vladimir Horowitz. The last supposition would be correct. Liszt was that kind of pianist himself, and he turned out concert paraphrases of anything and everything from the *Faust* waltz to Palestrina motets. Whether he was quite the master of musical distortion that Horowitz is, history does not record; but I think there is little doubt possible that a kindship of spirit exists between the two pianists. One has only to hear Horowitz play Liszt's music to recognize that.

Do not think, please, that my use of the word *distortion* implies that Mr. Horowitz's interpretations are wholly false and reprehensible. Sometimes they are and sometimes they are not. His Bach is no worse and no better than Stokowski's, on which I take it to be modeled. His Brahms may be less light-minded on other occasions than it was last night. His Chopin varied a good deal during the evening. The B-

flat minor Sonata was violent, coarsely conceived, melodramatic. He made its Funeral March sound like a Russian
boat song by accenting all the off-beats of the bass, and he
turned its serene middle section into the most affected of
nocturnes. His Études, however, were recognizable and, of
course, quite brilliant, as they should be; and the A-flat
Waltz (an encore) was as normal as his Liszt.

Supernormal would be a better word for the way he renders the works of the great Hungarian Romantic. He
seems to have a perfectly clear understanding of what they
are about and a thorough respect for them. He exaggerates
when exaggeration is of the essence, but he never tampers
with their linear continuity. He makes all the right effects,
and he makes them in the right places. The only distortion
is one of aggrandizement. He plays the Liszt pieces faster
and louder and more accurately than anybody else ever
plays them. Sometimes he plays the music of other composers that way too, and the effect is more tremendous than
pleasant. In Liszt it is both tremendous and pleasant, because Liszt's music was written for that kind of playing
and because Mr. Horowitz really loves and understands
that kind of music. It is the only kind that he approaches
without fidgeting, and last night it was the only kind the
audience didn't cough through.

If I speak chiefly of interpretation, it is not that I am
wanting in admiration of Mr. Horowitz's justly acclaimed
technical powers. But these powers are exploited by a violent and powerful personality that is, after all, a part of his
virtuoso equipment. Paderewski had and Artur Rubinstein
has a strength of crescendo comparable. E. Robert Schmitz
has an equal cleanness of articulation and a more even trill.
Josef Lhevinne's octaves and general marksmanship are at
least as good. And almost any of the more poetic virtuosos,
Rudolf Serkin or Robert Casadesus, for example, has a
lovelier tone. But none of these pianists is so free from respect for the composer's intentions, as these are currently
understood. Horowitz pays no attention to such academic
considerations. He is out to wow the public, and wow it he
does. He makes a false accent or phrasing anywhere he
thinks it will attract attention, and every brilliant or rapid
passage is executed with a huge crescendo or with a die-

away effect. It is all rather fun and interesting to students of what I like to call the wowing technique. It is a great deal more than that, however, when he gets into his own arrangement of Liszt's arrangement for one piano of Saint-Saën's arrangement for two pianos of the latter's orchestral version of his own song called *Danse Macabre*. His rendition of that number is in every way the berries.

March 7, 1942

THE GLUCK CASE

¶ The Juilliard School used to give modern operas. They did but they don't any more, as the ditty hath it. Their latest production was Gluck's *Iphigenia in Tauris,* a work that sometimes passes in the modern world for the most classic of musical classics, but that in its own day was considered a triumph of novelty and of fashion. I have no quarrel with a pedagogical policy that eschews today's modernism in favor of that of a century and a half back. I am all for bringing up the young on the ancient models of things, even though this may imply glorification of the house of Atreus. The young take more things in their stride than we do maybe, anyway, including what Mr. John Peale Bishop once rhymed as "Iphigenia's incestuous desires." The purpose of this article is not to correct anybody's morals but to offer a warning to whom it may concern that Gluck's operas are not quite such model matter for musical imitation as their historical prestige might suggest.

That prestige is as much a result of publicity as it is of intrinsic musical excellence. Gluck had a gift from his prodigious early years of making himself a center of controversy and of intellectual excitement. He perfected this gift in Italy, where he learned, as well, a great deal about sheer theater and became a skilled harmonist and orchestrator. Counterpoint he never mastered, but he got to be extremely expert at musical prosody.* Arriving in Paris with this far from negligible equipment for dramatic composition, he proceeded to make himself a protagonist and eventually the victor in one of those Parisian wars about aesthetics that have always been characteristic of French intellectual life.

The Gluck-Piccinni quarrel was really a revival, or continuation, of the famous *querelle des bouffons,* which had been going on for half a century. Everybody from Rameau to Jean-Jacques Rousseau had taken part in it. Its chief point of controversy was the respective virtues of the French and Italian operatic styles. The former prized correct declamation above melodic charm and admitted symphonic interludes as serviceable to dramatic expression. The latter prized tunefulness and easy theatrical effect and refused to consider music as wholly subservient to literature. The French side called the Italian school irresponsible and frivolous; the Italian defenders (Jean-Jacques among them) found the French opera static, pompous, and dull.

Piccinni was a charming composer, in many ways a more gifted musician than Gluck; and he was fabulously successful at the Opéra. Gluck's backers were mostly literary people. What they wanted was a composer who could placate the melody-fanciers without sacrificing correct declamation or obscuring the literary content of a dramatic poem. Gluck was exactly what they needed, an Italian-trained composer with a healthy German respect for the French language. And so they turned him on to the business of staging a contemporary literary movement by pretending merely to revive the past.

This latter game is old French strategy. Racine had taught manners, language, and moral conduct to the bourgeoisie and to the court of Louis XIV by pretending merely to retell the plots of Seneca and Euripides. The authors of the Enlightenment were busy preparing (quite consciously) a political revolution; but to conceal the novelty of their

---

* Debussy, in his famous *Lettre ouverte à Monsieur le Chevalier W. Gluck* (*Monsieur Croche, antidilettante;* Paris, 1921), accuses the Austrian composer of incorrect French prosody. Textually, he says: *"Entre nous, vous prosodiez fort mal; du moins, vous faites de la langue française une langue d'accentuation quand elle est au contraire une langue nuancée."*

reflections about society, economics, and law they pretended that they were merely studying ancient Greece and
Rome. When Greco-Roman analogies were insufficient
they brought the prestige of the natural sciences into play
and based their argument on a wholly fictitious figment
known as the "natural man." Gluck took advantage of this
argument in his famous preface to *Alceste* to pretend that
his music was superior to that of all other composers because, whereas theirs was merely music and perishable, like
all that follows aesthetic fashion, his could never die, being
a true depiction of "nature" itself. (By "nature" he meant,
as any man of the eighteenth century did, what the nineteenth called "human nature" and what our own is likely
to term "psychology.") I have heard Salvador Dali defend
his painting with the similar argument that it was superior
to mere "art" because it was an exact picture of his own
dreams (dreams being the only "reality" surrealism admits).

All this is sales talk. Dali is an intellectually fashionable
painter, as Gluck was an intellectually fashionable composer. The more they try to explain this fact away,
the more it becomes clear that their relation to a literary
movement is fuller justification for the frame of their work
than either their original power or their intrinsic skill,
though in neither case is the latter element negligible. For
all his talk of "reforming" the opera, Gluck did nothing of
the kind. Dr. Paul Henry Láng, of Columbia University,
likes to maintain that he had no influence on any subsequent operatic composition. Berlioz certainly admired and
studied the orchestral writing in Gluck, because he quotes
liberally from it in his *Treatise on Instrumentation*. Wagner used him as a battle cry for his own career, which he
also called a "reform," and rewrote some of the scores. All
this has accomplished exactly what Gluck's own polemics
accomplished: namely, to keep him famous, though his
operas are given more and more seldom. The revival of interest in pre-Revolutionary French opera that has accompanied our own searchings among seventeenth- and eighteenth-century composers for reference points in defense of
modernism has occasionally foundered on Gluck, for the
simple reason that Lully and Rameau, its real masters, are
not easily singable by modern voices. And so managers and
conductors are likely to make a great point of reviving

Gluck and pretending that it is pre-Romantic opera.

This is not true. The literary content of Gluck's librettos is the purest Classic Revivalism; and the Classic Revival, like the subsequent Medieval Revival, is one of the more sentimental and obscurantist aspects of the Romantic movement. Particularly is this true in music, where there were not even any ancient texts to revive. Gluck's choral passages are Protestant hymnody of the school popularized in America by Lowell Mason. His arias are watered Handel. His characters are artificial without being even symbolic. His recitative, the second-best element of his musical composition (after the instrumentation, which is tops, in spite of his abuse of string tremolando) is definitely inferior to that of Rameau, on which it is modeled. Because of his contrapuntal deficiency, his music is lacking in animation and in interior life. His melodies follow the harmony rather than generate it. The whole is lacking in surprise. Every number is predictable after four bars.

The most nearly individual note in his music is one derived from its literary and fashionable associations. That is a sort of sugary pastoral flavor that permeates his whole concept of classical antiquity. Everybody on the stage walks around as blithely as if he were about to become an ancestor, or a founding father of some future republic. The Atridae even, that bloody and incestuous clan, express themselves musically with all the placidity of a prosperous agricultural family. They complain about hard times, of course, as is the habit of such families; but they are really mostly busy impressing everybody with how noble they are in their suffering.

Many people find Gluck's music enchanting. Some of these like it because they like sugar from any period. Others like it because they think they get a glimpse through it of pre-Revolutionary operatic style. To these latter I suggest that they beg, bully, and bargain with the producing agencies till they get a chance to hear the operas of Rameau and of Handel. Once acquainted with these, I doubt if they will ever take Gluck's classical antiquity seriously again, just as there is no possibility of really liking his camouflaged Romanticism with anything like the warmth we feel toward the full-blooded article in Mozart and in Beethoven.

As a career boy, he made his fortune and got knighted

by the Pope. He was a second-class composer, nevertheless. As a successor to the great of his century he was as distinctly an anticlimax as are the well-known lines from Iphigenia's first aria in Tauris (a companion piece to our own "for God, for country, and for Yale"):

> J'ai vu se tourner contre moi
> les dieux, ma patrie et mon père.

March 8, 1942

THE SEASONS IN BROOKLYN

¶ Rarely have I passed a pleasanter summer. I refer to the second section of Haydn's *The Seasons,* which I heard last night at the Brooklyn Academy of Music. Spring was cheerful and autumn lusty, winter lugubrious and grand. But it was the long, lazy summer that I loved most of all.

Musical literature contains no finer collection of landscape painting than Haydn's homage to the year. There is virtually one of everything. A sunrise, a frog, a quail, a storm, a harvest, a vintage complete with love and waltzing, a communal spinning-song, every kind of weather known to the temperate regions, and finally a hymn of praise to God and truth and to the reviving earth. There are people, too, plain farm people, giving the measure of man at all times to this Romantic landscape with figures.

No two pieces of it are alike. The musico-pictorial invention is constant and enormous. The accuracy of the pictures and the economy of musical notes with which they are drawn are surprising and impressive. Debussy himself was no more reticent or more powerfully suggestive. Both he and Mendelssohn were less humane.

Grand indeed is the drinking-waltz entitled "Joyful, joyful the liquor flows." The winter spinning scene is the most interesting piece of its species I have ever heard. The prel-

ude to winter is an atmospheric piece of the most effective
kind. Its title: "The Thick Fogs at the Approach of Winter," might be by Erik Satie. "The Farmer's Joyful Feeling
about the Rich Harvest," another instrumental interlude,
is everything its title says. The storm is as grand as Beethoven's in the "Pastoral," the sunrise as noble as in Prokofiev's *Scythian Suite*. But nowhere that I know is there so
full and melodious an outpouring as the long summer aria
for soprano, "O, how pleasing to the senses." Neither
Bach nor Mozart ever uttered so steady a flow of rich song.

The Seasons represents Haydn at his most imaginative
and ingenious, the oratorio (or cantata) formula at its least
stuffy, and the art of musical landscape painting at its most
complete.

March 19, 1942

CONDUCTING REVIEWED

¶ Except for the regular visits of the Boston and
the Philadelphia orchestras, New York has heard no outside symphonic ensembles this season. But we have heard
conductors from everywhere. We have heard none of these
(excepting Koussevitzky and Ormandy and possibly
Barbirolli) under ideal conditions. By this I mean that they
have mostly been heard conducting orchestras they had not
selected or trained, orchestras that are not their orchestras.
Under such circumstances the finer details of execution, if
not absent altogether, are always lacking in the spontaneity
that is a product of long association between the musicians
and their leader. On the other hand, the leaders (and the
musicians too) have all been heard under identical conditions, so that comparisons of musicianship and of style are
more fairly based than usual. The Philharmonic and the
City Symphony have been running what it is legitimate to
consider as a kind of competition which, if it did not exhibit
everybody at his best or anybody completely, did show

them all playing the same game with the same equipment.

There is no question, I think, that with standard Philharmonic equipment Mr. Koussevitzky has produced the best all-around result of the year. His work and that of the orchestra sounded assured, sensible, eloquent, correct. No air of improvisation and no unexpected technical emergencies marred its musicality or interrupted its flow. It was calm and powerful and efficient and well-bred. Its most impressive quality was its dependability. One knew from the beginning it was going to be all right, and it was. Buying a ticket to one of his concerts was like buying a ticket to a concert by Toscanini or buying a record by Beecham, a wholly calculable investment.

Everybody else who has led the Philharmonic this season has been, by comparison, a blind date. The great Stokowski, ordinarily a conductor of high technical finish, did some good work and some very bad. Artur Rodzinski, of Cleveland, a most efficient workman on the whole, did brilliant renditions of Hindemith and of Berlioz; but having spent more time rehearsing one of these than was proportionately allowable, he gave an unprepared reading of Mendelssohn's *Midsummer Night's Dream* that was higgledy-piggledy. Fritz Busch's work was neither musically nor technically quite up to big-time standards; and the same is true of Eugene Goossens's. Walter Damrosch was variable in his readings, but he got the loveliest sound out of the Philharmonic I have ever heard anybody get. Mr. Barbirolli, the Philharmonic's titular conductor, was conducting his own orchestra and so not fairly admissible to the guest competition. His work was very much as it always is, competent but a little rough; and his musical conceptions were lacking in nobility.

The Mitropolous concerts were wholly dependable technically. Musically they varied a good deal. Some of them were nervous and violent, others calm almost to the point of platitude. He played more of the important new music than any of the other leaders did, played it clearly and efficiently and for the most part convincingly. Of them all, his case remains the least decisive. He is a great workman, certainly. He is an interesting musician, certainly. The exact nature of his musical culture and personality remains, however, vague. He seems to be oversensitive, overweaning, overbrutal, overintelligent, underconfident, and wholly without ease. He is clearly a musician of class, nevertheless, and a coming man of some sort in the musical world.

The contrary from every point of view is Bruno Walter. Musically he is most dependable, though his effective range of repertory is small, being limited chiefly to the German romantics. His specialty is the late German romantics, Bruckner and Mahler, though his Schumann is fine and his Beethoven has juice. At one time he enjoyed considerable prestige for his conducting of Mozart, though his readings in this repertory have never been able to stand competition with Beecham's. Nevertheless, in the narrow field of his specialization Walter is a rich musical mind, a conductor whose work has breadth and depth and a certain grand sincerity. He is also a technician of high quality. Unfortunately, he is undependable technically. His concerts, even the best of them, are marred by a sloppiness of beat and a general indifference to shipshapeness of execution that tend to alienate those elements of the public that are not wholly absorbed by the music he is playing. At his best he is one of the great living interpreters. When not at his best, he is still an authentic musician and worth hearing. But the concentration of thought and energy that underlies his best work seems not always to be wholly at his command.

The City Symphony has worked under a great variety of leaders this year. The great ones, of course, have been Beecham and Reiner. The former is a flood, a volcano, an earthquake, and as unpredictable as any of these. The latter is as calculable as the stars and about as distant. It is too bad we didn't hear them both with the Philharmonic instead of several of the lesser musicians whom we did. But it was an invaluable privilege, of course, for the Mayor's boys to play under them. It is invaluable also to have two orchestras in New York completing each other's repertory and playing to somewhat different musical publics. The City Symphony has produced a great deal of new music and has been honored by the appearance of hitherto little-known soloists and conductors. Among the latter, Mr. Henri Pensis impressed me as being extraordinarily dependable both technically and musically, an artist of high intelligence and power. I fancy he, too, is some kind of coming man and that we shall be hearing more and more of him.

At orchestral concerts of less than heroic pretensions it is not fair to match conductors, because on these occasions the music itself is more the subject of everybody's interest than the executant style. But in a seasonal review of conducting one does remember, all the same, the excellent work of Fritz Stiedry and George Szell at the New Friends of Music, the liveliness of Daniel Saidenberg with his Little Symphony and of Harry Farbman with his so-called "Symphonietta," the thoroughly intelligent programing of new music by Miss Frédérique Petrides at the concerts of her "Orchestrette Classique," and the elegant renditions of classic small scores by Adolf Busch and by the French flutist René Le Roy. All these one is thankful for, all these and Alfred Wallenstein, too, who plays reams of fine music, new and old, over the radio and plays it admirably.

The season's finest orchestral playing, as a whole has been done by the Boston Symphony. The most satisfactory renditions I have heard of modern pieces were Mitropoulos's readings of Aaron Copland's *Statements* and of Hindemith's Symphony No. 1 with the Philharmonic. The most revelatory of an older work I should say was Beecham's rendering of Haydn's Ninety-ninth at a concert of the Philadelphia Orchestra, though his playing of the Berlioz "Chasse Royale" from *The Trojans in Carthage* at a concert of the City Symphony will run his Haydn a close second for vigor and finesse and sheer musical grandeur.

The best single conducting job I heard at the Metropolitan Opera this winter was Beecham's *Faust*. The best dramatic conducting I have heard outside the Met was Alexander Smallens's *Porgy and Bess,* though Fritz Busch's *Macbeth* at the New Opera Company merits a memento. For these and all similar blessings may we ever remain duly thankful.

April 19, 1942

THE "BRAHMS LINE"

¶ Johannes Brahms was not during his lifetime a popular composer. Even today his works are little known and less loved by the concert-going publics of France, Italy, Spain, Mexico, and the South American republics. In the German-speaking countries, in Scandinavia, in Holland, in England, and in the United States a certain kind of musician has long borne his music great love. But neither the Latin nor the Slavic musical civilization has so far absorbed it at all. Its popularity among us has been growing steadily of late until today it ranks in popular favor with the music of Tchaikovsky and of Sibelius. This season the Brahms symphonic works have far outnumbered in performance the works of Beethoven, of Mozart, and of Schubert. The emergence of Brahms as a popular symphonist concords (in time, at least) with the noticeable confluence of two musical currents; and the result of that confluence is certain to be worth watching. These currents are the growing conservatism of the "advanced" musical world and the deeply inveterate conservatism of the non-professional music public.

A devotion to Brahms has always been, at least in our century, the mark of a quite definite musical conservatism. Even in his own day, which is not far past, this was mostly so, too. His whole musical program was traditionalist. He aimed to reinvigorate the classic style rather than to transform it or to add to it. In this he was the direct (and bitter) opponent of Richard Wagner. Wagner considered the works of his predecessors and of his contemporaries as equally grist for his mill, and he considered the business of his mill to be the turning out of a new kind of music for new kinds of social usage. He called this "the music of the future." Brahms considered his role to be that of a preserver of the classic tradition against the destructive tendencies of Romanticism. He modeled his contrapuntal style on the practices of Bach and of Mozart; his formal layouts in the long works he copied directly out of works by Mozart and Beethoven. His only voluntary concession to Romanticism was in the direction of chromatic harmony, and that was fairly hesitant.

Brahms was not by instinct a popular figure. He rather despised the non-professional public, and he had more gift for tiny craft in music writing than for sustained eloquence. He was nevertheless obliged, even though an opponent of Wagnerian demagogy, to do something about sustained eloquence, because no German could have success as a serious composer who did not obviously continue in the line of Beethoven. Brahms worked at this line assiduously, and finally, in his forties, produced a symphony. Later he produced three more. It was hard work for him, because his musical imagination was more lyrical than heroic and his instrumental style more at home with the scrupulosities of chamber music than in the broader symphonic manner. Neither was he any such master of the orchestra as his more radical contemporaries, Wagner, Berlioz, and Liszt.

He succeeded by sheer determination, and by the constant imitation of classic models, in pulling off these works most creditably and in building up for himself in Germany, in England, and even in America a devoted public of musicians who considered him to be the direct heir of Bach and Beethoven. The justice of that opinion is not a matter for present dispute, but its existence has long been a fact. A curious recent development in the Brahms controversy is that instead of having to wait for acceptance by the whole intellectual music world (which would include, of necessity, the Latins and the Slavs), Brahms's music has now achieved popular acceptance here without benefit of clergy.

In this it has separated itself from the work of those composers who have reached the masses with all canonical benediction. Beethoven and Wagner and Bach and Mozart our public has been taught to love. And if the modernists have sometimes regretted their haste in throwing the weight of their prestige on the side of Richard Wagner in his (and his widow's) campaign to popularize his operas, the fact remains that all over the world they did it. Brahms they nearly always resisted, as they mostly resisted Tchaikovsky and Sibelius. In all three cases the general public in Scandinavia, in England, and in the United States has stepped in and offered its accolade spontaneously.

This fact might well take some of the wind out of Brahms's academic admirers, leave them defending a lost cause that is no longer lost and yet still not wholly won academically, if it were not for the fact that new support has suddenly come to them from an intellectual source, from the heart of modernism itself. Ever since about 1914 modern music has been decreasingly revolutionary in its aims and increasingly conservative in its procedures. The so-called "neo-classicism" of Stravinsky and Hindemith and other accepted leaders of the modernist movement, though by no means without value historically and even intrinsically, is none the less a position of defense rather than of attack. Its stabilizing tendencies are proved by the fact that it has enabled a great number of modernist composers to accept teaching posts in academic institutions, its cultural aim being frankly the incorporation of modern stylistic procedures into what is left, if any, of the classic tradition.

The joke of it all on the neo-classic modernists is that their program turns out to be exactly that of Johannes Brahms. Modern music has, in the words of a recent correspondent, writing of the Hindemith First Symphony, "executed a masterly retreat to the heavily fortified Brahms Line." Examine ten, almost any ten, modern symphonies and you will see, I think, that this is true. If my correspondent is right (and I think he is), it turns out that at the same time that our general public is taking to Brahms as a frankly popular symphonist like Tchaikovsky or Sibelius, the modernist intellectuals discover themselves to be following in exactly his pattern of basic tradtionalism with contemporary surfacing. They also find themselves faced, as Brahms did, with the necessity of climbing down from their tower of ivory tinycraft and doing something about symphonic eloquence. If they don't, the symphony public won't respect them; and if the symphony public doesn't respect them, they lose face in the college where they teach.

It is sad to see official modernism turn out to be, after all, doubly conformist and wholly conservative. Maybe after the war there will be musical advance from the Brahms Line again. But for the present both the general public and most of the intellectual musicians are immured behind its surprisingly solid bastions. And if it is not pleasant to see modernist composers timidly pulling their punches and, what is worse, striking in many cases below the public's belt, it is salutary to observe that same public rising spontaneously to the work of a man who, though not a grandly original master, was a musical workman of high integrity and unquestioned nobility of thought.

April 26, 1942

THE TOSCANINI CASE

¶ Arturo Toscanini's musical personality is a unique one in the modern world. One has to go back to Mendelssohn to find its parallel. A reactionary in spirit, he has none the less revolutionized orchestral conducting by his radical simplification of its procedures. Almost wholly devoted to the playing of familiar classics, he has at the same time transformed these into an auditory image of twentieth-century America with such unconscious completeness that musicians and laymen all over the world have acclaimed his achievement without, I think, very much bothering to analyze it. They were satisfied that it should be, for the most part, musically acceptable and at all times exciting.

Excitement is of the essence in Toscanini's concept of musical performance. But his is not the kind of excitement that has been the specialty of the more emotional conductors of the last fifty years. Theirs was a personal projection, a transformation through each conductor's own mind of what the conductor considered to be the composer's meaning. At its best this supposed a marriage of historical and literary with musical culture. It was derived from the conducting style of Richard Wagner; and its chief transmitters to us have been the line that is von Bülow, Nikisch, and Beecham. For musicians of this tradition every piece is a different piece, every author and epoch another case for stylistic differentiation and for special understanding. When they miss, they miss; but when they pull it off, they evoke for us a series of new worlds, each of these verifiable by our whole knowledge of the past, as well as by our instinctive sense of musical meaning. Theirs is the humane cultural tradition. And if their interpretations have sometimes been accompanied by no small amount of personal idiosyncrasy and a febrile display of nerves, that, too, is a traditional concomitant of the sort of trancelike intensity that is necessary for the projection of any concept that is a product equally of learning and of inspiration.

Toscanini's conducting style, like that of Mendelssohn (if Wagner is to be believed about the latter), is very little dependent on literary culture and historical knowledge. It is disembodied music and disembodied theater. It opens few vistas to the understanding of men and epochs; it produces a temporary, but intense, condition of purely auditory excitement. The Maestro is a man of music, nothing else. Being also a man of (in his formative years) predominantly theatrical experience, he reads all music in terms of its possible audience effect. The absence of poetical allusions and of historical references in his interpretations is significant, I think, of a certain disdain for the general culture of his individual listeners. In any case, whatever he may have inherited of nineteenth-century respect for individualistic culture was sacrificed many years ago to an emphasizing of those musical aspects that have a direct effect on everybody. It is extraordinary how little musicians discuss among themselves Toscanini's rightness or wrongness about matters of speed and rhythm and the tonal amenities. Like any other musician, he is frequently apt about these and as frequently in error. What seems to be more important than all that is his unvarying ability to put over a piece. Like Mendelssohn, he quite shamelessly whips up the tempo and sacrifices clarity and ignores a basic rhythm, just making the music, like his baton, go round and round, if he finds his audience's attention tending to waver. No piece has to mean anything specific; every piece has to provoke from its hearers a spontaneous vote of acceptance. This is what I call the "wow technique."

Now, what are we accepting when we applaud a Toscanini rendition? Not personal poetry, certainly; nor any

historical evocation; nor a literal reading of a classic score.
I think it is his power of abstraction we are acclaiming, the
abstraction of a piece's essential outline. If he has reduced
conducting motions to their basic outline, too, that is not
mere elegance on his part, nor ostentation either; it is a systematic throwing away of all refinements that might inter-
fere with his schematic rendition. His whole accent is on
the structure of a piece. Its thematic materials are the
building blocks with which that structure is erected. Expression and ornamentation are details to be kept in place.
Unity, coherence, and emphasis are the qualities that must
be brought out.

Both theatrical experience and poor eyesight are probably responsible for the Toscanini style. When one cannot
depend on reading a score in public, one must memorize
everything. And when one memorizes everything, one
acquires a great awareness of music's run-through. One runs
it through in the mind constantly; and one finds in that way
a streamlined rendering that is wholly independent of detail and even of specific significance, a disembodied version that is all shape and no texture. Later, in rehearsal,
one returns to the texture; and one takes care that it serve
always as neutral surfacing for the shape. For shape is what
any piece is always about that one has memorized through
the eye and the inner ear. Playing a piece for shape and
run-through gives (if the piece has shape at all) the most
exciting effect that can ever be produced. It is the same
procedure as that of directing a melodrama on the stage,
character and dialogue being kept at all times subsidiary
to the effects of pure theater, to the building up in the audience of a state of intense anxiety that is relieved only at
the end of the last act.

The radical simplification of interpretative problems that
all this entails has changed orchestral conducting from a
matter of culture and of its personal projection into something more like engineering. Young conductors don't bother
much any more to feel music or to make their musicians
feel it. They analyze it, concentrate in rehearsal on the es-
sentials of its rhetoric, and let the expressive details fall
where they may, counting on each man's skill and everybody's instinctive musicianship to take care of these eventually. Poetry and nobility of expression are left for the last,

to be put in as with an eyedropper or laid on like icing, if there is time. All this is good, because it makes music less esoteric. It is crude because it makes understanding an incidental matter; but it is a useful procedure and one wholly characteristic of our land and century. About its auditory result I am less enthusiastic than many. I find Toscanini's work, for the most part, spiritually unenlightening, except when he plays Italian music. But that is only a personal experience; many musicians find otherwise. And those of us who like more differentiation, more poetry, and more thought in our music, who find his much advertised fidelity to the notes of musical scores to be grossly exaggerated, his equally advertised "perfection" to be more so, and both of these aims, even when achieved, to be of secondary importance, even we must admit, nevertheless, the reality of Toscanini's musicianship and achievements. For good or for ill, and most probably for good, orchestral conducting will never be the same again.

I say most probably for good, because it is noticeable already that lesser conductors analyze music better than they used to and that this simple extraction of a work's formal essence tends to facilitate rather than to obfuscate differentiations of style and expression in the conducting of men whose musical experience is more limited but whose general culture is more ample than Toscanini's. Many of his contemporaries and most of his famous predecessors have had more interesting minds. Almost none has been so gifted a natural musician and so strictly professional a showman. He has simplified the technique of the art by eliminating all the hangovers of Late Romantic emotionalism and by standardizing a basic technique of musical rendition that is applicable to any piece in the world, whether one understands its spirit or not. This may be treason to culture, or it may be merely a radical purging of culture's own fifth column. I fancy it includes a bit of both. In any case, I believe that the introduction of a new cultural understanding into orchestral rendition, as one observes this in the work of Alexander Smallens, for instance, and in that of most of the other good American conductors, is as directly traceable to Toscanini's having previously eliminated practically all cultural understanding from it as the means of their

doing so have been facilitated by his radical simplifications
of conducting procedure.

Toscanini's influence lies, so far, chiefly in America. Europe follows Furtwängler and Beecham and great French
conductors like Monteux and Münch. It has no need of ex-
changing their interpretations or their working methods for
anything so oversimplified as Toscanini's. The Romantic
tradition has already transformed itself there into a modern
tradition that is as rich and as complex and as generally
satisfactory to the mind as the tradition of Wagner and
Nikisch was. That tradition is too complex for us. We admire the work of the great European conductors, but we do
not quite understand how it is done. A century of import-
ing them has not revealed their secrets to our local boys.
We watched Toscanini work for ten years at the Philharmonic; and now there are 30,000 symphony orchestras in
the United States, practically all of them led by the local
boys. He is the founding father of American conducting.
Whether we like or not the way he interprets music (and
I don't much, though many do), his place in our musical
history is certainly an important one.

In any European sense, he is not a complete musician,
as the late Karl Muck was, and perhaps not even a great
technician, as Reiner is, for example. He is too completely
self-taught to be wholly responsible to any Great Tradition.
But he is a thoroughgoing professional, although self-
taught; and he has shown our musicians how to be thoroughgoing professionals too, although self-taught. The
value of this contribution to our musical life cannot be
overestimated. Any influence Toscanini might possibly have
on European musical life would be anti-cultural. His ruth-
less clearing away here, however, of Romantic weeds and
unsuccessful implantations has made a space where conductors are already being grown locally. And a steady
supply of good American conductors to the local market
is the thing above all else needful right now to the public
understanding and the autochthonous development of
American musical composition.

May 17, 1942

SHOWER OF GOLD

¶ Wanda Landowska's harpsichord recital of last evening at the Town Hall was as stimulating as a needle shower. Indeed, the sound of that princely instrument, when it is played with art and fury, makes one think of golden rain and of how Danaë's flesh must have tingled when she found herself caught out in just such a downpour.

Landowska's program was all Bach and Rameau, with the exception of one short piece by Froberger. She played everything better than anybody else ever does. One might almost say, were not such a comparison foolish, that she plays the harpsichord better than anybody else ever plays anything. That is to say that the way she makes music is so deeply satisfactory that one has the feeling of a fruition, of a completeness at once intellectual and sensuously auditory beyond which it is difficult to imagine anything further.

On examination this amplitude reveals itself as the product of a highly perfected digital technique operating under the direction of a mind which not only knows music in detail and in historical perspective but has an unusual thoroughness about all its operations. There are also present a great gift of theatrical simplicity (she makes all her points clearly and broadly) and a fiery Slavic temperament. The latter is both concealed and revealed by a unique rhythmic virtuosity that is at the same time characteristic of our century and convincingly authentic when applied to the execution of another century's music.

It is when this rhythm is most relentless that I find Wanda Landowska's work most absorbing. Free recitative and the affetuoso style she does with taste, and she spaces her fugal entries cleanly. But music becomes as grand and as impersonal as an element when she gets into a sustained rhythmic pattern. It makes no difference then whether the music is dainty, as in the Rameau suite played, or dancy and vigorously expository, as in both the Rameau suite and the Bach B-flat Partita. It is full of a divine fury and irresistibly insistent.

There is no need of my reviewing the works played, which are all great music, save perhaps to pay tribute to Rameau, who got so much of the sweetness of France, as well as its grace and its grandeur, into his E-minor Suite. And to mention the romantic and rhapsodical beauty of a piece by Johann Froberger entitled *Lament Composed in London to Dispel Melancholy to be Played Slowly with Discretion.*

October 22, 1942

IT'S ABOUT TIME

¶ Mr. Toscanini has played four American pieces in a row. He did it yesterday afternoon at a concert given before an invited audience in Studio 8-H, Radio City, the program being broadcast as the season's first of the N. B. C. Symphony Orchestra. Whether this conductor, in his whole American career, which covers well over thirty years, has formerly played that much American music all together I am not sure. But undeniably his previous encouragement of local art has been microscopic. Well, it's never too late to mend. And yesterday's gesture, which one hopes is the beginning of some fuller amends, was gratefully received by a large hand-picked audience.

It was handsomely carried out, too, with all the attention to detail and careful effort to understand the spirit of musical works that are characteristic of Mr. Toscanini's conducting. If the renditions were not the most beautiful one could imagine, that is probably due to the fact that the N. B. C. orchestra is not the finest instrumental group in the world. It plays with attention, as all radio orchestras do; and some of the soloists are first-class. But the ensemble is far from homogeneous, and nowhere is there much extra beauty of tone. Also there were not yesterday enough strings to balance the brass and percussion, so that the tuttis all sounded clattery. Nevertheless, the renditions, if not especially lovely, were at all times spirited, neat, and snappy.

Loeffler's *Memories of My Childhood* is old-fashioned impressionism of the Franco-Bostonian school. It is full of trick orchestration, and its contrapuntal texture is respectable. It is literate music-writing, but it doesn't get off the ground. It meanders gracefully without ever taking flight.

Morton Gould's *Lincoln Legend* takes the air a little better, but it is always having to make emergency landings in swampy places. After sitting on some vaguely Middle Western landscape for a time, it gets off to quite a promising joyride with *John Brown's Body* and *The Old Gray Mare*; but a lack of something necessary constantly pulls it back to earth. It next does some desultory hedge-hopping and then finally bogs down not far from where it started. It, too, is full of trick orchestration, though less ojectionably than other works I have heard by this composer.

Paul Creston's *Choric Dance No. 2* sounds to me like a fine piece. The material is interesting, the development of it imaginative, the rhythm far from banal, and the sentiment sustained. His instrumentation is sonorous, well-calculated, and appropriate. The work has atmosphere, too. It sounds like a choric dance. It does not sound like somebody's memories of his musical education.

Gershwin's *Rhapsody in Blue* is a modern classic. It has stood tough treatment from lots of people, and it is still a beautiful and gay work. It got rough treatment yesterday, from Benny Goodman's opening lick to Mr. Toscanini's final wallop. Goodman established a tone of high virtuosity. Earl Wild, the piano soloist, carried this on and added an affetuoso radio manner that alternated brilliant and violent execution of the hotcha passages with a studied rubato in the lyrical ones that made one wish he would stop fooling around and let the show get on. Mr. Toscanini didn't have a chance to do much to the piece till the songlike theme with horn accompaniment came in.

Mistaking this for Tchaikovsky (it does sound rather like *Romeo and Juliet*), he leaned on it heavily and then began building up a Warner Brothers finale. It all came off the wagon like a ton of bricks. It was the *Rhapsody in Blue* all right, as what rendition isn't? But it was as far from Gershwin's own way of playing the piece as one could imagine. George played it straight, kept the rhythm going, even in the passages of free recitation, which he treated as comments on the more animated parts, not as interruptions of them. He didn't moon around, and he didn't get brutal.

I don't expect every artist to do every piece just as the author used to. If a work is any good, it can stand lots of reinterpreting. But I was a little sorry yesterday to hear this gay, sweet, rhapsodical number treated to a routine glamorizing that rubbed all the bloom off it and left its surface as glittery as a nickel-plated Apollo Belvedere.

November 2, 1942

STRAUSS AND WAGNER

¶ Three of Richard Strauss's operas—*Salomé, Elektra,* and *Der Rosenkavalier*—have provoked worldwide admiration. Their musical style has long been called by the vague term "post-Wagnerian." Their whole method, musical and dramatic, seems to me, however, to merit a more specific denomination. The German aesthetic most current in poetry, painting, and the theater arts during the epoch of their composition has always been known as expressionism or, in German, *Expressionismus.*

Considering the important role played in the very creation of these works by literary and theatrical modernism, it is only just to their composer to credit him with having something on his mind beyond a mere continuation or extension of the Wagnerian musical technique. Two of them were made in close collaboration with a poet, Hugo von Hofmannsthal. The other, *Salomé*, uses as libretto the German translation of a tragedy written originally in French by Oscar Wilde. It is not to be denied, I think, that however old-fashioned this sort of literature may seem nowadays, all three plays have a linguistic style and a moral (or amoral) consistency that make them more distinguished entertainment than any of the mythological poems that Richard Wagner (who was not properly a man of letters at all, in spite of his large literary production) ran up for himself. Wagner's best works are full even of musical inequalities, and the contrast between their musical vigor and their religio-philosophico-poetic flaccidness has always been a scandal. Strauss's three great ones (I do not know his others well) are all of a piece. You can take them or leave them, but you cannot separate their music from what it expresses.

Strauss's concept of dramatic composition, though derived from Wagner's, turns out in practice to give a quite different result. It begins, of course, by accepting the Wagnerian formulas of the convulsive accompaniment and of the expansion of time. I do not know where Wagner picked up the idea of scrapping all accompanimental formality, of eschewing, I mean, all orchestral figurations of an abstract character. Neither Gluck nor Beethoven nor Weber nor Meyerbeer nor Berlioz, from all of whom Wagner appropriated theatrical procedures, ever did anything of the kind. They made their accompaniments appropriate and expressive, but it never occurred to any of them to destroy their function as a sort of auditory proscenium by whose static structure the more sensitive and personal music of the characters themselves is framed.

Characterization and all personal expression are classically the role of the vocal line and take place on the stage, just as atmosphere and dramatic emphasis are that of the orchestra and belong in the pit. In Wagner, and even more in Strauss, the orchestra takes over the work of characterization, as well as that of emotional analysis and amplification, leaving little for the singing actors to do beyond a certain amount of intoned speech-imitation in the low register, punctuated by intensely pushed-out cries in the upper. Not appearing ridiculous while they stand around waiting for their emotions to be described by the orchestra has always been the acting problem of Wagnerian singers. Nobody minds the eight to twelve minutes of relative immobility during which the Countess Almaviva in Mozart's

Marriage of Figaro sings her "Dove sono" or Charpentier's Louise describes her own love life in an aria beginning, "Depuis le jour." But when Sieglinde, in the first act of *Die Walküre*, has nothing to do but cross the stage once while the orchestra plays a fifteen-minute footnote, it becomes evident to all that something should really be arranged to keep her occupied.

Strauss avoided this kind of situation by choosing stories about people who were not too dignified—who were, indeed, human-all-too-human (preferably outrageous)— and by putting the playwriting of these into skilled hands. He did not ask his artists either to stand around doing nothing or to do very much continuously expressive singing (they've enough to do getting the notes right). He gave them instead a literary and orchestral blueprint for acting all over the stage. Hence it is that, though the vocal line is always static and often musically nondescript, the visual drama, like the auditory orchestral one, is constantly and intensely convulsive. The convulsiveness all round is greater than in Wagner; can afford to be so because Strauss, a composer of much experience in the concert forms, can always make an act hold together, give it shape, progress, and conclusion, no matter how much violence goes on, even at a length, as in *Elektra*, of nearly two hours.

It is not my thesis that Strauss is the greater composer of the two. He is not. His thematic invention is too often bromidic and careless. He is a better musician than Wagner, yes, though not nearly so original or powerful a musical mind. His operas (or music-dramas) are certainly made after the Wagnerian model. But what happened to the Wagnerian model in Strauss's hands is something like this: he kept the convulsive accompaniment and the augmentation of time; but, feeling a need to correct the embarrassment to actors and to the public that Wagner had caused by taking most of its dramatic responsibility away from vocal expression, he called in expert literary men, who tightened up the plays, while they searched in legend and in abnormal psychology for subjects suitable to convulsive orchestral treatment by a master hand.

It is exactly this research into the lurid and its rendering in the cataclysmic style that constitutes the kind of German art known to its practitioners as *Expressionismus*.

Musically and musico-dramatically Strauss is its world master. It is not incorrect to call Strauss's music post-Wagnerian; it is merely insufficient. Because expressionism represents a rebirth rather than a mere survival of the Wagnerian music-drama, the term is sufficient only if we admit, as I see no reason for not admitting, that the whole expressionist movement came into existence spiritually, as well as temporally, after Wagner.

December 13, 1942

1943

FREE LOVE, SOCIALISM, AND WHY
GIRLS LEAVE HOME

¶ Yesterday afternoon's performance of *Louise* at the Metropolitan Opera House was one of mounting power. It began rather weakly with Raoul Jobin singing throatily and off pitch and Grace Moore posing in attitudes derived from still photographs of Sarah Bernhardt. It picked up with the entrance of Doris Doe, and it became a real dramatic exposition when Ezio Pinza arrived. The sweeping musical conception of Sir Thomas Beecham, who conducted, and the tonal beauty of the symphonic passages made it evident, too, that a musico-dramatic occasion of some magnitude was in progress.

The second act belonged to the conductor and to the ensemble, as it should, with Maxine Stellman adding a handsomely sung solo in the dressmaking scene. The third act was everybody's. Miss Moore began it with a good "Depuis le jour." She and Mr. Jobin then got through the conversation about socialism and their love-duet and had just gone into the house when the surprise party arrived with lanterns and dancers and a brass band. Here Sir Thomas and the chorus took over again and did a rousing "Coronation of the Muse," with Nina Youchkevitch dancing most prettily. Then Miss Doe came on; and everybody else left but Louise and Julien, the alto Mother giving at this point a well-sung and excellently acted summons for Daughter to come home and console sick Father. One felt one had been through quite a bit of excitement by this time, but the height of it was yet to come.

The last act was a triumphant rendition dramatically,

vocally, and musically by Miss Moore, Miss Doe, Mr. Pinza, Sir Thomas, and the orchestra of one of the most shocking family brawls I have ever witnessed. Everybody was superb. Indeed, this climactic summary of all the reasons why girls leave home was of a sweep and power that marked the afternoon as memorable. It also brought to this reviewer's notice the fact that the whole plot and libretto of *Louise* are literature.

It has long been supposed that Gustave Charpentier wrote his own text for this opera; and, indeed, no other author is named on the title page of the score. I do not know exactly how much work the composer did on the libretto; but the poet Max Jacob once told me that the plot of it was conceived and much of the dialogue written down in one evening at a dinner of Charpentier and some literary friends in a Montmartre restaurant, Jacob himself being present and participating in the communal creation. Also that the poet Saint-Pol-Roux was the one writer there who remembered to put his name to the work. He may also have done more on it at a later time, because Jacob assured me that Saint-Pol-Roux received performing-rights fees regularly for *Louise* through the Society of Dramatic Authors and Composers.

Whatever may be the exact history of this libretto, however, it is certainly not the work of a literary amateur. Its intrigue is tightly woven; its characterization is powerful; and the dialogue is simple, direct, and stylistically pure in a way hardly to be expected of a composer who has never shown elsewhere any unusual literary mastery. What is his and characteristic, of course, is the musical mastery, manifest throughout the opera, of all the implications of a brilliant literary text. The opera is built up with clear musical characterization, an intense expression of the atmosphere of its subject and a sound respect for the plain language of plain people. Its musical continuity is symphonic in character without being overcomplex; and its orchestral coloration is fanciful, appropriately picturesque, and expert. It if were not for the trumpery musical quality of two of the chief leitmotives—Louise's and Julien's—and the consequent monotony of their subsequent developments, the work might rank beside *Carmen* and *La Traviata* in operatic literature. Even so, when conducted with understanding and acted with some style, as it was yesterday (not to speak of much excellent singing), it is a pretty poignant piece of musical theater.

January 16, 1943

A GOOD START

¶ Operating on the principle that one good recital deserves another, the Town Hall chooses each year a debutant musician of noteworthy qualities and awards him an engagement the following year in its endowment series of musical events. Last year's laureate was William Kapell, pianist, nineteen years old at the time of his first Town Hall recital. Last night he gave his award recital; and pretty fine it was, I must say.

It is a mistake to expect of youth any unusual concentration of fire and poetry. This is more normally an attribute of middle age. What youth has, at its best, is a small, hard musical gift and a certain freshness of training. The latter is likely to be tensely efficient rather than beautiful, the former clearly visible through it rather than wholly expressed. In Mr. Kapell's case the technical proficiency is most impressive. He plays clearly and cleanly and powerfully, with good tone, and with an ample range of weights and colors. His natural musicality shows up in the rhythm and in his tonal proportions and balances, which are always interesting, occasionally quite novel. His temperament is evident in the way different pieces come out sounding like different pieces in spite of the fact that they are all approached with the same grandiose preoccupation.

Mr. Kapell was better in the modern works than in the classical ones. Scarlatti, Beethoven, and Mozart might have been three pseudonyms of one man, so little did he appear to feel any necessity for varying his stylistic approach to them. The Beethoven sonata, however, was notable for its final rondo, which was dry and precise, and high in coloristic relief. Everywhere, too, there was a sense of music's continuity, an overall conception that is characteristic of musicians with more than average mental powers. It was this continuous progress, indeed, that saved Mr. Kapell from superficiality in the pieces of Chopin and Liszt.

Prokofiev, Persichetti, and Fuleihan, however, were the writers who drew from him the fullest intellectual understanding. He made them all sound rather alike, I must say, as he had previously done with his classics and his Romantics. But they sounded as if he had chosen them for their resemblance to his own image of the modern world, not as if he were imposing an inappropriate similarity upon them. He gave, thus, a most unusual tone to his recital, namely, that of an unconscious but perfectly real modernism. And here his youth served him well. The middle-aged play old music as if they owned it; but they are mostly pretty inept, in spite of goodwill, at rendering the contemporary. Mr. Kapell walked through the ancients (if so we may refer to our predecessors) like an intelligent somnambulist, making no false steps, but seeming to be aware of nothing beyond the exactitude and grace of his locomotion. But when he played the music of his own time he woke up and made sense.

January 21, 1943

ACQUAINTANCE WITH WAGNER

¶ About once a year your reviewer ventures to dip an ear again into the Wagnerian stream. He thinks he ought to find out whether anything about it has changed since the last time or if anything has possibly changed in him that might provoke a reversal of judgment about it all and a return of the passionate absorption with which he used to plunge himself into that vast current of sound. This season's expedition took him to hear *Die Walküre* last Tues-

day at the Metropolitan Opera House. So far as he could
tell, nothing has altered since last he heard the work.

The tunes are the same tunes as before, some excellent
and some not so excellent. The symphonic development
of the leitmotives continues to vary in interest according
to the musical value of the leitmotives themselves. Those
that contain chromatic progressions, arpeggios, or skips of
a major sixth still become monotonous on repetition, while
those based on narrower skips and diatonic movement continue to support expansion without strain. Wagner never
learned the elementary rules of thumb that aided Bach and
Handel and Haydn and Mozart and even Schubert to estimate the strength of melodic materials. His rhythmic patterns are frequently monotonous, too; and he has a weakness for step-wise modulating sequences.

The instrumentation remains rich in sound and highly
personal. And if it often creates its theatrical excitement
by the use of mere hubbub, that excitement is still a dependable effect and the instrumental dispositions involved
are acoustically sound. It has long seemed to me that Wagner's original contributions to musical art are chiefly of an
orchestral nature. Indeed, orchestration is the one element
of musical composition in which Wagner had sound training, exception being made for the rules of German declamation, which he derived for himself by studying the works
of Mozart and Weber and Meyerbeer. His music-writing is
more varied in quality than is that of any other composer
of equal celebrity, even Berlioz; but no matter what the
quality, it always sounds well. It is always instrumentally
interesting and infallibly sumptuous.

Sometimes the musical quality runs high, too. There are
unforgettable moments of invention in any of Wagner's
operas, though the percentage of memorable pages out of
his whole production will probably be inferior to that in
Verdi and certainly far less than what one can find in Mozart.
And their excellence is not due wholly to orchestral oro-
tundity; he often wrote charmingly for the voice, as well.
He wrote rather more effectively, however, it seems to me,
for the higher voices than for the lower. His tenor and
soprano roles are more pleasing and more expressive than
his alto, baritone, or bass writing. His Ortruds and his

Frickas are always a slight bore; and King Marke, Wotan, Hunding, Fafner, even for habitual Wagnerians, are proverbially great big ones. He had little feeling for the heavier vocal timbres, and there is no real liberty in his handling of them.

Well, all that is all that. Wagner was a gifted and original composer, though an unusually uneven one. And his lack of early musical instruction is probably the cause of his major faults, though I doubt if ignorance can be held responsible for any of his virtues. He was not, as a matter of fact, an ignorant man; he was merely an autodidact, lacking, like most autodidacts, more in aesthetic judgment than in culture. He read voluminously and understood what he read; he reflected in a penetrating way about aesthetic matters, and he mastered easily any musical technique he felt he needed. His troublesomeness on the musical scene has always been due less to the force of his musical genius (which was recognized from the beginning) than to the fact that neither instinct nor training had prepared him to criticize his own work with the objectivity that the quality of genius in it demanded. As a result, every score is a sea beach full of jewelry and jetsam. Fishing around for priceless bits is a rewarding occupation for young musicians, just as bathing in the sound of it is always agreeable to any musical ear. But musicians are likely to find nowadays that the treasure has been pretty well combed and that continued examination of the remnants yields little they hadn't known was there before.

What continues to fascinate me is not Wagner's music but Wagner the man. A scoundrel and a charmer he must have been such as one rarely meets. Perfidious in friendship, ungrateful in love, irresponsible in politics, utterly without principle in his professional life, and in business a pure confidence-man, he represents completely the nineteenth-century ideal of toughness. He was everything the bourgeois feared, hoped for, and longed to worship in the artist. The brilliancy of his mind, the modernity of his culture, the ruthlessness of his ambition, and the shining armor of his conceit, even the senile erotomania of his later years, all went into a legend that satisfied the longings of many a solid citizen, as they had long before made him an attractive figure to aristocrats and intellectuals.

To know him was considered a privilege by the greatest figures of Europe, though many of these found the privilege costly. His conversation was stimulating on every subject; his wit was incisive and cruel; his polemical writing was expansive, unprincipled, and aimed usually below the belt. He was the most inspiring orchestral conductor and the most penetrating music critic of his century. His intellectual courage and the plain guts with which he stood off professional rivalries, social intrigues, political persecution, and financial disaster are none the less breathtaking for the fact that his very character invited outrageous fortune.

All this remains; it is available in many books. The music remains, too; and it is available at virtually every opera house in the world. It would not bring out the crowds or incite conductors and vocalists to the serious efforts it does if it did not have, in spite of its obvious inequalities, strength beneath its fustian still. To deny that strength were folly. To submit to it is unquestionably a pleasure. But what your reviewer would like most of all is to have known the superb and fantastic Wagner himself.

February 21, 1943

DISSENT FROM WAGNER

¶ A recent article of this column wherein it was suggested that the music of Richard Wagner was perhaps less interesting intrinsically than the personality of the man behind it has brought a certain amount of correspondence to the music desk, much of it, surprisingly, complimentary. The widow of a famous music critic wrote: "Your 'Acquaintance with Wagner' seems to me the last and best word on the gentleman. I read it with the greatest interest and shall keep it for future reading." A Bostonian composer mentioned Wagner's "overbearing confusion" and called

him "to me the least satisfactory of the larger musical phenomena."

Many persons, of course, consider Wagner the *most* satisfactory of the larger musical phenomena. That he *is* one
of the larger musical phenomena is not disputed. What has
long been argued about is the nature of the phenomenon
and its value to civilization. Its value to individual persons is a private matter, and the voting or ticket-buying
power of those persons is a statistical fact. Neither private
pleasures, however, nor public devotions prove anything in
art. Unless there is unanimous acceptance of a man's work,
which is rare, it is the people who don't like it that have the
last word in its evaluation.

There is no sounder proof of Shakespeare's central position in English literature, or of Dante's in Italian, than the
fact that nobody objects to it. Such a position in music is
occupied, through common consent, by a triumvirate—
Bach, Beethoven, and Mozart. Wagner's pretensions to universal authority are inadmissible from the very fact that the
music world is not unanimous about admitting them. Mozart is a great composer, a clear value to humanity, because
no responsible musician denies that he is. But Wagner is
not an absolute value from the very fact that Rossini denied
it and Nietzsche denied it and Brahms denied it and, in our
own time, Debussy and Stravinsky have denied it. This does
not mean that, with the exception of Rossini, all these composers (including Nietzsche) have not stolen a trick or two
from Wagner or accepted him as a major influence on their
style. They have. But the fact that they have accepted his
work with reservations is what proves my thesis.

Similar reservations are current about the music of
Berlioz, of Gluck, of Weber, of Verdi, of Mahler, Strauss,
Hindemith, Milhaud, and Aaron Copland, not to speak of
the symphonists that descend from Brahms—the line of
Tchaikovsky and Franck and Sibelius and Shostakovich
and Roy Harris. These men represent musical values of a
high order, but the values they represent are not satisfactory to all. They are therefore minor masters. J. S. Bach
and Handel and Haydn and Mozart and Beethoven and
Schubert and Chopin are major masters. So, very probably,
are Schumann and Debussy. Richard Wagner is not. He
could not be with so many musicians against him.

It is not the purpose of this essay to prove that liking
Wagner's music is a low taste. Its purpose is to demonstrate
that Wagner's music is a taste like any other, wholly legitimate but in no way sacred. The great masters are a bore
to many people; they actively annoy almost none. But the
minor masters annoy a great many people in a great many
ways. There are excellent musicians who simply cannot
stand the Berlioz bravura; others find it invigorating. There
are those who are ravished by the sweetness of Grieg, carried away by the emphases of Verdi, or deeply shaken by
the Tchaikovskian eloquence. To others all this is superficial. A Wagnerian bath is the cleansing flood for their
souls. Still others find refreshment in the acidities of Stravinsky or in the dry champagne of Scarlatti and of Couperin.

All tastes are legitimate, and it is not necessary to
account for them unless one finds it amusing to do so. Dis-
tastes are equally legitimate, including a distaste for music
itself. If one has a distaste for the great masters of music,
or a complete indifference to them, one is not a musician;
that is all. But if one is a musician and if one has serious
reservations about the music of any given composer, those
reservations are grounds for suspicion that such music is
not wholly straightforward. If the reservations are shared
by other musicians, even a few, over a reasonable space of
time, then that music has failed to convince the world of its
purity.

It is the thesis of this reviewer that the music of Richard
Wagner is an achievement somewhat less remarkable than
that of the undisputed major masters of our tradition. The
argument for this thesis is the simple syllogism that the
canonization of a major master in any art requires a
virtually unanimous vote of the initiates and that Wagner
has never got anything approaching such a vote. He hoped,
and many of his friends believed, that he would get it eventually, that the hesitant of spirit would come round. In the
decade succeeding his death they seemed to be about to.
The peak of his music's prestige within the profession occurred around 1890. The decline of this has been continuous ever since, though there was a notable rise in its popular
acceptance between the two world wars. It seems now most
unlikely that any thorough or intellectual rehabilitation of

Wagner will take place until the wave of his box-office popularity shall have subsided.

And so for the present there is no reason why he
shouldn't provide sport for his enemies as well as delight
for the faithful. Most of all, right now, his music needs de-
bunking and deglamorizing, so that some unprejudiced
analysis of its virtues may eventually be possible. The question is not whether Wagner is one of the "larger musical
phenomena." Of course he is. Or whether he is one of the
prime numbers in music, which he certainly is not. The
question is simply how do the scores stand up page by page
beside those of other standard dramatic composers from
Mozart to Massenet. When the parishioners take up that
little bingo game, there will be surprises for all, I promise,
many of them agreeable.

March 7, 1943

SUPERFICIALLY WARLIKE

¶ The Boston Symphony Orchestra, assisted by the
Harvard Glee Club and the Radcliffe Choral Society, offered
yesterday afternoon in Carnegie Hall a program without
much inner unity. Such external cohesion as it had consisted of indirect references to the war.

The title of William Schuman's secular cantata, *A Free
Song,* refers, I take it, since the composition is partly fugal
in style, not to musical freedom but to freedom of some
other kind, economic, social, religious, amorous, or political. The times being what they are, one would probably be
safe in betting it was the latter, though of certain evidence
I have none, the chorus's effective enunciation of the text
being zero in row U. The music's intrinsic interest seemed
also to this listener to add up to a not high figure.

Private Samuel Barber's Essay for Orchestra, No. 1, is a
pretty piece but not a very strong one. It resembles more a
meditation than it does the kind of reasoned exposition one

usually associates with the prose form of that name. Perhaps Mr. Barber thinks of the word *essay* in its contemporary sense of a reflective composition on some relatively trivial subject. Certainly his musical material here is not striking. Neither, unfortunately, is his development of it, though there is, as always in this composer's music, grace. The military note was added to this performance by the composer's presence, bowing, in uniform.

Aaron Copland's *A Lincoln Portrait* consists of a pastorale, a scherzo, and a melodrama. The first is plain but pleasant; the second, a sort of county-fair scene made up of phrases out of Stephen Foster, is brilliantly picturesque. Lincoln himself comes into the portrait only by quotation, when an actor (yesterday it was Mr. Will Geer) speaks, as finale, over a slight orchestral accompaniment selected passages from the addresses of the great President. Even if Mr. Geer had not seen fit to utter these in the flat and twangy accent used in theatrical productions to characterize Vermont storekeepers, they would still have seemed, for all their grandeur, an unhappy ending to a musical work.

It is not easy to make a portrait of a person no longer living, as any artist will tell you. But the problem, difficult or not, is what it is; and Mr. Copland has chosen to essay it. By leaving off in the middle and simply inserting quotations from Lincoln's speeches, he has achieved a result comparable to what a painter would achieve if, after sketching in a period background of some kind, he were to substitute for a full rendering of his subject a half-dozen snapshots taken at various epochs of the latter's life, including something from the war period, of course.

The afternoon ended with an excellent performance of Beethoven's Fifth Symphony, of which the principal motif is currently thought to resemble the letter V in Morse code—three dots and a dash. This motif really consists, in its most frequent statement, of four dots, and in its initial, or motto, form of three dots and something the length of about fifteen dashes, a signal not admitted, so far as I know, in any telegraphic alphabet.

April 4, 1943

HOT JAZZ AT THE GOLDEN GATE

¶ The Sunday afternoon concerts at San Francisco's C. I. O. Hot Jazz Hall are a result of some lectures delivered last spring by Rudi Blesh at the San Francisco Museum of Art. These were illustrated by records from Mr. Blesh's own collection, as well as by non-processed executions. For the latter there was brought here from Louisiana no less an artist than Willie "Bunk" Johnson, considered by many the finest of all trumpet players. Johnson was an original member of the earliest hot group known, Buddy Bolden's Ragtime Band, organized in 1893 in New Orleans. For many years its leader, he is celebrated in the histories of hot music not only for his integrity as an artist but for his mastery of that imperious trumpet tone chiefly familiar to laymen nowadays through the work of his pupil Louis Armstrong.

At the closing of the lecture series many lovers of the hot wished to keep Mr. Johnson around, but the local musicians' union, not favorable to the hot style, has made it difficult for him to work. Negroes and whites are not allowed to play together, for one thing, and the informal participation in public music-making of visiting artists is forbidden, for another. There is, moreover, some kind of general ruling against jam sessions. Mr. Harry Bridges, regional director of the C. I. O. and long a patron of cultural activities (the San Francisco Symphony Orchestra is playing for his membership next week), came to the rescue of hot art by arranging a place for it in his union clubrooms. As a result, Bunk Johnson's Hot Seven play every Sunday afternoon all afternoon in an auditorium now known as the C. I. O. Hot Jazz Hall under the management of the Hot Jazz Society of San Francisco. Persons not members of this society can join at the door if properly introduced. Last Sunday there were perhaps five hundred people, a youngish but not adolescent audience consisting of well-dressed working people, professors, a goodly number of service men, both enlisted and commissioned, and one pretty young lady in a welder's uniform, complete with metal hat. Dancing was permitted in the back of the hall, and drinks were available in an adjoining bar.

The music was executed in the style known as New Orleans. The bass, a tuba, played straightforwardly and right on the beat. The drums indulged in no fancy work. Neither did the banjo. Piano, clarinet, trumpet, and trombone improvised with the greatest freedom but also with an astonishing sobriety. Nobody tried to show how fast he could play or how high. At no point was there any attempt to swing the beat or to fake a fury. Neither did any soloist try to conceal the tune. Variations were developed musically out of it and never left its expression for mere flambuoyancy, though Billy Singleton, who played piano as guest in several numbers, did expert work in thirds and chromatic octaves. Bob Barton, a youngster, played trombone with a fine dirty tone. Ellis Horne, the clarinet, is an accomplished mature artist and no show-off.

Bunk Johnson himself is an artist of delicate imagination, meditative in style rather than flashy, and master of the darkest trumpet tone I have ever heard. He is also the greatest master of "blue," or off-pitch, notes it has been my pleasure to encounter. The degrees of his deviation from normal pitch are infinite, and the taste with which he exploits this variety merits no less a word than impeccable. His timbres, his intonations, and his melodic invention are at all times expressive, at all times reasonable, and at all times completely interesting. His work takes on, in consequence, and so does that of those working with him, depth, ease, and lucidity. Nothing could be less sentimental or speak more sincerely from the heart, less jittery or move around more freely. Certainly no music was ever less confused.

The basic rhythm of his band is so solid and so plain that its effect on players and public alike is the opposite of that nervous exasperation that is frequently a result of jazz performance. It stills, rather, the nerves and allows the mind free play in that purely auditory perception of feeling that is the alpha and the omega of music. I suspect Mr. Bridges is right. This sort of music is as cultural an activity as any and more so than most. Certainly it is more rarely to be encountered at a high degree of purity than the symphonic

stuff. Both kinds of music, of course, are deplorably commercialized these days. Its purity, nevertheless, a noncom-
mercial quality, is wherein any music's cultural value lies.

August 8, 1943

THE PERSONALITY OF
THREE ORCHESTRAS

¶ Orchestras are not wholly the product of their
conductors. Their conductors train them and put them
through their paces in public. But the conductor is one personality, and the orchestra is another (in private life a hundred others). A good orchestral concert is really more a
duet than a domination.

Our three great Eastern ensembles, for instance—the
Philadelphia, the Boston, and the New York Philharmonic
—are as different from one another as the cities that created
them and that forged them slowly into the image of each
city's intellectual ideals. Conductors from outside have been
called in to aid this formation, and a few of these have left
traces of their own taste on that of the cities they have
worked for. But chiefly their function has been to care for a
precious musical organism, to watch over it, to perfect it in
the observance of the musical amenities, and to allow it to
mature according to its own nature and in accordance with
its community's particular temperament. The conductor is
never a static participant in such a process. He matures, too,
in harmony with the community if he stays a reasonable
length of time, is nourished and formed by local ideals, becomes a part of the thing to which he has contributed his
abilities.

Serge Koussevitzky and Eugene Ormandy are cases in
point of my thesis. They have been ripened and refined by
their association with the Boston and the Philadelphia orchestras in a way that was not predictable at all during

their previous careers. It was obvious always that both would go far, but it was not indicated to prophecy that Koussevitzky, the temperamental Slav, would become a master of orchestral understatement or that Ormandy, the boyish and straightforward central European, would become a sort of specialist of delicately equilibrated orchestral sensuality. These developments, I am sure, are as legitimately creditable to environmental influence as to any previously manifested characteristics. Contact with orchestras of powerful temperament and specific orientation, as well as responsibility to cities of ancient and irreducible character—Boston, the intellectually elegant and urbane; Philadelphia, where everything, even intellectual achievement and moral pride, turns into a luxury, into a sort of sensuous awareness of social differences—contact, conflict, and collaboration between their strong European and the even stronger local traditions has given to these conductors their quality of being both the creature and the guiding hand of their own orchestras.

It is surprising (and most pleasant) to observe how two orchestras as accomplished as these can differ so completely in the kind of sounds they make. Boston makes thin sounds, like the Paris orchestras, thin and utterly precise, like golden wire and bright enamel. Nothing ever happens that isn't clear. No matter what the piece, no matter how inspired or how mistaken the conductor's understanding of it, the Boston execution is always transparent. So perfectly turned out is any of its executions that, whether becoming to the work or not, it has a way of separating itself from it. It neither conceals the work nor presents it; it walks down the street beside it, rather, very much as a piece of consummate dressmaking will sometimes do with the lady who thinks she is wearing it.

The Philadelphia sonorities are less transparent, and the tonal balance is less stable. Because the sounds that make it up are all rounder and deeper and more human. They breathe; they seem almost to have sentience. They have a tactile quality, too, like a skin you might touch; yet they are never heavy nor hot. They are warm and moist and alive compared to Boston's Swiss-watchlike mechanism. As a price of this vibrancy, however, the Philadelphia Orchestra is not always easy to conduct. It is probably the most sensitive orchestra in the world. The leader can get a fortissimo out of it by lifting a finger, and he can upset the whole balance of it by any nervousness. Boston is tougher, more independent. No matter how the conductor feels or what mistakes he may make, the orchestra always plays correctly, saves its own face and his. Philadelphia is less objective, less rigidly mannered. But at its best it gives a more touching performance, achieves a more intimate contact with its audience. Boston, for all its glacial perfection, has no intimacy at all. No matter where one sits, the music seems very far away.

Our Philharmonic is a horse of another color and one that has had far too many riders. It has been whipped and spurred for forty years by guest conductors and by famous virtuosos with small sense of responsibility about the orchestra's future or about its relation to our community's culture. It has become erratic, temperamental, undependable, and in every way difficult to handle. The sound of it has of late years been more like an industrial blast than like a musical communication. By moments there has been lovely work, but such moments have had an air of being accidental, the result of one day's well-being in the life of a neurotic. When the Philharmonic has been good it has sometimes been very good, but when it has been bad it has as often gone clean out of bounds.

Mr. Rodzinski has undertaken to heal its neuroses. At least we presume that is what he has undertaken. Because improvement is noticeable already in tonal transparency, and a faint blush seems to be appearing on the surface of the string sounds. Rhythmic coordination, too, though far from normal, is definitely ameliorated. It is to be hoped sincerely that progress will continue. But let no one imagine that forty years of ill-treatment are going to be wiped out in a season. The Philharmonic will have to be retrained from the ground up, schooled for dependability, and accustomed to being able to count on its conductor. Under a steady and responsible hand it should in time develop into a team worthy of its magnificent personnel and of its nation-wide public. What specific virtues it may eventually develop are unpredictable. At present its faults, like those of any spoiled child or horse, are more easily definable than its qualities.

But it would be surprising if an orchestra so carefully selected, functioning in a city so sophisticated musically as
New York, did not, once convalescence from old ills is firmly
established, manifest characteristics of specific originality.

October 17, 1943

FRENCH RHYTHM

¶ What makes French music so French? Basically,
I should say, it is the rhythm. German musicians and Italian musicians tend to consider rhythm as a series of pulsations. French musicians consider pulsations as a special effect appropriate only to dance music, and they train their
musical young most carefully to avoid them in other connections. In the Italo-German tradition, as practiced nowadays, the written measure is likely to be considered as a
rhythmic unit and the first count of that measure as a dynamic impulse that sets the whole thing in motion. In
French musical thought the measure has nothing to do with
motion; it is a metrical unit purely. The bar line is a visual
device of notation for the convenience of executants, but the
French consider that it should never be perceptible to the
listener.

The French conceive rhythm as a duality of meter and accent. Meter is a pattern of quantities, of note lengths. Its minimum unit in execution is the phrase. Accent is a stress that
may occur either regularly or irregularly; but in any case, it
is always written in. It may occur on the first note of a
measure; but in well-written music it will usually appear
more frequently in other positions, since any regular mark-
ing off of metrical units tends to produce a hypnotic effect.
French music, unless it is written for the dance or unless it
aims to evoke the dance, has no dynamic propulsion at all.
It proceeds at an even rate, unrolls itself phrase by phrase
rather like Gregorian chant.

It is more than probable that the classical Viennese symphonists were accustomed to this kind of rhythmic articulation and took it for granted. Pulsation came into Viennese
symphonic execution around 1830, after the waltz had come
to dominate Vienna's musical thought. At any rate, discern-
ing Germans have frequently pointed out the superiority of
French renderings of their own classics. Wagner found the
Beethoven symphonies far better played by the Paris Conservatory Orchestra than anywhere in Germany, and he
based his own later readings on those of the French conductor Habeneck. Alfred Einstein, German Mozart
specialist of our own day, has avowed in his book, *Greatness
in Music*, his preference for French renditions of that composer. And certainly German organists have not in our century played Bach with any authority comparable to that of
Saint-Saëns, Widor, Vierne, Guilmant, and Schweitzer.

This acknowledged superiority of the French approach to
classical German music is due, I believe, to the survival in
French musical practice of observances about rhythm, elsewhere fallen into disuse. Those same observances are responsible, I believe, for the flowering of music in France that
is the most noteworthy event in the musical history of the
last seventy-five years. French harmonic innovations have
been striking, but so were those of Richard Strauss and of
Arnold Schönberg, of Gustav Mahler, even. Everybody has
played around at inventing a new harmony. Scriabin in Russia, Ives in Danbury, Connecticut, were no less original harmonically than Claude Debussy. What their music lacks is
true rhythmic life. The only music of our time that can
compare in this respect with that of the school of Paris is
American hot jazz. And this is based on the same duality of
meter versus accent that underlies French music.

The French rhythmic tradition is at once more ancient
and more modern than any other. It includes the medieval
plainsong and the Benedictine restoration of this, in which
a quantitative syllabic execution without regular stresses
turns out to be expressive and interesting. It includes the
French medieval and Renaissance music that grew out of
plainsong, the schools of Champagne and of Burgundy. It
remembers its own Baroque and Rococo styles. It is least
aware, perhaps, of the domain that is the very center and

pivot of German musical understanding, the world of nine-teenth-century Romanticism, though Chopin, Liszt, and, curiously, Schumann it considers as its own. All these it thinks of, along with Mussorgsky and Stravinsky and Span-ish dance music and the popular music of Java and Bali and Morocco and the United States, as in no way foreign to it-self.

The binding element, the thread that runs through all these different kinds of music is an absence of pulsating rhythm. In Greek theory quantities are one element of rhythm; stress is another; cadence (or phraseology) is the third. Pulsation has no place in this analysis. It is a special effect, derived from round dancing, only to be added to musical execution when round dancing is clearly implied as the subject of a musical passage. Its introduction elsewhere brings in a singsong element that tends to trivialize musical rhetoric. Bach played by Schweitzer or Landowska, Mozart and Haydn played by Beecham (who is no Frenchman but who remembers the eighteenth century as it was) and mod-ern French music conducted by Monteux or played on the piano by Schmitz are anything but trivial.

Other artists in other repertoires have their charms and their especial powers, like Horowitz's Liszt, Toscanini's Wag-ner, Walter's Brahms. These always seem to me like cases of pure genius, supported (excepting possibly for Walter) by no major tradition. But the others not only are supported by a major tradition; they support it, too. They are constantly tending it, pruning it, watering it, grafting new shoots on it, gathering from it new fruits. The parent stem of that tra-dition is, I think, a certain approach to rhythm. That ap-proach is as ancient as Hellas, as far-flung as China, Marra-kech, and New Orleans, as up-to-date as boogie-woogie or the percussion music of John Cage. I take this occasion to speak about it because there is better access to it right now in New York City than there has been in some years and be-cause I hope some of our young musicians, both composing and executant, may be induced here and now to profit by the occasion. I believe this view of rhythm to be the open sesame of musical advance today exactly as it has been all through history.

November 14, 1943

AMERICAN RHYTHM

¶ John Kirkpatrick, who gave a piano recital last night in Times Hall, has a way of making one feel happy about American music. He does this by loving it, understanding it, and playing it very beautifully. He plays, in fact, everything very beautifully that I have ever heard him play. But people who play that beautifully so rarely play American music that Mr. Kirkpatrick's recitals are doubly welcome, once for their repertory and again for his unique understanding of it.

The loveliness of his playing comes from a combination of tonal delicacy with really firm rhythm. Exactitude with flexibility at all the levels of loudness is the characteristic of American pianism that transcends all our local schools of composition. It is what makes us a major musical people, and it is exactly the rhythmic quality that escapes our European interpreters. European tonal beauty, of course, more often than not escapes American pianists. Mr. Kirkpatrick's combination of European tonal technique with full understanding of American rhythm makes his playing of American works a profoundly exciting thing and a new thing in music.

Charles Ives's *Concord* Sonata was esteemed by Lawrence Gilman the finest piece of music ever written by an American, and it very well may be that. Certainly it is a massive hunk of creation; four massive hunks, in fact. Because it is really four symphonic poems, named respectively, "Emerson," "Hawthorne," "The Alcotts," and "Thoreau": four full-length portraits done with breadth, tenderness, and wit. "The Alcotts" is the best integrated of these and probably the most original, or indigenous, in its musical material and fancy. I suspect that concert audiences would take eventually to all these portraits if they were performed separately for a time, since the whole work is longer than the ones people are now used to listening to. In any case, here is music, real music; and Americans should have no difficulty accepting its subject matter or understanding its ingenuous grandeurs.

Of the other works performed last night Theodore Chanler's Toccata in E-flat major seemed to me the most finely conceived and the most delicately indited. Roy Harris's early Piano Sonata, opus 1, is a coarse work and laborious. The MacDowell *Woodland Sketches* seemed charming and poetic, as always, but a little soft in their melodic material.

The encores consisted of two works by Stephen Foster, *The Old Folks' Quadrille* and a flute piece called *Anadolia*; a Prelude by Robert Palmer; Arthur Farwell's *Navajo War Dance*, and a *Trumpet Aire* by James Bremner, a composer of Revolutionary times. All these were good to hear, especially Mr. Palmer's strongly knit Prelude and Farwell's handsome evocation of Indian themes and rhythms. The others were agreeably antiquarian. And everything Kirkpatrick played turned into a poem.

November 24, 1943

HIGH-QUALITY SINGING

¶ All through Jennie Tourel's recital on Saturday night at Town Hall one had the impression of being present at the take-off of some new and powerful airplane for a round-the-world flight. One was aware that her previous vocal performances here, her test flights, so to speak, had inspired high confidence. Word had gone round the music world that her work was excellent in a way far beyond that of the average good singer; and a packed-in houseful of that world was present to judge, to describe, and, hopefully, to acclaim it. Miss Tourel's conquest of this well-disposed but critical audience was of a completeness without any local parallel since Kirsten Flagstad's debut at the Metropolitan Opera House some nine seasons ago.

Miss Tourel is of a wholly different musical temperament from Miss Flagstad, the only basis for comparison between the two artists being the degree of their vocal mastery, which places them together in the top category of living vocal musicians—together and virtually alone. Miss Tourel, who is a young woman (not far off thirty, I should guess), is not quite the mistress of her throat and face muscles in big climaxes that Miss Flagstad was (already over forty when she came here). Her fault in this respect comes, I fancy, from a way she has of opening her mouth very wide without compensating at the lips for this excessive relaxation. My explanation may not be physiologically correct, but I do think there is a slight fault in Miss Tourel's jaw position that shows up when she sings high notes loud. I also fancy that that fault is neither grave nor irremediable. With this single reserve, I found her vocal performance impeccable.

The voice is a mezzo-soprano of wide range, warm in timbre and unbelievably flexible. Miss Tourel is mistress of a wider range of coloration in all ranges and at all volumes than any other singer I have ever heard. Her pitch is perfect in the most difficult modern music. Her legato skips are the kind of *bel canto* one dreams about. Her enunciation in all languages, even in so introspective a work as Debussy's songs to words by Baudelaire, is cleanly projected at all times. Her musicianship in every domain is so thorough that from the whole technical and intellectual aspect her work belongs clearly with that of the great virtuosos of music.

Her gift for languages is at the bottom of much of her stylistic virtuosity. On Saturday night she sang in Italian, French, Russian, English, Portuguese, and Spanish, making them all sound like themselves, coloring her vowels to the characteristic timbres of those languages, revealing their special music, and cherishing their particular ways of expressing feeling. She moved around in each tongue as if it were a whole landscape and climate, untranslated, untranslatable, and unique. In none of the European ones did I sense any accent. Certainly in her English there was none.

This extreme mental and emotional flexibility, commanding a vocal skill of transcendent nature and commanded by musicianship of the highest order, produced, in a program of diversified works, a variety of musical experiences that is rarely encountered in a soloist's recital. There are singers who have her stylistic knowledge, but they mostly have inferior vocal powers. There are other singers, though few, who sing that well; but they are mostly either inferior as musicians or limited in their expressive scope. Miss Tourel is, I believe, unequaled among living singers for the high concentration in one artist of vocal skill, sound musicianship, and stylistic flexibility.

November 24, 1943

1944

MÉLISANDE

¶ The characters in *Pelléas et Mélisande* are well-bred, well-to-do French people. They don't talk about their business much; but they own property, wear good clothes, and seem to be running a small kingdom. They have strong passions, kind hearts, good manners, and an intense family life. They understand love and approve of it. What they cannot deal with is any vagueness on the subject. Mélisande's attractiveness for them seems to be due partly to the fact that she has no family ties (they can thus adopt her completely) and partly to the fact that her affections and her amorous tendencies are both powerful and imprecise. She fascinates them; they never know what to think of her. She keeps them guessing not through any plan but simply through the fact, astounding and incredible to them, that she has no plan, no conscious motives of any sort.

This lack of project, of intention on her part does not prevent her from acting with utter straightforwardness. Her one interest in life is being loved; she demands love from everybody and gets it. She pays willingly any price asked and suffers cheerfully all the consequences involved, early marriage, childbirth, and death. She will do anything to avoid not being loved. She lies about a ring she has lost; she submits to a thorough beating from her husband; she refuses to hold a grudge against anyone at any time. Her famous remark at the end of the flagellation scene reveals how egocentric is all her sweetness. "I am not happy here" is her whole comment on the incident. A lonely girl with a floating libido and no malice toward anyone can cause lots of trouble in a well-organized family.

Her husband sees trouble coming quite early, goes to bed

of a minor ailment, and tries to think the situation out. "Mélisande, be reasonable!" is his last plea. She doesn't know what he means. After that, tragedy is inevitable. Attempts on the husband's part to discipline her and to spy on her friendship with his younger brother merely bring out the relentless quality in her character, her inability to accept any discipline whatsoever. He tries to murder his brother. Then he pleads with him as man to man. But by that time the brother's sentiments are sufficiently definite so that he cannot, as an honest Frenchman, go back on them. Mélisande would not have collaborated on a renunciation, anyway. She would never have got the idea. So the young man is ordered away on a trip. When his departure provokes a real love scene (husband having impatiently shut them both out of the house one evening), there is at last a visible justification for running the deceiver through with a sword.

Nevertheless, Mélisande has the last word. She gives birth to a child, forgives her husband his violence by saying there is nothing to forgive, and dies sweetly, like Little Eva, after refusing to answer all direct questions about her love life. The husband has wanted to know whether he killed his brother unjustly. Also, with a legitimate curiosity, whether there is any chance he is not the father of the baby. Her reply is equivocal, "We have done nothing to be blamed for." The aged father, an observer from the beginning rather than an actor in the tragedy, thereupon brings out the following pearl of wisdom and of comfort for his bereaved son: "It is terrible, but it's not your fault." The French family is thus juridical-minded to the last.

This recital has one purpose only, to remind my readers and all who saw the lovely performance of this opera last week at the Metropolitan that the role of Mélisande is not an easy one to play. It has never been easy, and very few singing actresses have ever made a success of it. Mary Garden and Maggie Teyte were memorable. I have heard others do it, but none convincingly. Mélisande must be childlike on the surface and amorous underneath. She must be both affectionate and self-centered. She must radiate an unaware sexual preoccupation. And she must move delicately. The opera is her show, hers and the conductor's.

Bidu Sayao, in the present production, comes nearer to making the opera her show than any other singer I know of has done, excepting always Garden and Teyte. She has worked out a line of movement that is expressive, and her fragile youth is touching. It is the first star role I have seen her carry off at all, her whole previous effectiveness having been in the domain of the soubrette. She has not learned yet to project her amorous feelings and her sorrows in heroine style, as if the future of the cosmos hung upon them. But she seems to have made a beginning. Also she has created a Mélisande that, if it is not one of the great ones, is convincing, nevertheless.

Martial Singher, as Pelléas, overpowers her in every way. His vocalism, his declamation, his stage presence, his whole musical and dramatic equipment are of another magnitude. Their scenes together are his scenes, though there seems to be no intention on his part of making them so. All the same, Miss Sayao does a good Mélisande. Her characterization represents not only a step forward for her as a serious actress but also a contribution second only to that of Mr. Singher to a beautiful performance of a great work. When one remembers how many fine sopranos have made no effect at all in the role (though they have dreamed all their lives of singing it), one is obliged to recognize Miss Sayao's achievement as being a far from minor one.

January 30, 1944

REAL MODERN MUSIC

¶ Arnold Schönberg's Piano Concerto, which received its first performance anywhere yesterday afternoon by the N. B. C. Symphony Orchestra, Leopold Stokowski conducting and Eduard Steuermann playing the solo part, is the first original work for large orchestra by this master to be heard in New York since quite a long time back. For many of our young music-lovers it is no doubt their first hearing of any orchestral work of its kind. One cannot be too grateful to Mr. Stokowski for giving himself the trouble to prepare it and for paying his radio listeners the compliment of presuming their interest. [Leopold Stokowski's contract as conductor of the N. B. C. Orchestra was not renewed for the following year. His assiduity toward modern composition is considered in musical circles to be the chief reason for this change.]

The piece, which lasts a shade under twenty minutes, consists of four sections neatly sewn together and played without pause—a waltz, a scherzo, an adagio, and a rondo. All are based on a single theme, though there is considerable development of secondary material in the scherzo. The musical syntax is that commonly known as the twelve-tone system, which is to say that the employment of dissonance is integral rather than ornamental. The expression of the work is romantic and deeply sentimental, as is Schönberg's custom and as is the best modern Viennese tradition.

The instrumentation, too, is characteristic of its author. It is delicate and scattered. The music hops about from one instrument to another all the time. It sounds like chamber music for a hundred players. There is plenty of melody, but no massing of instruments on any single line for giving the melody emphasis, as is customary in oratorical symphonic writing. The work is not oratorical, anyway. It is poetical and reflective. And it builds up its moments of emphasis by rhythmic device and contrapuntal complication, very much as old Sebastian Bach was wont to do. Its inspiration and its communication are lyrical, intimate, thoughtful, sweet, and sometimes witty, like good private talk. At no point is there grandiloquence or theater. The work derives much of its impressiveness from its avoidance of any attempt to impress us by force.

Its great beauty is derived partly from the extreme delicacy and variety of its instrumentation and partly from the consistency of its harmonic structure (a result of its observance of the twelve-tone syntax). Its particular combination of lyric freedom and figurational fancy with the strictest tonal logic places it high among the works of this greatest among the living Viennese masters (resident now in Hollywood) and high among the musical achievements of our century. With the increasing conservatism of contemporary composers about matters harmonic, many of our young people have never really heard much modern music. Radi-

cal and thoroughgoing modern music, I mean. It is too
seldom performed. Well, here is a piece of it and a very fine
one, a beautiful and original work that is really thought
through and that doesn't sound like anything else.

Eduard Steuermann played the piano part with all delicacy and love. There isn't much in it to show off with, but
the piano is there all the time. It weaves in and out rather
in chamber-music style, and Mr. Steuermann never overplayed it or underplayed it.

February 7, 1944

STRAVINSKY'S LATE BEETHOVEN

¶ Celius Dougherty and Vincenz Ruzicka, who
played two pianos last night at Town Hall, are enlightened
program-makers. It is unfortunate that irresponsible tempos
and a good deal of slappy tone-production marred what
might otherwise have been one of the season's musical
treats. Schubert's great F-minor Fantasy, a sonata by Purcell, and a Prelude and Fugue of Buxtehude gave the concert classical interest, while a new work of Mr. Dougherty's
composition on American sea chanties offered a not unpleasant repose before the modern-style severities of Stravinsky's
Concerto for Two Pianos Alone. The latter work, indeed,
requires a charming, even an urbane, interpretation if it is to
be absolved by contemporary audiences from the charge of
gratuitous ugliness, its very abstruseness being sufficient un-
pleasantness for many.

It is abstruse because, as in most of Stravinsky's music
from the last twenty-five years, its style is its subject. And
music-lovers brought up on the Romantic tradition of music,
in which the style is supposed to derive from the subject, are
confused by any other approach to the art. Nevertheless,
the use of style as subject, the evocation of past periods, the
modernistic usage of ancestral furniture and formulas, is as
vigorous a practice in contemporary music as it is in con-

temporary theater, contemporary architecture and decoration. The whole aesthetic of Johannes Brahms, indeed, whom many consider the bulwark of musical conservatism, is based on nothing less. Stravinsky cannot be reproached for his masterly distortions of classical shape and phraseology without the same indictment being held valid against the original neo-classic composer of them all, Brahms, who invented the looking-backward business.

Brahms's preferred subject matter was the style of Beethoven's middle period. The subject matter of Stravinsky's Concerto for Two Pianos Alone is, if I mistake not, the style of Beethoven's later period, in particular that of the last four or five piano sonatas. It contains a stormy sonata movement, an air with coloratura ornaments, and a set of extended variations ending with a fugue. The melodic material is angular and strong, the emotional content violent. The calmer passages are static and more than a little mannered. Transitions are operated brusquely and without grace. There is a certain willful barbarism about the relation of theme to accompaniment. The whole picture of the later Beethoven music, as you can see, is complete, with all its mannerisms and all its perfectly real seriousness. And Stravinsky's music has here, just as Beethoven's did beneath the mannerisms he had inherited from Mozart and Haydn and those he had acquired in the course of his own composing life, an undeniable integrity of expression.

I should like to say also a certain grandeur of expression, were it not for the fact that grandeur, just as in many of Beethoven's later works, is as much the *modus operandi*, the conscious manner of the piece, as it is a result of inherent excellence. It is even more than in Beethoven the subject matter, because the concerto is a study of another man's achievement. In Beethoven's case that achievement consisted in the extended expression of grandiose sentiments in a vocabulary of such astounding directness that musical scholars have never yet been able to agree how far plain rudeness, a deliberate avoidance of the amenities, was of the essence. I think last night's audience, though certainly impressed by his talent, felt equally uncertain about Mr. Stravinsky's desire to please.

March 23, 1944

EQUALIZED EXPRESSIVITY

¶ Artur Schnabel, who played last night in Carnegie Hall the second of three recitals devoted to the piano
music of Beethoven, has for some thirty or forty years made
this composer the object of his especial attention. He passes,
indeed, for an expert on the subject, by which is usually
meant that his knowledge of it is extensive and that his judgments about it are respected. Any issue taken with him on
details of tempo, of phraseology, of accent is risky and, at
best, of minor import. Minor, too, are criticisms of his piano
technique, which, though not first-class, is adequate for the
expression of his ideas. His ideas about Beethoven's piano
music in general, whether or not one finds his readings convincing, are not to be dismissed lightly.

Neither need they, I think, be taken as the voice of authority. For all the consistency and logic of his musicianship, there is too large a modicum of late-nineteenth-century
Romanticism in Mr. Schnabel's own personality to make his
Beethoven—who was, after all, a child of the late eighteenth
—wholly convincing to musicians of the mid-twentieth. No
one wishes to deny the Romantic elements in Beethoven.
But I do think that they are another kind of Romanticism
from Schnabel's, which seems to be based on the Wagnerian
theories of expressivity.

Mr. Schnabel does not admit, or plays as if he did not
admit, any difference between the expressive functions of
melody and of passage work. The neutral material of music
—scales, arpeggiated basses, accompanying figures, ostinato
chordal backgrounds, formal cadences—he plays as if they
were an intense communication, as if they were saying
something as important as the main thematic material. They
are important to Beethoven's composition, of course; but
they are not directly expressive musicial elements. They
serve as amplification, as underpinning, frequently as mere
acoustical brilliance. To execute them all with climactic

emphasis is to rob the melodic material, the expressive phrases, of their singing power.

This equalized expressivity ends by making Beethoven sound sometimes a little meretricious as a composer. His large-scale forms include, of necessity, a large amount of material that has a structural rather than a directly expressive function. Emphasizing all this as if it were phrase by phrase of the deepest emotional portent not only reduces the emotional portent of the expressive material; it blows up the commonplaces of musical rhetoric and communication into a form of bombast that makes Beethoven's early sonatas, which have many formal observances in them, sound empty of meaning and the later ones, which sometimes skip formal transitions, sound like the improvisations of a talented youth.

The work that suffered least last night from the disproportionate emphasizing of secondary material was the Sonata opus 111. Here Mr. Schnabel achieved in the first movement a more convincing relation than one currently hears between the declamatory and the lyrical subjects. And in the finale he poduced for us that beatific tranquillity that was a characteristic part of Beethoven's mature expression and that had been noticeably wanting, though there were plenty of occasions for it, in the earlier part of the evening.

March 28, 1944

SURREALISM AND MUSIC

¶ The spring number of *Modern Music* contains a reflective article on the place of music in modernist aesthetics by a man who has admittedly little taste for the art and no precise knowledge about it. The author of this essay is André Breton, founder, defender of the faith, and for twenty years pope of the surrealist movement in French poetry, at present head of the surrealist government-in-exile in New York City.

Mr. Breton defends his own antagonistic attitude toward music on the grounds that it is identical with that of most of the nineteenth- and twentieth-century French poets. He admits, however, the desirability of some fusion between it and his own art. And he recommends to musicians a "return to principles" comparable to that which has made surrealism for two decades now the chief movement of renovation in European poetry.

The first observation needs no rebuttal. It is, alas, only too true that since the divorce of poetry from music (Thomas Campion was the last in England to practice both with distinction) the poets have manifested consistently a certain bitterness toward the rival auditory art. They have indited odes to it aplenty, I know, and spoken of it on many occasions most feelingly; but their homage has rarely been without gile. Shakespeare very nearly gave the plot away when he referred to music as a "concourse of sweet sounds." (Imagine the explosion that would have occurred had any one dared in Shakespeare's London to call poetry a "running together of pretty words.") The great one eventually carried his campaign for the discrediting of music as a major art to the point of proclaiming it frankly "the food of love." His disinterestedness in this matter has not hitherto been questioned. But music died in England shortly after him.

What Mr. Breton, a poet, fails to consider here is the propaganda for the dignity and the grandeur and, most important of all, the meaning of music that was operated so successfully by the nineteenth-century philosophers. It is not the exceptional suffrages of Baudelaire and Mallarmé that have given to music its prestige in contemporary society but the systematic and relentless praise of its expressive powers by Hegel, by Schopenhauer, and by Nietzsche.

On the fusion, or re-fusion, of the two great auditory arts Mr. Breton adopts without argument the Wagnerian thesis that this is desirable. As a good Marxian he refuses the "reformist" program of closer collaboration between poets and composers, maintaining with some justice that poems "set to music" serve no valid artistic purpose and that opera librettos are and always have been a pretty silly form of literature. He seems to think that the fusion might be operated by some one man working at a high emotional temperature, and he suggests the passion of love as possibly useful to this end. What such a fusion would accomplish beyond a regression to primitive aesthetics is not proposed to us. One wonders if Mr. Breton envisages as desirable a similar fusion of the visual arts, the reunion of painting and sculpture, for instance, with or without a framework of architecture, the event to take place by no collaborative procedure. One wouldn't wish that dish on his dearest enemy. The musical theater is only now recovering from Wagner's megalomaniac seizure of all its creative privileges, and convalescence is still far from complete.

That music should take a lesson from contemporary French poetry and go back to principled operations is not a bad idea. That the functioning of the auditory invention be studied in its divergent manifestations of poetry and of music is an even better one. It is probable that persons of strong auditory memory vary in the relation that their auditory function bears to specific bodily regions. Audito-cerebral types are likely to make poets, orators, preachers, and even statesmen. Audito-visceral types, persons whose reactions to sound and to the memory of it are organic (which means emotional) rather than visual or muscular, make musicians. The audito-kinetic make dancers, acrobats, and the like. Persons for whom noise is merely a sexual stimulant, as it is for rats, may reasonably call music "the food of love"; and their type, though common, is a low one in the biological scale.

The fusion of divers artistic techniques through personal collaboration is an ancient procedure. Their simultaneous exercise by one person is an even more ancient procedure, a primitive one, to be exact. The desirability of reestablishing this in custom depends on the feasibility of trying to develop in human beings a generalized bodily reaction to sound in place of the specifically varied ones that seem to be at present a mark of the higher human types. The matter is worth investigating; but so far as anybody knows now, music is better off without its former legal and virtually indissoluble union to the word.

What Mr. Breton does not seem to have grasped about music is that, instead of being behind poetry in its evolution, it is in many ways more advanced. The dissociative process, which has made possible Mr. Breton's whole career and that of the poetic movement he presides over, has long since lost its novelty for composers. The composer who doesn't use it freely is simply not a very interesting composer; his work lacks fancy, surprise, richness, originality, depth. The right of poets to express themselves by means of spontaneous, subconsciously ordered sequences of material has seemed to many in our century a revolutionary proposition. It is, however, the normal and accepted way of writing music. Any imposition of logic upon this, whether in the form of allusions to classical rhetoric or in the observance of the only rigorous syntax known to our time, the twelve-tone system, is considered in some circles as dangerous radicalism.

The Romantic revolution, in short, was successful in music. It won real freedom for the composer. That it was not successful in literature is proved by the fact that Mr. Breton and his friends are still fighting for it. Haydn, Mozart, and Beethoven, sometimes foolishly spoken of as classicists, were the most radical of libertarians; and sonata form, their favorite continuity convention, was, as is well known, no strict formula at all but the slenderest possible framework for the display of musical fancy and for the expansive expression of spontaneous, nonverbalized feeling.

Music's modern movement is another thing from poetry's. The verbal art is still demanding liberty from intellectual restraints. The tonal art, that freedom long since gained and the things it was gained for saying long since said, has fallen, through the progressive lowering of its intellectual standards, into demagogic and commercial hands. Its modern movement is based on the demand that music be allowed to make some kind of plain sense again. We seek no loosening of our intellectual clothes; they are so loose now we can barely walk. What we want is readmission to intellectual society, to the world of free thought and clear expression.

Most of the surrealists' psychological devices for provoking spontaneity represent a return to Romantic musical practice. What they do not represent for the musical world is any kind of novelty. Musicians are only too delighted, I am sure, to lend them for a while to poetry, with all good wishes for their continued success.

April 2, 1944

A WEALTH OF DISSONANCE

¶ Music of dissonant texture is a particular cult of the International Society for Contemporary Music. The music of Arnold Schönberg is the prayer book for dissonance-lovers, especially those brought up in the central-European rite. The Church of St. Mary the Virgin has long been the seat, if not of dissonance, of dissidence from the banal in musical practice. Last night it housed a concert of the International Society that was pretext and framing for a new work by Schönberg, written for that most dissonant of all instruments, the organ, and played to perfection on New York's most brilliant-sounding organ by Carl Weinrich.

The organ is a dissonant instrument because it contains rows of pipes tuned to furnish the entire harmonic series, or most of it, upon the pressing down of any one key. The simplest major chord under such an arrangement becomes a highly complex sonority. Many churches, especially those with stone interiors, those with more height than width and those that contain complex sound-reflecting surfaces in the form of transepts, vaults, tribunes, and side aisles, are in themselves highly dissonant sound-boxes. The dying away of any sound in such resonant buildings being somewhat slower than instantaneous, the playing in them of rapid organ music, even though this be composed according to classical harmonic syntax, produces a complexity of reverberation that is virtually complete. Modern music does not sound one whit more discordant at St. Mary's, for instance, and didn't last night, than a toccata by the seventeenth-century Georg Muffat.

This is not to say that all organ music sounds alike. Music differs in tune and rhythm and progress (or form); and one harmonic sequence differs from another in glory, as well as in significance. But since any music played on the fuller combinations of a rich and bright-toned organ in a reverberating enclosure makes all the tones of the chro-

matic scale all the time, the calculated dissonance of modern
writing adds little to the effective dissonance that is inherent
to the acoustical set-up.

Schönberg's Variations for Organ, opus 40, finished in
1943, is not a twelve-tone piece. It is squarely, though chro-
matically, in D minor. It is coloristic in conception and gives
opportunity for diversified registration. Rhythmically it is a
bit halting, like most of this author's music. Harmonically
and contrapuntally it is full of fancy. The whole effect is that
of musical impressionism, an accumulation of fancy being
its aim rather than an impressive build-up.

Hugh Lamb's Fugue in E, on the other hand, though
equally dissonant, is not a color-piece; it is a line-drawing
that builds to a climax of complex sound by the march of
unrelenting counterpoint. Both works are rich to the ear;
but the Schönberg is lighter, wittier, more romantic in feeling, and intellectually the more distinguished. Lamb's is a
sound church piece; Schönberg's is poetry.

A String Quartet in B-flat by Sergeant Andrew Imbrie
preceded these organ pieces. It is a skillful work, dissonant
in sound, oratorical in its gesture, with good melodic material and a serious poetic tone. It, too, profited from the
resonant acoustics of the church; but even in a dry concert
hall I am sure it would have sounded well, because no
amount of acoustical glamour can conceal musical poverty.
Sergeant Imbrie's work showed no such poverty. It showed
original thought, sound workmanship, and dignified, highly
personal sentiments. [Sergeant Imbrie's String Quartet in
B-flat was later awarded the New York Music Critics' Circle
award as the best new piece of American chamber music
first performed in New York in the 1943–4 season.]

April 11, 1944

MASTERPIECES

¶ The enjoyment and understanding of music are dominated in a most curious way by the prestige of the masterpiece. Neither the theater nor the cinema nor poetry nor narrative fiction pays allegiance to its ideal of excellence in the tyrannical way that music does. They recognize no unbridgeable chasm between "great work" and the rest of production. Even the world of art painting, though it is no less a victim than that of music to Appreciation rackets based on the concept of gilt-edged quality, is more penetrable to reason in this regard, since such values, or the pretenses about them advanced by investing collectors and museums, are more easily unmasked as efforts to influence market prices. But music in our time (and in our country) seems to be committed to the idea that first-class work in composition is separable from the rest of music-writing by a distinction as radical as that recognized in theology between the elect and the damned. Or at the very least by as rigorous an exclusion from glory as that which formerly marked the difference between Mrs. Astor's Four Hundred and the rest of the human race.

This snobbish definition of excellence is opposed to the classical concept of a Republic of Letters. It reposes, rather, on the theocratic idea that inspiration is less a privilege of the private citizen than of the ordained prophet. Its weakness lies in the fact that music, though it serves most becomingly as religion's handmaiden, is not a religion. Music does not deal in general ideas or morality or salvation. It is an art. It expresses private sentiments through skill and sincerity, both of which last are a privilege, a duty, indeed, of the private citizen, and no monopoly of the prophetically inclined.

In the centuries when artistic skills were watched over by guilds of workmen, a masterpiece was nothing more than a graduation piece, a work that marked the student's advance from apprenticeship to master status. Later the word was used to mean an artist's most accomplished work, the high point of his production. It came thus to represent no corporate judgment, but any consumer's private one. Nowadays most people understand by it a piece differing from the run of repertory by a degree of concentration in its expressivity that establishes a difference of kind. And certain composers (Beethoven was the first of them) are considered to have worked consciously in that vein. The idea that any composer, however gifted and skillful, is merely a masterpiece factory would have been repellent to Bach or Haydn or Handel or Mozart, though Gluck was prone to advertise himself as just that. But all the successors of Beethoven who aspired to his authority—Brahms and Bruckner and Wagner and Mahler and Tchaikovsky—quite consciously imbued their music with the "masterpiece" tone.

This tone is lugubrious, portentous, world-shaking; and length, as well as heavy instrumentation, is essential to it. Its reduction to absurdity is manifest today through the later symphonies of Shostakovich. Advertised frankly and cynically as owing their particular character to a political directive imposed on their author by state disciplinary action, they have been broadcast throughout the nations as models of patriotic expression. And yet rarely in the history of music has any composer ever spread his substance so thin. Attention is not even required for their absorption. Only Anton Rubinstein's once popular symphony, "The Ocean," ever went in for so much water. They may have some value as national advertising, though I am not convinced they do; but their passive acceptance by musicians and music-lovers can certainly not be due to their melodic content (inoffensive as this is) or to their workmanship (roughly competent as this is, too).

What imposes about them is their obvious masterpiece-style one-trackness, their implacable concentration on what they are doing. That this quality, which includes also a certain never-knowing-when-to-stop persistence, should be admired by laymen as resembling superficially the Soviet war effort is natural enough. But that what these pieces are up to in any musical sense, chiefly rehashing bits of Borodin and Mahler, is of intrinsic musical interest I have yet to hear averred by a musician. And that is the whole trouble with the masterpiece cult. It tends to substitute an impressive manner for specific expression, just as oratory does. That music should stoop to the procedures of contemporary political harangue is deplorable indeed.

There are occasions (funerals, for instance) where the tone of a discourse is more important than its content, but the concert is not one of them. The concert is a habitual thing like a meal; ceremonial is only incidental to it. And restricting its menu to what observes the fictitious "masterpiece" tone is like limiting one's nourishment to the heavier party foods. If the idea can be got rid of that a proper concert should consist only of historic "masterpieces" and of contemporary works written in the "masterpiece" tone, our programs will cease to be repetitive and monotonous. Arthur Judson, the manager of the Philharmonic, remarked recently that the orchestral repertory in concert use today is smaller than it was when he went into concert management twenty-five years ago, and this in spite of the fact that orchestras and orchestral concerts are many times more numerous. I am sure that this shrinkage is due to a popular misconception about what constitutes quality in music.

If the Appreciation Racket were worth its salt, if the persons who explain music to laymen would teach it as a language and not as a guessing game, the fallacy of the masterpiece could be exposed in short order. Unfortunately, most of them know only about twenty pieces anyway, and they are merely bluffing when they pretend that these (and certain contemporary works that sort of sound like them) make up all the music in the world worth bothering about.

June 25, 1944

SCHÖNBERG'S MUSIC

¶ On September 13 Arnold Schönberg, dean of the modernists, will be seventy years old. And yet his music for all its author's love of traditional sonorous materials and all the charm of late nineteenth-century Vienna that envelops its expression, is still the modernest modern music that exists. No other Western music sounds so strange, so consistently different from the music of the immediately preceding centuries. And none, save that of Erik Satie, has proved so tough a nut for the public to crack. Only the early *Verklärte Nacht* has attained to currency in our concerts. The rest remains to this day musicians' music.

Musicians do not always know what they think of Schönberg's music, but they often like to listen to it. And they invariably respect it. Whether one likes it or not is, indeed, rather a foolish question to raise in face of its monumental logic. To share or to reject the sentiments that it expresses seems, somehow, a minor consideration compared with following the amplitude of the reasoning that underlies their exposition. As in much of modern philosophical writing, the conclusions reached are not the meat of the matter; it is the methods by which these are arrived at.

This preponderance of methodology over objective is what gives to Schönberg's work, in fact, its irreducible modernity. It is the orientation that permits us to qualify it as, also, in the good sense of the word, academic. For it is a model of procedure. And if the consistency of the procedure seems often closer to the composer's mind than the expressive aim, that fact allows us further to describe the work as academic in an unfavorable sense. It means that the emotional nourishment in the music is not quite worth the trouble required to extract it. This is a legitimate and not uncommon layman's opinion. But if one admits, as I think one is obliged to do with regard to Schönberg, that the vigor and thoroughness of the procedure are, in very fact, the music's chief objective, then no musician can deny that it presents a very high degree of musical interest.

This is not to say that Schönberg's music is without feeling expressed. Quite to the contrary, it positively drips with emotivity. But still the approach is, in both senses of the word, academic. Emotions are examined rather than declared. As in the works of his distinguished fellow citizen Dr. Sigmund Freud, though the subject matter is touching, even lurid, the author's detachment about it is complete. Sentiments are considered as case histories rather than as pretexts for personal poetry or subjects for showmanship. *Die glückliche Hand*, *Gurre Lieder*, and *Pierrot lunaire*,

as well as the string sextet, *Verklärte Nacht,* have deeply
sentimental subjects; but their treatment is always by detailed exposition, never by sermonizing. Pierrot's little feelings, therefore, though they seem enormous and are unquestionably fascinating when studied through the Schönberg microscope for forty-five minutes of concert time, often
appear in retrospect as less interesting than the mechanism
through which they have been viewed.

The designing and perfecting of this mechanism, rather
than the creation of unique works, would seem to have
been the guiding preoccupation of Schönberg's career; certainly it is the chief source of his enormous prestige among
musicians. The works themselves, charming as they are and
frequently impressive, are never quite as fascinating when
considered separately as they are when viewed as comments
on a method of composition or as illustrations of its expressive possibilities. They are all secondary to a theory; they
do not lead independent lives. The theory, however, leads an
independent life. It is taught and practiced all over the
world. It is the lingua franca of contemporary modernism.
It is even used expertly by composers who have never heard
any of the works by Schönberg, by Webern, and by Alban
Berg that constitute its major literature.

If that major literature is wholly Viennese by birth and
its sentimental preoccupations largely Germanic, the syntax
of its expression embodies also both the strongest and the
weakest elements of the German musical tradition. Its strong
element is its simplification of tonal relations; its weak
element is its chaotic rhythm. The apparent complexity of
the whole literature and the certain obscurity of much of it
are due, in the present writer's opinion, to the lack of
a rhythmic organization comparable in comprehensiveness
and in simplicity to the tonal one.

It is probably the insufficiencies of Schönberg's own
rhythmic theory that prevent his music from crystallizing
into great, hard, beautiful, indissoluble works. Instrumentally they are delicious. Tonally they are the most exciting,
the most original, the most modern-sounding music there
is. What limits their intelligibility, hamstrings their expressive power, makes them often literally halt in their tracks, is
the naïve organization of their pulses, taps, and quantities.
Until a rhythmic syntax comparable in sophistication to

Schönberg's tonal one shall have been added to this, his whole method of composition, for all the high intellection and sheer musical genius that have gone into its making, will probably remain a fecund but insupportable heresy, a strict counterpoint valuable to pedagogy but stiff, opaque, unmalleable, and inexpressive for free composition.

There is no satisfactory name for the thing Schönberg has made. The twelve-tone-row technique, though its commonest denomination, does not cover all of it. But he has made a thing, a new thing, a thing to be used and to be improved. Its novelty in 1944 is still fresh; and that means it has strength, not merely charm. Its usage by composers of all nations means that it is no instrument of local or limited applicability. Such limitations as it has are due, I believe, to the fact that it is not yet a complete system. So far as it goes it is admirable; and it can go far, as the operas of Alban Berg show. It is to the highest credit of Schönberg as a creator that his method of creation should be so valuable a thing as to merit still, even to require, the collaboration of those who shall come after him.

September 10, 1944

THE ORMANDY CASE

¶ The Philadelphia Orchestra, which last night at Carnegie Hall opened our indoor orchestral season, has a sound that is pungent and mellow like the smell of fall fruits. No other instrumental assembly has quite the quality of impersonal, almost botanical, beauty that this one possesses; and none of the other conductors who appear regularly before us has quite Eugene Ormandy's way of offering really excellent workmanship without personal insistence.

Persons who cherish star quality in public performers often feel let down by Mr. Ormandy, though it is surprising how satisfactory the work he does with his orchestra turns out to be on accustomed acquaintance. There is, indeed, no final flame of eloquence in it and no categorical authority. But there is always beauty and order and an approach to all kinds of music that, if it does not manifest the ultimate of sensitivity, is nevertheless marked by an understanding of all the musical languages that is at once sensuous and delicate.

With no preparation, for instance, by early training or by residence, for the playing of French music, and with, to this day, an incurably Viennese irregularity of rhythmic scansion, he manages to expose French music with less distortion of its original sense than almost any of the other interpreters do, saving only those of extended Parisian experience. He does this by cultivating in his orchestra the whole gamut of sounds and colorations of sound—not just the pushing or the throbbing ones—that are the full French orchestral palette. And he keeps these cleanly separate from one another, equilibrating and contrasting, as is the custom of the French conductors, rather than mixing them.

He just misses full identification with the French style in his rhythm. He has neither the instinct nor the training for exact quantities that are characteristic of French musicians and that are necessary above all for the lucid exposition of Debussy. And he does not quite seize the strophic nature of French musical discourse. What is meant for a simple breath, a hesitation, becomes too often a hiatus. His whole rhythmic outline is too flexible for full metrical clarity.

All the same, French works, as he plays them, come out less distorted than is usual here and with far more vibrancy of timbre than is common anywhere. The trumpet passages that start the march section in Debussy's *Fêtes,* for instance, were articulated last night so brightly, and yet so softly, that one might easily have taken them for an off-stage effect. I have never before heard trumpets to be played so quietly and still to sound like trumpets. (I learned later that a rubber washer, such as is used in water faucets, had been placed as bushing around the stem of each mute.)

The novelty of the evening was a Concerto for Orchestra (it might as well have been called an overture) by Zoltán Kodály, written for the fiftieth anniversary season of Chicago's Symphony Orchestra and performed there in 1941. This is a lively piece, gay and clean and fresh and soundly sonorous. Mr. Ormandy read it straightforwardly and with

full appreciation of the special Hungarian savor that char-
acterizes the work of this composer, who was, in fact, Mr.
Ormandy's teacher.

October 4, 1944

REPERTORY

¶ It is a commonplace of contemporary aesthetics
that music of marked originality is likely to be found shocking by the epoch that gives it birth. The inability is notori-
ous not only of the lay public but of trained musicians to
perceive beauty in any work of which the style is unfamiliar. And program makers are aware that this blindness
obtains not only with regard to contemporary composition
but with regard to the past as well. When one considers
the vast amount of music written since 1600 that is perfectly well known, published, and available for performance
and that is never given by our operatic or orchestral establishments, in spite of the eagerness of conductors to vary
their monotonous routine, one is obliged to conclude, I
think, that the tininess of our effective repertory is due to
psychological factors that are beyond anyone's power to
control.

Epochs, styles, and authors all have a way of becoming
invisible, of passing in and out of focus, rather, that is not
easy to explain. The facts of this matter constitute the history of taste. Our inability to cope with the unfamiliar is
equaled only by our inability to maintain interest in the too
familiar, in that which is no longer in any way strange. The
vogue of our popular songs is typical. Within a few years,
sometimes within one year, it is possible to observe in succession the enthusiasm, the indifference, and the ridicule
with which one of these is treated; and we have all experienced the renewed charm of some old song that has been
left in limbo long enough to be all but forgotten. There is

no way of preventing it; the things we get used to tend to become invisible. They are there all the time, and we know they are there, and we think we love them dearly; but if they were taken away we should half the time not remark any difference.

Schumann's music, for example, is in a decline of favor just now; nobody has a lively feeling for it any more. Interpreters find it more and more difficult to render, audiences more and more difficult to listen to. It is passing out of our focus. Debussy is in an even more curious phase. He is listened to increasingly, understood less and less. Haydn seems to be emerging from his recent obscurity and taking on contours again. Bach, after having been genuinely popular among the *cognoscenti* for thirty years, is losing a bit his appeal for intellectuals. Mozart has, in fact, taken Bach's place of late as the master most admired among connoisseurs. Wagner and Brahms have still a broadly based popularity but a markedly diminishing attraction for musicians. Verdi, though he has lost much of his former power over the masses, has acquired in the last twenty years a prestige in university circles that would have shocked profoundly the scholastic musicians of fifty years ago.

Always, in the case of such revivals, there is imposed a certain falsification upon the original. No matter how much we pretend we are restoring old works to their pristine state, we are obliged at the same time to modernize them somewhat if we expect our contemporaries to take them seriously. Returns to popularity of past styles in architecture and decoration have usually been accompanied, therefore, by complete resurfacing. The nineteenth century unpainted its Gothic monuments and left them a unified gray. It covered up the bare wood of its Louis XVI furniture with a bluish color known as Trianon gray. It built Greco-Roman houses everywhere and painted them white, which is still considered, indeed, to be the appropriate color for classical antiquity. In recent decades flamboyant Victorian interiors also have regained their charm through the use of white paint, which was practically never used on them originally but which our age finds cheerful and associates with asepsis.

The Bach revival of the 1830's, which Mendelssohn and Schumann fathered, translated this music into all the idioms of contemporary executant style, using Tourte bows for the orchestral suites and violin pieces, gigantic organs and choruses for the religious works, pianos for the domestic keyboard music, and employing a constant crescendo and diminuendo within all phrases, as was considered necessary at that time for true expression. Bach was modernized all over again in the early years of this century. His rhythm was made to sound more mechanical, dynamism was everywhere diminished, phraseology streamlined, the harpsichord revived, the old, small, bright-sounding organs restored to use.

A healthy traffic goes on nowadays in the reinstrumentation of eighteenth-century music of all kinds, but we have not yet done over the Romantics very much. Though the nineteenth century is dying slowly, there is vigor in its traditions still. Not for some time will they be forgotten so thoroughly that a resurfacing of the Romantic masters will be possible to envisage. When this does take place, they will lose, of course, the somber patina that a century of daily handling has laid upon them and appear as bright again to us as cleaned and revarnished masterpieces from the past do in a gallery of painting.

Meanwhile, we must put up with our own age, because, whether we like it or not, its habits are for us the facts of life. This age listens to a great deal of new music, likes practically none of it, but would not for the world forego hearing it. It respects a vast repertory of old music, complains no end at the infrequency with which most of this is heard, discourages firmly the introduction of any of it into the major programs. Exception is made for pre-Romantic works when wholly reinstrumented. It holds to its Romantics with determination, will no more allow them to be restyled than it would consent to having its grandmother's face lifted. Grandma is not kept dressed in the style of her 1880 coming out, however; a seemly adaptation to the mode is encouraged. She is constantly told how young she looks. She is given the place of honor at every ceremony and treated generally with the consideration that we observe toward those who we know will not be with us forever. Her frequentation is considered to be a privilege for all and of inestimable value to the young.

October 8, 1944

STRINGS BOWED; STRINGS PLUCKED

¶ Harpsichord and violin certainly make a lovely duet. As played last night by Ralph Kirkpatrick and Alexander Schneider in a recital of sonatas by Mozart and Bach at the Y. M. H. A. they produced one of the happiest musical evenings this critic has spent in a long time. Even when details of rendering were not fully to his taste the sound was always attractive to the ear. One could bear to listen to all the music all the time. And since at least two of the works played, the Mozart G- and A- major sonatas, are in themselves works of rare grandeur, one was grateful to the artists for giving them to us so nearly, so very nearly, intact.

By nearly intact I mean that there were rhythmic irregularities in the harpsichord playing and some imperfect cantilena on the violin. Tempo rubato, for instance, however slight, is scarcely appropriate to syncopated passages, as Mr. Kirkpatrick used it in the slow movement of the Mozart A-major sonata. And haste to get back to the nut of the bow will always produce a bumpy violin phrase. Both Kirkpatrick and Schneider are skilled technicians and experienced players of chamber music. Their work has ease, confidence, understanding, and some brilliance. What it lacks for full distinction and for the brio that it essays is equalized tension. It is clear but not wholly clean, highly presentable as reading but not very deeply thought.

Everything was played a little fast, as if speed were being used to conceal a want of exact rhythmic articulation. This procedure is less objectionable in Mozart than in Bach, because the Mozart last movements, at least, do demand a demonic fury, though velocity is not necessarily the best means for achieving this. In Bach it only produces confusion. The attempt to make a show-off, à la Paganini, out of that most methodical of workmen is false stylistically, psychologically, and musically. The fury in Bach is the fury of complete control, a relentlessness of exactitude rather than of sweep. A too facile approach to his complexities captures no heavenly citadel; it is merely barnstorming.

Rather wonderful barnstorming the whole concert was. The music was recondite but not too much so for comprehension. The playing was adequate and pleasantly superficial. The sound of it all was delicious, spicy, eminently digestible. If nothing was played with penetration, neither was anything gravely violated. The evening was a revelation of how delightful music can be without a thumpy pianoforte or violin E strings of wire. Also, the Mozart A-major violin sonata is worth going some distance for.

November 2, 1944

PIERRE MONTEUX

¶ Pierre Monteux's two-week visit as guest conductor of the Philharmonic-Symphony Orchestra has led music lovers of all schools (the critical press included) to two conclusions: namely, that this conductor has drawn from our orchestra more beautiful sounds and more beautiful mixtures of sound than any other conductor has done in many years, and that his readings of Brahms are highly refreshing.

It has been a long time, a very long time, since our Philharmonic sounded like an orchestra. It has always been an assemblage of good players; and the changes of personnel operated last year by Artur Rodzinski, on his accession to the conductorship, have improved further its musical potentialities. Sometimes of late the playing has been most agreeable. Sometimes, too, no matter who was conducting, the performances have sounded more like a reading rehearsal than like a prepared execution. This lack of dependability in the ensemble—so noticeable in contrast to the solid teamwork, no matter who conducts them, in the orchestras of Philadelphia, Boston, and Chicago—has long been a trouble. As far back as 1936 Sir Thomas Beecham, who served a half-season that year as guest, annoyed the directors considerably by replying, when asked to diagnose the musical ills of the organization, that though it contained many excellent players, it was not an orchestra.

Many conductors, Mr. Rodzinski included, have produced a pretty good balance of timbres and made music, usually unfamiliar music, sound pretty well. Arturo Toscanini has occasionally, without any beauty of sheer sound being involved, made familiar music sound unusually eloquent. It has remained for Pierre Monteux to achieve what many of us thought was hopeless. He has made the Philharmonic play with beauty of tone, many kinds of it, and with perfect balance and blending—to sound, in short, like an orchestra, a first-class orchestra requiring no apology. And he has also played music as familiar as that of Brahms and Beethoven (not to speak of Debussy) with not only a wonderful beauty of sound but a far from usual eloquence as well. His is the way a real orchestra *should* sound, the way the first-class orchestras of the world all *do* sound. And this is the way many musicians have long wished the music of Johannes Brahms could be made to sound.

It is a strange anomaly that although Brahms's symphonic music is extremely popular (in some years it tops even that of Beethoven for frequency of performance), almost nobody's reading of it is satisfactory. How to discern the rhythm that underlies its slow and its energetic passages, to make these sound in any given piece as if they are all parts of the same piece, is one of the unsolved problems in music. Certainly the meditative ones require to be read as inward rather than as extrovert sentiment. And certainly the animated ones and the passages of broad eloquence, such as the codas and finales, tempt any conductor to make oratory out of them. But alterations of introversion with extroversion do not make a unity in the reading of anything, and there is no reason to suppose that so experienced and so consecrated a musician as Brahms was basically incoherent in thought. It is far more likely that his exact poetic temper, being profoundly personal, escapes us.

In my time only the late Frederick Stock of Chicago has been able to envelop the Brahms symphonies with a dreamy lilt that allows the soft passages to float along and the loud ones to sing out as elements of a single continuity. A rhythmic propulsion that was steady without being rigid was the basis of these readings. Orchestral tone that was light in texture and wholly transparent was its superstructure. Mr. Monteux is less expert than Dr. Stock was at preserving a poetical and rhythmic unity throughout, but he is more expert than anybody at lifting the velvet pall that is accustomed in our concerts to lie over the Brahms instrumentation and allowing everything, middle voices too, to shine forth with translucency. His strings never obscure the woodwinds. His trumpets and trombones never blast away the strings. His horns, when force is indicated, play very loud; but their loudness is bright, not heavy; it is a flash of light rather than a ton of bricks.

Both these conductors have been celebrated for their renderings of French music, especially of Debussy, which requires a similar rhythmic continuity and identical refinements of balance. Sheer weight, like sheer brilliance, must always, in this kind of music, be avoided, because it destroys the translucency that is the music's main means of evoking an atmosphere. And the rhythm must be alive but steady, the cantilena floating on the delicate wavelike motion of this without effort or any insistence. Mr. Monteux, when playing both these composers, sometimes allows the slower passages to go dead. At these moments the rhythm stops supporting the flow of sound, all animation disappears, and the sounds themselves lose their ability to blend. But these moments are never long. As soon as the rhythm reasserts itself, the tonal fabric comes to life again and breathes like a sentient being.

Listening lately to Pierre Monteux conduct Brahms and Debussy on the same program brought to mind how much the music of these two authors is alike, or at least demands like treatment. The secret of their rhythm is very much the same secret. And nonviolation of their rhythm is essential and preliminary to producing among their orchestral sounds luminosity. That and the use of transparent, or nonweighty, orchestral tone. By what occult methods Mr. Monteux produces in our Philharmonic-Symphony Orchestra a real community of rhythmic articulation, not to mention the delights of delicate balance and blending that proceed from this, I cannot even guess. The guest conductors who have failed where he has succeeded would like to know, too, I imagine.

November 12, 1944

OVERTRAINED

¶ The Boston Symphony Orchestra's first concert of the season, which took place last night in Carnegie Hall, consisted of two works and lasted two hours. They were beautiful works and were handsomely executed. With the exception of the difficult horn passage in the trio of Beethoven's "Eroica" scherzo, your commentator could find no fault in the playing. And yet he was aware of the passage of time.

Serge Koussevitzky's tempos were not slow. In the Beethoven symphony they were, in fact, most gratefully animated. And the mechanism of orchestral articulation was, as always with this group, delightful to observe. Everything was right, including William Primrose, who played the viola solo of Berlioz's *Harold in Italy*. It was the old story, I am afraid, of familiar pieces so elegantly turned out that one scarcely recognized them. They were not deformed. Their clear spirit was not violated. They were simply so completely groomed that one was not aware of any spirit present. The slickness of their surfacing made them seem hollow and laborious underneath, which they are not.

The truth of the matter, in my opinion, is simply that the Boston Symphony Orchestra is overtrained and has been for several years. Its form is perfect, but it does not communicate. The music it plays never seems to be about anything, except how beautifully the Boston Symphony Orchestra can play. Perfection of execution that oversteps its purpose is a familiar phenomenon in art. That way lies superficiality and monotony. And music has no business sounding monotonous, since no two pieces of it are alike. Whenever a series of pieces or of programs starts sounding that way you may be sure that the execution is at fault, is obtruding itself.

One longs, in listening to this orchestra's work, for a little ease. It is of no use for all the sonorous elements to be so neatly in place unless some illusion is present that their being so is spontaneous. Music is not the result of rehearsal. It is an auditory miracle that can take place anywhere. When it occurs among disciplined musicians its miraculous quality is merely heightened. When the frequency of its occurrence in any given group starts diminishing, there are only two possible remedies. Either the members must play together more often, or they must get some new pieces.

Obviously, this group does not need more rehearsing. And it knows now all the pieces there are in standard repertory; it even knows all the kinds of pieces there are for large orchestra. There is nothing to be done about it. It has passed the peak of useful executional skill, and executional hypertrophy has set in. The pattern is a familiar one, and regrettable. But there is no use trying to deceive one's self about it.

November 16, 1944

VIOLENCE AND CHARM

¶ Rudolf Firkusny, who played a recital of piano music in Carnegie Hall last night, is a dynamic temperament with lots of punch in his fingers. He plays very loud and very fast most of the time. He plays most of the written notes, too, and often adds extra ones by accident. I once heard him play a concerto most prettily. But concerto playing doesn't show up faults of musicianship as a recital does. Last night's concert revealed a pianist with far from negligible (though not complete, by any means) keyboard mastery and a musical temperament of such banal violence as it has not often been my lot to encounter among reputable performers.

Excepting for two of the Chopin études, which were sensibly and agreeably read, everything—literally everything—was so deformed by speed and pounding that it was difficult to tell one piece from another. Under such circumstances it was not possible for one to have any clear impression of Martinů's Fantasy and Rondo beyond recognition of the fact that it is a work of serious intentions and some length. What a listener not familiar with Beethoven's "Waldstein" Sonata might have made of the piece is difficult to imagine. It was recognizable to your reviewer only by the notes of it, its expressive content, as rendered, being chiefly reminiscent of the movie pianism of his youth.

The first movement might have been entitled "A Day at the Races," with steeplechase hazards being got over at full speed and ponies constantly coming lickety-split down the homestretch. The rondo was like the accompaniment to a class-B Western. A young miss of pastoral upbringing had apparently been seized by a band of outlaws on horseback, taken to a lonely spot, and left there. She was very sad about this, and then the outlaws took her to an even lonelier place and tied her hands behind her. A gallant young cowboy, however, came to her rescue and galloped her away. On the ride home the two had a tender moment in which she thanked him for his trouble. And when they got back to town there was general dancing.

If you think I am making fun of either Beethoven or Mr. Firkusny, just try playing the "Waldstein" Sonata at 120 half-notes to the minute. You will see that the effect is somewhat as I have described it, especially if you play all the passages marked *f* as if they were marked *ffff*. The result is both piquant and trite. If you play a whole program through in this way you will discover that only so tough a work as this particular sonata is capable, under the speed-up and the pounding process, of sounding as if it had a subject at all. If Mr. Firkusny were less charming as a platform personality, it is doubtful whether his kind of music-making would be as appealing to music lovers as it clearly was, I must admit, to last night's audience.

December 14, 1944

1945

FAIRY TALE ABOUT MUSIC

¶ Richard Wagner's *Die Meistersinger von Nürnberg,* which was given again at the Metropolitan Opera House last night after an interval of five years, is the most enchanting of all the fairy-tale operas. It is about a never-never land where shoemakers give vocal lessons, where presidents of musical societies offer their daughters as prizes in musical contests, and where music critics believe in rules of composition, where they get mobbed for preferring young girls to young composers.

It is enchanting musically because there is no enchantment, literally speaking, in it. It is unique among Wagner's theatrical works in that none of the characters gets mixed up with magic or takes drugs. And nobody gets redeemed according to the usual Wagnerian pattern, which a German critic once described as "around the mountain and through the woman." There is no metaphysics at all. The hero merely gives a successful début recital and marries the girl of his heart.

And Wagner without his erotico-metaphysical paraphernalia is a better composer than with it. He pays more attention to holding interest by musical means, wastes less time predicting doom, describing weather, soul states, and ecstatic experiences. He writes better voice leading and orchestrates more transparently, too. *Die Meistersinger* is virtually without the hubbub string-writing that dilutes all his other operas, and the music's pacing is reasonable in terms of the play. The whole score is reasonable. It is also rich and witty and romantic, full of interest and of humanity.

The first of the successful operatic comedies for gigantic orchestra, like Verdi's *Falstaff* and Strauss's *Rosenkavalier,* it is the least elephantine of them all, the sweetest, the most graceful. For the preservation of these qualities in performance George Szell, the conductor, and Herbert Graf, the stage director, are presumably responsible. For the loan of some new scenery, which enhanced the final tableau, the Chicago Civic Opera Company merits our thanks. For careful singing and general musical good behavior all the artists deserve a modest palm.

January 13, 1945

EXPRESSIVE PERCUSSION

¶ John Cage, whose recent compositions made up the program of a concert given yesterday afternoon at the New School for Social Research, is already famous as a specialist in the use of percussive sounds. Two years ago the Museum of Modern Art presented pieces by him for a large group of players using flowerpots, brake bands, electric buzzers, and similar objects not primarily musical but capable of producing a wide variety of interesting sounds all the same. The works offered yesterday included an even greater variety of sounds, all prepared by inserting bits of metal, wood, rubber, or leather at carefully studied points and distances between the strings of an ordinary pianoforte.

The effect in general is slightly reminiscent, on first hearing, of Indonesian gamelan orchestras, though the interior structure of Mr. Cage's music is not Oriental at all. His work attaches itself, in fact, to two different traditions of Western modernism. One is the perscussive experiments begun by Marinetti's Futurist Noisemakers and continued in the music of Edgar Varèse, Henry Cowell, and George Antheil, all of which, though made in full awareness of Oriental methods, is thoroughly Western in its expression. The other is, curiously enough, the atonal music of Arnold Schönberg.

Mr. Cage has carried Schönberg's harmonic maneuvers to their logical conclusion. He has produced atonal music not by causing the twelve tones of the chromatic scale to contradict one another consistently, but by eliminating, to start with, all sounds of precise pitch. He substitutes for the chromatic scale a gamut of pings, plucks, and delicate thuds that is both varied and expressive and that is different in each piece. By thus getting rid, at the beginning, of the constricting element in atonal writing—which is the necessity of taking constant care to avoid making classical harmony with a standardized palette of instrumental sounds and pitches that exists primarily for the purpose of producing such harmony—Mr. Cage has been free to develop the rhythmic element of composition, which is the weakest element in the Schönbergian style, to a point of sophistication unmatched in the technique of any other living composer.

His continuity devices are chiefly those of the Schönberg school. There are themes and sometimes melodies, even, though these are limited, when they have real pitch, to the range of a fourth, thus avoiding the tonal effect of dominant and tonic. All these appear in augmentation, diminution, inversion, fragmentation, and the various kinds of canon. That these procedures do not take over a piece and become its subject, or game, is due to Cage's genius as a musician. He writes music for expressive purposes; and the novelty of his timbres, the logic of his discourse, are used to intensify communication, not as ends in themselves. His work represents, in consequence, not only the most advanced methods now in use anywhere but original expression of the very highest poetic quality. And this has been proved now through all the classical occasions—theater, ballet, song, orchestral composition, and chamber music.

One of the works was played yesterday by the composer, the other two by Arthur Gold and Robert Fizdale, duo-pianists. The perfect execution of these young men, their rhythm, lightness and absolute equality of scale, and the singing sounds they derived from their instruments, in spite of the fact that the strings were all damped in various ways,

made one wish to hear them operate on music less special,
as well. The concert was a delight from every point of view.

January 22, 1945

THE POETRY OF PRECISION

¶ Igor Stravinsky, who conducted the Philharmonic-Symphony Orchestra last night in Carnegie Hall,
prefaced a delightful little concert of his own works with a
spirited reading of Glinka's *Russlan and Ludmilla* overture
and a correct but on the whole pedestrian excursion
through Tchaikovsky's rarely explored Second Symphony.
Whether this work is worthy of the respect that the greatest
living Russian composer has long borne it is not a matter
on which this reviewer has any opinion. It is obviously a
well-written work, full of original fancy and clearly
expressed. Whatever feelings anybody may have about it
(and feelings are all most people have about Tchaikovsky)
are his own business. Myself, I was not enthralled; but I
am not a Tchaikovsky fan.

Having long been a Stravinsky fan and long an admirer
of the Piano Concerto that Beveridge Webster played so
brilliantly last night, your reviewer spent one of the pleasanter moments of the season rehearing it under the composer's direction. Noble of thematic invention, ingenious of
texture, and eloquently, grandiloquently sustained, this
brilliant evocation of Baroque musical attitudes has too
long been left on the shelf. It was last played here, if the
files in my office are correct, exactly twenty years ago. If
patrons walked out on it in scores then, as they did last
night, one can understand the hesitancy of conductors to
revive it. But if the ovation it received last night from those
who stayed (and they were a majority) means anything
prophetically, the concerto will one day be as popular as
Tchaikovsky's in B-flat.

The *Ode* retains its elegance on rehearing and gains in

intellectual interest, but it remains for this observer a little distant in sentiment. The *Norwegian Moods* are not distant at all. They are warm and picturesque and cheerful, wonderfully melodious and impeccably tailored. At present a sort of *Peer Gynt* suite for the musically sophisticated, they will shortly, I am sure, find themselves at home in the "pop" concerts. The *Circus Polka* has already done so. And indeed a lively picture it is of the sawdust ring. Apparently, the only music lovers who haven't enjoyed it are the elephants for whose dancing it was written. I am told that they scented satire in it, a bit of joking about their proportions (which they are extremely sensitive about) and didn't like working to it. They did not, however, walk out on it.

Mr. Stravinsky's conducting of his own works was, as always, a delight to those who take his works seriously. His rhythm was precise, his tonal texture dry, the expressivity complete. It was complete because only through the most precise rhythm and the driest tonal textures can the Stravinskian pathos be made to vibrate or the Stravinskian tenderness to glow. His is a poetry of exactitude, a theater of delicate adjustments and relentless march. Conductors who sweep through his works as if they were personal oratory of some kind inevitably find these going weak on them. Stravinsky admires Tchaikovsky but he doesn't write or feel like Tchaikovsky. How much added juiciness the latter can stand is an unsettled problem of interpretation. Stravinsky can bear none. It is all written in. His scores are correctly indited, and the composer's reading of them is the way they go. It is also the way they go best.

February 2, 1945

CHILDREN'S DAY

¶ Heitor Villa-Lobos, who conducted two of his Choros, Numbers 8 and 9, last night with the Philharmonic in Carnegie Hall, is one of the world's most prolific com-

posers. Also one of the most gifted. His works are innumerable and full of bright ideas. Their excellent tunes, their
multicolored instrumentation, their abundance of fancy in
general, and their easy but perfectly real modernity of
thought have made them universally acceptable as valid
musical creations of this century. For all the French influence on their harmonic texture (chiefly that of Milhaud),
they are also valid musical creations of this hemisphere.
They sound, as is, indeed, their composer's intention, most
convincingly like Brazil.

Choros Number 8, last heard here at the World's Fair,
sounds to me like rural Brazil, like rivers and plains and
mountains and Indian villages and jungles. The jungles
seem to have lots of trees in them, big ones and small ones,
also some snakes and wild animals. Certainly there are birds
around of all sizes. And I thought I spotted, as the civilized
note, a sturdy stock of European canned nourishment and
a few reels of the best Hollywood sentiment.

Choros Number 9, which was a North American première,
is more urban. It has dance music and crowds and general
gaiety and some wit and quite a lot more Hollywood sentiment. It is all very pleasant, and it is loosely enough constructed so that one doesn't have to pay attention all the
time. The composer conducted one through both pieces
with courtesy, making everything clear and keeping us interested. If one felt at the end like a tourist who has seen
much but taken part in little, one was grateful for the trip,
all the same. One could almost hear the voice of the travel-
ogue saying, "Now we are leaving beau-u-u-tiful Brazil."

We left it for the comfortably suburban Violin Concerto
of Paganini and some astonishingly accurate violin playing
by Zino Francescatti. And thus safely returned to Europe
and the nineteenth century, we paid ourselves an old-style
treat in the form of Liszt's great orchestral *Mephisto Waltz*,
which was certainly the original of Ravel's *La Valse*. A
wonderfully beautiful piece this, and not a bit devilish, just
sweet and romantic and full of an inward light. Our thanks
to Artur Rodzinski, who thought of playing it, and who
played it enchantingly.

February 9, 1945

THE SANGUINE TEMPERAMENT

¶ The concert that Sir Thomas Beecham conducted with the Rochester Philharmonic Orchestra in Carnegie Hall on Saturday night was a personal triumph for the English leader. The massive applause that greeted his readings of Haydn, of Beethoven, of Berlioz, and of his own ballet music (out of Handel) could only have been gratitude for the grandeur and buoyancy of those readings as such, since the orchestral execution of the Rochester society is certainly no marvel for fine finish. When, at the close of the concert, the audience demanded extra numbers (the Andante from Elgar's String Serenade and the March from Sibelius's *Karelia* suite were what they got), it seemed reasonable to suppose that what they wanted was not so much further acquaintance with the pleasant but roughish playing of the Rochester band as more of Sir Thomas's deeply joyous music-making.

This reviewer confesses to a similar predilection for the Beecham readings. His Haydn has gusto and sentiment along with its grace. It breathes with ease and steps a real measure. It is no line drawing of antiquity but a full evocation in the round of music that ·everybody knows to have passion as well as decorum, but that no other conductor seems able to bring to life with quite that ruddy glow.

The new Handel-Beecham suite, which received its first New York hearing on this occasion, is out of a ballet entitled *The Great Elopement,* undertaken for the Ballet Theater, but not yet produced. Here is no sullen expatriate Handel, yearning after the Germany he grew up in (and never liked) or after the perverse and monumental Italy of his youth. It is the British Handel, as square-toed as a country squire, as witty as a London playwright, as dainty as a beau of Bath, as expansive as the empire itself.

Beethoven's Seventh Symphony received the roughest execution of the evening but the most enlightened reading it has had in my lifetime. Nothing in its whole progress was either long or wrong. And when one remembered the innumerable booby traps for conductors with which that work is sown, it was with amazement and respect that one observed Sir Thomas sidestepping them all and going straight to the heart of the matter. This heart is the funeral-march Allegretto, the saddest, the most tragic piece Beethoven ever wrote, surrounded and framed by three of the most exuberant affirmations that exist. We have had choleric Beethoven of late and melancholy Beethoven and even some lymphatic. Myself I like it sanguine, because I think that is the kind of man Beethoven was. And Sir Thomas's Seventh Symphony, for all its studied proportions, was abundantly that.

March 10, 1945

BEETHOVEN'S FIFTH

¶ Beethoven's C-minor Symphony is the most famous piece of orchestral music in the world. Everybody knows it; everybody admires it. Other pieces have their devoted publics, but this one is accepted by all as the world masterpiece of monumental abstract, or "absolute," music. For the simplicity of its melodic materials, the nobility of its proportions, and its forthrightness of style it has been esteemed throughout the Western world for over a century now as a sort of Parthenon among symphonies. Yet what it means nobody really knows. It has been as much argued about as *Hamlet,* and it remains to this day as movingly obscure a work.

The Germans long ago associated its opening phrases with their favorite idea of Fate Knocking at the Door. The French have taken the work as a whole to be connected in some way with political liberalism. It was so completely appropriated as a theme song, in fact, by French socialists of the Second International that adherents of the Third and

Fourth have tended rather to keep quiet about its possible political significance. Of late more conservative politicians have taken it over as the slogan, or symbol, of military victory, specifically the victory of the United Nations.

The Germans were clumsy not to think of this first; the victory idea would have fitted perfectly with their already popular interpretation of the piece as having to do with fate. It could have become thus a forecast of their "manifest destiny." Perhaps they felt its author was not quite the right man to put forward as the advocate of unbridled submission to authority. In any case, their propagandists have pretty much let the work alone. Whether ours would have done well to let it alone, too, was the subject of considerable reflection on your reviewer's part week before last, when George Szell conducted the Philharmonic-Symphony Orchestra through a thoroughly demagogic and militarized version of it.

If thinking of the work as embodying faith and hope has helped conquered nations to resist tyranny, that is all to the good. An energizing moral result is more valuable than any misreading of the composer's specific thought is dangerous. Besides, the piece will recover from its present military service just as easily as it has from its past metaphysical and political associations. But as a musician I was interested to observe the amount of distortion that Mr. Szell was obliged to impose on the work in order to make it seem to be representing military struggle and final victory.

There is no intrinsic reason, in this work or in any other, for considering contrast to mean conflict. The expression of strength, even of rudeness, in one chief theme of a piece and of pathos or tenderness in another does not mean that there is a war going on between the two sentiments. The highly contrasted materials of the Fifth Symphony have always seemed to me as complementary rather than conflicting. They make it whole and humane, the complete picture of a man. And I cannot find in the last movement of it, for all its triumphal trumpets, any representation, thematic or otherwise, of the victory of either sentiment. I find, rather, an apotheosis in which the two are transformed into a third expression, which is one of optimism and confidence, a glorious but still dynamic serenity. Neither assertiveness nor lyricism wins; they simply decide to co-operate.

This is no picture of military victory. It is the purest Hegelian dialectic, by which thesis and antithesis unite to form a synthesis. It may be an enlightened way of resolving contrasts, or even of conflicts, this using of them as complementary floodlights toward a general luminosity. And it may be an enlightened way of envisaging postwar problems, including Germany itself, though I am suspicious of the Hegelian dialectic, which lends itself to much trickiness in handling. Like most other philosophic methods, it can be made to give any result the handler desires. But in no case is it involved with anybody's unconditional surrender. It offers exactly the opposite kind of solution to a military victory. It is a peace proposition all round. Nowhere in Beethoven's Fifth Symphony, moreover, is there any suggestion of military operations, though other works of his portray them plentifully.

In order to throw the symphony into a key of direct action, Mr. Szell has been obliged to emphasize the assertiveness of the masculine material and to sort of slip over the significance of its tender and gentle passages. He made the strings play loud and rough, with that fierce impact that the Philharmonic strings achieve so admirably. He managed to keep the horns, with some difficulty, up to a reasonable balance with these for three movements. With the appearance of the trombones, at the beginning of the last movement, the horns appeared as hopelessly outclassed in the weight-throwing contest as the woodwinds had been from the beginning. The whole disequilibrium made Beethoven sound no end authoritative and didactic as a composer, which he certainly was, but also hopelessly incompetent as an orchestrator, which he was not. And it is exactly the musical ineffectiveness of the orchestral contrasts that proved, in spite of the moral impressiveness of the rendering, that violence was being done to the spirit of the work, whatever one may consider this to be.

Lots of people don't mind that sort of thing at any time; it rather amuses them. And nobody at all minds when it serves a national emergency. We were all interested, I think, to hear this piece played right up to the hilt as a sword of

psychological warfare, as the symbol of military victory
that it has come to represent in Allied strategy. I doubt if
a more thoroughgoing job of the kind could be done on it;
certainly none has. And now that military victory seems to
be imminent in the European theater, where the Fifth Symphony has its chief psychological utility, it is hardly to be
expected that other conductors will attempt to carry it much
farther in this direction. It is always a satisfaction to have
visited the ultimate outpost of anything; and it is a pleasure
to have viewed once this oh, so familiar piece in a new light,
however false. But the expedition is about over now, and I
imagine that all the conductors, including Mr. Szell, will
be getting back to Beethoven's plain markings, or else
inventing a new distortion of them to please other times.

March 18, 1945

BRUCKNER

¶ Anton Bruckner, whose Seventh Symphony was
played last night in Carnegie Hall by the Philharmonic-
Symphony Orchestra under Artur Rodzinski, became a
cause in his own lifetime and has remained one ever since.
The public has never either accepted or rejected him. Musicians have always loved or hated his music; they have
never quite classified it. And yet its virtues and its weaknesses are admitted by all.

A high songfulness in the melody of it is one of its
charms. A great suavity of harmonic figuration (one can
scarcely call it counterpoint) is another. Real seriousness
of thought and a certain purity of spirit it undoubtedly has.
There is nothing vulgar, cheap, or meretricious about it.
And it sounds extremely well; it is graciously written.

On the other hand, the eight symphonies, which constitute the major body of Bruckner's work, are none of
them well integrated formally; they barely hang together.

And their unvarying pattern of four-measure phrases, brings them, like César Franck's two-measure monotony, dangerously close to a doggerel meter. Also, their melodic material, for all its grace, is derivative. Schubert, Brahms, and Wagner are never wholly absent from the memory as one listens. The music is intended, I think, to feel like Brahms and to sound like Wagner; and unfortunately it more often than not does just that.

It does another thing, however, which is probably not intentional but which gives it what personal flavor it has. It evokes, by orchestral means, organ registration. Bruckner uses his brasses exactly as an organist uses the reed stops; and he uses the woodwind more often than not as a choir-organ, or *positif.* His masterful cleanliness in the antiphonal deployment of the different kinds of sound is the work of a great organ player, which he was. The looseness of his formal structures is due, no doubt, to the same professional formation, as is certainly his unvarying use of the apocalyptic climax to finish off his longer works.

There is a pious theatricality about all Bruckner's symphonies that, combined with his constant reverence toward his masters, makes them most attractive. They represent aesthetically a philosophy of quietism, musically the ultimate of humility. They rest one; they are perfect to daydream to. Of real originiality they have, I think, very little.

April 6, 1945

SCHUMAN'S *UNDERTOW*

¶ William Schuman's ballet, *Undertow,* now being played by Ballet Theater, has enlarged our acquaintance with this composer's personality; and it may be about to add to the repertory of his concert works. Whatever may be the future of Antony Tudor's ballet, there is probably an effective suite to be derived from this score.

There is no question, I think, that American composers

by and large, at least those of the presently mature and
maturing generation, have done their most striking work
in the theater. Also that the best training available for serious musico-theatrical work is practice in the concert forms.
Interestingness of texture and soundness of continuity are
the minimal requirements of concert music, and a composer
cannot hold the attention of concert audiences without
these qualities. On the other hand, concentration on a specific subject, the depicting of it without expansion or di-
gression, which is the minimal requirement of music destined for theatrical collaboration, is exactly where American concert composition tends to fall down. It is weak in
specific expressivity, partly because our American training
in composition is formalistic, seeking abstract perfection,
even at the expense of direct speech, and partly because our
concert audiences are not sufficiently accomplished at
seizing the meanings in music to require of musical composition the kind of coherence that they demand, for instance, of literature.

Formed entirely by American teachers and American
audiences, William Schuman is a product of the American
musical scene. He has written symphonies, string quartets,
overtures, band pieces, and lots of choral works; and they
have all been performed by major musical organizations.
His workmanship is skillful, individual, striking. His expressivity has always been tenuous, timid, conventional.
His serious works have shown a respectable seriousness of
attitude without much private or particular passion, while
his gayer ones have expressed either a standard American
cheerfulness or the comforting bumptiousness of middle-
quality comic-strip humor. He has written easily, abundantly, and, in a technical sense, well; but his music has
been, on the whole, reticent, has communicated to the
public little about himself or about anything else.

Undertow has a sounder proportion of matter to means.
The story of this particular ballet has required, to begin
with, vivid rather than formalistic treatment. That story,
for all its inefficiencies as dramatic literature (it has a realistic but nonessential beginning and a nonrealistic, quite
unbelievable ending; with all that public opinion around,
the young man would certainly have been arrested for murder if he had committed one), has a serious subject, namely,

the pathos of sexual initiation. The music is full of frustration and violence. It has a static intensity in the passages of pure feeling and a spastic muscular energy in the passages that depict physical action that are completely appropriate to the subject and completely interesting. The climactic *pas de deux* is the most realistic piece about sexual intercourse we have had since Shostakovich's *Lady Macbeth of Mzensk*. And the contrapuntal accompaniment to the scene of gang love-making between one girl and four men is both exciting and convincing.

Whether Schuman has a real theatrical gift or merely some qualities that are useful in the theater, I am not sure. The whole score does not accompany the ballet as consistently as certain passages underline it strikingly. If Schuman were a born man of the theater, he ought to have given to the choreographer, or secured from him, a closer communion. But Tudor, who likes to work from ready-made music, may not be easy to do a duo with. Further dramatic works from Schuman will no doubt reveal further his qualities. For the present he has shown a gift for expressing the lurid; and the lurid has afforded him a more ample field for exploiting his full powers as an artist than the formalistic, middle-ground modernism of his concert style and the boisterous-but-not-much-else Americanism of his assumed concert personality have done. Also, his gift for massive orchestration, which lends so easily a merely demagogic air to his concert works, becomes an element of magnificent emphasis when applied to a melodramatic subject in a theater.

And so, viewed freshly through his new-found medium, Schuman turns out to be not at all the composer of small expressive range and assumed monumental proportions that his concert music has long led one to consider him, but a man of high, of spectacular expressive gifts who has been constricted by the elegant abstractions of the American concert style—and a little bit, too, perhaps, by his youth. The concert forms have been good schooling for him, but he has never expressed himself in them with any freedom. The theater gives him elbow room. His mind can move around in it. And his feeling-content, his compassion, as well as his inveterate love for depicting physical movement, take on an unexpected strength under the theater's channelization of them to purposes of specific meaning. *Undertow* is not a masterpiece of music, any more than it is of choreography. But it is full of music that says something. It speaks. It can even be listened to. I think it will be remembered.

April 29, 1945

TWO BALLETS

¶ The week of ballet that Martha Graham and her dance company have been offering at the National Theater has given New York finally a hearing of Aaron Copland's *Appalachian Spring* and of Paul Hindemith's *Hérodiade*. The Copland subject is marriage preliminaries in nineteenth-century rural America. The style is pastoral, the tone, as is appropriate to the pastoral style, blithe and beatific. The material is folklore, some of it vocal, some violinistic. The harmonic treatment, based chiefly on open fourths and fifths, evokes our sparse and dissonant rural tradition rather than the thick suavities of our urban manner. The instrumentation is plain, clean-colored, deeply imaginative. It is designed not only to express the moods of the story but to amplify the characteristics of the dramatis personae. It is both poetically effective and theatrically functional. It is also musically interesting; it has style.

Every aspect of the work is musically interesting, though all of it is not equally intense as expression. If there is by moments, even in energetic passages, a static quality that does not seem to be advancing the story, that same immobility, when it comes off right, gives us both the very particular Copland miracle and that blithe Elysian-Fields note that is ideally the pastoral manner.

Aided as little, in the past, by her musical as by her pictorial collaborators, and devoted, by temperament and by preconception, to the rendering of emotion (specifically, feminist emotion) rather than of character, Miss Graham's work has long leaned toward the introspective and the psychologically lurid. Copland, in *Appalachian Spring,* has, by the inflexibility of his pastoral landscape mood, kept her away from the violence of solitary meditation and drawn her toward awareness of persons and sweetness of manners. Paul Hindemith, long acquainted with the traps that Miss Graham's Germanic approach to the theater presents, has led her away from them by another means. He has given her a subject that is lurid enough for any taste but that is objectively rather than subjectively so. By this simple device he has forced her to represent a real and visible person rather than a state of mind about one. And, of course, in such a situation, she turns out to be, as one has long suspected, not only an expressive dancer but a great actress, one of the very great among living actresses, in fact.

The piece, called *Hérodiade* (though the English form *Herodias* might have been preferable), is derived from Mallarmé's French poem of that title. It represents the boudoir afternoon of a woman who is beautiful, sensual, intellectual, proud, passionate, rich, and middle-aged. She consults her mirror and converses with her maid, frankly, without illusion and without despair. And then she dresses for the evening. The music is sumptuously evocative, rich, complex, civilized. Also solidly sustained architecturally. If it is reminiscent, in the central portion, of Strauss's *Salomé,* with its jumping-all-about-the-place melodic line, who is to say that that hypertrophied and decadent manner is inappropriate to the Herod family? Mallarmé's conception is stiffer and more concentratedly sumptuous, and so is Miss Graham's. But the Hindemith score, though not completely distinguished, is a fine piece. And it has inspired Miss Graham to the creation, for once, of a character that is real enough, I should think, for other dancers to undertake.

May 20, 1945

THE ORGAN

¶ The modern pipe organ and its repertory make a strange dichotomy. The instrument itself is the most elaborate, the most ingenious, the most complex, and the most expensive of all instruments. Also one of the most common. Hamlets that never saw a bassoon or a French horn or an Australian marimba or even a concert grand pianoforte will occasionally house a quite decent one. City people give them away like drinking fountains and stained-glass windows. And yet, in two centuries scarcely twenty pieces have been written for the organ that could be called first-class music. The learning, the taste, the engineering knowledge, and the skilled handicraft that go into the manufacture of even a reasonably satisfactory instrument are enormous. Nevertheless, not one major composer, since Sebastian Bach died in 1750, has written for the organ with any notable freedom or authority. Very few have written for it at all.

César Franck, perhaps, did the best, though none of his half-dozen best organ pieces is as commanding a work as any of his half-dozen best chamber and orchestral works. Also, Franck's position as a major composer in any medium is doubtful. The organ got much of their best work out of Frescobaldi and Couperin and Handel and Bach, not to mention a hundred other composers of the Baroque age. Since that time it is chiefly the second-rate that have written for it. Mozart, a skillful organist himself, never wrote a solo piece for the instrument (though Grove's *Dictionary of Music and Musicians* lists seventeen sonatas for organ, "usually with violin and bass, intended to be used as graduales" in the Church service). Mendelssohn wrote six solo sonatas for it that are sound music, if a little stuffy. Brahms wrote eleven chorale-preludes, his last opus number, of which two are genuinely inspired, though neither of these is particularly well conceived for the instrument. And there

are twelve organ pieces by Franck that are respectable as
music. The rest of the post-Baroque repertory has been
written by the Gounods, the Saint-Saënses, the Regers, the
Viernes, the Widors, and their like—at its best, second-rate
stuff by second-rate composers. Among the modern masters, only Schönberg, and that just once, has produced a
work of any grandeur for the organ.

The cause of this neglect lies, I think, in the nature of the
instrument itself, which has nowadays little but a glorious
moment of history to offer. For the organ, like many another instrument of ancient lineage, did have its hour of
glory. This hour, which lasted a good century and a half,
say from roughly the year 1600 to quite precisely 1750,
covers the whole of that period commonly known to the
fine arts as the Baroque. And though in the visual techniques the high Baroque style is associated chiefly with the
Counter Reformation of the Catholic Church, the musical
Baroque penetrated, both in Germany and in England, to
the heart of Protestantism itself.

That was the age that created the fugue, the aria, the
free fantasia, the opera, the oratorio. It invented the violin,
too, and carried to an apogee of musical refinement the
keyed instruments, notably the organ and the harpsichord.
It was the age of oratory in music, of the grandiose, the
impersonal, the abstract. When it gave way in the middle
of the eighteenth century to the beginnings of a more personalized romanticism, certain of its favorite media ceased
to have effective power. The oratorio, for instance, has
never recovered from that change in taste; nor have the
fugue and its running mate, the free fantasia, ever since had
quite the authority they enjoyed before. The opera survived
by going in for personal sentiment in the arias and by giving
up all that was merely grandiose in the set pieces. The violin
also, played with the new Tourte bow (an invention of the
1770's), took on an appropriate sensitivity of expression.
But the harpsichord fell wholly out of use, a new keyed
instrument, the fortepiano, offering possibilities of voluntary accent and of crescendo that were far more attractive
to the Romantic mind than the equalized articulation and
terraced dynamics of its predecessor.

The organ survived the Romantic revolution, but it lost
its primacy among musical instruments. It remained (and

remains still) firmly intrenched in its privileges as a hand-maiden of religion; but it has never since dared venture far, as the rest of music has done, from the protecting walls of the Church. It plays today the tiniest of roles in the concert hall and in the theater, while attempts to give it a new (and secular) prestige through its exploitation in department stores and cinemas have merely ended by robbing it of what little secular dignity was left to it after a century and a half of cloistered servitude.

Nevertheless, the instrument went on growing. It hypertrophied, to be exact. All through the nineteenth and early twentieth centuries it got bigger and bigger. It grew row after row of additional pipes, which included every possible reminder of other instruments, including the human voice; and the manufacturers imperiled its very existence by weighing it down with every imaginable labor-saving device. It went to leaf and flower, grew very little musical fresh fruit. In our time a movement to restore to use the surviving organs of the Baroque age, which are fairly numerous in Europe, and the construction of new instruments modeled after these, have given us a new enlightenment, just as a similar revival in harpsichord-building has, about Baroque keyboard music. This revival, for all its antiquarian nature, has played a role in the drama of modernism. Whether it is capable of reinvigorating the organ as an instrument of contemporary expression I do not know. But certainly the communion it has provided with the Baroque keyboard repertory, which is one of the world's very greatest musical literatures, is a closer one than was previously available. And that has brought fresh ideas into modern writing, just as the studies of medieval chant which the Benedictines of Solesmes carried out in the late nineteenth century had given a new life both to harmony and to the French vocal line, and just as the Greek studies of the late Renaissance in Italy had rendered possible in the year 1600 the invention of the opera.

And so the organ, in terms of its once central position in musical advance, is today, as it has been for nearly two centuries (and in spite of its continuing to be manufactured in ever more and more pretentious format), as dead as the harpsichord. But, as in the case of the harpsichord, an inspired resuscitation has given today's world of music a source of knowledge, of real acquaintance with the auditory past, that has brought the instrument back to a worthy and possibly to a proud position in our creative life. Not that there is anything intrinsically unfortunate about having worked so long for religious establishments. But religious establishments have for so long dallied on the sidelines of musical advance that sacred organ composition, like any other musical enterprise limited to Church patronage, has usually found itself outclassed intellectually in the world of free artistic enterprise. And thus it is that antiquarianism and scholarship, for all their supposed sterility, have, by enabling us to hear Bach fugues as Bach himself heard them, made to music a gift that no other agency could have done, would have done, or, to stick to the simple fact, did do.

August 5, 1945

OLIVIER MESSIAEN

¶ "Atomic bomb of contemporary music" is the current epithet for Olivier Messiaen. Whether France's thirty-seven-year-old boy wonder is capable of quite so vast a work of destruction as that unhappy engine I could not say. But certainly he has made a big noise in the world. And the particular kind of noise that his music makes does, I must say, make that of his chief contemporaries sound a bit old-fashioned.

What strikes one right off on hearing almost any of his pieces is the power these have of commanding attention. They do not sound familiar; their textures—rhythmic, harmonic, and instrumental—are fresh and strong. And though a certain melodic banality may put one off no less than the pretentious mysticism of his titles may offend, it is not possible to come in contact with any of his major productions without being aware that one is in the presence of a major musical talent. Liking it or not is of no matter; Messiaen's

music has a vibrancy that anybody can be aware of, that
the French music world is completely aware of, that has
been accepted in France, indeed, for the postwar period
as one of the facts of life.

Messiaen's pieces are mostly quite long; and their textures, rhythmic and harmonic, are complex. In spite of their
length and their complexity their sounds are perfectly clear.
They are nowhere muddy in color but always sonorous.
Their shining brightness takes one back to Berlioz. So
also does their subject matter. "Dance of Fury for the Seven
Trumpets," "The Rainbow of Innocence," "Angel with Per-
fumes," "The Crystal Liturgy," "Subtlety of the Body in
Glory," "Strength and Agility of the Body in Glory," "God
with Us," and "Vocal Exercise for the Angel Who An-
nounces the End of Time" are some of the simpler subtitles.
And the renderings of these are no less picturesque than
Berlioz's description of doomsday (in the Dies Iræ of
his Requiem Mass) for chorus and full orchestra plus
twenty-eight trumpets and trombones and fourteen kettle-
drums.

Messiaen is a full-fledged romantic. Form is nothing to
him, content everything. And the kind of content that he
likes is the convulsive, the ecstatic, the cataclysmic, the terrifying, the unreal. That the imagery of this should be derived almost exclusively from religion is not surprising in a
church organist and the son of a mystical poetess, Cécile
Sauvage. What is a little surprising in so scholarly a modernist (he is organist at the cultivated parish of La Trinité
and a professor of harmony at the Paris Conservatory) is
the literalness of his religious imagination. But there is no
possibility of suspecting insincerity. His pictorial concept of
religion, though a rare one among educated men, is too intense to be anything but real. Messiaen is simply a theolo-
gian with a taste for the theatrical. And he dramatizes theological events with all the *sang-froid* of a man who is completely at home in the backstage of religious establishments.

The elaborateness of Messiaen's procedures is exposed in
detail in a two-volume treatise by him called *The Technique
of My Musical Language,* (*Technique de mon language musical;* Alphonse Leduc, Paris, 1944). The rhythmic devices
employed, many of them derived from Hindu practice, are
most sophisticated. The harmonic language is massively

dissonant but not especially novel. It resembles rather the piling of Ossa on Pelion that formerly characterized the work of Florent Schmitt. There are layer cakes of rhythms and of harmonies but there is little linear counterpoint. The instrumentation is admirably designed to contrast these simultaneities and to pick them out. Derived from organ registration, it exploits the higher brilliancies (as of mixture stops) to great advantage. The weaker elements of Messiaen's style are his continuity, which, like that of many another organist-composer, is improvisational rather than structural, and his melodic material, which is low in expressivity. The themes are lacking in the tensile strength necessary to sustain long developments because of his predilection for weak intervals, especially the major sixth and the augmented fourth, and for contradictory chromatics.

Among the works which one hopes will soon be heard in New York are *Forgotten Offerings* (*Les Offrandes oubliées*) for orchestra, by which Messiaen became known way back in 1935 as a major talent, and *The Nativity of Our Lord*, nine meditations for organ, published in 1936. These pieces have charm and youth in them and a striking virtuosity of texture. Among the more recent works of some length are *Seven Visions of the Amen*, for two pianos; *Twenty Admirations of the Infant Jesus* (unless I mistranslate *Vingt Regards sur l'enfant Jésus*), for solo piano; *Three Short Liturgies of the Divine Presence* (they last a good half-hour, all the same), for women's voices and orchestra; and a *Quartet for the End of Time,* which was composed during his German captivity.

The most satisfactory of these works to me is the two-piano work. The most impressive to the general public, however, is the orchestral one, which was first presented last April at a concert of *La Pléiade* in the Salle du Conservatoire. I have heard a recording of these liturgies, made from a subsequent broadcast under the direction of Roger Désormière; and though certainly they have a spasmodic flow (and no little monotony) they do make a wonderful noise.

The instrumentation, though top-heavy, is utterly glittering. It consists of vibraphone, celesta, maracas, gong, tam-tam, nine sopranos singing in unison, piano, *les ondes Martenot* (a form of theremin), and strings. The three sections are entitled: "Antiphon of Interior Conversation (God present in us . . .)," "Sequence of The Word, Divine Canticle (God present in Himself . . .)," and "Psalm of the Ubiquity of Love (God present in all things . . .)." The text employed by the singers is of Messiaen's composition, as were also program notes printed on the occasion of the first performance. Of the "Antiphon" he writes:

"Dedicated to God present within us through Grace and the Holy Communion. After a most tender beginning ('My Jesus, My Silence, Abide with Me'), accompanied by the songs of distant birds (on the piano), there follows a contrapuntal middle section of great polyrhythmic and polymodal refinement. ('The Yes which sings like an echo of light.' 'Red and lavender melody in praise of The Father.' 'Your hand is out of the picture by one kiss.' 'Divine landscape, reverse your image in water.')"

All these are clearly a believing organist's ideas. César Franck and Anton Bruckner, though neither had Messiaen's humor, worked from just such preoccupations. I once described this religio-musical style as the determination to produce somewhere in every piece an apotheosis destined at once to open up the heavens and to bring down the house. Certainly the latter action is easier to accomplish in modern life than the first. And certainly Messiaen has accomplished it several times in the *Liturgies*. The success of his accomplishment is due to a natural instinct for making music plus the simplicity and sincerity of his feelings. These are expressed, moreover, through a musical technique of great complexity and considerable originality. The faults of his taste are obvious; and the traps of mystical program music, though less so, are well known to musicians, possibly even to himself. Nevertheless the man is a great composer. One has only to hear his music beside that of any of the standard eclectic modernists to know that. Because his really vibrates and theirs doesn't.

September 23, 1945

PURGING THE "COLLABOS"

¶ Who collaborated with the enemy and what sanctions are being meted out to those who did are the subject of constant queries to reporters working in those European countries that were occupied during the war by German troops. A full answer is impossible till the purgings have been completed. They are being applied in France to the musical confraternity in the following manner:

Let us distinguish, to begin with, collaboration from treason. Any citizen who betrayed state secrets to the enemy, who denounced Communists, Jews, Allied agents, or members of local resistance movements or who by maladministration allowed works of art or other national wealth to fall into enemy hands is a traitor to his country and must be punished. Collaboration is more difficult to define and consequently to judge. It is doubtful, indeed, whether there is any basis in law for judging it at all. Certainly the facts are so confusing—because everybody has at some point or other made some compromise, and because even the most cynical among the "collabos" have all concealed Jews in their houses or helped French young people to avoid deportation—that no clear division is possible of sheep from goats.

Nevertheless, every social group and professional body feels the need of expressing its disapproval of those members whose conduct toward the enemy has been lacking in moral dignity. Consequently, in those cases where the law does not apply, sanctions have been left to the social groups and professional bodies whose moral prestige has been lowered by such conduct. At the beginning a good deal of spontaneous direct action by the Resistance troops took place; but most of that has ceased now, and purging is orderly. It is not, however, a state action except in treason cases. The French have avoided, as far as possible, defining collaboration as a political crime, because that would have involved them in the very abuse of power that they hated most in the German and Vichy administrations, namely, political arrest.

There is today no legal hindrance to the public appearance of musicians who collaborated, excepting of those who are under provisional arrest. They can accept any engagement offered and they can organize any concert they wish, short of hiring for it state-owned premises, like the Théâtre de L'Opéra. Even here the hindrance is one of administrative discretion, not of legality. There are certain things that are hard to do, however, such as to work for the state radio or for the state theaters. All the state theaters were purged a year ago by committees of their own members. Singers and instrumentalists formerly working at the Opéra, for instance, whose conduct has been judged unpatriotic by their own Musicians' Resistance Committee are not being allowed to work in that house for the present. The committee has not been oversevere. Every group, in fact, has tended toward tolerance in the judgment of its own members.

Every group has tended equally toward intolerance in judging the conduct of others. It is not the musicians and dancers, for instance, who are preventing the return to the Opéra ballet of Solange Schwartz and Jean Peretti and Serge Lifar. It is the stagehands' union, which threatens to strike every time the subject is broached. Since nobody wants a public controversy with so powerful a union on any subject (and particularly not on that one), the stagehands remain masters in fact of the situation, though purging musicians is properly no right of theirs, any more than purging the backstage is any right of the orchestra. The Soviet Embassy is at the moment, for reasons unknown, being kind to Lifar (a White Russian); and it seems likely that pressure from that source on the Communist cell within the stagehands' union may eventually bring about his return to the Opéra, for which there is some public demand. The orchestra of the Opéra-Comique has recently refused to perform a work by Marcel Delannoy which the management had planned to revive this fall, though the composer is under no formal ban of any kind, official or unofficial.

The musical profession and the musical public, at least in Paris, are eager to forget the whole collaboration story, if not to forgive, and to get back the use of music's full effectives, throwing just a few of its more outrageous sinners to the wolves of superpatriotic opinion. Already the cultural department of the Foreign Office is sending to England as propagandists for French music many artists it does not dare yet to bless at home. And the composer Henry Barraud, musical director of the state radio, has on several occasions used artists who are on the radio's black list. He has used them because he needed them and because he considers the present procedure of radio black-listing to be unjust.

The radio purges have been the strictest of all, because they have been made not by musicians but by Resistance politicians, and because they follow a logical method. Playing publicly in the symphony orchestras involved no trading (technically) with the enemy, because these are cooperative associations. Neither did working at the state opera houses, because there one was employed by one's own government. (The stagehands are forgetting, however, in their present moralistic fervor that they accepted tips from Germans at the German-organized gala performances.) Performing at Radio-Paris, however, which was German-run, entailed open acceptance of money from the enemy, of working directly for him.

Now it happens that the bookkeeping of Radio-Paris is intact. So, instead of allowing the musicians' union or some similar professional body to make up the black lists, the government office in charge of the radio (I think it is the Ministry of Information) simply black-listed everybody who had ever received a check from Radio-Paris. The time an artist has to remain in Coventry is two weeks for each broadcast he made under the Germans. In some cases the period is brief; in others it mounts as high as seven years. In the case of choirs, quartets, dance bands, and other name groups only the leader is black-listed, because he is the one who received the money. There is no way of punishing the associates who broadcast with him, because their names are not on the Radio-Paris books.

The system, as you can see, is both logical and completely unfair. It is unfair because judgment has been imposed on artists by nonartists in a matter where no crime, but only professional misconduct, is charged. It is unfair also because it has chosen its scapegoats from lists that are not complete. And it is unfair because it has condemned, on a technicality, a very large part of the profession with a severity that neither the profession itself nor public opinion condones. The poor musician or entertainer who, in order to eat, occasionally performed French music (he was not allowed to perform German) at Radio-Paris may not be the noblest form of man. But to penalize him financially and morally, while not pushing at all the workers at state theaters who performed occasionally, under orders, German music that the French state paid for is one of the injustices that is bringing the whole operation of purging musician collaborators into disrepute. If the discussions of it that I have heard (and during my recent two months in Paris I heard many) indicate a general trend in French opinion, I think that the purging of the artistic professions is likely to be dropped within another year and that practically everybody will be glad.

November 18, 1945

A MIRACLE AND A MONUMENT

¶ Maggie Teyte, who gave her second Town Hall recital of the season last night, is both a miracle and a monument. To have retained both her beautiful singing voice and complete mastery of it over a period of some thirty-five years (I last heard her in 1912 at the Chicago Opera) is the miracle. The monumental nature of her work comes from the fact that she remains virtually alone today as an exponent of the French vocal style of the period that preceded the other war. If you want to hear the Debussy songs and the Ravel songs and Fauré sung by a vocalist who still knows what they sounded like in the epoch that saw their creation, there is no other living artist that can evoke them for you so authentically or so vividly. And if you want to hear the French singing style as Jean de Reszke invented it, as Muratore and Mary Garden practiced it, you will have to elbow your way into Town Hall the next time Miss Teyte gives a recital.

That style is based technically on being able to sing any vowel in any color and at any degree of loudness or softness on any note of one's voice. It is based interpretatively on reading aloud. It is intoned elocution that uses so large a variety of vocal coloration that in no single piece is the gamut ever exhausted. Each song is a little drama, a slice of life that takes place in its own poetic climate, uses its own special and appropriate palette of sound. This vocal impressionism is of the utmost auditory richness, and also of the most intense poetic clarity. Such musical variety combined with ease of understanding, such apparent naturalism, is a summit of vocal art from which the singing of our epoch has long since declined. Miss Teyte alone has the key to it, the discipline of it, the workmanship and the knowledge to expose it before us.

It is a dramatic art. There is nothing personal or introspective about it, excepting that most of the repertory that shows it at its best is music of introspective subject matter. But introspective subject matter requires for its clear projection the most impersonal dramatic technique. Otherwise you get only obscurity. There is nothing inspirational about Miss Teyte's musical procedures. Her renderings are the product of discipline, reflection, and lots of rehearsal. Imagination and exactitude are what make them so dramatic. And naturally, they are not dramatic in any inappropriate sense. She projects poetry without getting theatrical. It is as if somebody were singing very beautifully and reading very beautifully at the same time.

It would be hard to say which among the songs she sang offered the greatest revelation. Her Fauré was marked by a wonderfully unifying rhythm. Her Debussy had the real Debussy immobility, the rocklike reality of emotion that is the essence of Debussy. Her Ravel had a wiry delicacy that I have not heard applied to these songs since Eva Gauthier used to sing them for us with such fine awareness of their essential parody.

Perhaps the grandest dramatic achievement of the evening was the letter scene from *Pelléas et Mélisande,* which Miss Teyte added at the close. This was so simple, so clear, and so relentless, so plain at the same time, that one was reminded of how touching *Pelléas* can be whenever any-body lets us hear the words of it.

In face of such thoroughly conscious workmanship it seems almost unnecessary to mention Miss Teyte's personal charm. But that charm is itself so gracious, and Miss Teyte's schooled temperament as an actress is so warmed by it, that the very sweetness of her woman's personality becomes a valid part of her work as an artist. It is something of the kind, I am sure, that has made possible the miracle by which time has touched her singing so little.

December 29, 1945

1946

AMERICANISMS

¶ For all the vaunted virtuosity of the American symphony orchestras, your correspondent has long wondered what, if any, has been, or is likely to be, their contribution to art. American ensemble playing on the popular level has given to the world two, perhaps three, expressive devices of absolute originality. One is a new form of tempo rubato, a way of articulating a melody so loosely that its metrical scansion concords at almost no point with that of its accompaniment, the former enjoying the greatest rhythmic freedom while the latter continues in strictly measured time. Another characteristically American device is playing "blue," using for melodic expression constant departures from conventionally correct pitch in such a way that these do not obscure or contradict the basic harmony, which keeps to normal tuning. Simultaneous observance of these two dichotomies, one metrical and one tonal, constitute a style of playing known as "hot." And although precedents for this are not unknown in folklore and even in European art custom, our systematization of it is a gift to music.

Another device by which our popular ensembles depart from European habits is the execution of a volume crescendo without any acceleration of tempo. It is possible that Sebastian Bach may have played the organ without speeding up the louder passages, but Bach did not know the volume crescendo as we conceive it. He only knew platforms of loudness. The smooth and rapid increase of sound from very soft to very loud and back again is an invention of the late eighteenth century. It is possible, even today, only with a fairly numerous orchestra or chorus, on a pianoforte, or on the accordion. It is the basic device of musical Romanticism; and the nineteenth century invented a fluid rhythmic style, in which pulsations were substituted for strict metrics, to give to the planned crescendo a semblance of spontaneity.

It was the conductor Maurice Abravanel who first called my attention to the rarity of the nonaccelerating crescendo in European musical execution. It has long been used to suggest armies approaching and then going off into the distance, its rhythmic regularity being easily evocative of marching. But aside from this special employment it is foreign to Romantic thought. If you want to get a laugh out of yourself, just try applying it to Wagner or Chopin or Liszt or Brahms or Beethoven or even Debussy. These authors require a fluid rhytmic articulation. And though one may for rhetorical purposes, as when approaching a peroration, get slower instead of faster as the volume mounts, it is obviously inappropriate in Romantic music to execute a subjectively expressive crescendo or decrescendo without speeding up or slowing down.

The modern world, even in Europe, has long recognized the rhythmically steady crescendo as, in theory, a possible addition to the terraced dynamics of the eighteenth-century symphony. In fact, however, European composers have never, to my knowledge, used it without a specifically evocative purpose. Of the three most famous crescendos in modern music not one is both tonally continuous and rhythmically steady. Strauss's *Elektra* is tonally continuous, rising in waves from beginning to end; but it presupposes no exact metrics. Stravinsky's "Dance of the Adolescents" (from *The Rite of Spring*) and Ravel's *Bolero* do presuppose a metrically exact rendering, but they are not tonally steady crescendos. They are as neatly terraced as any Bach organ fugue.

The completely steady crescendo is natural to American musical thought. Our theater orchestras execute it without hesitation or embarrassment. Our popular orchestrators call for it constantly and get it. Our symphonic composers call for it constantly and rarely get it. The conductors of European formation, who lead most of our symphonic ensembles, simply do not understand it. Very few of them understand metrical exactitude in any form. American music, nevertheless, requires a high degree of metrical exactitude, emphasized by merely momentary metrical liberties. Also lots of crescendo, which is our passion. The music of Barber and Schuman and Piston and Hanson and Copland and Harris and Bernstein and Gershwin and Cowell and Sowerby and Randall Thompson and William Grant Still is full of crescendos. It is also full of rhythmic and metrical irregularities. But none of it is romantic music in the European sense, because the crescendos and the rhythmic irregularities are not two aspects of the same device. The separation of these devices is as characteristic of American musical thought as is our simultaneous use of free meter with strict meter and free with strict pitch. These three dichotomies are basic to our musical speech.

Hearing Howard Hanson or Leonard Bernstein conduct American music is a pleasure comparable to hearing Pierre Monteux conduct French music or Bruno Walter interpret Mahler and Bruckner. The reading is at one with the writing. Our foreign-born conductors have given the American composer a chance to hear his own work. Also, they have built up among the public a certain toleration of American music, or encouraged, rather, a toleration that has always existed. But they have built up also a certain resistance to it which did not exist here previous to the post-Civil-War German musical invasion. This resistance comes from a complete lack of adaptation on the part of the European-trained to American musical speech. They understand its international grammar, but they have not acquired its idiom and accent.

In so far as they are aware that there are an idiom and an accent (as several of them are), they are likely to mistake these for localisms of some kind. They are nothing of the sort; they are a contribution to the world's musical language, as many postwar Europeans are beginning to suspect. American popular music has long been admired abroad, but American art music is just beginning to be discovered. It would probably be a good idea for us here to keep one step ahead of the foreign market by building up a record library of American works in authoritative renderings by American-trained artists. Also to accustom our own public to this kind of authoritative collaboration. We shall need both a professional tradition and broad public support for it if we are to accept with any confidence the world-wide distribution of American music that seems to be imminent.

Actually we are producing very nearly the best music in the world. Only France, of all the other music-exporting countries, operates by stricter standards of workmanship and of originality. Not Germany nor Italy nor Russia nor England nor Mexico nor Brazil is producing music in steady quantity that is comparable in quality to that of the American school. And we are a school. Not because I say so, but because we have a vocabulary that anybody can recognize, I think, once it is pointed out, as particular to us.

January 27, 1946

GOING CONTEMPORARY

¶ Prokofiev's Fifth Symphony, which the Boston Symphony Orchestra played last night in Carnegie Hall, remains on second hearing chiefly interesting to this listener as a neo-Romantic work by a formerly neo-Classic-and-Impressionist composer. Its more picturesque sections, which are the second and fourth movements, present no novelty of any kind, though they are good Prokofiev, the first of these being a sort of Soviet-style blues, or Muscovite one-step, and the other a finale in the composer's best calisthenic vein. Both are brightly, if a little weightily orchestrated. The last has even more reminders than mere coloration of Strauss's *Till Eulenspiegel*.

The first and third movements, which are less striking, deal with a more difficult problem, namely, making a piece of some length out of pliable material. The third movement, a lament, or elegy, is less successfully developed than the first. Slow movements have never been Prokofiev's forte, and of late years he has taken more and more to concealing their lack of expressivity (and of rhythmic variety) with an overlay of cinema sentiment.

The first movement, however, is as neat a piece of sym-

phonic workmanship as has been exposed to us locally in
many a day. The rounded, graceful theme of it is no theme
at all in a classical sense. It is a motif that generates a flow
of music. This is not made up of themes or of formal melodies; it is rather a constant outpouring, an oratorical discourse that never repeats itself but that springs always from
the original motif, or source, and that returns constantly
to it for refreshment.

The movement is a neo-Romantic work because it faces
the central problem of neo-Romanticism, which is the making of sustained music out of non-angular material. This is
a technical statement of the neo-Romantic meaning-
problem, which is that of sustained personal lyricism. But
the two problems are one. The neo-Classicists of the 1920's
used either angular or motionless material. Any neo-
Classicist who, knowingly or unaware, has got involved
with rounded or flowing material has found himself up to
his neck in personal lyricism, the most treacherous of contemporary aesthetic currents. That Prokofiev has not, in this
work, found himself out beyond his depth either technically
or emotionally is proof that he is not an old man yet. That
he has walked out after one movement on all the serious
difficulties proves also that he is not quite at home in contemporary waters.

February 14, 1946

NEW HIGH

¶ Duo-pianism reaches heights technical and artistic in the work of Arthur Gold and Robert Fizdale, who
gave a recital last night in Town Hall, hitherto unknown to
the art. Such consistent beauty of tone and sweetness of
sound, even in fortissimo passages, such refined precision of
rhythm and grace of phraseology, such masterful penetration of the nature of music, of the differences between one
piece and another, between one composer's thought and

another's, such a thoroughly musical approach to music and to concert-giving produced an evening that left one elated, not tired of ear and mentally worn down, as is the common effect on this listener of two-piano recitals.

The program, save for a charming duet by Johann Christian Bach, was strictly modern. The novelties were a sonata by Paul Bowles and one by Alexei Haieff. Mr. Bowles's piece consists of a lively and a slow movement in his most poetic early-Ravel vein and a finale in imitation of African drum sounds. The effect of the whole is that of a strong musical work that is nowhere lacking in charm. Mr. Haieff's piece, though longer, is less serious and less forceful. Its textures are expert; but its thematic material wears thin under repetition, and its extended conservatory-style format (à la Anton Rubenstein) is inappropriate to the tight, modern-music-style angularity of its tune content.

Among the other modern works Satie's *Three Pieces in the Shape of a Pear* seemed to this observer the most richly packed with plums. Composed in 1903, these are still an unexhausted source of pleasure for listening and of lessons in musical composition. Seemingly unpretentious, they contain not one measure of banality, not a phrase that is not profoundly expressive and original. Beside their firm and gracious rightness, Stravinsky's Sonata for Two Pianos, also a work of gentle character, seemed lacking in concentration, though the latter is, compared to most contemporary works for that medium, expressively pretty compact. Its musical intention, if I mistake not, is to evoke Bach's "Goldberg" Variations.

John Cage's Dance for two prepared pianos is a rhythmic composition of tiny thudlike sounds that recalls Indonesian gamelan music. It is distinguished and beautiful and makes one feel good. Vittorio Rieti's *Second Avenue Waltzes*, of which three were played, are the original version of his ballet, *Waltz Academy*. They are graceful and melodious and not banal, even when they quote (knowingly) Verdi's *La Traviata* and Ravel's *La Valse*.

February 16, 1946

AGGRESSIVE BUT HARMONIOUS

¶ Verdi's *Otello,* revived yesterday afternoon at the Metropolitan Opera House after a four-year interval, is an "effective" musico-theatrical work very much in the vein of Ponchielli's *La Gioconda.* Indeed, the latter piece, which preceded *Otello* in composition and in production by eleven years, is probably responsible, along with the revised (and theatrically successful) version of Boïto's *Mefistofele,* which appeared a year before that, in 1875, for the violent theatricalism of this particular work, of which Boïto himself was the librettist.

The word "violence" comes constantly to tongue in speaking of *Otello.* And yet, as Italian opera plots of the late nineteenth century go, there is not much visible violence in this one. The spectacle is, on the whole, statuesque. But violence is present, nevertheless. It is present in the attitude of the composer toward his audience, which for three acts is allowed no respite from aggression. Every remark is exaggerated, every sentiment blown up into a passion. And since the passions, however they may differ in origin and social reference, all have exactly the same amount of emotional content (the maximum) and a virtually identical (at that intensity) expressive content, the first three acts of *Otello,* for all their masterful orchestral detail, are as monotonous in their insistence on applause-at-any-price as any Broadway musical or floor show.

The fourth act is less wearing. It takes its time, makes its points one by one, and allows, in consequence, a certain awareness of the actors as characters in a play. It allows one time to feel sorry for them, even. If Verdi, at seventy-four, had not lost the melodic invention that flowed throughout his early and middle years, the last act of *Otello* might well be as deeply touching as those of *La Traviata* and *Il Trovatore.* The repose and the leisurely timing are

there, the whole shape and progress of a noble act; but its
"Ave Maria" is a far cry from the great *"Miserere."*

February 24, 1946

NEW STAR

¶ Verdi's *La Traviata,* as sung last night at the
Metropolitan Opera House, presented for the first time in
those premises the admirable Dorothy Kirsten as Violetta.
Miss Kirsten's handling of the role, already favorably known
from the City Center, brought liveliness and beauty in no
lesser degree to the grander establishment. Backed up by a
first-class orchestra and chorus, with Cesare Sodero conducting, and surrounded by such excellent singers as Robert Merrill and Armand Tokatyan, she appeared to this observer as definitely a singing actress of the first category.

Miss Kirsten is still young, of course; and her star quality
is almost brutally brilliant. But she is not afraid of her voice,
which is big, beautiful, and well trained, or of her person,
which she projects dramatically with confidence not only in
herself, which is common enough these days, but in the
reality of her role, which is all too rare on the operatic
stage. She seems to have the material, vocal, personal, and
intellectual, for a great operatic career. If she has any vocal
disadvantage (and this is not grave), it lies in her singing
the closed vowels, the Italian *e* and *i,* less perfectly than she
does the darker, open ones, the *a* and *o.* Her scales are
clean, her range is wide, her marksmanship impeccable.
And whether she is uttering a musical line or crossing the
stage, she means it.

March 8, 1946

MÉHUL'S *JOSEPH*

¶ Etienne-Henri Méhul's *Joseph,* which was revived at the Paris Opéra on Friday, June 7, is one of the
most famous stage works in the world and one of the least
familiar. Composed in 1806 and first presented to the Parisian public in February 1807, it enjoyed a wide popularity
in Germany for several years before the French discovered
that they had a classic on their hands. Its last Paris revival
in dramatic form took place in 1896. There were two concert performances in 1935 at the Salle du Conservatoire.
It was for these last that Henri Rabaud composed the recitatives used in the present production. The work in its
original form had been an *opéra-comique,* with spoken
dialogue.

Alexandre Duval's poem is not, however, at any point
comic. Nor does it tell a love story. It simply narrates, in
pastoral vein, the story of Joseph and his brethren. The
music of Méhul's score is straightforward in style, quite
without displays of local color, noble but not pompous,
varied in expression, and remarkably touching. The characters, when they sing, have life in them; and they express
themselves with an astonishing simplicity. There is not a
vocal high note or arpeggio in the whole opera. But its
musical composition is not, for all that, unsophisticated.
There is, indeed, in Méhul's music a contrapuntal life that
is lacking in that of Gluck, his master, and that gives to his
simplest hymn or romanza an intrinsic musical interest
that supports expressivity without thickening the texture.

The unobtrusiveness of Méhul's musical mastery is particularly advantageous to the ensemble pieces, where the
individuality of the characters is preserved at no sacrifice
to apparent simplicity. The chorus of Joseph's brothers,
for example, is a notable piece of contrapuntal writing without any of the baroque ornateness that we are used to associate with the contrapuntal style. The whole opera, in

fact, like many another triumph of French workmanship, is deceptively plain. And it achieves by a masterful but abstemious use of the more elaborate musical procedures a humanity of expression that is as sweet today as it was nearly a century and a half ago.

Méhul's career as a composer, which covered the years 1787 to 1817, comprised the Revolution, the Directory, the First Empire, and Napoleon's fall. His style, which was formed in the Revolutionary years, is comparable to the neoclassic manner in architecture and decoration that was practiced contemporaneously in France and that we call in America the "Federal style." A republican simplicity was its ideal; clean, light colors were its taste; the Rights of Man was its Bible. Méhul, Gossec, and Cherubini perfected the style together. Though they all left handsome works behind them, the style itself did not survive the Bourbon Restoration. The dynamism of Beethoven and the violence of Berlioz made it seem, by comparison, picayune to the Romantic age. It is a noble style, all the same, and one that has left its ideals of personal modesty and of professional perfection on the tradition of the Paris Conservatory, where all three masters worked, and where they left their perhaps most lasting mark on music.

Méhul's *Joseph* is not passionate and grand, like Beethoven's *Fidelio,* nor fun, like Rossini's *Barber of Seville,* though as a professional job it is probably superior to either. It is a quiet piece and a well-nigh perfect one. It remains after a hundred and forty years one of the sweetest in all dramatic literature. Its revival just now, in a period of musical, as well as of political, unrest, was a more than merely bright idea on the part of the Opéra's directors. It seems to point a moral to the effect that art, at least, can be efficient without having recourse to sensational measures. The appropriateness of its subject matter, too, which treats of displaced persons and Jewish resettlement, is inescapable.

June 23, 1946

AFTER THIRTY YEARS

¶ Richard Strauss's *Ariadne on the Isle of Naxos,* which was given its first professional New York performance last night at the City Center of Music and Drama, is considered by many to be its composer's masterpiece. That it is the work of a master there is no doubt. If it lacks, perhaps, the lurid vigor of *Elektra* and *Salome* or the straight sex appeal of *Der Rosenkavalier,* it has a clarity of musical texture that is missing from these earlier works. It is indeed a pleasure to hear Strauss's music pruned of the 10,000 useless notes per act with which he was accustomed to clutter up his scores. *Ariadne,* though thin of expressive substance, has great charm, both melodic and harmonic; and its small, clean orchestra is a perpetual delight.

Last night's performance of the work under Laszlo Halasz was a pleasure all round. The orchestra was lovely; the singers sang with style; the staging, if not especially chic, was at the same time neither dull nor clownish. The work was not played for laughs or for easy applause; it was presented as a serious piece. And the audience responded with gratitude to the compliment paid its intelligence.

The work itself, from both the literary and the musical points of view, is what Marxians would probably call "decadent capitalist art." It is shallow of substance and utterly sophisticated. It is a masterful display of learning, skill, and deliberate charm, all luxury and no meat. It evokes the eighteenth century through the conventions of the Reinhardt baroque. It aims, one learns from the librettist Hofmannsthal's own publicity, at a certain profundity, which this writer finds scant, and at a humor which he finds facile. Musically it is a joke about how much fun it is to play around with the classical techniques.

From any point of view it is good to listen to, because it is a completely successful work. About what its place in musical history will be a century from now I have no guess.

But for thirty years it has had a unique place in contemporary music, and the City Center has contributed to New York's intellectual life by making us acquainted with it. Whether in all those thirty years the Metropolitan Opera, upon whom the responsibility for our operatic culture has chiefly rested, could ever have produced it I do not know. Their setup is, of course, almost unbelievably inefficient; and the work requires skill and lots of rehearsal. In any case, the fact remains that *Ariadne auf Naxos* is New York news this morning and its City Center performance musically good news.

October 11, 1946

WARM WELCOME

¶ Dame Myra Hess, who played a pianoforte recital yesterday afternoon in the Town Hall, has, as a musician, instinct and intelligence. She has the quality which in France is called *musicalité,* the gift for making music sound like music. Also, she is a workman of taste and refinement. She takes convincing tempos, phrases soundly, analyzes a work correctly, executes it with ease. What she lacks is temperament, the power always to respond in public to her music's own sound and to add, inevitably, communication. She plays intelligently and she has a natural nobility. But she doesn't easily "give," as the young people would say.

Her playing yesterday of a Bach French Suite was pleasant, of two Beethoven works (the Six Variations, Opus 34, and the A-flat Sonata, Opus 110) pretty but distant. It was as if, having known them all her life, she were reminding other musicians of how they went. She did not so much play them as strum them. She exposed them clearly, sounded them out agreeably, but abstained from any personal involvement with their expressive content. The result was hard for a listener to keep his mind on. And her

constant imposition of slight crescendos and descrescendos
on every phrase removed from musical design its expressive
urgency, reduced all to a restful lullaby.

Halfway through the Brahms F-minor Sonata, 'Opus 5,'
a change took place. She got into the scherzo through its
rhythm, stopped strumming and really played the piece.
From there to the end of the work she made music
squarely, forthrightly, convincingly, instead of just dreaming about it in a flowing robe. One realized then that her
celebrity is not due merely to her admirable wartime activities. Here her work had a plainness of speech, an impersonal grandeur that was served rather than diminished by
refinements of touch and phraseology.

Dame Myra is no devotee of the big tone, though she can
play loud enough when she needs to. It is the breadth of
her musical thought that gives dignity. For all the gentleness of her sentiments, the grace of her musical ornaments,
the wit of her dry little scale passages, she is not a finicky
player. She is sensible, straightforward, and noble, when
she gets warmed up.

Yesterday she was rather slow warming up, though the
massive audience had warmed to her from the beginning,
had stood up, indeed, to welcome her. Perhaps the speech
she made at the end of the first half of the program, in
which she thanked America with such sweet sincerity for its
moral and financial help in continuing throughout the war
daily free concerts at the National Gallery in London, had
broken down her previous emotional reserve. In any case,
she was first-class when she finally got going.

                                              October 13, 1946

GERMAN COMPOSERS

¶ Musical composition in Germany and Austria, relieved from Nazi censorship by the Allied invasion, has
gone back to where it left off when Hitler came in. This is

not to say that nobody in those countries wrote any good music during the Nazi years. I mean rather that the newer music now available there by print or performance bears a closer relation to that current in pre-Nazi times than most of the music honored by the Third Reich did. In other words, the break with the modernist tradition that accompanied the triumph of National Socialism is being repaired under the aesthetically less dictatorial Allied Military Occupation.

The mending job will not, however, be complete, with no seams visible, because certain powerful influences on central Europe's music life that were exiled in the mid-1930's will never, can never return. The principal of these is that of the twelve-tone trinity—Schönberg, Berg, and Webern. The first of these masters, now resident in California, is seventy-two years old and not in perfect health; the other two are dead. And though their influence might be expected to go on through their works and their pupils, the curious fact is that in Germany it does not. There is a little of it left in Austria, where the pre-Schönbergian atonalist, Josef Matthias Hauer, survives, along with two or three Webern pupils. The younger Austrians mostly follow other leaders, other styles. In Germany this reporter inquired diligently without encountering one twelve-tone writer or finding any German musician who knew of the existence of one in the land.

The influences of Paul Hindemith and of Kurt Weill, on the other hand, both resident in the United States, are considerable. That of the former is less notable on musical composition, curiously, than on pedagogy. Musicians who write like Hindemith are not so plentiful as those who teach his theory. In the process of getting the conservatories started again, a revision of German music teaching seems to be desired. And since personnel is lacking for the teaching of atonal theory, this school of composition is not represented on the faculties. But the Hindemith textbooks are held in high respect and seem likely to form the basis of the most advanced pedagogy. Hindemith's works are held in honor, too, but rather as proof of their author's personal gift than as models being followed. In any case, though Hindemith is a burning subject of discussion in music circles, it is his undeniable influence on music teach-

ing that is chiefly defended and attacked rather than his
direct influence on musical composition. Evidences of the
latter are, though not wholly lacking, more rare. In Germany, as here, he has formed more good teachers than he
has successful composers.

Kurt Weill, though not a theorist at all, seems to have
left a strong mark on German music. At least, there is an
influence around that is not easily explainable through
any of the existing pedagogical traditions and that this de-
tective strongly suspects to come out of *Mahagonny* and
Der Dreigroschenoper. The academic German styles today
are two, the Hindemith style and the Reger style, both contrapuntal. Like all contrapuntal styles, these are more entertaining to write in than to listen to; they lack expressivity. The rival style, which leans more on melodic and
rhythmic device, is lighter of texture, more varied in expression, less pompous, and more easily digestible.

The most successful writer in this vein is Karl Orff, who
lives near Munich. His works are chiefly dramatic oratorios, which is to say, choral works with orchestral accompaniment that require (or at least are enhanced by) staging. Their texts are elaborately cultural, their musical textures almost willfully plain. One, called *Carmina Catulli*,
consists of odes by Catullus, in Latin, interspersed with
modern recitatives, also in Latin, by the composer. Another,
Carmina Burana, uses student songs in medieval Latin
mixed with Old German. An opera entitled *Die Klüge* has
a rhymed text by the composer. Another now nearing completion, *Die Bernauerin*, is in Bavarian dialect. The direct
musical model of all these works is Stravinsky's *Les Noces*.
They employ lots of rhythmic chanting, and the orchestral
accompaniment is percussive. The music is simplified, however, to a point where the basic musical elements—melody, harmony, and counterpoint—are almost nonexistent.
The rhythm itself, even, has not much intrinisic interest.
What holds these works together is first-class handling of
words and their excellent orchestration. Otherwise they
are monotonous. Surprisingly, enough, they have considerable success in performance, even on the radio, where
stage spectacle is not there to help out.

More interesting musically, though also an example of
the simplification for expressive purposes that I credit to

Kurt Weill (radio work is also, no doubt, an influence), is the music of Boris Blacher and of his pupils. Blacher is half-Russian by birth, a child refugee of the Revolutionary years. He is musical director at present of the Russian-run Berlin radio station. His music, though aware of both Stravinsky and Satie, is gayer than that of either. At its simplest it is full of musical interest; at its most complex it is still full of life, clear and expressive. His suite, *Concertante Musik* (Bote and Bock, Berlin, 1938), would be an ornament to anybody's orchestral program. His pupil Gottfried von Einem, an Austrian, writes operas in which rumba rhythms turn up at the most tragic moments, not always inappropriately. Blacher's work and von Einem's have a touch of wit that is welcome in German music. Blacher himself is the most vigorous single musical influence now present in the country.

Blacher and Orff are the most original composers whose work this reporter encountered in Germany. Whether Orff can remain long acceptable to musicians I cannot say, though I doubt that he will. Blacher is growing in interest and influence. Hindemith, whether he ever returns or not to the land of his birth and major successes, will certainly continue to occupy there for many years a position of prestige.

October 13, 1946

ATONALITY IN FRANCE

¶ French music today presents a novel development, namely, the successful implantation on Gallic soil of Schönbergian atonality. By successful I do not mean that the public likes it. This kind of music is genuinely popular nowhere. I merely mean that it is being written in France by French composers, written skillfully and, within the composing fraternity, taken seriously.

Twelve-tone-row atonality, invented in Austria during

the first decade of this century and perfected there during the succeeding two, has since spread all over the world. A sort of musical Esperanto, it is current practically everywhere now except in Russia, where state policy discourages the recondite. In our hemisphere from Iceland to the Tierra del Fuego and in the western European enclave from Norway to Jerusalem and to Gibraltar, no country, no musical region now lacks its twelve-tone school. And if the cult seems to be dying out in the Austro-German regions that nurtured its beginnings, its adoption by France and Italy, following on earlier successes in South America, means that this new language of Germanic origin has taken root at the very center and stronghold of the Latin tradition.

Schönberg's music has long been known in Paris to a few initiates, of course; and his *Pierrot lunaire,* which Darius Milhaud gave there as early as 1922, has several times produced a striking effect. So has Alban Berg's *Lyrische Suite,* for string quartet. But the other music of these masters has made slow progress in acceptance by musical Paris. Its acquaintance and real understanding have been postponed for some eventual rainy day.

That day seems now to have arrived, and the brighter young, reacting against outmoded nationalism, are passionately involved with the new international style. Some embrace it, and some resist with vehemence. But all are having to deal with it, and many are practicing it. It has ceased to be a curiosity and become a cause. And the principal persons available who actually learned its technical procedures in Vienna—Max Deutsch, a pupil of Schönberg, and the young René Leibowitz, who once had some lessons from Anton Webern—are enjoying a prestige as mentors that their somewhat literal and stiff adherence to the system's rules would probably not have gained for them as composers.

The most pretentious of the young atonalists is Serge Nigg, a former pupil of Messiaen. He has written in the strict technique of the twelve-tone-row a piano concerto that is far from easy to listen to but that is also a work of far from negligible ponderousness. No less ingenious and learned but more digestible as a musical dish is a Sonata for Flute and Piano by Pierre Boulez. This young man is the most brilliant, in my opinion, of all the Parisian under-twenty-fives. Whether he remains attached forever to *"la musique sérielle et dodécaphonique,"* as the French term precise adherence to the twelve-tone-row syntax, he is bound to write interesting and lively music, because he has a talent for that. And the practice during formative years of the strictest counterpoint available to the modern world cannot fail to liberate by discipline the creative faculties of any genuinely gifted musician.

The attractions of the system are, I think, two. Its first delight is its seriousness. No composer primarily occupied with merely pleasing or with getting on in the world ever takes it up. It is not easy to listen to; no public likes it. Its adoption is proof that one wishes to write music for music's own sake and that one is willing to sacrifice money and quick fame to that end. One can accuse the twelve-toners of scholasticism, but no one can say they are not consecrated.

Its second fascination is its dangerousness. It presents all the perils of complete consistency. Consistency can lead artists to high triumphs of style, but it can also lead them into sterility. Nobody knows yet whether atonality is a new road to expressivity or an impasse of noncommunication. With the Austrians it has been a fair medium for the communication of limited sentiments. Outside of Austria it has so far remained pretty closely involved with the sort of psychoanalytic depiction of intimate sentiments that was its chief achievement in Vienna. If any nation in the world can enlarge this music's scope, that is the French. They should be able to give it sweetness, lightness, charm, ease, and to adapt it even more successfully to the theater than Alban Berg has done in *Lulu*. (His *Wozzeck*, though highly chromatic, is not entirely a twelve-tone work.)

The discipline should have a good effect on French music, too, which is in danger right now of falling into eclecticism of style. French music needs tightening up both in thought and in technique. And the international atonal style needs loosening up. Its expressivity is too tenuous, too introspective, too hopelessly standardized; and its technical practice lacks freedom. The French are good about freedom and good about objectivity. The Italian atonalists are already adding to it that soaring lyric line that is the joy of Italian music. If the French can add to the new idiom

precision of thought, taste, drama, and the power of evocation, the twelve-tone world will seem less oppressive to
music lovers than it does just now.

Atonality is the last of the modernisms remaining unacceptable to the general public. Straussian *Expressionismus,*
Debussyan impressionism, the dissonant neo-Classic style,
and the neo-Romantic rounded contours are all a part of
standard musical language. Even the symphony orchestra
public, the last bastion of lay conservatism, takes them as
normal. If the French can't make an airplane that will fly
with the twelve-tone syntax, nobody can. But if they suc-
ceed in doing so, then the last battle of modernism will
have been won; and our century can enter on its second
half with no regrets. A modern classic period will no doubt
then ensue, with everybody writing in an amalgamated
modern style. A very few years more should suffice to
determine whether the twelve-tone manner is to be part of
this style or not.

October 27, 1946

BRILLIANT FAREWELL

¶ The final concert of our New York City Sym-
phony's all too brief season took place last night at the City
Center of Music and Drama. The program, devoted to Stravinsky, was anything but a stale one, the *Firebird* suite
being the only number on it that is current in repertory.
Leonard Bernstein, the conductor, made a pretty speech.
Divers soloists from the orchestra played expertly chamber
works by the White Russian master. And Mr. Bernstein led a
handsome and (for once) thoroughly prepared performance of the rarely heard dramatic oratorio, *Oedipus Rex*.

The latter, which your scribe had not encountered since
its first performance in Paris nearly twenty years ago, is the
same troublesome work it was then. It has not aged be-

comingly, as *L'Histoire d'un soldat*, from 1917, has, nor
lost its savor altogether, like the *Ragtime*, of 1919, both of
which were represented on the program. It is a great big
lump of wonderful music, some of which never did come
off right and still doesn't.

It is noble, grandiose, complex, massive, stony. Only a
master could have written it; and only a master with purely
instrumental turn of thought, like Stravinsky or Sebastian
Bach, could have written it so ungratefully for the human
voice. A linguistic problem is somewhat responsible for the
vocal ineptitudes; but so is the composer's imperfect acquaintance with vocal ranges; and so is a certain stylistic
willfulness on his part that he hoped, I presume, would
conceal the faults of the original literary conception.

The text, believe it or not, is a translation into modern
Sorbonne Latin of a French adaptation of an English literal
translation of Sophocles. It is no wonder that all literary
quality got lost in the process. There was not much Stravinsky could do with such a text but to make it sound as much
as possible like Russian. Last night Mr. Norman Corwin went
further and, using a public address system, recited between
the numbers a sort of explanation, translated from Jean
Cocteau's French, which is quite elegant, into radio American, a far from distinguished idiom.

For all its final ineffectualness, and forgetting Mr. Corwin, the work has considerable expressive power and a musical seriousness of the grandest kind. It is full of real invention, also of outmoded stylistic affectations. The latter, imitated mostly from Verdi and from Handel, just barely, in
some cases, escape the comical. The former, plus its
strong dramatic plan, saves the work from silliness.

Neither saves the singers from giving an effect of swimming in molasses, because their solos are all conceived as if
the human wind instrument were a trumpet or a keyed
trombone. Linear shape and ornament are expected to
produce all the expressivity, verbal color and vocal sweetness being omitted wholly from the requirements. Even the
male chorus, save for a few really terrifying percussive moments, did not sound as if the music they were singing was
their music, though Robert Shaw had obviously prepared
them thoroughly. The work is not well written vocally, sim-

ply that. But it is nobly conceived. Hearing it occasionally
is a privilege, and Mr. Bernstein is to be thanked for giving
it to us.

Mr. Bernstein, along with tantrums and occasionally im-
modesty, has given us lots of good music, especially in the
domain of modern revivals. One will miss the concerts
of his orchestra. Their programs have been more distinguished intellectually than those of any similar group, in
spite of the brilliant season the Philharmonic has lately
been offering. And the relation of all this to the City Center audience has been of a vivacity unique in the orchestral
world. Also, Bernstein conducts like a master when he
knows and really likes a score.

November 26, 1946

MONEY'S WORTH

¶ Alexander Brailowsky's recital of piano music
last night in Carnegie Hall was a model of the "good show"
produced by legitimate means. He dramatized the music
that he played, and he dramatized the excellence of his
execution. He dramatized these as a harmony, too, not as a
conflict of opposing elements. Everything he played was
consequently a human, as well as a musical, pleasure. Not a
very deep pleasure, perhaps, but a real one.

Mr. Brailowsky has a natural gift for making music, un-
tainted by intellectuality, and a masterful hand. His instincts are as gracious as his technique is sound. He exploits
sentiment without getting hot around the collar, brilliance
and brio with a visible delight. He paces a piece, any piece,
as if it were an act of a play, builds it up, tapers it off, without hurry and without lingering. And he plays the right
notes.

No audience can fail to respond to such competence,
such courtesy. This member of last night's audience responded most vigorously to the Liszt Sonata, which offered
the further delight of an apt stylization. This consisted of

executing all its rolling and rumbling figurations with the driest, cleanest, and most exact modern finger mechanics. To the mere power of its climactic moments, which was already considerable, there was added thus an incisiveness that this work rarely enjoys; and its Romantic fury took on, in consequence, a diabolic quality at once terrifying and completely appropriate.

Mr. Brailowsky's Chopin benefited from the same clarity of articulation; and so did his Hummel Rondo, his Mendelssohn, Debussy, and Ravel. A Brahms Intermezzo, though cleanly read, lacked intimacy. And the Bach organ Toccata and Fugue in D minor (in the Busoni transcription) rather missed out all round. This is a clocklike piece, not a storm in the mountains. Its themes and its figurations are all mechanistic. Its expressive power in performance comes from playing up this mechanical quality rather than from trying to conceal it. Any organ transcription, moreover, must derive on the pianoforte any overpowering effect that is desired from a relentless rhythm rather than from mere pounding.

With these two exceptions, the evening was full of good musical value. No revelations, mind you. Mr. Brailowsky projects little original poetry and almost no novel meanings. But he makes music harmoniously, brilliantly, and quite soundly enough for anybody's price of admission. He is an honest virtuoso.

December 6, 1945

KING OF THE GYPSIES

¶ Tossy Spivakovsky, who played a recital last night in Carnegie Hall, is a sensationally effective violinist when he is effective and a major disappointment when he is not. The gypsy style is his meat; there he is forceful, varied, brilliant, and explosive. His classical violin playing has a certain grandeur, too, a hard nobility in slow passages. But it is so lacking in both flexibility of expression and, when he plays fast, accuracy of pitch that one cannot but regret the sacrifice he has made to achieve power in the other style.

The sacrifice has to do with his adoption of a right-hand position that is unique among reputable artists and, so the professionals tell me, heretical. He grasps the bow by bending his thumb clean round the nut and flexing the other fingers over it at the outer joints. In this position he has the full weight of his forearm available for bow pressure with small chance of producing an unsteady sound. Hence the nobility of his sustained cantilena. Hence also the unusual force he can put into off-center tonal effects, such as are produced by playing right on the bridge or way down on the fingerboard.

This strong but insensitive bow position, which lacks the cushion usually provided by a relaxed first finger, deprives him of two major expressive devices, the long light bow and the short light, or bouncing, bow. He is obliged, in legato playing, to alleviate the bad acoustical effects of excessive arm weight by drawing his bow too fast across the strings; and his wrist position is too inflexible to allow him much play in the lighter qualities of spiccato and saltando playing. He changes the direction of his bow about twice as often as another good player needs to. He does it most skillfully, but he breaks up a phrase unnecessarily all the same. He also attempts to compensate for diminished phrasing interest by excessive vibrato.

A strong but indelicate bow arm, lots of vibrato, and an unusual mastery of off-center colorations, combined with the agilities and high pitches available to very long fingers, all go to make up the gypsy style of violin playing. Spivakovsky is admirable in works written for this style or in something resembling it. His performance, for instance, of Bartók's Violin Concerto several years back, with Artur Rodzinski and the Philharmonic, was a memorable performance of a memorable work. Last night he played with equal brio the same composer's Four Rumanian Folk Dances and Copland's entertaining *Ukulele Serenade*. Everything else, in spite of occasional moments when slow sound was handsomely sustained, was disappointing.

December 12, 1946

1947

A WAR'S END

¶ *Modern Music,* quarterly review edited by Minna Lederman and published by the League of Composers, has ceased publication after twenty-three years. Musicians and laymen who are part of the contemporary musical movement will of necessity be moved by this announcement, because *Modern Music* has been for them all a Bible and a news organ, a forum, a source of world information, and the defender of their faith. It is hard to think of it as not existing, and trying to imagine what life will be without it is a depressing enterprise.

No other magazine with which I am acquainted has taken for its exclusive subject the act of musical composition in our time or sustained with regard to that subject so comprehensive a coverage. This one reported on France and Germany and Italy and England and Russia and Mexico and the South American republics, as well as on its own United States. It covered musical modernism in concerts, in the theater, in films, radio, records, and publication. Jazz and swing procedures were analyzed and Calypso discovered in its pages. Books dealing with contemporary musical aesthetics were reviewed. The only aspects of music excluded from it were those that make up the ordinary layman's idea of music, namely, its interpretation, its exploitation as a business, and its composition before 1900.

Modern Music was a magazine about contemporary composition written chiefly by composers and addressed to them. It even went into their politics on occasion. When our entry into the recent war brought to certain composers' minds the possibility that perhaps our government might be persuaded not to draft all the younger ones, thus

husbanding, after the Soviet example, a major cultural re-
source, Roger Sessions disposed of the proposal firmly by
identifying it with the previous war's slogan "business as
usual." And when, on the liberation of Europe, consciences
were worried about musician collaborators, a whole symposium was published, exposing all possible ways of envisaging the problem. Darius Milhaud, as I remember, said
that traitors should be shot, regardless of talent or profession. Ernst Křenek pointed out that Shostakovich, who
had accepted from his own government artistic correction
and directives regarding the subject matter of his music,
was the prince of collaborators. While Arnold Schönberg
opined that composers were all children politically and
mostly fools and should be forgiven.

In the atmosphere of sharp aesthetic controversy that
pervaded the magazine and with its constant confrontation
of authoritative statement and analysis (for there is practically no living composer of any prestige at all whose
works have not been discussed in it and who has not written for it himself), wits became more keen and critical
powers came to maturity. It is not the least of many debts
that America owes Minna Lederman that she discovered,
formed, and trained such contributors to musical letters
as Edwin Denby, Aaron Copland, Roger Sessions, Theodore
Chanler, Paul Bowles, Marc Blitzstein, Samuel Barlow,
Henry Cowell, Colin McPhee, Arthur Berger, and Lou
Harrison. My own debt to her is enormous. Her magazine
was a forum of all the most distinguished world figures of
creation and of criticism; and the unknown bright young
were given their right to speak up among these, trained to
do so without stammering and without fear.

The magazine's "cessation of hostilities," as one of its European admirers refers to the demise, is explained by its
editor as due to "rising costs of production." Considering
previous difficulties surmounted, I should be inclined to derive the fact from a deeper cause. After all, the war about
modern music is over. Now comes division of the spoils.
Miss Lederman's magazine proved to the whole world that
our century's first half is one of the great creative periods
in music. No student in a library, no radio program maker,
dallying with her priceless back issues, can avoid recogniz-

ing the vast fertility, the originality, ingenuity, and invention that music has manifested in our time.

January 12, 1947

IN THE ROYAL STYLE

¶ The Collegiate Chorale, conducted by Robert
Shaw, gave last night in the Hunter College Auditorium
an uncut performance of Bach's B-minor Mass. Though this
lasted nigh on to three hours, your reporter experienced no
fatigue and observed no sleepers. Indeed, it has not previously been his privilege to hear so thoroughly delightful
a reading of this majestic work, though he has attended
many. How Mr. Shaw worked his miracle on this most recalcitrant of pieces is the subject of this morning's sermon.

He started by organizing his musical effectives in proportions not unlike those available in the German eighteenth-
century courts, for one of which the work was originally
planned. A chorus of sixty mixed voices (American amateur female sopranos are not as loud as trained German
boys), an orchestra of strictly chamber proportions, a harpsichord, an organ used with extreme discretion, and the
necessary soloists were quite sufficient for volume and not
excessive for the florid style. He further reduced the orchestral effectives in accompanying the solos and duets to
single instruments or, in the case of string backgrounds, to
two on a part. And then he rehearsed the choruses for lightness and clarity, the vocal soloists for harmonious blending
with the instrumental soloists that accompany them.

As a result, the accompanied solos, in reality small chamber ensembles, took their place in the choral framework
very much as the concertino group in a concerto grosso is
set off against the larger instrumental body. The work became thus a dialogue, an antiphony, each kind of music
being beautiful in its own way, the two kinds giving amplitude and perspective to the whole.

That whole turns out to be, as one might have expected, not at all a giant Lutheran cantata, nor yet a liturgical Mass, but a grand and sumptuous court oratorio on the subject of the Mass. Its grandeur lies in its vast proportions and in its completely simple expressivity, its sumptuousness in the extreme and formal floridity of the musical texture. Its layout is huge but perfectly clear; its style is the ultimate in ornateness. It is at once enormous and graceful, like the palace architecture of its time, complete with gardens, ponds, statues, and vistas.

Mr. Shaw preserved these proportions and all their grace by simply limiting his forces to a size capable of achieving grace. He added, moreover, a grace of his own in the firm lilt of his beat. His rhythmic alacrity evoked a court ballet. The *"Cum sancto spiritu"* that ends the Gloria was as gay as a hornpipe; and the bass aria, *"Et in spiritum sanctum,"* from the Credo, tripped along none the less reverently for being light on its feet. Just as the alto Agnus Dei might easily have rocked a cradle.

Rhythmic courage, tonal exactitude, pretty balances, and sweetness all round allowed the proportions of the work to take on full majesty without any heaviness. If Mr. Shaw and his admirable colleagues will give us such a performance annually, Bach's choral masterpieces will cease in short order to be merely edifying and become humane, as I am sure, from last night's performance of the Mass, they were conceived to be. The sacred music of the great masters is not designed to shake humanity; that is a function of the theater. It is made to please God by fine workmanship. This one was planned, as well, to get its author a job at the Saxon court.

January 29, 1947

LANDSCAPE MUSIC

¶ The Dallas Symphony Orchestra, Antal Dorati, conductor, gave yesterday afternoon in a program broadcast by N. B. C. the first performance of a work in four movements by Paul Hindemith entitled, *Symphonia Serena*. The symphony, this composer's second, is a large essay in pastoral vein. Eschewing voluntarily all personal pathos, the composer has aimed, I think, at a direct rendering of landscape. No land or seascape so specific as that of Debussy's *Ibéria* or *La Mer* is invoked; but the piece is a pastoral symphony all the same, a formal communion with nature not dissimilar in approach to Mendelssohn's "Italian" and "Scottish" symphonies. Whether the landscape is one with or without figures is hard to say, though there is certainly an echo present in the slow movement. All the same, there is no such broad humanity included as that which joins in the village dancing of Beethoven's Sixth Symphony.

The first movement seems to be about the countryside, perhaps a walk through this in spring or summer; at one point water, possibly a rivulet or cascade, is suggested. The second, a scherzo for wind instruments based on a quickstep theme by Beethoven, is light in texture and extremely animated. Possibly insect life may be its subject. The third is a dialogue for two string orchestras, two solo strings (a violin and a viola), and two more of the same playing offstage right and left. Its sentiment is tender, sweet, and not without a deliberate nobility. Echo effects evoke a décor with some distance in it. A certain pathos of expression indicates a spectator. The last movement, which is one of considerable thematic complexity, is certainly dominated by the sound of birds.

The entire piece is contrapuntally complex in the sense that almost no theme is ever stated without a countertheme in contrasting rhythmic values being present. This proce-

dure gives objectivity to the expression, impersonality and
reserve. The work is distinguished of texture and most
agreeable in sound (the dissonant diatonic is its syntax). It
will take its place in the repertory of evocation rather than
in that of symphonic sermonizing. Exactly what that place
will be is difficult to predict; but if manliness of spirit and
sound workmanship have any carrying power in our land
and century, that place will be one of honor. Hindemith's
Symphonia Serena is a solid, conservative work from the
studio of one of the solidest and most conservative workmen alive.

February 2, 1947

MODERNISM TODAY

¶ Musical modernism, as this has been understood
for fifty years, is nowadays a pretty dead issue. Its masters
are all famous and their works are known to the public. Its
libertarian attitude toward dissonance, rhythmic and metrical irregularities, and unconventional sonorities is no longer
revolutionary. Children are brought up on these liberties;
and even symphony subscribers, a notoriously conservative
group, accept them as normal. The only form of modernism that remains to be imposed (or finally refused) is atonality.

In such a situation, with little left to fight for, what future is there for the composing young beyond a prospect
of inevitable conformity? How can they avoid being placed
in the public's present scheme of things as mere competi-
tors of their elders? How can they be fresh and original
and interesting in their own right? Having observed them
pretty carefully during the last ten years both here and
abroad, I have come to the conclusion that they are doing
exactly what anybody could have figured out by pure logic
that they would do. They have taken up the only battle
left, namely, that of atonality and its allied techniques.

Not all the young, I grant you, are atonalists. There are neo-Classicists and neo-Romantics and even a few retarded impressionists among them. But a generation takes its tone from those who branch out, not from those who follow in footsteps. And today's adventurous young, believe me, are mostly atonal. This position has more to offer them in artistic discovery and less in immediate royalties than any other available, excepting only the tradition of pure percussion. The latter is for the present so limited in scope and so completely occupied by John Cage that there is not much room left in it for anybody else.

The atonal techniques, however, are more ample. One can move around in them. And the young of England, France, Italy, and the Americas have recognized that fact. Germany and Russia, on account of their lack of expressive freedom in the last ten and more years, are slower in taking up the new manner. There are still too many older ones that have not been accepted there yet. But in the countries where intellectual freedom is the norm, young composers are busy with nontonal counterpoint.

Nontonal music, any music of which the key and mode are consistently obscure, has so far always turned out to be contrapuntal. It cannot be harmonic in the conventional sense, because chords pull everything back into a tonal syntax. And if harmonic in an unconventional way, through dependence on percussive and other pitchless noises, it becomes contrapuntal through the necessity of writing for these in varied simultaneous rhythmic patterns, these being its only source of formal coherence.

Counterpoint within the conventional scales can be of three kinds. That practiced in Europe from the twelfth through the fifteenth century is known as quintal, which means that, read vertically at the metrical accents, the music will be found to contain chiefly intervals of the fourth and fifth. Tertial counterpoint, which was the official style from the sixteenth through the nineteenth century, exhibits principally thirds and sixths when read this way. Secundal counterpoint, which is characteristic of our time, stacks up on the down beats as mostly seconds and sevenths.

Any of these styles can be used with either a diatonic or a chromatic melodic texture. The twelve-tone syntax, the strictest form of chromatic writing, can even be made to

come out harmonically as tertial counterpoint. The music
of the chief living neo-Classicists—Stravinsky, Milhaud, and
Hindemith—is diatonic secundal counterpoint. That of
Schönberg is mostly chromatic secundal counterpoint. On
account of this music's lack of a full acceptance by the general public such as that of the neoclassicists enjoys, it remains, with regard to the latter, though it was conceived,
in point of time, earlier, in an "advanced" position. The
more vigorous movements among today's young are, in
consequence, all more closely related to Schönberg than to
the others.

The newer music offers a divergence, however, from
Schönberg's practice in its consistent preoccupation with
nondifferentiated counterpoint, a style of writing in which
all the voices have equal obligations of expressivity and
identical rights in rhetoric. The dramatizing of counterpoint into melody, bass, countermelody, and accompaniment is abolished in this style for an equalized texture that
recalls the music of the pre-Renaissance period. There are
advantages here to intimacy of expression, since the composer can speak in this technique as personally through a
vocal or string ensemble as through a solo instrument. The
disadvantage of it is that it is not easily applicable to diversified ensembles, where variety of timbre and technique imposes a certain differentiation of melodic style
from one voice to another.

The new music, therefore, is mostly homophonic in
sound, or instrumentation. It is personal in expression, too,
and contrapuntal in texture. Its counterpoint is secundal
and generally chromatic. If it were not the latter, it would
resemble more closely than it does official, or neo-Classic,
modernism. It can appear tonal or nontonal when examined closely; and it can follow or not Schönberg's twelve-
tone syntax, which this composer himself does not always
follow. But its chromaticism invariably approaches atonality. This last, let us remember, is not a precise or easily
attainable end. It is rather an ultimate state toward which
chromaticism has always tended. Its attractiveness to our
century comes, I think, from its equalization of harmonic
tensions. We like equalized tensions. They are the basis of
streamlining and of all those other surface unifications that

in art, as in engineering, make a work recognizable as belonging to our time and to no other.

February 2, 1947

THE PHILHARMONIC CRISIS

¶ Artur Rodzinski has gone and done it. For years the knowledge has been a secret scandal in music circles. Now he has said it out loud. That the trouble with the Philharmonic is nothing more than an unbalance of power. Management has usurped, according to him, certain functions of the musical direction without which no musical director can produce a first-class and durable artistic result. He has implied that no conductor, under present conditions, can keep the orchestra a musical instrument comparable to those of Boston and Philadelphia. He points to Arthur Judson, a powerful business executive who manages the orchestra as a side line, as the person chiefly interested in weakening the musical director's authority. He is right; he is perfectly right; he could not be more right. An orchestra can use one star performer and one only. And such a star's place is the podium, not the executive offices.

The American symphony orchestra, like the American government, is an operation of three powers. Its trustees are the power responsible to the community. They provide (or collect) money and determine how it is to be spent; they hire a manager to handle the business details of concert giving; and they entrust to a conductor the production of music for these. The manager in his office and the conductor before his orchestra both have full authority to run their departments, the trustees preserving a veto power over policies only. The trustees, a self-perpetuating body, are thus the initiators of the orchestra as a project and the court of final appeal about everything regarding it.

The musical director's job is the most responsible post

of its kind in the world. He has all the authority of a ship's captain. Hiring and firing of musicians, their training and discipline, the composition of all programs and their public execution are his privilege. Any visiting conductor or soloist is a guest in his house. The manager's job is purely organizational, a routine matter that anyone can handle who has a knowledge of standard business methods and some diplomacy. The latter is essential for him, serving constantly, as he does, as go-between in whatever brush-ups occur between the conductor and the trustees. Since the symphony orchestra is a nonprofit-making institution serving the community in a cultural capacity, its trustees must be men and women of culture and of unquestioned civic responsibility, its conductor a musician with courage and judgment as well as technical skill, its manager a model of integrity and of tact.

The Philharmonic case is simple. Arthur Judson is unsuited by the nature and magnitude of his business interests to manage with the necessary self-effacement a major intellectual institution doing business with his other interests. He is also a man of far too great personal force to serve effectively as a mediator between a proud musician and the equally proud trustees. That is probably why no conductor ever stays long enough with the Philharmonic to accomplish the job that everybody knows should be done, namely, to put the orchestra permanently on an artistic equality with the other American orchestras of comparable financial resources.

Artur Rodzinski has done more for the orchestra in that respect than any other conductor in our century has done. Mahler and Toscanini were greater interpreters, were not such great builders. If Stokowski and Munch, also great interpreters, have been able this winter, as guests, to play upon the orchestra in full freedom and to produce from it sonorous and expressive beauties of the highest quality, that achievement has been made possible by Rodzinski's personnel replacements and his careful training. Such an achievement on the part of guest conductors has not heretofore been possible. Today the Philharmonic, for the first time in this writer's memory, is the equal of the Boston and Philadelphia orchestras and possibly their superior.

Stabilization of these gains is the next step indicated.

With that in mind the trustees in December voted Mr. Rodzinski a long-term contract "without strings attached." One gathers that the contract he actually received contained not strings but chains, that his right to decide who besides himself shall conduct his orchestra, to confer with his guests about their programs, even to determine in full freedom his own was seriously jeopardized. It seems doubtful that any conductor would leave so important a post unless the working conditions were about to become intolerable. So far, they have not been that for him, and the orchestra's improvement under his leadership has proved that they were not.

What awaits his successor is anybody's guess. Dramas and heartbreaks probably, unless the trustees decide to hire another such orchestra builder and give him full power to go ahead and build. In that case, it is scarcely worth while to have provoked the present conductor into resigning. (The contention that he resigned merely because a better job was offered him is not credible, because there is no better job.) In any other case, the Philharmonic will decline as an orchestra as inevitably as winter will return. There is only one way to have a first-class orchestra and that is to let the conductor run it. If he fails, he can be replaced. But while he lasts he has to be given full musical authority as that is understood in the major symphonic establishments.

Rodzinski's career will not be gravely interrupted, we hope, by his courageous gesture. New York will miss him and regret his musical benefits bestowed. The last and greatest of these will have been the most valuable of all, if his exposure of what has long been known in music circles as a scandal and a shame shall encourage the trustees to correct it. There is no reason why the Philharmonic should not remain what it is now, the tip-top executant musical organization of the world. All it needs is a competent and energetic musical director and a disinterested management.

February 9, 1947

YOU CAN LISTEN TO HIM

¶ Stravinsky's *Rite of Spring*, which closed last night's concert of the Boston Symphony Orchestra in Carnegie Hall, is probably the most influential work of music composed in our century and the most impressive in performance.

The work does not stand much interpretative tinkering. The more rigid its beat the greater its expressive power. What it needs is clean rhythm, clean tonal balances, and understanding. Its subject, human sacrifice, is too grand and terrible to permit personal posturing. And Leonard Bernstein, often a sinner in that regard, gave it none. If he did not extract from the score one tenth of the detailed refinement that older hands at it do—conductors like Monteux and Ansermet and Désormière—he nevertheless got the rhythm right and made the meaning clear. One felt that he loved the music, understood it, and submitted his will in all modesty to its discipline.

The work is not a clear masterpiece, like the same composer's *Petrouchka*; but it is more original. It cuts farther below the surface of musical convention, goes straight to the heart of the whole stylistic problem of Romanticism, comes out both deeply expressive and completely impersonal. Its complex rhythmic interest, its high harmonic tension, and its rigid orchestral textures are justly famous. Its patent of nobility, however, lies in the extreme beauty of its melodic material. Partly Russian folklore and partly inventions in the same manner, its themes are short, diatonic, and narrow. They rarely cover a larger range than the perfect fifth. They are as plain as granite and as resistant to time. If the work did not lose intensity in the early part of its second half, it would be the solidest single monument of music our century has erected. Just possibly it is that in spite of everything.

February 13, 1947

THE AMERICAN SONG

¶ English-speaking singers are trained and grow to maturity on one of the most curious musical literatures in the world. German vocalists cut their professional teeth on the lieder of Romantic masters and, if the voice is strong, on airs from Weber and Wagner. The Italians, to a man (or woman), sing Puccini and Verdi and very little else. The French have their Fauré, their Gounod, and their fragments from Massenet. All this is perfectly reputable music. The Continent has its popular religious pieces, too, like Jean-Baptiste Faure's *The Palms*, Adam's, *Minute chrétien*, and Bach's *My Heart Ever Faithful*, also its glorified folklore like Irish mother songs and Italian boat pieces.

But just cross the Channel, and you find that the basic vocal repertory is not either the classics or the indigenous folk lyric. It is a commercial product known variously as "ballads" or "art songs" or just "songs," though it is not in a proper sense any of these things. You hear it in homes, at banquets, in recitals, and over the BBC. In its manlier forms it is a hearty baritone number about how "when we were young and I went down to Rio." Its tender mood deals with gardens and somebody referred to as "YOUUU." For a light touch children are introduced who resist medicine or dislike the cook, though they never go so far as to refuse spinach. The American version of this vast Anglo-Saxon musical literature admires trees and sunsets, believes that marriages are made in heaven, faces the future with confidence, and enjoys playing cowboy.

There is nothing wrong, of course, about any of these ideas. They represent ethnic aspirations and touch infallibly the English-speaking heart. What is curious about the musical literature in which they are embodied is its stylistic vulgarity, its technical and aesthetic ineptitude. The literary aspect of it, though often banal in verbiage, is as to sentiment perfectly sound and humane. But take a look, I ask

you, at the musical settings; or listen to them at recitals. A
sunrise is described in the idiom of *Tristan und Isolde*, trout
fishing in that of *Pelléas et Mélisande*. A nursery incident
may be blown up till it suggests *The Sorcerer's Apprentice*.
As for mating, you would imagine the whole population
sex-starved if you believed in the amorous intensity of our
"art-song" harmonizations. The musical vulgarity of the
literature I am describing is due, as a matter of fact, not
only to its exaggerated passional make-believe but to its
practice of describing everything, literally everything, in
the musical language of love.

The stuff needs only comparison with the Continental
equivalent for the technical ineptitude to be patent. The
rhythmic inflections of the English language are more often
than not correctly observed and neatly dramatized. But
vowel quantities are handled with as complete disregard
for their exigence as could well be imagined. An otherwise skillful song by the late Carl Engel asks that three
beats of slowish time, plus a retard, be occupied to pro-
nounce the word *stop*. And one by Bainbridge Crist, quoted
in this composer's far from uninteresting brochure, *The
Art of Setting Words to Music*, asks that the word *kiss* be
held on a high F for something like five seconds. If you
think my criticism finicky, just try this trick out; and you
will discover that the result is neither English nor music.

The aesthetic fault most commonly committed in American vocal music is the confusion of genres. Setting a simple love lyric as if it were an operatic aria removes all
poignancy from the poem. Dramatic expression in music
requires a dramatic situation in the text. The Continental
song literature from Mozart through the German Romantics to Fauré, Debussy, Ravel, Sauguet, and Poulenc deals,
in any one piece, with a single person in an unequivocal
mood. No event, inner or outer, takes place; and no conclusion is arrived at, though the sense of the whole may be
summed up in a final couplet. These are the classical limits
of lyric poetry. The ballad form, as in *Der Erlkönig*, is
equally set and stylized by its stanza construction. Epic recitation and dramatic narrative demand still another musical form. I accuse the English and American composers
(especially the Americans) of having hopelessly confused
one kind of poetic expression with another in their vocal

concert music. I am not naming any names, because they are practically all guilty. Just listen, if you want examples, to the American group of any singer's recital program. Or take a look at what your kid sister is given by her vocal teacher.

Is it any wonder that our American singers are not masters and mistresses of their art, when the repertory they all learn music through is so incompetently composed? They don't know that English vowel lengths, like Continental ones, are immutable. They don't know that poetic expression, no matter what its subject, falls into four or five styles, or genres rather, and no more. They don't know that lyric poetry does not permit an aggressive mood, that impersonation of the poet by the interpreter is unbecoming to it, that it can be recited or sung but never acted, though the ballad style can, on the contrary, be dramatized up to the hilt.

How can they know these things when the composers of the music that is virtually their whole fare write as if they didn't know them either, and when singing teachers, for lack of a better repertory, give them for study year after year pieces that nobody can vocalize correctly or interpret convincingly because they are incorrectly composed? They are incorrect as to vowel quantities, false to the known aesthetics of poetry, and irresponsible in their misapplication of a climactic and passionate musical style to virtually any subject, even the sacred. America is full of beautiful young voices and high musical temperaments. The singing teachers are not bad either, on the whole. Students often learn from them to vocalize the long vowels quite prettily. After that they commit every fault. What about our composers sitting down and writing them something that can be sung without fault? Our playwrights write plays that can be acted. Our painters paint pictures that can be hung, looked at, lived with. Our better composers write fair symphonies and thrilling ballets. But the human voice they have left in second-rate hands. There are probably not twenty American "art songs" that can be sung in Town Hall with dignity or listened to there without shame. Nor are there five American "art composers" who can be compared, as song writers, for either technical skill or artistic responsibility with Irving Berlin.

February 16, 1947

FARCE AND MELODRAMA

¶ *The Medium*, an opera written entirely (words and music) by Gian-Carlo Menotti, is about the private life of a woman who evokes by trickery, for paying customers, visions and voices of the dead. Caught up in her own psychic ambience, and aided by alcohol, she imagines she feels a hand on her throat. Terrified by this experience, she renounces her racket and exposes it to her clients. They refuse to believe that what they had wanted to believe in was false. At this point, the medium goes hysterical and murders a dumb boy who was previously part of her household and an aid in her trickery setup.

No such reduction of the plot can give an idea of how absorbing this work is. I have heard it three times and it never fails to hold me enthralled. Mr. Menotti's libretto and his music form a unit that is deeply touching and terrifying. And if the second act is a little reminiscent as theater (though not as music) of the second act of Puccini's *La Tosca,* the piece in no way suffers by comparison with that infallible piece of stage craft. The play wrings every heart-string, and so does the music. I cannot conceive the whole work otherwise than as destined for a long and successful career.

The Telephone, or *L'Amour à Trois*, is a skit about a young man whose girl friend is so busy talking to people on the telephone that the only way he can get her attention for a proposal of marriage is to go out to the corner drugstore and call her up himself. It is gay and funny and completely humane. Both operas, indeed, are infused with a straightforward humanity that is a welcome note of sincerity in contemporary operatic composition. Their librettos are skillfully made, and their music is skillfully composed. But that is not the main point. Their unusual efficacy as operas comes from their frankly Italianate treatment of ordinary human beings as thoroughly interesting.

February 19, 1947

THE KOUSSEVITZKY CASE

¶ Serge (or Sergei) Koussevitzky, conductor of
the Boston Symphony Orchestra since 1924, is an aristocrat
among American conductors and in Boston music circles
something of an autocrat. Born seventy-two years ago in
Russia and reared there in poverty (his family, though
Orthodox Jews, never lived in a ghetto), he has attained
wealth, world-wide fame and the highest distinction in his
profession. As a virtuoso on the double-bass viol and as a
conductor his ranking, by any standards, has been for many
years among that of the very greatest in our time. As a composer he has contributed to the reputable literature of his
instrument. As a publisher and a patron of contemporary
music he has probably made a more lasting contribution to
the art than any other single person living, excepting five or
six composers. His place in its history is already assured and
glorious.

Just to make assurance doubly sure, the Boston immortality machine has started issuing this winter what looks like a
series of books bearing the papal imprimatur of the good
doctor (LL.D., *honoris causa,* Harvard, 1929, and elsewhere). M. A. DeWolfe Howe, official biographer to the
Bostonian great, has furnished *The Tale of Tanglewood,
Scene of the Berkshire Music Festivals* (Vanguard Press,
New York, 1946, $2), prefaced by Mr. Koussevitzky him-
self. And Hugo Leichtentritt, a musicologist of repute and a
former Lecturer of Harvard University, has fathered *Serge
Koussevitzky, the Boston Symphony Orchestra and the New
American Music* (Harvard University Press, Cambridge,
Mass., 1946, $3).

And now to supplement these two books, which are
clearly official and more than a little superficial, arrives a
full-length biography of the maestro which is neither. It is
entitled simply *Koussevitzky,* by Moses Smith (Allen,
Towne, and Heath, New York, 1947, $4). Announced for
sale on February 15, its distribution has been held up for

the time being by an injunction that prohibits its publication, sale, and distribution till Justice Shientag of the New York Supreme Court shall have determined whether the book's circulation will do its subject "irreparable harm." If the present writer, who has read an advance copy received before the injunction was issued, is in any way typical of the American reading public, it certainly, in his opinion, will not. The only possible harm he can envisage to so impregnable a reputation as that of Serge Koussevitzky is that already done by his own efforts to suppress the book.

Moses Smith, a trained newspaper man, for many years music critic of the *Boston Evening Transcript*, as well as a friend of Mr. Koussevitzky, has produced a far more thorough study, a better work of scholarship than either Mr. Howe or Mr. Leichtentritt, scholars both by trade. There seems little in the book of factual statement that is subject to question. Whether Mr. Koussevitzky, in view of his great devotion to the memory of his second wife, Natalie, is made unhappy by mention of his first marriage, hitherto not publicized in America, is scarcely germane. Neither is his possible sensitivity to reports of his quarrels with musicians and with blood relatives. These are, as a matter of fact, common knowledge; and they legitimately form part of the whole story of his musical life, just as his first marriage does of any complete biography.

Judgments and opinions, expressed over any writer's signature, are, of course, personal. The conductor's legal complaint objected to Mr. Smith's statement that Koussevitzky had succeeded as a conductor in spite of imperfect early training in musical theory and score reading. This also, if I may make so bold, has long been common knowledge among musicians. Nor is the estimable doctor unique among the conducting great for being in a certain sense self-taught. Leopold Stokowski, Sir Thomas Beecham, and Charles Muench, great interpreters all of them, did not come to conducting through early mastery of the conservatory routines. They bought, muscled, or impressed their way in and then settled down to learn their job. They succeeded gloriously, as Koussevitzky has done. All honor to them. They have all, Koussevitzky included, contributed more of value to the technique of their art than most of the first-prize-in-harmony boys ever have.

But great pedagogues, and the good doctor is one, do hate hearing that their own education has not been conventional, though it rarely was. And all great artists loathe criticism. They do; they really do. What they want, what they need, what they live on, as Gertrude Stein so rightly said, is praise. They can never get enough of it. And sometimes, when they have come to be really powerful in the world, they take the attitude that anything else is libel. Dr. Koussevitzky's complaint, as I remember, did not use the word "libel." It spoke of possibly "irreparable injury." Well, criticism is often injurious; there is no question about that. Many a recitalist, receiving unfavorable reviews, finds it more difficult to secure further engagements than if the reports had been less critical. Minor careers have been ruined overnight that way. Major careers are rarely harmed by criticism, because major artists can take it. They don't like to; but they have to; so they do. All the same, it is the big boys, the great big boys that nothing could harm, that squawk the loudest. I know, because I have been in the business for several years now.

Mr. Smith's book makes Koussevitzky out to be a very great man indeed, but it also makes him human. Gone is the legend of his infallibility. Renewed is one's faith in his sincerity, his consecration, his relentless will to make the world permanently better than he found it. Nobody, I am sure, can read the book through without admiring him more. And the faith of the pious need not be shaken by reading that he has not always been toward his fellow man just and slow to anger. Civilization would be just a racket if we had to learn all we know about the lives of great men from their paid agents.

Mr. Koussevitzky is not the only first-class conductor in the world, though he is one of the best. Nor is he the only first-class conductor the Boston Symphony Orchestra has enjoyed. Nor does he any longer play the double bass in public, though when he did he was, by common consent, world champion. His unique position in a world full of excellent conductors, many of them devoted to contemporary music, is that he has played more of it, launched more of it, published more of it, and paid for more of it than anybody else living. That is the clear message of Mr. Smith's biography. Everything else, a petulant gesture here and there,

a musical or family quarrel, a pretentious remark, a vain-
glorious interview, the present court action—all these
things serve the picture; they bring him more vividly to life.
How can anyone mind knowing them? Only he himself,
apparently, hasting fearfully toward Parnassus, though his
throne there has long been reserved for him, and involved,
no doubt, in a publicity apotheosis that has already begun,
would see any value in posing before an already worshiping
universe without the customary habiliment of one human
weakness. His lawsuit, of course, adds to the tableau that he
has essayed so carefully to compose just that.

February 23, 1947

VARIETY WITHOUT LOUDNESS

¶ Suzanne Bloch gave last night in Times Hall a
concert of Renaissance music in strictly pre-Baroque instrumentation. There were solos for lute, duets for two
lutes, music for a quartet of the same, vocal solos and duets
accompanied by them, and divers compositions that included a recorder, a viola da gamba, and a pair of virginals,
as well. There was also solo music for the virginals, for
though the phrase seems self-contradictory (a pair of anything playing a solo), the virginals are, at least linguistically, a plural instrument, like scissors.

Gerald Hayes, an English writer about old music and old
instruments, states in one of his books that there is in existence more first-class music for the lute than has ever been
written for any other solo instrument. Certainly the music
played last night was all first-class and thoroughly delightful. And if Miss Bloch undertook none of the Elizabethan
fantasies that compare for length and variety with the Viennese piano sonatas of the Classical period, she gave us a
highly digestible selection of charm numbers from all over
Europe.

The lute is a hand-plucked instrument related in sonority both to the mandolin (which is not hand-plucked) and to the Spanish guitar (which is). Like the mandolin, it plays melodies effectively and even counterpoint. Unlike the guitar, it cannot easily play chords across the board. It has too many strings to allow chord playing by any but selective means. Consequently, though the instrument resembles the guitar somewhat in sound, it has none of the latter's romantic abandon. It is a plain and noble instrument that lends itself to the execution of music of the highest complexity, rhythmic, harmonic, and contrapuntal. It sounds rather like a harpsichord without a keyboard mechanism.

Since wide variations of loudness as an expressive (and even rhetorical) device are an invention of the seventeenth century, no music written before that time counts on them for effect. The chamber music of Renaissance times was regularly and systematically quiet. Its interest is melodic, harmonic, contrapuntal, and rhythmic, but never dynamic. It can be played and sung for hours without any strain on the listener's nervous system, because loudness was never a part of its pattern.

The music-making that Miss Bloch and her associate artists offered last night was like a cultivated conversation rather than like an exhortation of any kind. It was fanciful, instructive, intimate, gay, delicious, and vast for vistas opened. It was not emotionally portentous, but it was deeply refreshing. Contemporary life has need of music based on ingenuity and sentiment, music in which dynamic strain plays no part.

March 5, 1947

NEW AND GOOD

¶ Roger Sessions, whose Piano Sonata No. 2 was played last night by Andor Foldes in a League of Composers concert at the Museum of Modern Art, is in spite of

considerable renown as a talked-about composer and a long
history of success as a pedagogue, little known through his
music. His production is small; and the few works available
are seldom performed, because they are difficult to play and
not easy to listen to. They are learned, laborious, complex,
and withal not strikingly original. They pass for professor's
music, and the term is not wholly unjustified. Because the
complexity and elaboration of their manner is out of all
proportion to the matter expressed. Nevertheless, they are
impressive both for the seriousness of their thought and for
the ingenuity of their workmanship. They are hard to take
and even harder to reject. They represent the most embar-
rassing problem in American music, because though they
have unquestionably quality, they have just as certainly almost no charm at all. And we have no place in our vast system of musical distribution for music without charm.

The piano sonata played last night by Andor Foldes (and
dedicated to him) is Mr. Sessions's second. The first dates
from nearly twenty years back. Like the first, it is composed
in a dissonant tonal style. Unlike the first, it is in melodic
idiom largely chromatic. Like all of this composer's music, it
bears no clear marks of its national or local origins. It could
have been written anywhere in the world—in Leningrad,
Shanghai, Paris, Buenos Aires, Vienna, Rome, or Melbourne
—as easily as in Berkeley, California, where it actually was
composed, and by a man of any race and clime as easily as
by a one-hundred-per-cent New Englander. Its speech represents the international neo-Classic style at its most complete and eclectic, though the feelings expressed in the work
are derived from the violence-and-meditation contrast beloved of the German Late Romantics.

It is not music of direct melodic or harmonic appeal for
the uninitiated; nor yet has it great stimulus value for modernists, who have already heard elsewhere practically everything in it. All the same, it is interesting to listen to, because it is wonderfully, thoroughly sophisticated. The slow
movement, moreover, is almost atmospheric. Operating in
a small range of pitch, with little variety of rhythm and, for
once, no great variety of musical device employed, Sessions
has achieved here a completely absorbing tranquillity. The
work is not likely to be popular, I should think, either soon
or ever. But it is not a negligible composition, and Roger

Sessions has reminded us through it that his very existence as a musician is a far from negligible contribution to the history of music in America.

March 17, 1947

BIRTHDAY SALUTE

¶ Arturo Toscanini will be eighty years old on Tuesday, March 25. The occasion is notable not merely for the fact that age has not withered nor custom staled his infinitely satisfactory musicianship, but also for the reminder that he is today, exactly as he has been for twenty years, the first conductor of the world. His primacy in the field of opera has been clear for nearer forty years, since his appearance at the Metropolitan Opera House in 1908, in fact. Since 1926, when he first conducted the New York Philharmonic Orchestra, his mastery of the concert style has been equally unquestionable. From that day till now it has not been possible for any musician or musical observer to list the great living conductors of an age that has been glorious for great conducting without putting Arturo Toscanini's name squarely at the top.

His most remarkable quality as a public perfomer has always been his dependability. He never lets his audience down nor lets music down. When announced to appear, he appears. When he conducts any work, however familiar, unfamiliar, difficult of execution, facile of sentiment, no matter what kind of work or by whom, he knows the score and gives it as careful, as polished a reading as if his whole musical life depended on that single work. It is this unusual dependability, indeed, that has given rise to the legend of his musical infallibility. Actually he misses the point of a piece, misunderstands a composer's thought as often as any other musician. Where he does not fail is in the ability to call forth on any platform the full resources of his own musical interest and attention. Music, any music, all music stimulates in him as automatically as in the proverbial circus horse the full functioning of his professional capacities.

Those capacities derive not only from a nervous stability superior to that of any of the other great living conductors, but also from a musical instinct as simple and as healthy as that of a gifted child. Toscanini, and let us make no mistake about it, is a natural musician. His culture may be elementary, but his ear is true. He makes music out of anything And the music that he makes is the plainest, the most straightforward music now available in public performance. There is little of historical evocation in it and even less of deliberate emotional appeal. It is purely auditory, just ordered sound and very little else. There is not even much Toscanini in it. For in spite of his high temperament, this musician is strangely lacking in personality.

That is why, I think, he has based his interpretative routine on as literal as possible an adherence to musical texts. A respect for the written note and the adherence to any composer's clearly indicated intent have always been the procedure of first-class conductors. But the composer's expressive intent is more often than not far from clear; and musical notation, particularly as regards phraseology and rhythmic inflection, is extremely imprecise. Imagination and a deep historical culture are the classical approaches to the problem of invigorating the music of the past. Toscanini has no such culture to channelize his imaginative faculties. He is not in any sense an intellectual. He is not ignorant; he has heard, read, and played vast quantities of music; and his mind is as sound as his body. But he has not the humane letters of a Beecham, a Reiner, a Monteux, the refined sensuality of a Stokowski, an Ormandy, the moral fervor and sense of obligation toward contemporary creation of Koussevitzky. He simply sticks as closely to the text as he can and makes music.

Actually, of course, he takes as many liberties with a text as any other executant. He neglects Beethoven's metronome marks, as everybody else does. He corrects a balance for clarity's sake. He speeds up a finale for general excitement. He has gravely falsified, moreover, the musical tradition of our time by speeding up the Mozart minuet movements to a point where all memory of the court dance has disappeared from them. What he does not do is to personalize his interpretations. He adds a great deal of excitement to any piece, but that excitement is of a purely auditory and cerebral, rather than of an expressive character. His appeal is thus deeply contemporary to an epoch which has accepted abstractions in art, in science, and in politics as the source of its most passionate loyalties.

Nobody else in our time has been so simple or so pure toward music as Toscanini. He will not loom large, I imagine, in the history books of the future, because he has mostly remained on the side lines of the creative struggle. And music's history is always the history of its composition. Toscanini has radically simplified the technique of orchestral conducting, and he has given a straightforwardness to all interpretation in our time that cannot fail to facilitate the execution problem for living composers. But his involvement with the formation of our century's musical style, with the encouragement of contemporary expression in music, with the living composers, in short, whose work will one day constitute the story of music in our time, has been less than that of any of today's other orchestral great. He has honor and glory now, but by posterity his work will probably pass unremunerated.

March 23, 1947

LURCHING AND MUGGING

¶ Richard Strauss's *Salome*, a musical version of Oscar Wilde's play, was produced last night at the City Center of Music and Drama. The orchestral version used was one for slightly reduced forces, reported to have been made by the composer. The musical execution was shipshape and most agreeable to the ear. The visual production, though no more absurd than most, was a hodgepodge of stylistic elements, running from Assyrian architecture to Hollywood kimonos split down the front and gilt leather G-strings. There were pasteboard goblets aplenty, too, and artificial peaches that got thrown about like pincushions, and for once a realistic head of the prophet. That helped, though Brenda Lewis, who sang the title role, didn't seem to know quite what to do with it when she had got it.

Somebody should teach opera singers not to lurch. This movement is never graceful and rarely convincing. Frederick Jagel did it oftenest last night, though the others indulged when they couldn't think of anything else to do. He suggested Soglow's Little King rather than a figure of erotic tragedy. Miss Lewis did a good deal of lurching, too, and lots of leaning backwards. The constant projecting forward of the pelvis may be a sexy movement, but it is not a sensuous one. It is a concomitant rather of commercialized vice than of seduction. In a role of this kind it betrays, indeed, a certain innocence, a child's concept of the lascivious.

Miss Lewis's Dance of the Seven Veils was full of good will, though of real style it had none. Where she failed as an actress most gravely was in the final scene with the head. She might have been singing it a lullaby. And she took her last lines standing and looking upward, as if she were playing Joan of Arc. Her miming of this sensational scene was not in any sense puritanical. It was sexy enough, as I said before; but it gave no suggestion of sensuality. No small part of its ineffectiveness came also from her constant attempt to act with the face, a procedure known commonly as "mugging" and one that has no place in opera. In opera the face is used for singing; one acts with the body. It would be interesting to hear this excellent singer, for that she certainly is, in a role more becoming to her temperament.

April 17, 1947

INTELLECTUAL CONTENT

¶ Music, a creation of the human mind, has its appeal for all the faculties of the mind. Its direct communication is to the feelings, of course. But the methods by which continuity is sustained and interest held are a result of thought taken. And though it is desirable that this thought be not too evident, it does have a listener interest over and above its functional efficiency, because any construction of the human mind is fascinating to the human mind. This is the workmanship aspect of music, the quality that adds beauty to expression. And so if the power of provoking specific emotional effects can be referred to as music's expressive content, the power of provoking cerebration, of interesting the mind, may legitimately be called, I think, its intellectual content.

The intellectual content of anything—of music, painting, poetry, oratory, or acting—consists of references to tradition, to the history of its own technique as an art, of a wealth of allusions, indeed, to many things under the sun. Expressive content is personal, individual, specific, unique. It cannot be borrowed. If it is not spontaneous it is not sincere, hence not, in the long run, convincing. But intellectual content is all borrowed; it is only the choice and the appropriate usage of allusions and devices that give them validity in any work. Exhibited overostentatiously, they merely prove vanity. Aptly applied they enrich the texture and delight all.

The richness of music's intellectual substance varies from composer to composer. It is greater in Bach, for instance, than in Handel, though the latter, predominantly a man of the theater, has a plainer and more direct emotional appeal. Mozart's frame of reference, likewise, is more ample than that of Haydn. It is characteristic of both Bach and Mozart to use dance meters without the idea of dancing being the only thought communicated. Bach writes between an organ toccata and its fugue a siciliana which is at the same time a religious meditation. And Mozart writes in a piano sonata (oh, how often) a slow movement which is both a minuet and a love duet, as well as a piano solo.

The best opera composers have usually avoided, in writing for the lyric stage, any duality of allusion that might weaken the impact of the expressive content. The best concert composers, on the other hand, are those who employ the techniques of multiple meaning, adding thus to simple expressivity contrapuntal interest and the perspective effect of contradictory evocations. It is Beethoven's gift for work-

ing opposites in together that gives to his concert music its
phenomenal power of suggesting drama. Beethoven has for
this reason intellectual content to a high degree. He did not
refer much, except in his later works, where he employed
constantly the deliberate archaism of fugal style, to the history of composing techniques; but he did manage by careful handling of the contemporary techniques, to make one
thing mean many things (as in the variation form) and to
make many things mean one (as in the ten-theme symphony form). He holds attention to this day, in consequence. He keeps the listener occupied.

Wagner's operas have the highest intellectual content of
any. I don't mean the philosophical tomfoolery of his librettos, either, though this was necessary to him as a pretext for elaborateness of musical texture and for the whole
psychological refinement that was his chief legacy to the
stage. Puccini's operas have probably the lowest intellectual content of any, though their plots are far from stupid.
Their expressive content, which is chiefly self-pity, is powerful by its simplicity. But the emotional composition of this
has little depth of perspective, and the musical textures employed are of small interest as workmanship.

Tchaikovsky, Sibelius, and Shostakovitch are demagogic
symphonists because the expressive power of their work is
greater than its interest as music; it does not fully or long occupy an adult mind. Debussy and Stravinsky are fascinating to the adult mind. They stimulate feelings and provoke
thought. Schönberg and Hindemith are overrich of intellectual interest in proportion to their feeling content; they
are a little dry, in consequence. Bartók, Milhaud, and Copland strike a sound balance between mental and emotional
appeal, even though their intensity in both kinds is less than
one could wish it were. Roy Harris oscillates between extreme intellectuality, for which he has little gift, and a banal,
a borrowed emotionalism, which he cultivates out of a
yearning for quick-and-easy success. At his best, however,
he is both moving and interesting. Olivier Messiaen is a similar case, though his musical gift is greater and his mind
more ingenious.

The music of the great masters is always good both ways.
One could go on for columns describing the music of past
and present masters in terms of its vital equilibrium, its bal-

ance of heart and head. And one could get into some pretty arguments. Brahms, Bruckner, Mahler, César Franck, Ravel, and Liszt are tough cases to judge. So are the great men of jazz. Schubert, Schumann, Mussorgsky, and Fauré are more clear. They were truly great artists, though all suffered from technical deficiencies.

What makes possible the writing of good music, beyond that talent for handling sound that is required for being a musician at all, is emotional sincerity and intellectual honesty. Both can be cultivated, of course; but no man can quite lift himself by his boot straps. Unless he has a good heart (the psychiatrists nowadays call this affectivity) and a vigorous mind, he will not write any music capable at once of touching the human heart and interesting the human mind. Art that does not do both dies quickly. And longevity is the glory, perhaps even the definition, of civilization's major achievements.

April 20, 1947

"LA MÔME" PIAF

¶ The presence among us of Edith ("la Môme") Piaf, currently singing at the Playhouse, is a reminder, and a very pleasant one, that the French *chanson* is an art form as traditional as the concert song. It has a glorious history and a repertory. Its dead authors and composers have streets named after them. Its living ones, just like the writers of operas, symphonies, and oratorios, enjoy a prestige that is not expressed in their income level. Its interpreters are artists in the highest sense of the term, easily distinguishable in this regard from the stars of commercialized entertainment.

If the official art music of our time expresses largely the life and ideals of the bourgeoisie and penetrates to the basic strata of society *from above*, the *chanson* is almost wholly occupied with depicting contemporary life from the viewpoint of the underprivileged and comes to us *from below*. The habitats of the official style are dressy places with a sanctimonious air about them. The *chanson* lives in neighborhood "music halls," as the French call them, or what we refer to, using a French term, as "vaudeville" houses. The *chanson* has nothing to do with farm life, either. Farm workers, unless they are itinerants who spend their winters in town, sing, when they sing at all, an older repertory, that which we denominate folklore. The *chanson* is a musical art form of the urban proletariat.

Its social origins and preoccupations are expressed not only in the words of the songs but also, in performance, by a vocal style opposed in method to that of the vocal studios. The latter consider high notes their greatest glory and make every effort, in training the voice, to spread the quality of these downward through the middle and chest ranges. The *chansonniers* use principally chest resonances, carrying these as high in the vocal range as possible and avoiding pure head tone as rigorously as singers of the official school avoid an unmixed chest tone. Head tone is used, if at all, for comic or character effects, to represent the voices of children, of the not very bright, and of the socially hoity-toity.

Miss Piaf represents the art of the *chansonnière* at its most classical. The vocalism is styled and powerful; her diction is clarity itself; her phrasing and gestures are of the simplest. Save for a slight tendency to overuse the full arm swing with index finger pointed, she has literally no personal mannerisms. She stands in the middle of a bare stage in the classic black dress of medium length, her hair dyed red and tousled, as is equally classical (Yvette Guilbert, Polaire, and Damia all wore it so), her feet planted about six inches apart; and she never moves, except for the arms. Even with these her gestures are sparing, and she uses them as much for abstractly rhetorical as for directly expressive purposes.

There is apparently not a nerve in her body. Neither is there any pretense of relaxation. She is not tense but intense, in no way spontaneous, just thoroughly concentrated and impersonal. Her power of dramatic projection is tremendous. She is a great technician because her methods are of the simplest. She is a great artist because she gives you a clear vision of the scene or subject she is depicting with a minimum injection of personality. Such a concentration at once of professional authority and of personal modesty is no end impressive.

If Miss Piaf had not impressed me so deeply with the authenticity of her repertory and her convictions about its rendering, I should have used my column today for praising Les Compagnons de la Chanson, a male chorus of nine singers who precede her on the program. They sing folksongs to the accompaniment of athletic pantomime with a perfection of drill, vocal and muscular, that is both sidesplitting and utterly charming. If anybody wants to find a political reference in their song about a bear that terrified the village but became, when legally elected, as good a mayor as his predecessor, I presume such an interpretation could be discovered without too much effort, since otherwise the number has little point. Their imitation of an American radio quartet accompanied by a swing band, however, needs no further point than its excellent satire. Their work in every number is funny and unusually imaginative. "La Môme," or "Pal" Piaf, to translate her cognomen, may be strong meat, artistically speaking, for American theater audiences, but Les Compagnons are more the sort of act we can take without any effort at all.

November 9, 1947

LIVELY REVIVAL

¶ Marc Blitzstein's *The Cradle Will Rock*, which was performed last night at the City Center under Leonard Bernstein's direction, remains, ten years after its first New York success, one of the most charming creations of the American musical theater. It has sweetness, a cutting wit, inexhaustible fancy, and faith. One would have to be untouchable (and who is?) by the aspirations of union labor to resist it. Last night's audience did not. No audience I have ever seen, in fact, ever has.

It was inevitable that the piece (call it, if you will, an opera, a musical comedy, or a play with music) should be revived; and it is a sound idea to revive it just now. In a year when the Left in general, and the labor movement in particular, is under attack, it is important that the Left should put its best foot forward. There is no question, moreover, but that the Left's best foot is its Left foot. In the opinion of this reviewer, Mr. Blitzstein's *Cradle* is the gayest and the most absorbing piece of musical theater that America's Left has inspired. Long may it prosper, long may it remind us that union cards are as touchy a point of honor as marriage certificates.

The Cradle is a fairy tale, with villains and a hero. Like all fairy tales, it is perfectly true. It is true because it makes you believe it. If the standard Broadway "musical" plugs what Thurman Arnold called "the folklore of capitalism," this play with (or "in") music recites with passion and piety the mythology of the labor movement. It is not a reflective or a realistic work. There is not one original thought or actual observation in it. Everybody is a type, symbolizes something; and the whole is a morality play. Its power is due in large part to the freshness, in terms of current entertainment repertory, of the morality that it expounds. That morality is a prophetic and confident faith in trade unionism as a dignifying force.

An equally large part of its power comes from its author's talent for musical caricature. He makes fun of his characters from beginning to end by musical means. Sometimes his fun is tender, as in the love duet of the Polish couple; and sometimes it is mean, as in the songs of Junior and Sister Mister. But always there is a particular musical style to characterize each person or scene; and always that style is aptly chosen, pungently taken off. The work has literary imperfections but musically not one fault of style.

Its presentation last night followed the style of its 1937 production, save for the substitution of Mr. Bernstein at a small orchestra in place of Mr. Blitzstein at a small piano. As before, there were costumes but no scenery. As before, the system of presentation was completely effective, though the orchestra added little musically. The cast was fair, some of it excellent, notably Will Geer and Howard da Silva, who had sung Mr. Mister and Larry Foreman in the original performances. Others were less than ideal, but that made little difference. The work is a tough one and hard to spoil.

November 25, 1947

MAURICE RAVEL

¶ Ten years ago next month, December 28, 1937, Maurice Ravel died. He was not old, only sixty-two. Many people living knew him well. I knew him myself a little. He was cultivated, charming, companionable, neither timid nor bold, in no way difficult. That is why he is not today, nor was he during his lifetime, a misunderstood man or a misunderstood composer. For all its complexity of texture, wealth of invention, and technical originality, his work presents fewer difficulties of comprehension than that of any of the other great figures of the modern movement. Satie, Debussy, Schönberg, Webern, Stravinsky all remain, in many facets of their expression, hermetic. Ravel has never been obscure, even to the plain public. His early work produced a shock, but only the shock of complete clarity. Anybody could dislike it or turn his back, still can. Nobody could fail, nobody ever has failed to perceive at first sight what it is all about.

What it is all about is a nonromantic view of life. Not an antiromantic view, simply a nonromantic one, as if the nineteenth century had never, save for its technical discoveries, existed. All the other modernists were children of Romanticism—worshipful children, like Schönberg, or children in revolt, like Stravinsky, or children torn, like Debussy, between atavism and an imperious passion for independence. Even Satie felt obliged to poke fun at the Romantics from time to time. But for Ravel there was no such temptation, no Romantic problem. When twentieth-century models failed him he had recourse to eighteenth-century ones. And he used these not at all to prove any point against the nineteenth century, but simply because they were the most natural thing in the world for him to be using. Couperin, Rameau, and Haydn were as close to him as Chabrier and Fauré, his immediate masters.

Maurice Ravel was not interested in posing as a prophet, as a poet, or as a writer of editorials. He was no sybil, no saint, no oracle nor sacred pythoness. He was simply a skilled workman who enjoyed his work. In religion a skeptic, in love a bachelor, in social life a semirecluse, a suburbanite, he was not in any of these aspects a disappointed man. He was jolly, generous, a wit, a devoted friend, and as much of a *viveur* as his none too solid health and his temperate tastes permitted. His was an adult mind and a good mind, tender, ironic, cultivated, sharply observant. He was kind but not foolish, humane but not sentimental, easygoing but neither self-indulgent nor lazy. There was acid in him but no bile; and he used his acid as a workman does, for etching.

He considered art, and said so, to be, at its best, artifice, and the artist an artisan. For all the clarity that his music embodies, its crystalline lucidity in every phrase, it probably expresses less of personal sentiment than any of the other major music of our century. He worked in the free impressionist style, in the straight dance forms, in the classic molds of chamber music, and for the lyric stage. His masterpiece is a ballet. Always he worked objectively, with the modesty of an architect or a jeweler, but with the assurance of a good architect or a good jeweler. He was equally master of the miniature and of the grander lay-outs. At no necessary point does his expression lack either subtlety or magnitude. It lacks nothing, as a matter of fact, except those qualities that are equally lacking, for instance, in La Fontaine and in Montaigne, namely, animal warmth, mysticism, and the darker aspects of spirituality.

Ravel was a classical composer, because his music presents a straightforward view of life in clear and durable form. The straightforwardness and the clarity are, I think, obvious. The durability will be no less so if you consider the hard usage that *La Valse, Daphnis et Chloë* (at least the Second Suite from it), the Bolero, the *Pavane for a Dead Princess*, the Piano Sonatina, and *Scarbo,* a pianists' war horse, have been put through already. I call them durable because they stand up under usage. And they stand up under usage because they are well made. They are well made because they are clearly conceived and executed by an objective and responsible hand. The hand is objective and responsible in the way that it is because it is a French hand, one that inherits the oldest unbroken tradition in Europe of objective and responsible artisanry.

Ravel's music represents, even more than does that of Debussy, who was more deeply touched than he by both the Slavic and the Germanic impulses toward a spiritualization of the emotional life, the classic ideal that is every Frenchman's dream and every foreigner's dream of France. It is the dream of an equilibrium in which sentiment, sensuality, and the intelligence are united at their highest intensity through the operations of a moral quality. That moral quality, in Ravel's case, and indeed in the case of any first-class artist, is loyalty, a loyalty to classic standards of workmanship, though such loyalty obliges its holder to no observance whatsoever of classical methods. It is an assumption of the twin privileges, freedom and responsibility. The success that Ravel's music has known round the world is based, I am convinced, on its moral integrity. It has charm, wit, and no little malice. It also has a sweetness and a plain humanity about it that are touching. Add to these qualities the honesty of precise workmanship; and you have a product, an artifact, as Bernard Berenson would call it, that is irresistible.

France has for centuries produced this kind of art work and, for all the trials of the flesh and of the spirit that she is suffering just now, is continuing to produce it. Rosenthal, Sauguet, Poulenc, Jolivet, Barraud, Rivier, and the dodecaphonic young, these and dozens more have vowed their lives to sincerity of expression and to high standards of workmanship. The music of Milhaud and Messiaen has even grander aspirations. But all French composers, whether they care to admit it or not, are in debt to Ravel. It was he, not Gounod nor Bizet nor Saint-Saëns nor Massenet, nor yet César Franck nor Debussy, who gave to France its contemporary model of the composer. That model is the man of simple life who is at once an intellectual by his tastes and an artisan by his training and by his practice. He is not a bourgeois nor a white-collar proletarian nor a columnist nor a priest nor a publicized celebrity nor a jobholder nor a political propagandist, but simply and plainly, proudly and responsibly, a skilled workman. Long may the model survive!

November 30, 1947

CONSERVATIVE INSTITUTION

¶ The symphony orchestra, among all our musical institutions, is the most firmly established, the most widely respected and, musically speaking, the most efficient. It is not, however, either the oldest or the most beloved. The opera and the singing society, I should think, have better right to the latter titles. Nevertheless, the orchestra is what all music, its prestige, its exploitation, and its teaching, turns round. It is the central luminary of our contemporary musical system.

Someone, I cannot remember who, suggested several years ago that the strength of the institution comes from the fact that the concert orchestra is a representation in art, a symbol, of democratic assembly. Certainly it is so conceivable. And certainly its rise is contemporaneous historically with the rise of parliamentary government. The fact that its most glorious period, as regards composition, the working years in Vienna of Haydn, Mozart, and Beethoven, was a time when, in that place, there was no parliamentary government at all, does not disprove the identification. It merely suggests that the parliamentary ideal, as represented then by England, was strong enough to influence democratic-minded men everywhere and that its picturing through music, an art difficult to censor, is more than probable in a country which would not have tolerated at the time any such representation through the less hermetic techniques of painting or of literature.

In any case, these men in Austria, not the composers of liberal England or of revolutionary France, transformed the court symphony into the popular symphony. Never

again, after they had lived, was the symphony an elegant
or decorative form. It was larger, louder, more insistent,
more humane, broader of scope, and definitely monumental. Its performance ceased to be a private entertainment and became a public rite. Also, there has remained
with the symphony ever since an inalienable trend toward,
in the broad sense, political content.

Professional symphony orchestras today remain associated with a political unit, the city. They are a privilege and
symbol of civic pride. States and central governments rarely
support them. Even municipalities do not like contributing
taxpayers' money to them, though in a few American cities
—Baltimore, Indianapolis, and San Francisco—there is a
budgetary provision for such aid. Normally they are a civic
proposition, and their deficits are met by public-spirited
citizens. Rarely are great orchestras associated with our
religious or scholastic foundations (as our finest choruses
are more often than not) or directly with the world of big
business and finance and fashion (as our best opera companies have always been). They are wedded to our great
cities. They are monuments of civic pride and symbols not
only of musical achievement but of their communities' whole
cultural life.

There are really two kinds of orchestras, the monumental and the directly functional. The latter kind exists in large
numbers connected with educational institutions and with
the amateur musical life of neighborhoods and of semirural
communities. In 1937 there were about 30,000 of these in
the United States alone. Their chief purpose is the musical
training or musical enjoyment of the players, though they
also provide in increasing numbers nowadays professional
players to what I call the monumental orchestras. The
latter are strictly professional and perform only for the edification of the listener.

The functional orchestras, being educational in purpose,
play a larger repertory than the others do. And their style
of execution is less standardized. The monumental orchestras, being more ceremonial by nature, are highly standardized in both repertory and execution, internationally
standardized, in fact. The players, the conductors, the
pieces played (save for a very small number that represents
local courtesies) can be removed from one orchestra and

inserted in another anywhere in the world. Even language is no barrier to rehearsal efficiency. Indeed, it is exactly their international standardization that enables our orchestras to represent localities, to symbolize to the whole world the cultural level—by internationally recognized standards —of the particular city that supports any one of them.

The civically supported symphony orchestra is the most conservative institution in the Western world. Churches, even banks, are more open to experiment. The universities are daring by comparison. This does not mean that new music does not get played by the orchestras. The rendering of contemporary works along with familiar classics is one of their firmest traditions. No orchestra can live that plays only the music of dead composers. As a matter of fact, no orchestra ever essays so radical a policy. The public objects to modern music, naturally, because modern music, however great intrinsic musical interest it may present, simply can never compete as edification with the hallowed past. But the same public that objects to hearing modern music objects far more vigorously to being deprived of the privilege. Just as the musical execution of our symphony orchestras is the most conservative and correct that money can buy, so also is the repertory they play, a certain appearance of musical progressiveness being required by tradition itself.

The encouragement of musical advance, however, is not the chief purpose of symphony orchestras. The first-line trenches of that lie elsewhere. They lie in many places, but always the rapidest progress of musical invention takes place where the attention of so large and so pious a public is not present to discourage the inventor. Small groups of musicians working under private or university patronage can produce more novelty in a year than will be heard at the subscription concerts in twenty. Invention takes place sometimes even under the very eye of a large public, provided that public is looking at something else.

If theatrical entertainment is there to give novelty a *raison d'être,* as at the ballet or at the opera, or if the occasion is not too respectable socially, as in jazz dives, then the circumstances for musical invention are at their most favorable. The symphony orchestra favors musical advance officially, but it dare not offer much of it at a time. It must advance slowly, because it deals with a large public, which necessarily is slow of comprehension, and because the basis of its whole operation is the conserving of tradition anyway. Stability rather than variety is what the faithful chiefly demand of it.

Our symphony orchestras, historically viewed, are solider than our banks. They are always getting born; they rarely die. Constantly threatened with financial disaster (a talking point during campaigns to raise money or in union negotiations), they almost never cease operations. Nor will they, so long as civic pride exists and so long as democratic government through parliamentary procedure shall seem to us a beautiful ideal and worthy of representation in art.

December 28, 1947

1948

JOAN OF ARC IN CLOSE-UP

¶ The performance itself was perfection, that of Honegger's *Joan of Arc at the Stake,* as given at last night's Philharmonic concert under the direction of Charles Munch. The piece itself is what the French call a "big machine"—a work of some musical and literary pretentions set for orchestra, chorus, soloists, and speaking voice. The inventor of the formula, so far as I know, is Berlioz. Its local version is the Norman-Corwin-style radio number. Its most successful European practitioners, among the living, are Arthur Honegger, who composed the present score, and Paul Claudel, author of the present text.

Joan at the Stake aims to please all, save possibly the Marxian Left, by exploiting religious and patriotic sentiments without doctrinal precision. It appeals to the theater instinct in us all by the realistic evocation of horror scenes. It appeases the lover of modern music with bits of polytonal composition. It impresses all by its elaborate mobilization of musical effectives. It offers, in short, virtually everything a concert can offer but bets on nothing.

The weakness of the work lies exactly in its failure to bet, to make clear whether we are listening to a musical work on a literary text or to a literary work with musical commentary. The fact that the title role is a speaking role, not a singing one, is the chief source of this ambiguity. Another is the lack of musical shape in the set-pieces.

These are full of expressive variety and abundant of apt musical invention, but they are tied tightly to a text that has itself little of formal shape or progress. The music illustrates the text in running commentary but does not take it in hand, add unity and emphasis. As a result, the work makes rather the same effect that a film of the same length (seventy-five minutes) might. It is picturesque at all moments, varied, and vastly detailed; but it lacks the monumentality that its oratorio layout would seem to impose. It is all in close-ups. At no point do we get a panoramic view, an epic breadth in the narrative.

This is why, for all the fine fancy in Honegger's music, *Joan at the Stake* remains somewhat trivial. It is closer in feeling to devotional than to dramatic literature. It is like some garrulous meditation on the Stations of the Cross. Its convulsive tone is striking, but there is not the dignity in the whole conception that one might expect from a musician of world-wide prestige dealing with a subject so familiar, so touching, and so grand. The effort to please everybody possible in every possible way has left the whole effort touched with a flavor of insincerity, that same flavor we all know so well from our own "big machines" of radio and the films.

January 2, 1948

ON BEING AMERICAN

¶ What is an American composer? The Music Critics' Circle of New York City says it is any musical author of American citizenship. This group, however, and also the Pulitzer Prize Committee, finds itself troubled about people like Stravinsky, Schönberg, and Hindemith. Can these composers be called American, whose styles were formed in Europe and whose most recent work, if it shows any influence of American ways, shows this certainly in no direction that could possibly be called nationalistic? Any award committee would think a second time before handing these men a certificate, as Americans, for musical excellence. The American section of the International Society for Contemporary Music has more than once been reproached in Europe for allowing the United States to be represented at international festivals of the society by composers of wholly European style and formation, such as Ernest Bloch and Ernst Křenek. And yet a transfer of citizenship cannot with justice be held to exclude any artist from the intellectual privileges of the country that has, both parties consenting, adopted him, no matter what kind of music he writes.

Neither can obvious localisms of style be demanded of any composer, native born or naturalized. If Schönberg, who writes in an ultrachromatic and even atonal syntax and who practically never uses folk material, even that of his native Austria, is to be excluded by that fact from the ranks of American composers, then we must exclude along with him that stalwart Vermonter, Carl Ruggles, who speaks a not dissimilar musical language. And among the native-born young, Harold Shapero and Arthur Berger are no more American for writing in the international neo-Classic manner (fountainhead Stravinsky) than Lou Harrison and Merton Brown are, who employ the international chromatic techniques (fountainhead Schönberg). All these gifted young writers of music are American composers, though none employs a nationalistic trademark.

The fact is, of course, that citizens of the United States write music in every known style. From the post-Romantic eclecticism of Howard Hanson and the post-Romantic expressionism of Bernard Rogers through the neoclassicized impressionism of Edward Burlingame Hill and John Alden Carpenter, the strictly Parisian neo-Classicism of Walter Piston, the romanticized neo-Classicism of Roy Harris and William Schuman, the elegant neo-Romanticism of Samuel Barber, the sentimental neo-Romanticism of David Diamond, the folksy neo-Romanticism of Douglas Moore, Randall Thompson, and Henry Cowell, the Germano-eclectic modernism of Roger Sessions, the neo-primitive polytonalism of Charles Ives, and the ecstatic chromaticism of Carl Ruggles, to the percussive and rhythmic research fellows Edgar Varèse and John Cage, we have everything. We have also the world famous European atonalists Schönberg and Křenek, the neo-Classic masters Stravinsky and Hindemith. We have, moreover, a national glory in the form of Aaron Copland, who so skillfully combines, in the

Bartók manner, folk feeling with neo-Classic techniques that foreigners often fail to recognize his music as American at all.

All this music is American, nevertheless, because it is made by Americans. If it has characteristic traits that can be identified as belonging to this continent only, our composers are largely unconscious of them. These are shared, moreover, by composers of all the schools and probably by our South American neighbors. Two devices typical of American practice (I have written about these before; are the nonaccelerating crescendo and a steady ground-rhythm of equalized eighth notes (expressed or not). Neither of these devices is known to Europeans, though practically all Americans take them for granted. Further study of American music may reveal other characteristics. But there can never be any justice in demanding their presence as a proof of musical Americanism. Any American has the right to write music in any way he wishes or is able to do. If the American school is beginning to be visible to Europeans as something not entirely provincial with regard to Vienna and Paris, something new, fresh, real, and a little strange, none of this novel quality is a monopoly, or even a specialty, of any group among us. It is not limited to the native-born or to the German-trained or to the French-influenced or to the self-taught or to the New-York-resident or to the California-bred. It is in the air and belongs to us all. It is a set of basic assumptions so common that everybody takes them for granted. This is why, though there is no dominant style in American music, there is, viewed from afar (say from Europe), an American school.

National feelings and local patriotisms are as sound sources of inspiration as any other. They are not, however, any nobler than any other. At best they are merely the stated or obvious subject of a piece. Music that has life in it always goes deeper than its stated subject or than what its author thought about while writing it. Nobody becomes an American composer by thinking about America while composing. If that were true Georges Auric's charming fox trot *Adieu New-York* would be American music and not French music, and *The Road to Mandalay* would be Burmese. The way to write American music is simple. All you have to do is to be an American and then write any kind of music you wish. There is precedent and model here for all the kinds. And any Americanism worth bothering about is everybody's property anyway. Leave it in the unconscious; let nature speak.

Nevertheless, the award-giving committees do have a problem on their hands. I suggest they just hedge and compromise for a while. That, after all, is a way of being American, too.

January 25, 1948

THE ULTIMATE OF LUCIDITY

¶ Debussy's ballet *Jeux* (or *Games*), lately conducted by Ernest Ansermet with the N. B. C. Orchestra, was written in 1912 and produced by Diaghilev in 1913 (the scenarist and choreographer, Nijinsky, also dancing the male role). As a ballet it died right there. As an orchestral piece it has also been somewhat neglected by conductors, even in France. The last orchestral work to be fully orchestrated by Debussy himself, it represents at its ultimate that tendency toward the attenuation of musical materials into a luminous and golden dust of which *La Mer* and *Images* are earlier examples. It glows like mercury vapor or a sunset in Texas and is as immaterial to the touch. Sonorously it is a piece for two harps, four flutes, and subdivided strings, in which the rest of its large orchestra merely amplifies climactically the basic coloration. Expressively it is an apotheosis of the waltz. Formally it is a masterpiece of continuity that employs no classical continuity device for its own sake but that holds together in the most surprising way. Its musical language, starting out with twelve-tone chords and continuing to the end in polyharmony and polyrhythm, achieves an effect close to atonality and remains today advanced.

Jeux is a unique work, an ultimate work, an end, and maybe a beginning. Executed with Ernest Ansermet's equally

unique and ultimate lucidity, it is also one of the most ravishing pieces imaginable.

January 26, 1948

THE PROBLEM OF SINCERITY

¶ If art is a form of communication, and music the
form of art best suited to the communication of sentiments,
feelings, emotions, it does seem strange that the clear communication of these should be beset with so many difficulties. Perfection of the technical amenities, or at least an
approach to it, is more commonly to be met with in the
concert hall than is a convincing interpretation of anything.
They play and sing so prettily, these recitalists, work so hard
and so loyally to get the notes of the music right that it is a
matter of constant astonishment to me how few of them
can make it speak.

Composers, too, have trouble communicating, especially
American composers. They make you great, big, beautiful,
shapely structures; but it is not always clear what purpose,
with regard to living, these are intended to fulfill. One has a
strange feeling sometimes, right in the middle of a concert
season, that the music world, both the composers and their
executants, are just a swarm of busy ants, accomplishing
nothing to human eyes but carrying grains of sand back
and forth. How much useful work anybody is doing, of
course, is hard to know. But seldom, oh, so seldom, does a
musical action of any kind speak clearly, simply, without
detours.

Part of this inefficiency comes, I am sure, from the prestige of Romantic attitudes in an unromantic age. From the
violinist in a Russian restaurant who hopes to be tipped for
pushing his violin into your shashlik to the concert pianist
who moons over the keys or slaps at them in a seeming fury,
all are faking. They are counterfeiting transports that they

do not have and that in nine cases out of ten are not even the subject of the music. For music of passionate and personal expressivity is a small part indeed of standard repertory. There is a little of it, though very little, in Mozart, a bit more in Beethoven, some in Mendelssohn, a great deal in Schumann and Chopin, less in Brahms, and then practically no more at all till you get to Bartók. Its presence in Bruckner and Mahler, though certain, is obscured by monumental preoccupations. Berlioz, Liszt and Wagner, Strauss and Schönberg, even Debussy and the modernists operate mostly on a level of complexity that prevents an efficient interpreter from going too wild and the meaning from getting too private. It is not that technical difficulties prevent introversion. But the simple fact that the subject of most music is evocation obliges both composer and executant to objective procedures.

Music of personal lyricism, Schumann, for instance, can be played or sung without antics and often is. But it cannot be rendered convincingly without personal involvement. This poses the problem of sincerity. You can write or execute music of the most striking evocative power by objective methods, provided you have an active imagination. You can represent other people's emotions, as in the theater, by the same means, plus decorum. But you cannot project a personal sentiment that you do not have. If you fake it knowingly, you are dramatizing that which should be transmitted directly; and if you fake it unknowingly, you are merely, by deceiving yourself, attempting to deceive your audience.

Sincerity is not a requisite for theatrical work, for evocative work, for any music that is, however poetic, objective in character. Taste, intelligence, and temperament are the only requirements. These will enable you to get into any role and out of it again, to perform it perfectly, to communicate through it. They are not sufficient for a proper rendering of Schumann's songs or of the Bartók quartets. These you must feel. What gives to lieder recitals and string quartet concerts their funereal quality, when they don't come off, and their miraculous excitement, when they do, is the absence or presence of authentic feeling in the interpretation.

Any sincerely felt reading must be a personal one. Ob-

jective music has, more often than not, traditional readings
that are correct. All traditional readings of the music of
personalized sentiment are, by definition, incorrect. Because
sentiments, feelings, private patterns of anxiety and relief
are not subject to standardization. They must be spontaneous to have any existence at all, spontaneous and unique.
Naturally, experienced persons can teach the young many
things about the personalized repertory. But there is no set
way it must be rendered, and any attempt to impose one on
it takes the life out of it. The exactly opposite condition obtains regarding objective music. This benefits enormously
from exact procedures and standardized renderings, from
every thoughtful observance and precision. Personal involvement in it, the injection of sentiment, is a great foolish-
ness.

The whole question of sincerity hangs on a difference
between those feelings with which one can become temporarily identified by imagination and those which are one's
own and relatively permanent. The former, which make for
drama, constitute nine-tenths of the whole musical repertory and nine-tenths of any mature composer's available
subject matter. Mixing the two kinds get nobody anywhere.
Treating personal music objectively gives a pedantic effect.
Treating objective music personally gives a futile effect.
Nevertheless, on account of the prestige that historical Romanticism enjoys, the latter procedure dominates our concert halls. All over America artists are endeavoring to treat
the repertory, the vast body of which is objective music,
and composers are treating the monumental forms, too, as
if their personal fantasies about these were a form of communication. On the other hand, more often than not they
treat personal music to a routined and traditional streamlining that prevents it altogether from speaking that language of the heart that is speech at all only when it comes
from the heart. They should leave the stuff alone unless
they are capable of spontaneity. Once rid of their romantic
pretenses, too, they would certainly do better with the rest
of the repertory. For composers the urgency is even greater.
Let them do theater and evocations to their hearts' content.
But in the domain of private feelings, fooling around with
those one does not have is suicidal.

February 8, 1948

SUCCESS TACTICS

¶ Benjamin Britten's *Peter Grimes,* which was added last night to the repertory of our Metropolitan Opera, is a success. It always is. Given in any language in a house of no matter what size, it always holds the attention of an audience. As given last night "the works," so to speak, which is to say, the full mechanism, musical and scenic, of a mammoth production establishment, it still held the attention. This is not to minimize the excellences of the present production, which are many, or the care that has gone into it, which is considerable. It is merely to point out that the steam-roller processing that our beloved Met, geared to Wagner, puts any new work through is one of the severest known tests for the strength of theatrical materials. If Mr. Britten's work came out scarcely in English, vocally loud from beginning to end, and decorated in a manner both ugly and hopelessly anachronistic, it also came through the ordeal with its music still alive and its human drama still touching.

Make no mistake about *Peter Grimes.* It is varied, interesting, and solidly put together. It works. It is not a piece of any unusual flavor or distinction. It adds nothing to the history of the stage or to the history of music. But it is a rattling good repertory melodrama. And if the executant artists, beginning with Emil Cooper, who conducted, going on through Frederick Jagel and Regina Resnik, who sang the tenor and soprano leads, to the smallest role in a large cast and even including the chorus, treated the work with no consideration for its special or poetic subject matter, but rather as disembodied, or "pure," theater, just "wow" material, that is exactly what the composer himself has done, what his score invites and asks for.

There is everything in it to make an opera pleasing and effective. There is a trial scene, a boat, a church (with organ music), a pub (with drinking song for the full ensemble), a storm, a night club seen through a window (with boogie-woogie music off stage and shadow play), a scene of flagellation, a mad scene, and a death. There are set-pieces galore, all different, all musically imaginative, and mostly fun. And there are a good half-dozen intermezzos, most of which are musically pretty weak but expressive all the same.

The musical structure of the opera is simple and efficient. Everything and everybody has a motif, a tune or turn of phrase that identifies. The entire orchestral structure, and most of the vocal, is pieced together out of these in the manner of Italian *verismo*. The harmony is a series of pedal-points broadly laid out to hold together the bits-and-pieces motif continuity. There is no pretense of musical development through these motifs, as in Wagner. They are merely identification tags. The music is wholly objective and calculated for easy effect. That is why it works.

It works even in spite of its none too happy handling of English vowel quantities. It sacrifices these systematically, in fact, to characteristic melodic turns, as if the composer had counted from the beginning on translation. A good part of the obscurity that was characteristic of last night's diction, in spite of the singers' visible efforts to project sung speech, was due to the deliberate falsity of the prosodic line. Mr. Britten is apparently no more bothered about such niceties than he is by the anachronisms of an almost popishly High Church service in an English fishing village of 1830 and an American jazz band in the same time and place. He has gone out for theatrical effects, got them, got his success. So did the Metropolitan. And still *Peter Grimes* is not a bore.

February 13, 1948

THOROUGHLY CONTEMPORARY

¶ Eugene Istomin, who played a recital of piano music last night in Carnegie Hall, is a schooled technician, a natural musician, and a very young man. The first two advantages keep his work interesting and alive. The other state gives it a certain immaturity that weakens from time to time its expressive tension.

Like many another young person of today, he is not at his best in Romantic repertory. He respects it, plays it with what grace and sentiment he can muster; but he cannot really keep his mind on it. Only the music of his own century draws forth his full mental powers. Just as most of the older pianists, especially those brought up away from the centers of contemporary creation, fake their moderns, when they play them at all, so Mr. Istomin is obliged to fake his Romantics—his Schumann, his Chopin, and his Beethoven. The former's *Abegg* Variations he got through on sheer virtuosity. But his Chopin Preludes and his *Moonlight* Sonata were the work of a skillful and gifted child, nothing more.

Even two preludes of Rachmaninoff and one by Debussy were read with more plain animal warmth than imaginative penetration. It was Ravel who brought out the young man's full expressive powers. The latter's triptych, *Gaspard de la nuit,* which has tripped up both technically and expressively many a mature master, was just homework to this gifted youth. He played this intricate and difficult work so cleanly, so delicately, so powerfully, with such variety and beauty of touch, such easy understanding of its sense and motivations, with such command and such sincerity that it is impossible, on the basis of that rendering alone, to deny him recognition as an artist of the highest possibilities.

It is not fair to ask the young people of today, simply because they are in accord with their time, to drop the Romantic repertory and the Classical sonatas. The whole of music is their province, and they must get to know it as best they can. All the same, the modern world is where they live and feel at home. Their dealings with Romanticism are a child's version of an old wives' tale, or a city boy's dream of the Far West. They are Romanticism's drugstore cowboys, or at best college students who know the heroic days out of books and photographs. But they do know their time, love it, and take it for eternal, just as the Romantics did theirs. That is why they can make beauty of its masterpieces. That part of their work is real and thoroughly grand. The rest is just culture. And it is on the whole healthier for art that the contemporary in spirit should be authentic and the revivals of past time a product of intellectual ingenuity than that the reverse should obtain. Mr. Istomin is, in this sense, a healthy spirit as well as a good musician.

February 21, 1948

COMPOSERS IN TROUBLE

¶ The Russians are at it again. First there appears in the left-hand column of *Pravda's* front page a criticism of the nation's leading composers. They are charged with "formalistic" tendencies, with being influenced by the "decadent" West, with neglect of Russia's "classical" tradition, with failure to maintain the ideals of "socialist realism" and to ennoble as they ought the Russian people. Next the Central Committee of the Communist Party issues a formal denunciation by name and in detail. Next the offending works are removed from the theaters, the symphony concerts, and the radio. Then the composers under attack write open letters to *Pravda* and to the Central Committee thanking them for the spanking, confessing all, and expressing full intention, with the kind advice of the Committee, to reform. After that there is nothing for them to do but "purify" their music, to write new works that will hopefully be in accord with that "new look" that has been the stated ideal of Soviet musicians (and their political leaders) for the last twenty years. Then in a reasonable time they will mostly be back in favor.

For a Soviet composer there is no other solution. Publication and performance being a monopoly of the state, he cannot, nor can any group of composers, operate as a minority appealing to public opinion for justification. Never forget that in Soviet art there is no underground, no unofficial movement, nor, for the present, any possiblity of one. This being so, and all observers agree that it is, let us examine, from previous occasions, what is likely to happen to Prokofiev, Shostakovitch, Khachaturian, and company while they remain out of favor.

While Shostakovitch was being disciplined in 1936 and 1937 for the "bourgeois" tendencies that Stalin himself had noticed in *Lady Macbeth of Mzensk,* his works intended for wide consumption were not performed or sold. His chamber music, however, continued to be played and printed; he continued to write it with no alteration of style; and he went on receiving a salary from the Composers' Union. He lived in Moscow, as before, got married, went on working. He was poor and unhappy, drank heavily, we are told by people who visited him; but he was not destitute. He also wrote during this time two symphonies, both of which were rehearsed and performed privately, the last of them only, however, his Fifth, being accepted for public audition. That he had lost no popularity in the meantime was proved by the enormous lines that for three weeks before it was given stood to get seats for the new symphony.

In the case of the literary purge that has been going on since 1936, the majority of those being disciplined have lived in about the same circumstances as Shostakovitch had ten years earlier. Graver cases, however, especially those involving political disaffection or extreme and recalcitrant individualism, have received graver sanctions. Zoschenko, Pasternak, and Akhmatova, for example, were expelled from the Writers' Union. This meant a cutting off of their income and the loss of priority on a Moscow apartment. Until ration cards were abolished it meant also the loss of access to a reasonably nourishing diet. I have not heard of a verified case of a mere writer being sent recently to the Siberian salt mines, as was done with political offenders in the mid-1930's. Expulsion from the Writers' Union (or the Composers' Union) remains, however, a grave form of excommunication, not only for its moral stigma and for the virtual exile from intellectual company but also for the great physical dangers entailed. It has not yet been employed against any of the composers recently denounced.

Whether Shostakovitch and Shebalin, professors at the Moscow Conservatory, will be temporarily retired from their posts I cannot say, though it is rumored that they have already left. Certainly Kharapchenko, the director, has lately been discharged. And it seems likely that Khachaturian, president of the Composers' Union, may find it difficult to remain at that post while under a disciplinary cloud.

What have they done, these composers, to provoke denunciation and disciplinary action? And what moral right has the Central Committee to order their even temporary disgrace? Well, what they have done is to fail, in the judgment of the Party leaders, to conform to the aesthetic of Soviet music in its relation to the whole public, as this was laid down by the musicians themselves back in 1929. That conception is, in our terms, certainly a false one; but it is already an old one, and it is certainly nothing imposed from above. The Russian Association of Proletarian Musicians worked on it for five years before they got it stated the way they wanted it. And though the Association itself was dissolved in 1932, the declaration of 1929 remains to this day the basic aesthetic of Soviet music, of the proper relation of any Soviet composer to decadent "bourgeois" Western culture and to the rising masses of Russia.

In this conception, a composer is a writer of editorials. He is supposed to elevate, edify, explain, and instruct. He is to speak a language both comprehensible to all and worthy by its dignity of a nation-wide public. He is to avoid in technique the overcontrapuntal and the overharmonic, in expression the abstract, the tricky, the mystical, the mechanical, the erotic. He is to turn his back on the West and make Russian music for Russia, for all of Russia, and for nothing beyond. His consecration to this aim is to be aided and reinforced by public criticism, as well as by the private counsels of his colleagues. Judgment as to the accomplishment of the aim is not, however, his privilege nor that of his critics. That belongs to the Communist Party, which has the responsibility for leadership and guidance in artistic as in all other matters. The composers, in other words, have determined their own ideal and accepted, along with the ideals and forms of the society in which they live and work and which they have helped toward the achievement of its present internal solidity, the principle that the professional body alone, and still less the listening public, is not the final judge of music's right to survive.

This idea is not in accord with our Western concept of the integrity of the professions. Nevertheless, it is that of the Soviet government and of all, so far as we know, Soviet musicians. The hasty *mea culpa* of the Soviet artist in trouble with the Central Committee shocks the Western mind, but I see no reason to doubt its sincerity. Seven of the boys are in a jamb right now, and I suspect most of them will get out of it. I sincerely hope they will, because they are good composers and because I like to see good composers writing and getting played and published. Myself I have never taken much stock in Soviet music. I am too individualistic to like the idea of an artist's being always a servant of the same set-up, even of so grand a one as a great people organized into a monolithic state. I don't like monolithic states anyway; they remind me of the great slave-owning empires of antiquity.

But my tastes are not involved in the matter. Soviet music is the kind of music that it is because the Soviet composers have formally and long ago decided to write it that way, because the Communist party accepts it that way, and because the people apparently take it. When the Party clamps down on it for "deviation," who am I to complain if the composers of it themselves don't? Whether they could do so with any hope of success, of course, is doubtful. All we know from previous occasions is that he who confesses and reforms quickest gets off the lightest. I do not find, given the whole of Russian political and aesthetic theory, that the procedure is undignified; and apparently the composers do not find it so, however much they may regret having to submit to the sanctions. It seems likely that they would feel far worse, even if they could survive, excommunicated from the intellectual life and deprived of their forum.

Russians mostly, I imagine, believe in their government and country. Certainly these great, official public figures do.

They could not, in so severe and censored a period, have become national composers by mere chicanery. That is not what bothers me about them. Nor yet that they are always getting into trouble from excess of musical fancy. What worries me, and has for twenty years, is that, for all their devotion, noble precepts, faith in their fatherland, and extraordinary privileges, their music, judged by any standard, is no better than it is. I only hope, against all reason and probability, that a similar preoccupation on the part of the Central Committee is at least a little bit responsible for the present disciplinary action. Russian music may or may not need ideological "purification." But it certainly needs improvement.

February 22, 1948

FULFILLMENT EXPERIENCED

¶ Webster Aitken played last night in the Town Hall one of his most rewarding recitals of piano music. The program, as is so often the case with this artist, was a severe one. A lesser technical and musical master could hardly have got through it, much less held the absorbed attention of his audience. But Mr. Aitken left us all, I think, with a feeling of fulfillment. It is not often in the concert hall that one experiences so deep a satisfaction.

Save for two Scarlatti sonatas that served for little more than to warm up the pianist's hands and to quiet the audience, everything was thoroughly rendered and thoroughly communicated. Charles Ives's Four Transcriptions from *Emerson,* dated 1920, is a normal-length piano sonata fashioned by its author out of the first movement of his vaster *Concord* Sonata. Like much of Ives's music, it is fascinating harmonically but not very personal in expression; rhythmically, too, it is a little dead. It is a polyharmonic evocation of German Romanticism rather than, to my perception, a portrait of its subject. It can scarcely be a portrait of Mr. Ives's feelings about his subject, either, since its emotional content is all too familiar in other, and many other, contexts. Its chief originality is its chord structure, which is both consistent and interesting. I doubt if it will ever be a very useful repertory piece, for all its airs of grandeur. It is, as expression, too banal.

Elliott Carter's Piano Sonata, written in 1945 and 1946, might just possibly be a work for the repertory. This is a sustained piece full of power and brilliance. Its relatively quiet moments, though a shade reminiscent of both Copland and Stravinsky, are not entirely, in feeling, derivative; and as figuration they are quite personal. The brilliant toccatalike passages, of which there are many, are to my ear completely original. I have never heard the sound of them or felt the feeling of them before. They are most impressive indeed. The whole work is serious and not superficial. It would be a pleasure to hear it again, and soon.

Gian-Carlo Menotti's Ricercare and Toccata, composed in 1942 but not previously heard in New York, is perhaps a bit superficial, compared to the Carter sonata. But it is so brilliant, so cheerful and generally pleasant that one was grateful for its presence, along with the Scarlatti pieces, on a program of more weighty works. The chromatic Ricercare, in fact, was melodically most graceful. This listener would have liked it to go on a little longer.

The evening ended not with light fare but with Beethoven's Sonata, Opus 111, no less. Here Mr. Aitken gave a reading not at all traditional but one restudied in the light of tradition. He did not moon over the easy slow passages or slow up for the hard fast ones, as is customary. He gave the whole a rhythmic structure and an emotional progress. If one regretted slightly at moments its relentlessly metallic coloration, one was grateful at all times for the clarity and the force of his transcendent execution. Also for his real Beethoven culture. The piece sounded a little hard, but we are told Beethoven played like that. And its hardness was of crystal and granite, not that of stale Christmas cookies. Mr. Aitken is the most masterful of all our American pianists, and his musical culture is the equal of anybody's from anywhere.

March 13, 1948

BRILLIANT AND DIFFUSE

¶ Gregor Piatigorsky, our most popular touring cellist, played to a large audience last night in Carnegie Hall. He played a distinguished program and was more than warmly received. The soloist's execution was brilliant and his accompanist, when audible, excellent. And yet somehow the evening was not quite a first-class musical occasion.

The trouble seems to be that Mr. Piatigorsky is more expert than imaginative. He is a virtuoso in the old style. He has a huge sound, huge hands to reach about the cello's fingerboard with, and a vast variety of tone color. His musical sense is a cultivated one, too. He would seem to have everything. Everything, at least, but concentrated thought. He rarely keeps to the same mood for fifteen seconds. In the midst of a smooth cantilena like that of the Fauré *Elégie* he suddenly introduces the biting-bow declamatory style. To the sustained and interior poetry of the Debussy Sonata he adds an oratorical crescendo, returns to the poetry, then pushes his bow into more crescendo, plays handsomely in duet with the piano in the pizzicati passages, then utters a phrase of interlocked harmony with the pianoforte as if he were all alone on the stage. He plays one phrase like an angel and then scratches the next as only a six-footer with a long bow-arm can scratch. He makes beautiful sounds and ugly sounds, complete sense and no sense, fine music and commonplace music all in one piece, in any piece. His talent and mastery are tops; but he does not seem always to have his mind, though it apparently is a good one, on what he is doing.

From the Boccherini Sonata in C major through the Prelude and Fugue of the Bach C minor Suite, the Chopin Sonata, and the Debussy Sonata to the final oddments, not one piece was read with sustained expressive power; and yet not one reading was without its commanding traits. An enormous competence and a certain indifference marked them all. In spite of a receptive audience, the artist seemed unable to call forth that concentrated attention on his own work that is, if not the whole state of inspired artistry, its sine qua non.

Perhaps your reporter is lending his own incomplete attention to the proceedings to a sincere and hard-working soloist. He hopes not. And he thinks not, since he is ascribing to the artist not lethargy so much as a nervous, almost a mercurial discontinuity of thought. If that were of a continuous intensity, Piatigorsky would be continuously fascinating. As it is, or as it was last night, this listener found him both fascinating and tedious, impressive and banal all at once.

March 20, 1948

CLAUDE DEBUSSY

¶ Thirty years ago last Friday, on March 26, 1918, Claude Debussy died in his fifty-sixth year. Though his three decades of artistic productivity lie on both sides of the century-mark, just as Beethoven's did a hundred years earlier, musically he is as clearly a founding father of the twentieth century as Beethoven was of the nineteenth. The history of music in our time, like any other history, is fully to be reviewed only in the light of all its origins and all its roots. Nevertheless, modern music, the full flower of it, the achievement rather than the hope, stems from Debussy. Everybody who wrote before him is just an ancestor and belongs to another time. Debussy belongs to ours.

It is doubtful, indeed, whether Western music has made any notable progress at all since his death. Neo-Classicism, the evoking of ancient styles in general and of the early eighteenth-century styles in particular, he invented. Polytonal writing existed before him. Even atonality, if we define this as the consistent employment of contradictory chromatics, is present in his later works, notably in the ballet

Jeux. No succeeding composer has augmented his dissonant intensity, though some have made a louder noise. Stravinsky's early picturesque works and his later formalistic
ones are no more radical in either sound or structure than
Debussy's landscape pieces and his sonatas. Schönberg's
twelve-tone row, though Debussy never knew about it, is
merely a rule of thumb to make atonal writing easy. Expressively it has added nothing to any composer's gamut of
sensibility. If, as Busoni believed, one could reconstruct the
whole German Classic and Romantic repertory out of Sebastian Bach alone, certainly modern music, all of it, could
be rebuilt from the works of Debussy.

What music has lost since Debussy's death is sensitivity of
expression and expressivity of instrumentation. Our feelings
are more brutal and our statements about them less precise.
Similarly, our language of chord dispositions and musical
sounds is less competent, less richly evocative than his. We
have all gone in for broader, cruder effects. We have had
to, because his way of writing was at the end of his life almost unbearably delicate. Refinement could be pushed no
further, though Anton Webern tried and succeeded at least
in not falling far short of Debussy's mark. But the others
could not face going on in that way. Sensibly they turned
to easier paths. The fact remains, nevertheless, that Debussy's
work is more radical than theirs and, in the ways both of
expression and of the use of musical materials to this end,
more powerful.

Curiously enough, Debussy's employment of orchestral
sound, though commonly described as "colorful," was not
so envisaged by him. Variety of coloration is certainly present, and knowingly, in his piano writing. Like that of Schumann and that of Mozart, it is full of the imitation of both
orchestral and naturalistic sound-effects. But he avowed the
aim of *Fêtes,* for instance, to be monochromatic, "a musical equivalent of the *grisaille,*" which is a watercolor or ink
brush-drawing done entirely in grays. The secret here is
that Debussy did not, in this piece or in any other, ever,
save for the purpose of avoiding them, seriously respect the
gamut of orchestral weights. He used the orchestral palette
as the impressionist painters used theirs, not for the accenting of particular passages but for the creation of a general
luminosity. And the surface tension of his scores in per-

formance is no less equalized than that of a Renoir, a Pissarro, a Monet canvas. Something like this must have been what he meant by comparing them to a *grisaille*.

Debussy's instrumentation, though it is an advance over Berlioz, is derived from the latter's practice, from the use of sound as a purely acoustical phenomenon. He depersonalizes all instruments. His piano writing, too, though an advance over Chopin's, is derived from that of the Great One. It is not designed, like that of Liszt, for ease of execution but all for delighting the ear and for making music mean things. His melody is Massenet purified, plainsong, and memories of popular song. His counterpoint, though rarefied almost to the point of non-existence, is straight out of Mozart by way of the Paris Conservatory. Every line communicates. Even his harmony, for all its imaginative quality and its freedom, is made up out of Satie plus a taste for the archaic. Maybe there is just a touch of Mussorgsky, too. But his profound originality lies in his concept of formal structure. Where he got it I do not know. It may have come out of Impressionist painting or Symbolist poetry. Certainly there is small precedent for it in music. It remains, nevertheless, his most radical gift to the art.

This formal pattern is a mosaic texture made up of tiny bits and pieces all fitted in together so tightly that they create a continuity. The structural lines of the composition are not harmonic, not in the bass, but rhythmic and melodic. Debussy freed harmony from its rhetorical function, released it wholly to expression. He gave everything to expression, even structure. He did not sculpt in music or build architectural monuments. He only painted. And no two of his canvases are alike. They are all different and all intensely communicative. The range of their effective expression is the largest our century has known, the largest that music has known since Mozart. Piano music, the song, the violin sonata, the cello, chamber music, the opera, the oratorio, the orchestral concert piece all receive from his hand a new liberty, say things and mean things they had never said or tried to mean before. His power over all the musical usages and occasions comes from his complete disrespect for the musical forms and from his ability to replace these by a genuinely satisfactory free continuity.

That France, classically the land of freedom, should have

produced a model of musical freedom is only natural. All
the same, Debussy, even for France, is something of a miracle. No composer ever wrote with such absence of cliché,
detailed or formal. And few have achieved such precision,
such intensity, such wide range of expression. His music is
not only an ultimate, for our century, of sheer beauty.
It is a lesson to us all in how to make use of our liberty.

Isidore Philipp, the great piano pedagogue, now in his
middle eighties, tells of a visit received in Paris from Béla
Bartók, then a young man. He offered to introduce the
young Hungarian composer to Camille Saint-Saëns, at that
time a terrific celebrity. Bartók declined. Philipp then offered him Charles-Marie Widor. Bartók again declined:
"Well, if you won't meet Saint-Saëns and Widor, who is
there that you would like to know?" "Debussy," said Bartók.
"But he is a horrid man," said Philipp. "He hates everybody
and will certainly be rude to you. Do you want to be insulted
by Debussy?" "Yes," said Bartók.

March 28, 1948

THE STYLE IS THE SUBJECT

¶ The musico-intellectual world turned out in considerable numbers for last night's concert in Town Hall of
the Chamber Art Society. Igor Stravinsky's music and presence were the attraction. The program gave us four works
rarely heard, covering a period of twenty years in the composer's middle and later middle life, from 1920 to 1941.
Two of these, the *Symphonies of Wind Instruments,* from
1920, and the *Danses Concertantes,* of 1941, were conducted by himself. The Symphony in C, of 1940, and the
Capriccio for Piano and Orchestra, of 1929, were led by
Robert Craft. Elly Kassman played the solo part in the
latter work. Execution throughout was excellent.

The wind piece, dedicated to the memory of Claude Debussy, was given in a recently made revision. Though it re-

mains a striking piece chiefly for its dissonant and almost motionless chorale at the end, throughout it is a deeply expressive work in mortuary vein. The other pieces, neo-Classic in character, are less directly expressive, being chiefly evocative of scenes, periods, and circumstances from the history of musical composition.

The Capriccio, derived from Weber's Konzertstück, is a brilliant potpourri of Schumann, Chopin, Liszt, Delibes, and probably some others. The *Danses Concertantes* evoke the ballet music of Adam in particular and of the mid-nineteenth century in general. The Symphony in C is modeled after the Viennese classical works in that form, after Haydn, Mozart, and the early Beethoven.

The Symphony is the noblest of the three works, by its grandly simple material, its shapeliness, and its elevated tone. The others are a bit frivolous, though plenty of fun, and more than a little discontinuous. Even the Symphony falls apart a bit in the last movement. All the same, it is a handsome piece, as the Capriccio is a jolly and brilliant one and the *Danses Concertantes* an attractive one for anybody who likes to get sentimental about the ballet.

Stravinsky's neo-Classic music having never had a real audience success, as his impressionistic early theater works have had, his friends and disciples tend to defend it as a cause rather than to discriminate one piece of it from another. Last night's concert gave us a chance, however, to do just that by providing three celebrated and varied examples of it in a row. My choice among these, if I must make one, is the Symphony in C. Another's will be the Capriccio or the *Danses*. The attractiveness of Stravinsky's whole neo-Classic production lies, however, less in the expressive power of a given work than in the musical language in which they are all written.

This is a compound of grace and of brusqueness thoroughly Russian in its charm and its rudeness and so utterly sophisticated intellectually that few musicians of intellectual bent can resist it. The general public has never cared much about modern neo-Classicism, but does listen to it more easily than it used to. I don't think musical ticket buyers are overfond of indirectness, and certainly most of anybody's neoclassic works are indirect. Every now and then, however, one of them forgets its game of reminding you about the history of music and starts saying things of its own. To me the Symphony in C does that, just as the wind instrument *Symphonies,* on the whole an inferior work but not an eclectic or derivative one, have always done.

April 12, 1948

HIGH COSTS

¶ The depression has hit the music business and no doubt about it. Records, books, and concert tickets are getting harder to sell; and the money for giving prestige recitals in New York is less plentiful than it was during the war. The cost of such recitals, moreover, has doubled in the last three years. A Town Hall event, professionally managed and publicized modestly, used to cost the artist about a thousand dollars. It now comes to nearer two thousand. Costs are higher all round; but management, aware of the public's diminished purchasing power, does not dare ask higher prices for admission. Buyer resistance is already formidable. Only a few nationally advertised artists and organizations can today fill any New York hall without resorting to "paper."

Even rich organizations like the Philadelphia Orchestra and the Metropolitan Opera Association have threatened suicide. I must say they have brought their troubles on themselves. Not that any group in the country is solely responsible for the rise in prices, not even Congress. But it has long been evident that artistic enterprises which conduct their operations on the models of business must accept the unhappy consequences of a business depression. If our symphony orchestras were more clearly a part of our real cultural life, like the universities, and less a mere front for the music industries, for radio, recording, and concert management, they would be in a better position than they are today to face deficits. Their intellectual function would be worth more as capital. As I remarked several years ago about the Metropolitan Opera, such groups do best when they conduct themselves and think of themselves as successful money-spending enterprises, not as unsuccessful money-making ones.

Neither should they get mixed up in class warfare. It is unfortunate that supposedly philanthropic and cultural foundations serving art and public instruction should appear in the role of labor's enemy. They should economize where and when they can, naturally; and they should negotiate the most favorable contracts they can. They should not waste their funds. But neither should they assume before the whole public any attitude that renders the motivation of their trustees and administrators suspect to a large part of that public, namely, to all those citizens, many of them music consumers, who make up the trade union movement or who believe in its value to our economy.

I mean by this that the negotiation of labor contracts between unions and nonprofit-making institutions should be carried on without recourse to the major arms of the labor-capital struggle. Symphony orchestras have gone on strike in the past, but rarely successfully; and the action has usually, as in the case of the Boston Symphony Orchestra's strike back in 1920, been costly to unionism in terms of public opinion. The Metropolitan Opera's threat of last August to suspend operations and the Philadelphia Orchestra's announcement of last Monday, canceling its whole concert season, risk a similar unfavorable result for management, since both are dangerously close to what is called in industry a lockout. (In neither case was complete liquidation of the enterprise proposed.) That Philadelphia's Local 77 of the Musicians' Union so understood the move was clear from their reply that they were "unwilling and unable" to accept the orchestra board's decision. Both sides left the door open to further negotiation.

The present writer is holding no brief for either contestant. He is simply pointing out that two philanthropic musical enterprises have recently risked unfavorable public opinion by behaving as if they were businesses, as if no obligation to the public had ever been assumed, as if their governing boards were free to discontinue a valued cultural operation on no other provocation than that of a threatened deficit. It is such a board's duty to negotiate contracts, accept the results, and meet deficits. It is also their privilege to call for public support in meeting deficits. It is their duty, moreover, to ask for such support, to give the public its chance to pay up, before cavalierly announcing the interruption of a public service.

The Philadelphia management has long complained that the Musicians' Union local takes to itself an unfair negotiating advantage by delaying each year to propose its terms until just before the season opens. The union, too, may well at present consider the orchestra's directors to have acted unfairly in threatening the public with a stoppage of the concerts merely to avoid the trouble of raising the money for a wage increase. Wage increases are everywhere in discussion; in a time of high prices their demand need surprise no one. Whether granted or not, they have to be considered. I know nothing of the horse trading that must certainly have gone on between management and the union in Philadelphia, or what exasperation provoked the orchestra board to cancel, at least in announcement, its whole concert season. I merely repeat that I find the gesture unbecoming, as was certainly that of the Metropolitan Opera board in threatening last summer to omit a season from its history.

I find the gesture unbecoming because it uses us, the public, as a pawn in the game of costs. We do not care what symphony orchestras cost; our interest is in what and how they play. If an administration is efficient (and one has every reason to believe that Philadelphia's is), then the proper price of musicians, like that of railway fares, hall rent, musical scores, trucking, and publicity, is simply whatever such a management can get the best for, no more and no less. If prices all round are more than we, the public, are able to cope with, then we do without an orchestra or put up with a cheaper one. But we do not like having trustees tell us they are stopping our concerts simply because they find some necessary element of the enterprise, in their opinion, overpriced. What have they in mind as their trust, one wonders, when they assume what is, after all, our privilege? Are they acting as trustees of all our interests and of music's place in the intellectual tradition, or are they merely playing trustees of private capital in capital's age-old war with labor?

FRENCH LOVELINESS

¶ Few musical delights are so deeply satisfying, both sensuously and intellectually, as a good French orchestra, in form, playing French music under a good French conductor; and the Orchestre National, playing last night in Carnegie Hall under Charles Munch, was exactly that. From beginning to end the concert was both electrifying and delicious. For any who might have had doubts about the ability of this, or of any other European orchestra, to bear comparison with our million-dollar-a-year groups, such hesitations were relieved after the opening overture (Berlioz's *Corsaire*) and not at any time again brought to mind.

In certain ways, this orchestra, playing at its best, does better work than we are accustomed to hear. The clean unanimity of its string playing, the exactitude of its string and woodwind balances, the shading and stability of its percussion section and, of course, the matchless phrasings and other tonal refinements of the French woodwind soloists are standards of comparison that our orchestras, pre-occupied in many cases by the appeals of emphasis and warmth, do not always try to meet. On the question of brass, America follows the German taste for heavy round sounds. The French thinner brasses, which operate as woodwinds in soft passages and in loud ones as a stronger counterpart to the nasal timbre of strings, oboes, and bassoons, are consciously avoided in this country, even in the performance of French music.

How brilliant, how tender and how poetic French music can sound when played in the French way is a rare experience for us. The French orchestral style is one of equilibration, of clear balances and clean colors, of poetic luminosity rather than of animal warmth. And the whole repertory of French music composed since Berlioz has been designed to profit by this delicate performing style. When French orchestras are not in form or well led, which is all too often, they are without vitality. When they are really playing well under a good leader, and playing French music, they offer orchestral sound at its maximum of sophistication.

October 18, 1948

IN WALTZ TIME

¶ Arnold Schönberg's Five Orchestral Pieces, which Dimitri Mitropoulos conducted at last night's concert of the Philharmonic-Symphony Orchestra in Carnegie Hall, were written in 1909, nearly forty years ago. Previously they have been played in New York, I believe, one and three-fifths times. They are among the more celebrated works of our century, and yet few musicians or music lovers have heard them. The present writer, though the owner of a printed orchestral score for twenty-five years, listened to them last night with a virgin ear. Having followed the performance score in hand, he is able to certify that Mr. Mitropoulos and the Philharmonic boys read them to perfection and faithfully. His opinon of the work is that it deserves every bit of its world-wide prestige and none of its world-wide neglect.

The orchestral sound of the work is derived from French impressionism in general and from the music of Debussy in particular. The orchestra is delicate, coloristic, and clean, at no point emphatic or demagogic. There is not in it one doubling of a note for purposes of weight. Harmonically the work is dissonant and atonal, though there is no twelve-tone row in it. Contrapuntally and rhythmically its texture resembles that of the Brahms intermezzi, though it offers a more advanced state of the technique.

That technique tends toward fragmentation of the musical material through rhythmic and contrapuntal device. Schönberg here carries it close to the state of ultimate pulverization that his pupil Anton Webern achieved fifteen years later. Rhythmic contradictions, the gasping, almost fainting utterance of intense emotion in short phrases conventional of curve, the chromatic character of these phrases —all this is out of Brahms, though the harmony is far harsher and the sound of it all, orchestrally, is French.

The expressive character of the Five Pieces is deeply sentimental, in spite of a touch (and more) of irony. Four of the five are in triple time. Composed, as they are, almost wholly of phrases consecrated by Vienna to waltz usage, your reviewer is inclined to consider them a sort of apotheosis of the waltz. He realizes that their waltz structure is no obvious or perhaps even consciously intended communication. All the same, except for the one called "The Changing Chord" (in reality an unchanging one), which is an essay in pure orchestration, he finds them evocative of waltz moods and waltz textures, an etherealization of a theme that is at bottom just good old Vienna.

October 22, 1948

MODERN PIANO PLAYING

¶ In a program marked throughout its execution by intelligence, musicianship, sensitivity and solid brilliance, Yvonne Léfébure's playing of Liszt's transcription of Bach's great A minor organ fugue and of Debussy's rarely played *Images* stood out as unusual experiences for this listener. Her Mozart was sound, her *Tombeau de Couperin* of Ravel distinguished, her Beethoven Sonata (opus 110) grand enough, and her Fauré perfect. Her Bach and her Debussy, however, seemed to your reviewer a sort of ultimate in both sense and sensibility. Also in the evocation by pianistic means of the quality and color of other instruments.

This orchestrating, so to speak, of the literature of the piano is the specific approach to piano playing that differentiates our century's practice of the art from that of its immediate predecessor; and modern piano music, of course, has mostly been composed with that approach in mind. Debussy, Ravel, and their followers are of orchestral evocation wholly conceived. So also, I am convinced, is Mozart's piano writing; and so certainly, in terms of the organ, are Liszt's arrangements of Bach, as well as, in evoking the sound of the *zimbalon*, his Hungarian Rhapsodies.

Modern piano technique exploits, for the purpose of suggesting a great variety of kinds of sound, a great variety of kinds and heights of touch. One of Miss Léfébure's most impressive achievements as a technician is the accuracy with which she can strike whole chords from a height of fifteen inches above the keyboard, strike them with perfect note-balance and agreeable tone at any speed and at any degree of loudness or softness. Her musical differential between time and accent also aids orchestral evocation, because melodic passages, as on the bel canto instruments, are played without down-beat stresses, the accentual pattern being rendered, as in real orchestral playing, by sharp pings, deep bell-strokes and other articulations recalling those of harp, bow-heel, and the orchestra's percussion group.

This kind of piano playing is far from unfamiliar to us, though our own pianists do not do it so well, on the whole, as the French do. What makes Miss Léfébure's work so thoroughly exciting and fresh are the soundness and the penetrating nature of her musical mind (like those of the very best French artists), the rightness of her rhythmic instincts (like Benny Goodman's or Wanda Landowska's), and the breadth of her musical conceptions. There is fecund drama, too, between the strength of her temperament and the discipline of her preparation. She catches fire but does not burn up. She is at all times spontaneous, but she never improvises a reading. She is a first-class pianist, a first-class musician, and an artist. She is of our time, moreover, even playing Bach.

November 15, 1948

CONTEMPORARY FRENCH MUSIC

¶ Erik Satie's *Cinéma*: *Entr'acte,* which opened last night's program at the Juilliard School (the second in a series devoted to contemporary French music), is in the judgment of this reviewer, the finest film score ever composed. The film itself, made by René Clair after a scenario of Francis Picabia, is a brilliant piece of work but completely, if also delightfully, a period piece. Produced in 1924 as a divertissement joining two scenes of a ballet, *Relâche* (composed by Satie and decorated by Picabia), it takes us back to the still innocent last days of Dada, before surrealism had turned our fantasies sour, sexy, and mean. It is not about anything at all but being young and in Paris and loving to laugh, especially at funerals. In those days there was still comic cinema, too.

The excellence of the musical score composed to accompany with real orchestral sounds this otherwise silent film (these were played last night by two pianists) is due to Satie's having understood correctly the limitations and possibilities of a photographic narrative as subject-matter for music. Also to the durable nature of his musical invention. The whole is made out of short musical bits like building blocks. These are neutral enough in character to accompany appropriately many different scene moments and images, but also interesting enough as music to bear a great deal of repetition without fatiguing the listener. These minute musical blocks are organized into a sort of rondo form, as squarely terraced as a New York skyscraper and every bit as practical in function.

Satie's music for *Entr'acte,* consequently, is not only beautiful in itself. It is also efficient as expression; it is appropriate to the film. It avoids banality of sentiment not by avoiding sentiment but by keeping its expressivity objective, by never becoming subjective, never identifying itself with any person on the screen. By remaining ever as cool and clear as René Clair's photography itself, it remains also as clear in meaning and as satisfying intrinsically. I do not know another film score so durable, so distinguished, so complete.

Francis Poulenc's secular cantata *Le Bal Masqué,* on poems of the late Max Jacob, a piece in six sections for baritone and chamber orchestra, shows us a master of musical exuberance at the climax of his youthful period. It was composed in 1932, about the last year anybody in Europe was really carefree, and it is musical highjinks from beginning to end. Its pasticcio of urban banalities, melodic and rhythmic, is rendered personal and interesting by the extreme elegance of the vocal lines and of the instrumental textures. Thin, clean, brilliant, frank, and delicate, its charm, its good humor, its wit and poetry, like those of Satie himself (though the invention is less jewel-like and original than Satie's), is as fresh as the day the piece was written.

December 2, 1948

1949

A BRILLIANT ASSUMPTION

¶ *Jazz: A People's Music*, by Sidney Finkelstein (Citadel Press, New York, 1948. $3), has one distinguishing feature among books on jazz. It attempts to explain the nature of this music, its development and its vigor under persecution in terms of Marxist sociology. The idea that jazz is a music of revolt and of America's economically submerged is perspicacious and merits a more elaborate documentation than the author has provided for its defense. The use of the word "people" to define the lower economic levels of our society is a Stalinist obscurantism that prevents by moral intimidation detailed investigation of the field it pretends to delimit. Nevertheless, there is certainly some relation between jazz and the class structure of American society, a relation not at all to the discredit either of this music or of the people who make it, though the circumstances in which their lives are led are often, from any bourgeois or social-worker point of view, appalling.

Aside from its class-angle approach, Mr. Finkelstein's book is not very original or acute. As another volume on the subject, it can be read by the pious and placed on the sacred shelf; but I do not think there is much in it not elsewhere available, beyond its brilliant basic assumption. And certainly there is far more reviewing of famous recorded performers and performances in it than proves anything. That aspect makes it just another Appreciation book. I do wish the author had developed further his social view of a major musical phenomenon.

January 9, 1949

PRINCE OF IMPRESSIONISM

¶ Cries of "Bravo!" sounded in Carnegie Hall last night as Ernest Ansermet, conducting the Philadelphia Orchestra, brought to a close the final dazzling pages of Debussy's *La Mer*. The whole concert had been dazzling, indeed, and not through any playing of tricks on audience psychology or any of the grosser forms of tonal appeal. The great Swiss conductor had held us all enthralled, as he had the orchestra itself, by sheer musicianship, by knowledge, by understanding, by a care for aural beauty and for exactitude.

In appearance a simple professor, touched up perhaps toward both Agamemnon and the King of Clubs, he is at once a sage, a captain, and a prince. With wisdom, firmness, and grace he rules his domain; and that domain is the music of impressionism. For other leaders the center of the world may be Beethoven or Brahms or Wagner. For him it is the music of Debussy and all that borders thereon. No one living, not even Monteux, can command him in that repertory. Smooth as a seashell, iridescent as fine rain, bright as the taste of a peach are the blends and balances of orchestral sound with which he renders, remembering, the lines, the backgrounds, and the tonal images of the great tonal painters who worked in France round the turn of our century.

Mozart he plays with love and with light, too; and he began last night with the "Prague" Symphony, just to show us how a classical rendering can be clean and thoroughly musical without being dry or overcrisp. The Philadelphia players found his company on that ground a privilege and gave of their best, which is the world's best. But it was only royalty on a visit. With Stravinsky, Fauré, and Debussy the king was back in his land, in his own house reigning, informed, understanding, understood, obeyed from a glance.

Stravinsky's *Song of the Nightingale*, arranged from an

opera score and reorchestrated into a symphonic poem in 1919, may well represent this composer at his highest mastery of instrumental evocation. Musically, nevertheless, the work is weak from lack of thematic integration and harmonic structure. It gives pleasure as sound, page by page, palls as musical continuity in the concert room. It needs to be played from time to time because it is a work of the highest and most striking fancy, but heaven preserve us from it as a repertory piece.

Fauré's *Pelléas et Mélisande* suite, on the other hand, is a work of deep loveliness that could stand more usage in repertory than it gets these days. When played with such sweet harmoniousness and such grace of line as it was last night, one wonders why one had forgotten how touching it can be.

Debussy's *La Mer* brought the wonders of the evening to a radiant close. It is a piece this reviewer has always found a shade disappointing; but it is a popular repertory work; and if one has to hear it, Ansermet's reading of it is more welcome than most. Actually, while listening to it, this unfriendly witness forgot all about his prejudices and enjoyed himself thoroughly, almost as thoroughly as during the Mozart and the Fauré.

January 19, 1949

SPECIALTY OF THE HOUSE

¶ Richard Wagner's *Twilight of the Gods,* as performed on Wednesday night at the Metropolitan Opera House, lasted from half-past seven till five minutes of twelve (a saving of five minutes on the normal run); and there was not, for this listener, a dull moment in the second half. The first act and a half were talky, save for two fine orchestral interludes. Dramatically and musically the script just will not move along. But beginning about the middle of the second act, with the entrance of the male chorus, the stage takes on animation, ensemble singing adds brilliance to the musical effect, and the whole work grows in grandeur until the final curtain falls. A wealth of musical thought and an opulent elaboration of musical textures pile up for two hours, till it is impossible, given a reasonably good musical rendering, to leave the theater without some feeling of full-ness, of fulfillment.

Wednesday's rendering was, moreover, far better than reasonably good. It was first-class clean through, thoroughly grand and wonderful. The orchestral direction of Fritz Stiedry, the singing of Helen Traubel, Set Svanholm, and Dezso Ernster, were what anybody could know for mem-orable. Refinement, power, and beauty marked the reading in all its leading roles; dignity and musicianship in the sec-ondary ones gave shape to the whole. Even the stage move-ment, deliberately static and statuesque, was executed with decorum. And the scenery, new last year, is still, along with the costumes that go with it, an integrated design and reasonably clean.

It becomes increasingly evident to this observer that Wagner's works are the branch of repertory to which the Met, in the present decade, is best adapted. The German-language singers available there are far superior to those whose preparation has destined them chiefly for Italian, French, or English-language work. So are the present staff conductors. And eminently suitable is the size of the house and stage. Wagner fills the place with resonance and visibil-ity. Big sounds, big scenic effects, fires, mountains, vast sun-sets, demolitions, and characters whose emotions and con-flicts are as huge and as impersonal as those of any leviathan—all are at home in that house and becoming to it.

Set Svanholm's slender figure is of no help to Wagner, though his handsome singing is. Wagner's music dramas are conceived for a theater of whales. These move slowly, re-lentlessly, on an epic scale, require space, offer sounds of infinite power and complexity to fill up that space. At the Met, they and the house are of a proportion. Italian opera has never since Caruso's death been loud enough for it, and French opera never has been loud like that at any time.

The management and executants, moreover, seem to take Wagner for music's central figure. They work more carefully

for him, more confidently, and with more dignity, project
a sense of having studied everything more thoroughly than
is apparent in the rest of the repertory. Occasionally another composer gets a fair deal; but Wagner always gets
the best of everything—the best playing, the best singing,
the best scenery, the best direction and lighting, the most
impressive effects of every kind. It is as if only he were
worthy the deployment of so vast a machine. The contrast
between these works and the rest of opera, as given year
after year in that house, is striking and revelatory. Not of
Wagner's musical primacy, however. Mozart remains a
greater composer and Verdi just possibly an equal. But it
does show us what the Met, its whole set-up and management, are good for. Good *for* because good *at*.

January 21, 1949

YESTERDAY'S MODERNISM

¶ The League of Composers concert, which took
place last night in the Museum of Modern Art, lasted till
eleven o'clock; and your reviewer, the night being rainy,
did not reach his desk till fifteen minutes later. Consequently, in order to cover a concert of some intellectual
importance, he is going to take the liberty of stating his
judgments in summary, stenographic fashion. But first it
must be listed that all the executions were excellent, unusually distinguished being the piano playing of Grant Johannesen, the violin playing of Nikolai Berezowsky, and the singing of Arline Carmen. Especial thanks are due also to Fred-
eric Waldman, who conducted the Varèse piece perfectly,
at least to these ears.

The Varèse work, entitled *Hyperprism,* is real "modern
music" of twenty years back; and it still makes its point.
That point is that beauty does not require cantilena, harmony, contrapuntal imitation, or deliberate pathos. It can
be made with elements commonly considered to be noise,

and it does not even have to confine its sound sources to the conventionally ignoble. Trumpets, trombones, flutes, horns, piccolos, and the classical instruments of percussion give out purer sounds than flower pots and brakebands. Consequently they are useful. But out with their sentimental connotations! They are there as sound sources, not as poetic references.

The sounds that Varèse makes in this piece are handsome in the abstract. Their composition is rhythmically interesting, moreover; and with no cue as to the work's particular meaning, your listener found it absorbing, convincing, beautiful, and in every way grand. That the League of Composers, which fought this composer bitterly and all too successfully twenty years back, should revive him now is poetic justice. Let no one think, however, that they have just made his acquaintance or that they are recalling any historical benefaction of theirs.

As recalling former successes of the modern-music movement, the League gave us last night three jolly pieces by Leo Ornstein, from 1916, rhythmically thoroughly alive, if harmonically nothing difficult. Three piano pieces by Roger Sessions, though harmonically sophisticated, were as dead as the day of their birth. Roy Harris's Concerto for String Quartet, Clarinet and Piano, is still, twenty years later, real chamber music, with no more faults than are to be found in Brahms and with all the virtues. And Stephan Wolpe's songs, the evening's only first performance, are knockouts in the vein of yesterday's modernism and up to date in their use of Hebraic texts, references to Israel being the last word today in successful public relations. They are really quite good songs, but so are Orstein's pieces good piano music. It was hard to know, indeed, among all these period-style compositions, exactly where real quality lay, excepting for the Varèse work, which, by any standards I know, is great music.

January 24, 1949

STIFFLY CONDUCTED

¶ Stravinsky's ballet *Orpheus* had not been heard here as a concert piece till the composer conducted it last night in Carnegie Hall. When Ballet Society produced the work last season the score made a deep impression. At last night's performance of the Boston Symphony Orchestra it struck this observer again as an unusually rewarding work.

Though dominated at all times by the strings of the orchestra, its sonorous variety runs high. Constantly static of harmony and rhythm, it evokes action, all the same, as well as feeling. Wholly diatonic in style, it has a harmonic plainness and melodious grace that are just right for a subject out of classical mythology. Mostly the music is slow, too; but from beginning to end it is all so interesting, so full of expressive life, that monotony is at no point present. A magical sort of work it is, because it creates a spell. That spell resembles a little the mood of Satie's *Socrate,* as if the whole air were become suddenly motionless and vibrant.

The Concerto in D for String Orchestra, usually considered a minor work, delighted all by its jollity and animation. Indeed, it was the only piece that Mr. Stravinsky led last night with any ease. Perhaps his lively way with it explains its happy reception. In any case, it was the one moment of the evening when fun got loose. The other works were all tragic of theme; and they were tightly, laboriously led.

Soulima Stravinsky, playing the twenty-five-year-old Piano Concerto, read it correctly, gave us the notes. Igor Stravinsky, conducting it, somehow squeezed all the life out of it with his stubborn and hesitant beat. The same was true in the Ode, which began the program. Granted that three sad pieces and one jolly one do not make an ideal menu, I think the great man was not in his best form. He let his sonorities thicken unblended and his phrases bog

down from lack of afflatus. Nothing moved along except
the String Concerto. Many, discouraged, left the hall.

February 17, 1949

RUSSIANS RECOVER

¶ Dmitri Shostakovitch, the most popular of living
Russian composers, inside the Soviet Union or out, has apparently been reinstated in the favor of the Politburo. A
year ago he had been removed from that favor, along with
five other well known composers—Prokofiev, Khachaturian,
Miaskovsky, Shebalin, and Popov. He had also been removed, along with some of these others, from public office.
Shostakovitch and Miaskovsky ceased to teach composition
at the Moscow Conservatory. Shebalin was replaced as head
of that institution by A. Sveshnikov, a choral conductor.
Khachaturian lost to Tikhon Khrennikov the position of
Secretary General of the Union of Soviet Composers. He
also ceased to be head of its Orgkomitet, or organizing committee. This group, working in close collaboration with the
Committee on Arts of the Ministry of Education, has huge
power, since it decides what works will be printed and recommends works for performance to opera houses, symphony orchestras, and touring virtuosos.

Prokofiev, who did not teach or hold any official post,
was ostracized by the simple means of removing nearly all
his works from the opera and concert repertories. The same
measure was applied, of course, to the other purged composers, but less drastically. Shostakovitch's First and Fifth
symphonies, Miaskovsky's Symphony on White-Russian
Themes, Khachaturian's Cello Concerto, and divers other
pieces by the denounced "formalists" have gone right on
being played, at least occasionally, since the purge.

Last year's offense, let us recall, was not the first for
Shostakovitch. Back in 1936 he had been subjected to disciplinary measures of a similar nature lasting a year and a

half. His chief offense had been the opera *Lady Macbeth of
Mzensk* and his work of restitution the Fifth Symphony.
This time the troublesome piece was his Ninth Symphony;
and his comeback has been accomplished through two film
scores, *The Young Guard* and *Michurin*. The first of these
is a heroic and optimistic melodrama about the exploits of
the Komsomol during the defense of the Don Basin. The
other is a biography in color of a Soviet hero, I. V.
Michurin, founder of Soviet anti-Mendelian biology.
Though neither film has yet reached the Stanky Theater,
they have passed the musical judges; and two musical excerpts from *The Young Guard* have been printed in
Sovietskaya Muzyka of October, 1948.

The cases of Khachaturian and Shostakovitch are simpler than that of Prokofiev. The former's "illness," as the
Russians like to refer to any artistic deviation, is only recently contracted and is 50 per cent non-musical, anyway.
This half is a result of his political position. As a Party member, president of the Orgkomitet, and Secretary General of
the Composers' Union, he was naturally held responsible for
whatever protection the "formalists" had enjoyed prior to
their denunciation. A first offender, a man of charming personality, and a convinced Bolshevik from the periphery of
the Union (Armenia), he represents to the Politburo the
achievements of a national-culture policy dear to its initia-
tor Stalin. Of all the purged six, he has been the most played
since his purge. As a Party member, he has continued, moreover, to serve on Union subcommittees. Professor T.
Livanova (sole woman member of the Presidium of the
Composers' Union) dealt with him indulgently in the July,
1948, number of *Sovietskaya Muzyka*. His successor as Secretary General of the Composers' Union, T. Khrennikov,
also patted him on the back (for effort) in his "state of the
Union" message of January 1, 1949.

If Khachaturian appears now as on his way out of trouble, Prokofiev seems to be in no such position. Not a
product of Soviet culture but of the pre-revolutionary
Czarist regime, a traveled man long resident in such centers of "bourgeois corruption" as Paris and the U.SA.,
an associate of the Russian émigré enterprise, Serge
de Diaghilev's Ballet Russe, and a resident of the Soviet
Union only since 1933, this composer is being referred to

more and more in the Soviet press as an incorrigible case. The recently deceased Boris Asafiev, Acting President of the Composers' Union (Stalin being Honorary President), also Khrennikov and Marion Koval, editor of *Sovietskaya Muzyka* and a party-line whip, have all denounced him. Consistently and, one surmises, deliberately nowadays, his name is linked with such "servile and corrupt musical businessmen" as Stravinsky, such "degenerate, blackguard, anti-Russian lackeys of the Western bourgeoisie" as Diaghilev. His latest opera, moreover, composed under the purge, has been found unacceptable.

The latter, based on a story by Boris Polyevoi and entitled *The Life of a Real Person* (libretto by the composer's companion, Mira Mendelssohn), deals with a Soviet flier and hero who lost both legs in the war. In December of last year the conductor Khaikin, who seems to admire Prokofiev deeply, organized in Leningrad a public reading of the opera. He apparently overstepped in this case his prerogatives, for the Leningrad papers scolded him severely; and Khrennikov called the incident "a fatal one for Prokofiev." Khrennikov specified further that "this opera shows that the traditions of Western modernism have captivated his consciousness." Moreover, "to him an acute dramatic situation is an end in itself; and the overplay of naturalistic details seems more important than the creation of musically truthful and convincing images of a Soviet hero with his life-asserting, ebullient will and his bold outlook into the future." Khrennikov also regrets that Prokofiev did not submit the work to his comrade-composers for criticism before its unfortunate concert hearing. The critic of *Izvestya*, Mr. Kukharski, dismisses the piece as "impractical, ivory-tower workmanship" and the composer as "an artist who has severed all connections with real Soviet life." *Pravda* thinks it "doubtful" whether one "can expect anything to satisfy the needs of the great Soviet people" from a "composer whose work is penetrated to the core" by "Western formalist decay."

In contrast to the apparently incurable maladjustments of Prokofiev (who is physically ill, as well, for he seems to have had last spring another stroke like the one he suffered in 1946), Shostakovitch is clearly on the road to recovery. Not only is he being sent to us on a mission; he has also been praised by the head of his union for his "successful" film music. His position last year was grave. As a second offender he might easily have lost his apartment. Koval actually suggested at a Composers' Union meeting as late as last October that those afflicted with "decadent, bourgeois tendencies . . . could very profitably move out of Moscow to the periphery of the vast Soviet land and get their inspiration from a close contact with the life of the people in the provinces, in collective farms and factories." Happily, however, Mr. Shostakovitch encountered nothing so drastic as forced residence on the "periphery" of the Soviet Union.* His case was argued in the magazines; his confession was accepted at face value; his penitential work has been judged good. And so (the United States willing) he is going to be sent to visit us.

Koval has analyzed his chronic "illness" as follows. Shostakovitch's great natural gift has been perverted by:

1. Discordant German counterpoint (presumably the Hindemith style).

2. Introducing into the "sacred soil of the pure classic Russian tradition jazz neurosis and Stravinskyan rhythmical paroxysms."

3. Inability to write "singable" melodic lines.

4. Naturalistic approach to subject matter. (The love scene in *Lady Macbeth* shocked some here, too.)

5. "Limitless adulation of a chorus of sycophants" (in other words, success).

He can, however, be cured by the following regimen:

1. Avoiding "dissonance."

2. Avoiding any harmonic syntax more advanced than that of the late Sergei Rachmaninov.

3. Learning to write "easy" tunes.

4. Avoiding dependence on "abstract" instrumental and symphonic forms.

5. Writing more songs.

6. Strictly abstaining from jazz rhythms, paroxystic syncopation, "fake" (meaning dissonant) polyphony, and atonality.

7. Writing operas about Soviet life.

---

* By " 'periphery' of the Soviet Union" Russians usually understand Siberia.

8. Turning his attention in general to the song of the great Soviet people and forgetting about the West.

Whether sending him to visit the West is the best way to make him forget about it is not for a mere Westerner to judge. Certainly his Western admirers will give him an unforgettable welcome. But before we submit him to the temptations of a bourgeois publicity-apotheosis, let us remember him as last described from home sources, piously glorifying Soviet science. In *Pravda*'s art magazine of January 1, 1949, he is mentioned as having written successful music for a charming episode in the film *Michurin*. The biologist is therein described as "standing high above a blooming apple tree and in total self-oblivion conducting a rapturous, wordless chorus of the Voices of Nature." "These Voices," it is added, "have been clearly heard and well expressed by the composer." Hollywood itself could not, I am sure, provide a musician with a more glorious opportunity than the scene here described; nor could any composer wish for a more auspicious way to salute the U.S., hereditary home of "formalistic decadence," than by indulgence in such unashamed hamming.

The above, or, rather, the information contained in it, is derived from a report of some length on the Russian musical press, furnished me, with translations, by the composer Nicolas Nabokov. I regret that space restrictions forbid more extensive quotations from this entertaining material, but I think I have incorporated the gist of it.

February 27, 1949

MASTERPIECES REVIVED

¶ Carl Ruggles's *Angels* was the high point of the concert presented last night in Times Hall by the National Association for American Composers and Conductors. Other works had elegance or musical distinction, and all were handsomely executed. But Ruggles's piece is a masterpiece and one almost wholly unknown today. Its revival after more than twenty years was accompanied by the kind of intellectual excitement that has ever attended its performance, plus the deep joy of the young just making its discovery.

Angels is part of a longer work entitled *Men and Angels,* composed in 1921. This section, as rescored in 1938, is a sustained and tranquil motet for four trumpets and three trombones, all muted. The texture of it is chromatic secundal counterpoint. Its voices, nondifferentiated as to expressive function, are woven together by thematic imitation. The dissonance-tension is uniform throughout, hence, in the long run, harmonious, though that tension carries the maximum of dissonance possible to seven voices. Complete avoidance of the dramatic and the picturesque gives to the work a simplicity and a nobility rare in the music of our time. Its plain nobility of expression and the utter perfection of its workmanship place Ruggles as one of our century's masters, perhaps the one among all from whom the young have most to learn just now.

Lou Harrison conducted reverently, admirably. It was a lovely occasion, in every way out of the ordinary.

February 28, 1949

BÉLA BARTÓK

¶ Béla Bartók's music, always respected by musicians, seems now, some three years after his death, to be coming into its reward of love. Not only is the number of musicians who are attached to it increasing; laymen are beginning to bear it affection. Every orchestra plays a Bartók piece now once a year, and his string quartets appear regularly on the chamber music programs. The Juilliard String Quartet played three of these last month, will complete the cycle of six at Times Hall on Monday evening, the twenty-eighth of this month.

This examiner has never been deeply impressed with the technical originality of Bartók. His major virtues, in my view, lie in the expressive domain. He was a master, of course. He had a good ear and abundant fancy. He knew the technical innovations of our century, used most of them, invented innumerable small adaptations or variants of them. But there is very little of textural ingenuity in his music that could not have been derived by any active musical mind from the works of Debussy and Stravinsky. Exactly such a mind, that of Manuel de Falla, did derive a comparable rhetoric from those sources, employing Spanish local color as Bartók did Hungarian and achieving a musical result not essentially different, a nationalistically oriented Impressionism admirably suited to evoking the dance.

Bartók, however, though he began as a picturesque composer, had another string to his harp. He wrote chamber music of a reflective character. Impressionism was paralleled in his practice not by neoclassic constructions, as was the practice of Western composers (even de Falla, in his harpsichord concerto, essayed the formal), but by expressionism, by an outpouring of private feelings that is related as an aesthetic method both to the loose formal observances of nineteenth-century Central European chamber music and to that extreme subjectivity of expression that is characteristic of Arnold Schönberg's early works.

The formal preoccupations of Western neoclassicism do not lend themselves easily to emotional effusion, and neither do the techniques of picturesque sound. Emotional outpourings work best with loose structures and a gray palette. So Bartók kept his continuity loose, abbreviating it more and more into a semblance of tight form, and neutralized his color. At heart, however, he loved bright colors; and in his concertos he continued to employ them. In his later quartets he replaced surface color with emotional vividness. And if this last is less lurid and private than it is in Schönberg's chamber works, it is no less tonic.

Hans Heinsheimer, visiting in Boston the premiere performance of Bartók's Concerto for Orchestra, has recounted how at the end of the piece a neighbor turned to her husband and said, "Conditions must be terrible in Europe." She was right, of course. They were, especially in

Central Europe, where Bartók had lived. And she was right in sensing their relation to the expressive content of Bartók's music. It is here, I think, that his nobility of soul is most impressive. The despair in his quartets is no personal maladjustment. It is a realistic facing of the human condition, the state of man as a moral animal, as this was perceptible to a musician of high moral sensibilities just come out of Hungary.

No other musician of our century has faced its horrors quite so frankly. The quartets of Bartók have a sincerity, indeed, and a natural elevation that are well-nigh unique in the history of music. I think it is this lofty quality, their intense purity of feeling that gives them warmth and that makes their often rude and certainly deliberate discordance of sound acceptable to so many music lovers of otherwise conservative tastes. Nobody, as we know, ever minds expressive discord. The "modern music" war was a contest over the right to enjoy discord for its own sake, for its spicy tang and for the joy it used to give by upsetting applecarts. Bartók himself, as a young man, was a spice lover but not at all an upsetter. He was a consolidator of advance rather than a pioneer. As a mature composer he came to lose his taste for paprika but not for humanity. His music approached more and more a state of systematic discord, rendered more and more truly and convincingly the state of European men in his time. His six string quartets are the cream of Bartók's repertory, the essence of his deepest thought and feeling, his most powerful and humane communication. They are also, in a century that has produced richly in that medium, a handful of chamber music nuggets that are pure gold by any standards.

March 20, 1949

BRILLIANT CONDUCTING

¶ Eleazar de Carvalho, conducting the Juilliard
School of Music, gave a sensationally successful performance of the Berlioz *Symphonie Fantastique*. Earlier in the
evening he had thoroughly muffed Schönberg's Kammersymphonie, and before that, your informant had messed
up his own coverage by arriving late (what with wet streets
and a concert that really began on time) for Harold
Shapero's *The Travellers* overture. Carvalho's New York
début, nevertheless, offered compensations.

Exasperated by his own miscalculation, your investigator
was inclined toward sympathy with that of the young
Brazilian conductor in the Schönberg work. The fact remains, however, that Mr. Carvalho failed to induce his fifteen instrumentalists to make any kind of balance that
sounded like chamber music. He forced them to force their
tone, strove for effects of dynamism unattainable with single
strings and woodwinds and in general threw his weight
around pretty carelessly. The Kammersymphonie, all tenderness, formality, and meditation, resisted such treatment.
Neither the work nor the interpreter came out of the match
to advantage.

Both shone in the *Fantastique*. Note that almost any conductor makes a fine effect with the last two movements of
this piece, which are foolproof. But few, very few, ever get
much life into the first three. Mr. Carvalho, I must say, let
the first go static on him by arbitrarily holding back the
beat every few measures, but in the waltz he found a trajectory and kept to it. His balances everywhere were clear,
moreover; and his orchestral tone was consistently agreeable, in spite of a certain violence in expression that is essential to a live reading of this work. The *Fantastique* is not
an easy work to conduct at all, much less to interpret convincingly. Mr. Carvalho proved himself a leader of unusual

skill and unusual platform power in a performance memorable for clarity and pacing.

Faults the young conductor has aplenty. Like many another Koussevitsky pupil he swims in molasses, chews the air, and in general pleads for personal attention. He puts on a ballet of hands, moreover, that is affected and of questionable value to the players. Like many another barehanded leader, too, he throws an overheavy and over-detailed beat. All this is of no gravity whatsoever to a musician of his brains and temperament. What is cardinal to conducting is an ability to make other musicians make music. That Mr. Carvalho has. He can even prevent them from doing so, as he proved in the Schönberg work, when he misconstrues a piece and miscalculates sonorous limits. A conductor with a future, I say, and already worth listening to.

March 26, 1949

HOLLYWOOD'S BEST

¶ Aaron Copland's musical accompaniments to a film called *The Red Pony* (by Milestone, out of Steinbeck) are the most elegant, in my opinion, yet composed and executed under "industry conditions," as Hollywood nowadays calls itself. Mr. Copland himself, Hollywood's most accomplished composer, has not in his earlier films—*Of Mice and Men, The North Star,* and *Our Town*—produced for cinematic drama a musical background so neatly cut and fitted.

It is the perfection of the musical tailoring in this picture that has made clear to me in a way I had not understood before just where the artistic error lies in the industry's whole manner of treating musical backgrounds. Honegger, Auric, Milhaud, and Sauguet in France, William Walton in England, Kurt Weill in Germany, Prokofiev and Shostakovitch in Soviet Russia have all made film music that was more than a worthy contribution to film drama. Here privately produced or government-produced documentaries have occasionally made film and music history, but our industry-produced fiction films have not included in their whole lifetime five musico-dramatic productions worthy to rank beside the fifty or more European films that as musico-dramatic compositions merit the name "work of art."

It is not talent or skill that is lacking here. It is not intelligence, either, or general enlightenment on the part of directors and producers. The trouble goes deep and has, I think, to do with our distribution rather than with our production system. But first let me talk a bit about *The Red Pony*.

The film itself, as a visual narrative, is diffuse; it tries to tell more stories than it can bring to a conclusion. Also, it has too many stars in it. It is about a boy and a pony, both admirably played. What the child star and the animal need is acting support. What they get, however, is not acting support at all but the glamour competition of Robert Mitchum and Myrna Loy. As a result, the composer has been obliged to hold the show together with music. There are some sixty minutes of this; and Mr. Copland has made it all interesting, various, expressive. If he has not made it all equally pointed, that is not his fault. He has met beautifully and effectively all the possible kinds of musical demand but one. That one is the weak spot in all American fiction films. It is a result of our particular treatment of the female star.

Wherever Copland has provided landscape music, action music, or a general atmosphere of drama he has worked impeccably. Wherever he has essayed to interpret the personal and private feelings of Miss Loy, he has obscured the décor, stopped the action, killed the story, exactly as Miss Loy herself has done at those moments. His music at such times goes static and introspective, becomes, for dramatic purposes, futile. In a landscape picture, which this is, interpreting emotion directly in the music destroys the pastoral unity of tone. Miss Loy's sadness about her marital maladjustment might have been touching against a kind of music that suggested the soil, the land, the farm, the country life —all those attachments which, not shared by her husband, are the causes of her sadness. But the sadness itself, when blown up to concert size and deprived of specific musical allusion, loses point.

American films have occasionally omitted all such fake *Tristan und Isolde* music, using simply dialogue or sound effects to support the stars' close-ups. It is much easier, moreover, to handle musically a male star in emotional crisis than a female one, since our mythology allows character and even picturesqueness to the hero. Our heroines, on the other hand, are supposed to be nymphs—all grooming, all loveliness, all abstract desirability, though capable of an intense despair when crossed in love. It is not easy to make a successful picture about one of these goddesses unless the contributing elements—music, costumes, furniture, housing, male adoration, effects of weather, and triumphs of technology—are made to contribute to the myth. Our industry, our whole design, manufacture, and distribution of fiction films, is the commerce of this goddess's image. She is what Hollywood makes and sells. It is easy for a classically trained composer, one for whom art means reality, to enhance the reality of scenic backgrounds, to animate passages of action, to emphasize dramatic values, to give shape and pacing to any narrative's progress. But it is quite impossible for him to be a salesman of soul states in which he does not believe.

No composer working in Hollywood, not even Copland, has ever made me believe that he believed in the reality of our female stars' emotions. That is the spot where American films go phony, where they fail of truth to life. In so far as this spot is a box-office necessity (and with million-dollar budgets it may well be a necessity), it is impossible for the film industry to make a musico-dramatic work of art. The film, as Europe has proved, is an art form capable of using to advantage the best composers. The film as produced by the American industry has never been able to show any composer at his best. *The Red Pony,* in spite of its mediocrity as a film drama, comes nearer to doing this than other American fiction films I have seen. It is the nearness of its miss, indeed, that has made me realize where the fault in our Hollywood musical credo lies. It lies in the simple truth that it is not possible to write real music about an unreal emotion. An actress can communicate an unreal emotion, because tears, any tears, are contagious. But no composer can transform a feeling into beauty unless he knows in his heart that that feeling is the inevitable response of a sane human being to unalterable events.

April 10, 1949

THE NEW GERMANY AND ITALY

¶ New musical styles from Italy and Germany were the subject of last night's League of Composers concert in Times Hall. Boris Blacher's *Romeo and Juliet,* the freshest among the novelties, the most different from standard modern models, is a radio opera based on a cutting of Shakespeare's tragedy in Schlegel's German translation. It was given last night in an adaptation, made partly by the composer, to the original English verses. These fit their musical setting surprisingly well. The choral and solo parts are everywhere in this opera the point of attention. They are musically most expressive and always rhythmically animated. The instrumental accompaniment is expressive, too, though sparse. With sagacity and skill, Mr. Blacher has reduced this to a skeleton that is functionally no less complete for its extreme thinness. Everything contributes toward throwing the text into high relief. The result is moving and genuinely distinguished.

Blacher represents the new Germany in music. He turns his back on harmonic and contrapuntal complexity and on the romantic afflatus in expression, on all heaviness, obscurity, and introversion of sentiment. He cultivates the elements that have long been absent from German composition, namely, rhythmic life, instrumental wit, harmonic and contrapuntal succinctness, naturalistic declamation. With the simplest of means, he makes a straightforward communication.

His influences are chiefly Satie, Kurt Weill, and Stravinsky, though he has neither the commercial folksiness of Weill nor the intellectual ambition of Stravinsky. The sophisticated plainness of his music is close to that of Satie, though Blacher's does not shine with quite the same white light. It is invigorating like milk and apples, clean, sensible, healthy, and just what German music needs after a century of over-eating.

Whether the twelve-tone style is what Italy needs just now I am not so certain. Possibly the twelve-tone style, however, can profit from an Italian voyage. Certainly Luigi Dallapiccola gives to its characteristic broken melodic line a grand lyric quality that is becoming. His *Sex Carmina Alcaei* are a group of poems from the Greek set for soprano voice and about ten instruments. They are vocally ornate, instrumentally delicate and warm of expression. They are lovely, elegant, sweet, and just the right amount recondite.

Guido Turchi's String Quartet, written two years ago at the age of thirty-one, is the work of an unusually gifted and skillful young man. Dedicated to the memory of Béla Bartók, it imitates the Hungarian master chiefly in its use of spooky sonorities. These are applied with imagination and a light hand. The last movement has a rhythmic life in it too. The whole piece is graceful, sensitive, serious.

April 11, 1949

BEECHAM AT 70

¶ On the 29th of April Sir Thomas Beecham was seventy years old. The British Broadcasting Corporation, in honor of the event, put on a week of concerts, opera and divers other events dedicated to the great man. Naturally he took part in most of them, for the doughty knight (and baronet) is no passive recipient. If this writer knows that joyful energy, he was all over the place, conducting everything, making speeches, cracking jokes, delighting everybody, terrifying everybody, horrifying the thin-skinned, and solemnly alerting his country to the dangers of musical negligence and irresponsibility.

A glorious festival it has been, I am sure, and one impossible to imagine taking place here. Toscanini's eightieth birthday, the seventieths of Koussevitzky, Walter, and Monteux, all were passed off with a few editorials in the press and a sanctimonious mention on the radio. Even

Koussevitzky's retirement from the Boston Symphony Orchestra after twenty-five years netted him in New York one public dinner and one platinum watch. The truth is, of course, that no musician means to America what Beecham means to Britain. The music life of America has come to maturity through the efforts of many. Today's vigorous music life in England is traceable in virtually every branch to Beecham.

His taste and his talents, aided in the beginning by his father's benefactions, made Covent Garden for thirty years a synonym for quality in operatic production. His insistence on playing the works of his countrymen brought British composers, from Delius to Vaughan Williams, a world public. His loving attention to Handel, Haydn, and Mozart revolutionized the contemporary attitude toward these composers and changed them, as Albert Schweitzer did with Bach, from formal classics into a living force. He was at the heart of the movement, too, that revivified the Elizabethan and pre-Elizabethan music of England, restored England's glorious musical past to her living tradition.

Wherever a musical job needed doing, there was Sir Thomas, sleeves rolled up, doing it. Folklore studies, the Renaissance revival, the masters of the Classical period, neglected Romantics like Berlioz, moderns from Strauss to Stravinsky, the discovery of Sibelius, importation of French masters and of the Russian ballet, the encouragement of British composition. British soloists, British ballet, opera in English, modern music concerts, touring opera companies, everything sound in music from the most scholarly research to the most radical experimentation has benefited from his enlightened assiduity.

To build a musical new Jerusalem in England's green and pleasant land has from youth been his aim; or, failing this, to make of that country, which has for a century and more borne music an unrequited love, a fit place for musicians. And if England is not today quite yet a musical Garden of Eden, the erosion of her once-rich musical resources has been arrested. From now on she can take a place among the world's music-producing countries comparable to that she has long occupied among the consumers. I am not saying that the whole British revival is Sir Thomas's work, for some of it began before he was grown. I merely wish to point out that he has been the greatest single animator, living or dead, in that whole astonishing movement. It is no wonder that his country owes him honor, pays him thanks.

In the course of giving to England all the music there is in all the kinds, this man of taste, talent, and energy became not only an impresario but also a great conductor. As the former (and also as a philanthropist), he provided survival for Britain's four chief orchestras during World War I. As the latter, he has toured the world ever since, offering to the astonished continents the spectacle of a British musical artist comparable in every way to the best from any land and superior to most. Germany found his Mozart a revelation. France has considered his renderings of French opera, from Berlioz to Debussy, as exemplifying perfection and authority. Russians have taken his Moussorgsky and his Korsakov, Italians his Verdi and his Rossini right into the body of their tradition. The present writer is witness, too, that when he plays American music he gets it right.

Beecham's interpretative and technical skills are available at their highest in that most modern branch of the executant's art, gramophone recording. Sir Thomas is not always at his best in the concert hall. When he is in form, there is nobody so live, so loving, so gracious. But sometimes he gets excited and falls short of his own standards. Not so in the recording studio. There he works in calm, rehearsing, playing back, retaking each record-side over and over till every sound in it is a musical sound and contributes to the whole piece's meaningful design. The result is a body of recorded music unequaled by that of any other conductor.

Considering his excellent health and undiminished vigor, we may hope for a great many more fine concerts and recordings from Sir Thomas, as his enemies may also look for lots more trouble from him, and for a long time. His quarrels, his lawsuits, his indiscreet public addresses are signs of that vigor, its overflow. But the vigor itself is in the music he makes, in the humane culture of his mind, in the warmth of his sentiments, in the liveliness of his wit and spirits, in the huge and undaunted devotion of a great man

and a grand seigneur to all that music means, ever did, ever
will, or ever could mean in the life of a great people.

May 8, 1949

A STRING OCTET AND
A TEMPLE SERVICE

¶ The San Francisco Bay region's summer music
season differs notably from that of most other urban centers
in the high seriousness of the programs offered. Not led
by climatic intensities to center itself about outdoor circumstances and the intellectually easy-to-take, its repertory
regularly includes material that would do honor to any
community at any time. Among the new works presented
this year, two by Darius Milhaud have had a striking effect
on listeners. Unusually impressive both by weight and by
volume, their presentation, as well as their composition,
represents musical achievement of a high order. It was
your correspondent's privilege recently both to hear and
to examine the French master's String Octet and his Sacred
Service for the Jewish liturgy.

Milhaud's String Octet is really two String Quartets, numbered in this composer's production Fourteenth and Fifteenth. Intended to be played both separately and together,
they were recently so presented in first performance by the
Budapest and Paganini Quartets at the University of California in Berkeley. Your correspondent was not present on
that occasion; but he listened later, score in hand, to a tape
recording of the execution. He also heard the two Quartets
played, both separately and simultaneously, by students of
Roman Totenberg at the Music Academy of the West in
Carpinteria. Their sound, let it be said right off, is an un-
commonly tonic musical experience.

Any composer's main problem in writing such a double-
barreled work is to differentiate the musical expression of
the separate units, to make of them two communications

which, when combined, offer a third. The degree to which
Milhaud has solved this problem your correspondent would
not like to be hasty about estimating. The mere hearing of
the double piece, the following of it in sound, is so complex
an exercise that judgments of an aesthetic nature must wait
upon really learning the piece. Nevertheless, it is clear already that the degree of successful meaning-projection is
high.

Quartet No. 14 is a more straightforward lyrical expression than No. 15. The latter has, I think, poetry of a deeper
meditation. Both are composed, as is Milhaud's custom,
with the freest use of double harmonies. Even heard alone,
they sound pretty dissonant. Heard together, they make a
bumping and a jostling that is full of vigor but not at all
easy to analyze with the ear. Double harmonies become
triple and quadruple to produce a kind of sound that might
easily, in the hands of a less skilled polytonalist, have
turned into a colorless or muddy gray. It is unquestionably a
technical achievement on Milhaud's part to have kept so
complex a texture full of light and brightness to the ear.

The first movement of Quartet No. 14 is flowing in character, moderate in animation. That of No. 15, though the
tempo of execution is necessarily the same as that of the
other, is a light and lively scherzo. In simultaneous performance, the first of these movements tends, I think, to dominate the expression, the second to make commentary on it.
The harmony of the two pieces is not always, measure by
measure, the same harmony. Consequently, when played as
an octet, their sound is fresh.

The two middle movements are even more different.
That of No. 14 is a sort of lullaby, that of No. 15 a mystical
landscape or pastoral that hardly progresses at all, so intense is its inner dream life. Technically, No. 15 is a four-
part reversible canon that after completion turns round on
itself and proceeds crabwise back to its beginning. During
this latter operation No. 14 performs a thoroughly developed fugue. The effect of the whole, surprisingly, is one
of intense luminosity. I am inclined to consider this movement, in all of its forms, the most striking of the three.

The last movement is a jolly rondo in both Quartets; and
though no thematic material is ever passed from one to the
other, the expressive content in the two is roughly similar.

Hearing them together offers a new experience chiefly from
the huge fun involved in the way the eight parts elbow one
another around. The whole Octet, indeed, is fun to listen
to, fun to follow in score, fun to practice swimming around
in. Its ultimate value to repertory I have no prescience
about, but it seems clear even now that here is a unique
composition by a master and that its gustation can offer to
music lovers a kind of auditory delight not at all common
these days.

Milhaud's Sacred Service, also a double-barreled work,
though not one involving superposition, consists of settings
for cantor, chorus, and orchestra of both the Friday Evening and the Sabbath Morning Services from the Jewish liturgy. About half the musical matter is common to the two,
the rest separately composed. No melodies of traditional
origin are employed (save for one briefly), and no evocation of Near East orientalism is allowed to sentimentalize
or to localize a musical conception of universal applicability.
The style, though personal to Milhaud, is easily comprehensible anywhere. The service is occasionally bitonal in harmony, often a flowing counterpoint of two or three parts
freely juxtaposed, now and then noisily evocative of crowds
and of jostling alleluias. But for all its occasional brilliance,
the service is marked throughout by a tone of intimacy wholly
appropriate to the Jewish temple and deeply touching. Its
grandeur and its plainness impressed this listener as being
somehow related in spirit to those of Purcell and his Elizabethan forebears in their settings of Anglican worship
forms.

September 18, 1949

PIANO PLAYING AS MUSIC

¶ Mieczyslaw Horszowski played the piano last night in Town Hall, and that is news. This extraordinarily sensitive and powerful musician, though he lives no farther away than Philadelphia (where he teaches at the Curtis Institute), seldom crosses the Delaware for our benefit. When he does, it is a good day for us, for few pianists play with such beauty, such distinction, such unfailing seriousness of thought.

The first quality one notices in his work is the beauty of the sound that it makes, the genuinely musical character of all that strikes the ear. The second is grace, the airy way he treats a melody and its ornaments, throwing up the latter like spray round the coastal contours of the former, using two kinds of tone, one resonant and weighty, the other light as bubbles, the presence of both making depth, perspective, roundness.

Then little by little one grows aware of the man's strength, physical, emotional, intellectual. He does not let the composer down. He goes straight to the meaning of a piece and gives it to you. His ways are subtle but never devious, his readings at once elaborate and straightforward. For all his preoccupation with detail, which is great, he indulges no personal or outlandish fancy. The whole complex variation of tonal color, accent, and phraseology that goes to make up great piano playing is dominated by a grand line that sweeps through a piece, holds it firm and clear, makes it meaningful, keeps it a composition.

Two works were particularly happy under this breadth of conception last night; Beethoven's Sonata in B flat major, opus 106, a far from easy piece to keep in motion, and the Chopin B-flat minor Scherzo, which regularly falls apart in lesser hands. Everything played had shape, as well as beauty of sound, depth and clarity of communication.

Least communicative—and that through no fault of

Horszowski—was Villa-Lobos's *Homage to Chopin* a seasonal offering that seems little likely to survive the frost.
Surprisingly full of drama was Haydn's hackneyed Andante
(with variations) in F minor. Utterly welcome at this time,
when everybody rattles off Chopin in his own version of the
standard international touring style, was a certain Polish-
ness in the pianist's understanding of that composer. National origins here, instead of presenting a difficulty to sur-
mount, offered occasion for added picturesqueness of style,
especially in the mazurkas, without intruding on their
period elegance.

October 20, 1949

RELIGIOUS CORN

¶ Olivier Messiaen's *Three Short Liturgies of
the Divine Presence,* which received their first American
hearing last night under the direction of Leopold Stokowski, have been known to musicians here and in Europe for
some five years as their composer's most generally successful work in large form. By successful I mean both typical of
his procedures and having a direct audience appeal.

Somehow a good deal of that appeal got lost last night
in the broad spaces of Carnegie Hall. Though small of instrumentation, the piece needs to sound loud and full and
penetrating. Heard that way, its rhythmic and instrumental
variety holds immediate attention. Heard at a distance, its
trite melodic content and static structure dominate. There is
no question that this work is the product of a delicate ear
and an ingenious mind. Its aesthetic value has not seemed
entirely convincing to the purely musical world, though laymen have usually cast their vote in its favor. My own opinion is that its author is a case not unlike that of Scriabine.
That is to say that he is a skilled harmonist and orchestrator, full of theories and animated by no small afflatus, but
that there is a sugar in his product which keeps it from con-
gealing.

The two composers have an identical preoccupation with ecstasy and an identical inability to keep a piece moving along. Their religious inspiration has no energizing force; it is drug-like, pretty-pretty, hypnotic. In Messiaen's case all the paraphernalia of commercial glamour are mobilized to depict the soul in communion with God—a ladies' chorus, divided strings, piano, harp, celesta, vibraphone, Chinese cymbal, tamtam and of course an electronic instrument playing vibrato (in this case the Ondes Martenot). The sounds of such an ensemble, however intelligently composed, can not transport this listener much farther than the Hollywood cornfields. Placing them at the service of religion does not ennoble them; it merely reduces a pietistic conception of some grandeur to the level of the late Aimee Semple McPherson.

November 19, 1949

GLOOMY MASTERPIECE

¶ The star of last night's Philharmonic program was the late Alban Berg, author of the violin concerto played by Joseph Szigeti. Mr. Szigeti himself, who also played a Bach concerto (the G minor), and the other composers represented all fitted modestly into a background for this striking work. Only Dimitri Mitropoulos, who conducted, stuck out a bit. Apparently in one of his febrile moods, he kept getting between each work and its rendering, standing out against it, till closing the eyes, with all the risks of somnolence entailed, became the only escape. Even then one could not avoid an awareness that everything was being overplayed, overpushed, overdramatized, overexpressed. Everything, at least, but the Berg Concerto, itself so powerful, so lucid an introspection that even a tortured and twisting conductor could not overshadow its gloom.

German expressionism at its most intense and visceral is the work's aesthetic. The twelve-tone-row technique is the method beneath its coherence. Pure genius is the source of its strength. Somber of coloration, its sound is dominated ever by the soloist, the string section, and the horns. Based on a row that outlines a circle of fifths, the constant recurrence of this easily noticed progression brings some monotony to the texture. Expressive chiefly of basic pleasure-pain and tension-relief patterns (the reason for my calling its expression visceral), its few cerebral references (to a Viennese waltz in the first movement and to a harmonized Bach chorale in the last) stand out like broken memories in a delirium.

The piece is too continuous, of course, too consistent to represent mind-wandering. It is a work of art, not a madman's dream, though its gloom is almost too consistent to be real. Nevertheless, it would not be fair to suspect a piece clearly so inspired in musical detail of essential second-rateness. One must, I think, take it or leave it as a whole. Your reviewer has long been willing to take it, to enjoy its musical fancy, and to admire its coloristic intensities, without, however, at any time finding his emotions transported. Such an experience often accompanies the hearing of works removed from one's personal sensibilities by space and time. It does not prove a thing against a masterpiece.

Alban Berg is dead; he has joined the classic masters. One does not have to vote about his work, to love it or to hate it. It exists in perfection, for whatever use we may care to make of it. I suspect that the world will be making more and more use of this particular piece.

December 16, 1949

PERSONAL DISTINCTION

¶ Margaret Truman made her first appearance as a concert artist in New York at a short broadcast of semi-popular music that took place last night before an invited public in Carnegie Hall. She sang one brief aria from Puccini's *Gianni Schicchi* and two familiar Christmas carols. The rest of the program was of negligible interest to a reviewer.

Miss Truman herself presents surely a greater personal than musical distinction. One was prepared for the grace, warmth, and refinement of her presence; but this reporter, having seen only the grinning photographs that present-day publicity sanctions, was not at all prepared for the beauty of her face in repose. Few artists now appearing before the public have Miss Truman's physical advantages, and almost none other has her dignity.

Her vocal advantages are far less impressive. The voice is small in size and range and not at all beautiful. The lower notes of it do not project, and the upper ones are hollow. Nowhere is there any vibrancy or richness. She seems to sing carefully, is obliged to, indeed, by the poverty of her resources. Her English enunciation in one of the carols was remarkably clear. Of temperament, of the quality that enables a musician to bring music to life, she seems to have none at all. Her singing did not communicate last night as powerfully as her personality did. Only at the end of each piece, when she stopped singing and smiled and became the lovely Miss Truman again, did she make real contact with the guests of the evening.

December 21, 1949

1950

THE FIRST FIFTY YEARS

¶ The first decade and a half of this century were a glorious time for music. Creative originality has rarely run so high. In the flowering of modernism that took place during that time, the prize blooms were from three gardens. France gave us Debussy and Ravel, the impressionist technique of detailed musical description. Austria produced Schönberg and his school, the expressionist aesthetic, the use of atonal harmony as a psychological microscope. Russia's cultural ambitions also received international blessing through the ballet successes of Serge de Diaghilev, whose original offering was the nationalistic primitivism of Igor Stravinsky. When the first World War interrupted for four years artistic expansions in all forms, the garden of musical modernism was already laid out.

During the two decades that followed, the structure rose. The modern techniques got disseminated rapidly, in part through the aid of mechanical media such as the gramophone and the radio. They were popularized, vulgarized, generalized, taught in the schools. Neoclassicism was the official aesthetic everywhere. Originally a Romantic invention and tainted for the modernists by its associations with Mendelssohn and Brahms, this had been rediscovered by Debussy and the Impressionists, who used it not for faking the past, as the Romantics had done, but for evoking it, for making hand-colored picture-books out of it.

The atonal school during this time was not very successful. Its practitioners did not get the good teaching jobs, and their works rarely made the big concerts. The first upturn of their fortunes would seem to date from the late 1920's, when Alban Berg's opera *Wozzeck* began making the big opera houses, at least in Central Europe. The racial and political persecutions that began in Germany shortly after this retarded, I think, the rising movement, though they hastened its dissemination throughout the Western world. The Schönberg school at this time became a sort of musical underground. When the smoke of World War II blew away in 1945, that underground turned out to have been an aid in what we may call, to carry out a metaphor, the musical liberation of France.

Today atonalism is on the rise again, and the neoclassic school wanes. In the final edifice of our century's music, it seems probable now that atonal harmony, completed by the new researches in asymmetrical rhythm, will have a place in the upper structure comparable to that already assigned to it in the ground plan. Impressionism and expressionism, in other words, are approaching integration. It is not yet predictable whether that integration will be a European achievement, like their invention, because both movements have today a world-wide practice. The French, the Italians, the Americans, and the Argentines are equally adept at their handling.

The most remarkable changes in the musical scene that have become visible since World War II are the removal of the world center of music's distribution from Europe to America and the emergence of an American school of composition. In 1900 everything good in music came out of Europe—works, even of popular music, executants, styles, ideas, teachers, publications. Today we own the world market in light music and export as much of the rest as anybody. New York has not yet monopolized contemporary "serious" publication, but it determines the world price of executants and pedagogues. It has become the musical stock exchange, the center of stabilization for musical opinion. It establishes reputations and fees, crowns careers with the ultimate honor just as Paris did in 1900, as Vienna did in 1800, and as Venice had done a century before that.

The 1950 picture, by nations, reads something like this. Three countries produce new music abundantly in good quality—France, Russia and the United States. The Russian production, on account of political interference, is lacking in scope just now, in elbow room both techical and expressive. The other two countries produce in all the kinds and keep up experimental effort. They lead the world, in fact, for "advance" in all directions. Italy, Argentina and Chile are also among the advanced; but none of these countries is doing much in the vein of public-pleasing serious music. That is Russia's specialty and a little bit England's, with Benjamin Britten a local Shostakovitch. Neither country, however, produces this kind of work at as high a level of sincerity and refinement as France's Poulenc and Messiaen (the latter also an innovator).

Germany, Austria, Central Europe in general form a small part of 1950's musical scene. Greece, Spain and Mexico have the beginnings of a musical movement and an avid public; but their social institutions are unfavorable. Brazil and Canada are good public. The former has excellent composers but no school, no style, no source save indigenous folklore. The republic of Israel is music-mad from top to bottom. It offers, however, chiefly executants and a warm audience. Its composing time is far from ripe.

I do not think musical execution has improved in fifty years, but the number of skilled executants available today is much larger than it was. The number of symphony orchestras is also larger, hugely. The number of opera houses is smaller. Neither do I believe that musical pedagogy has improved at the top, though there is far more good instruction available in provincial centers than there used to be. Opera—its singing, its production, its composition—has declined spectacularly. So has ballet since Diaghilev's first five years in France, 1909–14. The films, which scarcely existed in 1900, have, on account of their higher cost and the consequent necessity of appealing to a very large public, made a virtually negligible contribution to the history of music.

Radio's services and those of the gramophone have been rather to distribute than to create. They have helped the spread of knowledge, hastened the using up of works, activated composition very little. In Europe, however, the state radio, aware of its cultural privileges, has by-passed the small audiences of metropolitan *élites* that used to serve as opinion formers for advanced movements. Broadcasters now speak straight to the nation. In America radio plays no such cultural rôle, being wholly in the hands of salesmen.

In conclusion, one may say that nothing has improved since 1900 save the size of the musical machine. The world situation of music has altered in every detail, and in most cases there has been a loss of distinction. Even the audience, though much larger and, in the provinces, better informed than it was, is less subtle, less intelligent, less sure of itself. As for Sunday articles, they are written nowadays by people like me. In the early years of this century the critical fraternity contained Ernest Newman, a better historian, and Claude Debussy, a better composer.

January 8, 1950

DRAMATIZING THE STRUCTURE

¶ Clifford Curzon, who played yesterday afternoon in the Town Hall, is far and away the most satisfactory interpreter I know of the pianoforte's Romantic repertory. Horowitz may play Liszt with a more diabolic incandescence, and anybody can fancy himself a specialist of Chopin. But Schubert and Schumann are composers whom almost nobody plays convincingly any more. Certainly no one brings them to life with quite the delicacy and the grandeur of Mr. Curzon.

He prefaced them yesterday afternoon with a Mozart sonata, as if to show us how his special treatment of the Romantics had been arrived at. If I understand correctly, he has approached them not so much with a romantic feeling about them as with a taste for classic rhythmic and dynamic layouts. His Mozart sonata (the G minor, K. 457) was treated as a symphony. Huge varieties of shortness in the articulation of notes, of color in the sound, of loudness levels sharply differentiated gave it the variety and the proportions of an orchestral score. Metrical steadiness without the imposition of any regular downbeat gave freedom to the Mozart stresses (as written), gave rhythmic perspective and objectivity to the musical shape. He exposed the work as a wide and solid building, made no effort to use it for personal meditation.

The Schubert Sonata in D, opus 53, a far wider and more personally conceived structure, he walked around in. He did not get lost in it or allow us to forget its plan, but he did take us with him to the windows and show us all its sweet and dreaming views of the Austrian countryside, some of them filled with dancing folk. The terraced dynamics and the abstention from downbeat pulsations, just as in the Mozart piece, kept the rendering impersonal at no loss to expressivity. On the contrary, indeed, the dramatization of it as a form, the scaling of its musical elements gave it evocative power as well as grandeur of proportion. And its enormous variety in the kinds of sound employed, its solid basses, and a dry clarity in the materials of its structural filling prevented monotony from becoming a concomitant of its vastness.

With the Schumann Fantasy in C, a work of intense personal lyricism and very little shape at all, Mr. Curzon's objective, orchestral approach turned out, surprisingly, to be just what was needed. It interfered at no point with eloquence or poetry. It merely held the piece together, gave it a color gamut, provided a solid setting and a rich frame for the passionate feelings that are its subject. Again the impersonal, the dramatic approach gave power to the work and breadth to its communication. By sacrificing all improvisatory, all minor-poetry attitudes, he gave us the piece as a large composition and as great poetry.

January 8, 1950

THE INTELLECTUAL AUDIENCE

¶ Anyone who attends musical and other artistic events eclectically must notice that certain of these bring out an audience thickly sprinkled with what are called "intellectuals" and the others do not. It is managements and box offices that call these people intellectuals; persons belonging to that group rarely use the term. They are a numerous body in New York, however, and can be counted on to patronize certain entertainments. Their word-of-mouth communication has an influence, moreover, on public opinion. Their favor does not necessarily provoke mass patronage, but it does bring to the box office a considerable number of their own kind, and it does give to any show or artist receiving it some free advertising. The intellectual audience in any large city is fairly numerous, well organized, and vocal.

This group, that grants or withholds its favor without respect to paid advertising and that launches its ukases with no apparent motivation, consists of people from many social conditions. Its binding force is the book. It is a reading audience. Its members may have a musical ear or an eye for visual art, and they may have neither. What they all have is some acquaintance with ideas. The intellectual world does not judge a work of art from the talent and skill embodied in it; only professionals judge that way. It seeks in art a clear connection with contemporary aesthetic and philosophic trends, as these are known through books and magazines. The intellectual audience is not a professional body; it is not a professors' conspiracy, either, nor a publishers' conspiracy. Neither is it quite a readers' anarchy. Though it has no visible organization, it forms its own opinions and awards its own prizes in the form of free advertising. It is a very difficult group to maneuver or to push around.

In New York it is a white-collar audience containing stenographers, saleswomen, union employees of all kinds, many persons from the comfortable city middle-aged middle class, and others from the suburban young parents. There are snappy dressers, too, men and women of thirty who follow the mode, and artists' wives from downtown who wear peasant blouses and do their own hair. Some are lawyers, doctors, novelists, painters, musicians, professors. Even the carriage trade is represented, and all the age levels above twenty-five. A great variety of costume is always present, of faces and figures with character in them. Many persons of known professional distinction give it seasoning and tone.

The presence of such an audience at a musical event is

no result of paid advertising or of standard publicity. Its representation is small at the Metropolitan Opera, the Philharmonic, and the concerts of the N. B. C. Symphony Orchestra, though it will go to all these places for special works. Dimitri Mitropoulos, for example, drew a brilliant audience for his recent performance at the Philharmonic of Strauss's *Elektra*. The smaller symphonic ensembles, the City Center opera, the New Friends of Music, and the League of Composers bring out lots of intellectuals. So do certain ballet performances and the spectacles of Martha Graham, though not, on the whole, for musical reasons. The International Society for Contemporary Music, the Composers' Forum, concerts and opera productions at the Juilliard School and at Columbia University, and certain recitalists are definitely favored. Wanda Landowska, harpsichord players in general, Jennie Tourel, Maggie Teyte, Martial Singher, Gold and Fizdale, sometimes Josef Szigeti are all notable for the interest they offer to persons of high mental attainments.

The conductors chiefly favored by this group are Reiner, Monteux, and Ansermet. The intellectuals often come in a body to hear them. They come individually from time to time to hear Toscanini, Koussevitzky, Bernstein. They have shown no consistent interest in Rodzinski, Mitropoulos, Munch, Ormandy, or in recent years Stokowski. Beecham's audience appeal, for all his high cultural equipment, remains strictly musical, though his recordings are collected by many persons from other professions.

Flagstad, too, is a purely musical phenomenon; and so is Horowitz. The latter, indeed, no longer pleases wholly even the musical world, if I read his public right. One sees fewer and fewer known musicians at his recitals, more and more a public clearly not familiar with standard piano repertory. The music world attends *en masse* Landowska, Schnabel, and Curzon. The last two, however, have never made full contact with the world called intellectual, the world of verbalized ideas and general aesthetic awareness.

Management's aim is to mobilize the ticket-buying and propaganda power of this world without alienating the mass public. The latter is respectful of intellectual opinion, which it learns about through the magazines of women's wear, but resistant to the physical presence of the intellectual audience. The varieties of fancy dress and interesting faces, the pride of opinion expressed in overheard conversations, the clannish behavior of these strange and often monstrous personalities are profoundly shocking to simpler people. Their behavior expresses both a freedom of thought and a degree of ostentation that are not available to the standardized consumer. Much as he would like to enjoy everything that is of good report, he is really most comfortable among his own kind listening to Marian Anderson. This is why the Philharmonic and the Metropolitan managements make little or no play for the intellectual trade and discourage efforts in that direction from the musical wing. They have a mass public of sorts already, do not need intellectual promotion. They seem to fear, moreover, that the intellectual influence, bearing always toward the left in program-making, may keep away more paying customers than it brings in.

Beneath all of management's dealings with the intellectual group lie two assumptions. One is that intellectuals like novelty and modernity. The other is that the mass public dislikes both. I think the first is true. I doubt the second. I am more inclined to believe, from long acquaintance with all sorts of musical publics, that it is management which dislikes novelty and everything else that interferes with standardization. I suspect that management's design is toward conditioning the mass public to believe that it dislikes novelty. Some success has already been achieved in this direction. If intellectual opinion has any carrying power beyond the centers of its origins, there is a job to be done, a war to be fought across the nation. The intellectuals' own survival, even, may depend on winning it. For unless these bright ones carry some weight in the forming of everybody's opinions and tastes, they are a useless body and can be by-passed by any power-group that wants to use art for its own ends.

January 15, 1950

STAR DUST AND SPUN STEEL

¶ Anton Webern's Symphony for Chamber Orchestra, the novelty of last night's Philharmonic concert in Carnegie Hall, was "advanced" music when first played here twenty years ago; and it still is. For all the world-wide spread of the twelve-tone technique that has taken place since then, it would be hard to find today five living adepts of it whose writing is so firm and so sophisticated as Webern's was. The audience effect of this work attested also to its vitality. Not only were repeated bows taken by Dimitri Mitropoulos, there was actually booing in the hall, a phenomenon almost unknown at the Philharmonic.

The piece itself offends, as it delights, by its delicacy, transparency, and concentration. The first movement, for all its canonic rigor, is something of an ultimate in pulverization—star dust at the service of sentiment. Each instrument plays just one note, at most two; then another carries on the theme. The theme itself is a row of tones isolated from one another by scale skips. The texture is thin, too. One note at a time, just occasionally two or three, is the rule of its instrumental utterance. And yet the piece has a melodic and an expressive consistency. It is clearly about something and under no temptation to fidget. Its form, I may add, is roughly that of a binary, or Scarlatti-type sonata; and its rhythmic pulse, save for a few retards in the second movement, is steady.

This movement (there are only two) is a set of variations on the work's whole twelve-tone row, first stated completely at this point. Rhythm is broken up into asymmetrical fragments. The melodic pulverization is less fine, however, than that of the first movement. Occasionally an instrument will articulate as many as eight or ten notes at a stretch. Some of these are even repeated notes. Metrical fragmentation has taken the place of melodic. The sonorous texture becomes even thinner at the end than anything one has heard previously. A tiny sprinkle of sounds; two widely spaced ones on the harp; and vaporization is complete.

There is every reason to believe the Philharmonic's reading of this tiny but ever so tough work to have been correct. Musicians following the score could question only the size, here and there, of some minute crescendo. The rendering was clear, clean, tonally agreeable, and expressive. Expressive of exactly what, would be difficult to say, as it is of any work. Nevertheless, consistency and self-containment, ever the signs of expressive concentration, were present to the ear, just as they are to the eye reading the score. Once again there was cause to be grateful to Mr. Mitropoulos for his assiduity toward neglected distinction and for his enormous loyalty to the text of a work rare, complex, and in every way difficult.

January 27, 1950

ATONALITY TODAY

¶ Every century, as Lou Harrison once pointed out, has its chromatic and its diatonic style. Atonality is our chromatic style. Indeed now that we have it in so highly evolved a form as twelve-tone composition, it seems to be the ultimate condition toward which chromatic harmony has always aspired. That condition is one of extreme fluidity, and its attraction for the pioneer-minded is that of the open sea. Classical scales and harmonic relations, in this conception, constitute reefs and treacherous currents and are hence to be avoided. Arnold Schönberg's twelve-tone-row syntax is a device for avoiding them. It is not the only one in existence, but it is the easiest to handle. Its simplicity and general practicability have caused its adoption by such a large majority among atonal writers that it may now be considered, I think, as the official, the orthodox method of com-

posing in tones without composing in tonalities. Other methods, however excellent or even superior, constitute devia-
ations from standard practice.

That practice is common to most of the mature music of
atonality's Big Three—Schönberg, Berg, and Webern. Now
two of these three are dead, and the other is seventy-five
years old. Their favorite syntactical device, moreover, now
available to all, is widely employed. Hence there is every
reason to consider the epoch of advance that they represent
to be a closed one. Certainly those of their musical progeny
who work by identical or nearly identical methods bear the
mark of the epigonous. Others, however, who accept the
twelve-tone row and its canonic application as their basic
method are not satisfied with this as a complete method.
For them it is satisfactory only as a way of arranging tones
with regard to their pitch. They wish a method equally con-
venient for ordering their length. Present-day efforts by
twelve-tone composers to build a rhythmic technique comparable to their tonal system have initiated a second period
in atonal research and composition.

If the first problem in atonality is to avoid familiar tonal
relations, its second is surely to avoid familiar metrical ones.
Complete renewal of the musical language and not a mere
abandonment of its decayed portions, still less a spicing up
of spoiled material, let us remember, is the aim of the atonal
group. Also we must not forget that the Big Three, with
slight exceptions in the work of Webern, made virtually no
effort at originality in the rhythmic direction. Here they remained conservative, though less by principle, I should
think, than from the fact that all advance needs to proceed
in an orderly fashion, one thing at a time. The rhythmic
achievements that now form the backlog of the second-
period atonalists, the knowledge they start from, came almost wholly from outside the atonal tradition.

These are many. The exactly written-out rubato of
Mahler, the fragmented developments of Debussy, studies
of Chinese, Javanese, East Indian, and other exotic musical systems, acquaintance with American ragtime and jazz,
the epoch-marking Danse Sacrale from Stravinsky's *Rite
of Spring* with its long, rhythmic phrases developed from
tiny cells or rhythmic motifs, the experiments of Varése
and others in pure percussion, the introduction into Western

music by Messiaen of a Hindu device for varying a meter's
minimum note-length—all have prepared the way for the
new atonalists. Since the new rhythmic efforts have not yet
brought about any standardization of rhythmic procedures,
the field of rhythm is still full of sectarian dispute. Anybody
with a new trick can imagine himself as in possession of the
golden key. So far, however, there is no golden key. The
period is a lively one, and all doors are still open, even to
tonal writers.

The ideal of nonmetrical rhythm, like that of atonality,
is asymmetry. Pierre Boulez states it as *d'éviter la carrure,*
that is to say, the avoidance of everything square. This
means that metrical repeating patterns are out and that
even the rhythmic canon by inversion, the hardest to hear
of all rhythmic imitations, requires violation of its exactitude by means of the Hindu added dot. There are problems
of rhythmic construction, too, that require solution, though
conservative twelve-tone composers like René Leibowitz
consider them subsidiary to tonal relations and not soluble
independently. John Cage employs a numerical ratio in any
piece between the phrase, the period, and the whole, the
phrase occupying a time-measure which is the square root
of the whole time and the periods occupying times propor-
tional to those of the different rhythmic motifs within the
phrase. This procedure, though it allows for asymmetry
within the phrase and period, produces a tight symmetry in
the whole composition and is not therefore quite the rendering of spontaneous emotion that the European atonalists
hope to achieve.

The expressive aim of the atonalists has always been a
romantic one, the depiction and provocation of intense,
introverted feelings. Berg's music, in this respect, is closely
related to that of Hugo Wolf and Mahler. Schönberg oscillates in his feeling allegiance between Wagner and Brahms.
Both go into a waltz at the slightest pretext or even with
none. Webern is more personal, more fastidious in his expression, as he is more original, more reflective in his ap-
plications of the twelve-tone technique. In both respects, and
also through his pulverization of sound into a kind of luminous dust, he is an Austrian cousin of Debussy. He it is, in
fact, and not Schönberg or Berg, whom the French atonalists tend most to revere and to stem from. He it is, too, who

will probably remain most loved among the founding fathers when the atonal world shall have got round to doing over the art of instrumentation. But that will not be for another decade, at least. Just now a new rule of rhythm is the instrument lacking for traveling the trackless ocean of atonality, where the brave adventurer has, by the very nature of his renunciation, no harmony to guide him. The twelve-tone-row technique is a radar for avoiding shoreline hazards, but it has not yet taken any composer beyond the sight of Europe's historic monument. For that a motor source will have to be found.

February 5, 1950

A POULENC CANTATA

¶ *Figure Humaine* (or *The Face of Man*) is a poem of 160 lines by Paul Eluard celebrating clandestine French resistance to the German conquerors. It is plain in meaning, lilting of meter, and both fanciful and familiar as to imagery. Irresistibly touching in sentiment, it is also a work of no mean literary sophistication, a devotional and patriotic text. Francis Poulenc's music, no less straightforward in melodious contours and dramatic accents, is its match for both simplicity and inventive workmanship. The former quality keeps the verbal prosody clear without phraseological distortions or undue extension of vowel sounds. The latter underlies a loose but ingenious linear construction in twelve-part counterpoint for unaccompanied double chorus. It has also added many delicate refinements to the harmony.

This harmony, like so much contemporary French writing, has an acoustical freedom that is more easily rendered by keyed instruments than by voices. Its progression from relatively consonant chords to highly dissonant ones and back again is not at all systematic. There is an accidental quality in the sound of it that resembles the seeming messi-

ness of a great deal of the best French draughtsmanship.
It looks careless, but it reads with utter clarity. This kind of
vocal music is not easy to sing, but it can be sung. And when
well sung, it has charm and a great freshness. *Figure Humaine* is a sweet, vigorous and lovely work; and the Schola
Cantorum, led by Hugh Ross, gave it to us just that way.

February 18, 1950

ON THE WHOLE, DERIVATIVE

¶ Leonard Bernstein's *The Age of Anxiety,* for
pianoforte and orchestra, conducted by himself in a Philharmonic concert with Lukas Foss at the solo instrument,
is a meditation on the poem of that title by W. H. Auden.
Scored with a sure and ingenious hand, its chief interest for
this observer lay in its orchestral timbres and their disposi-
tion. These are dominated, colored everywhere by the percussion choir and related sonorities of harp, piano, plucked
strings. The textures are transparent, easy to hear, picturesque, expressive. The rhythm is lively, too, in the animated
passages. Otherwise the work does not hold inevitably the
musical attention. Its form is improvisatory, its melodic content casual, its harmony stiff, its counterpuntal tension weak.
The piano writing is excellent; the figuration shines; the
whole sounds out beautifully; but the expressive content
seems to me (and I have read the score as well as heard it)
banal, derivative in feeling.

A lugubrious beginning and some desultory variations
on no theme are replaced half way through the piece by an
active section for the solo instrument and percussion in the
jazz style known as "Harlem party piano." This makes a
most brilliant effect in the Gershwin taste. Then comes a
finale out of Strauss's *Death and Transfiguration.* Over
the whole floats an intangible shadow of Mahler. As a study
in orchestration the work has interest for musicians. As a
ballet it may support choreographic fantasy. As a concert

piece it is lacking in the chief elements, or so it appears to me, that make for survival in repertory.

February 24, 1950

MUSICAL HORSE SHOW

¶ Victor de Sabata, if one may believe last night's concert of the Philharmonic, which he conducted, is what used to be called in horsy circles a great whip. Certainly he rode the orchestra hard and well, made it play soft and slow, loud and fast, stop dead in its tracks, change gaits, do everything but spell. He himself spelled out the scores for us clearly, unmistakably. If occasionally, as in the Berlioz *Symphonie Fantastique,* he seemed doubtful of our ability to catch the meaning, or, as in the Morton Gould Spirituals, to have missed it himself, there is no question but that he knew their notes backwards. Surely he is a skilled technician of the *haute école.*

His program, consisting entirely of showpieces, offered as its only rarity a *Preludio Magico* by Vito Frazzi, an Italian professor now in his sixties. This work, composed in the impressionistic taste and suavely orchestrated, is a civilized piece. It lacks a striking thematic content; but it is agreeable to listen to, with its spicy string-and-wind mixtures of sounds, its clean rhetoric and accomplished workmanship. It would have been even more a pleasure had the conductor not overplayed his brasses in the climax.

He overplayed everything, in fact, to such a degree that what with huge accents, imperceptible pianissimos, interminable pauses, and static slow passages, everything lost cohesion, came out void of line or progress. This kind of musical eagerness-to-hit-us-between-the-eyes could not wholly conceal from us the familiar thought content of Rossini and Berlioz, though it did occasionally bury the sound of the full string body under a brassy canopy. But Mr. de Sabata's incessant tampering with tempos caused him to

miss every trick in playing with Mr. Gould's seemingly simple but far from unsophisticated American metrics. This
composer's Spirituals for String Choir and Orchestra, over-
dressed as it is orchestrally and harmonically, has its
own rhythmic life, supports no imposition of any merely
theatrical animation. Itself all trickiness, the addition of
jugglery from another school plain breaks its back.

Thankfully, deadline considerations made joining Wagner's Valkyries in their Ride inadvisable for the reviewer.
One had been carried along by that time on quite enough
battle horses. One had admired the skill of the rider but lost
confidence in his sense of destination. He had put the orchestra through its paces over and over but not convinced
one of a single thing. So much musical skill combined with
so little musical taste would surely be of more brilliant effect in the theater than in the concert hall.

                                        March 3, 1950

A KNACK FOR LANDSCAPE

¶ Victor de Sabata, conducting the Philharmonic
last night, revealed an aspect of his mind that had not been
in evidence on the previous occasion of this reporter's attendance. I refer to his subtlety in the handling of landscape music.

Dvořák's *New World Symphony* received from Mr. de
Sabata a reading thoroughly live and fresh. Making no effort to confound this with the music of oratory and personal passion, as so many do, he gave it to us very simply
as the work of a European landscape painter charmed by
American subjects. He even restrained the lyric outpouring of woodwind soloists, kept the whole a picture. It was
rich in color, vibrant, full of light in the climaxes, everywhere atmospheric, pastoral, an outdoor piece. Hearing so
hackneyed a work sound fresh and new was a pleasure, because the work is intrinsically tender and imaginative. It

kept its distance, spoke in poetry, penetrated the spirit in spite of familiarity.

The technical methods by which this effect was achieved were the whole gamut of orchestral fine adjustments and balances that mark the work of skilled conductors. But the poetic idea behind the interpretation was proof of other qualities in Mr. de Sabata, of an intellectual distinction, a refined musical imagination far more in keeping with his European repute than any reading had indicated at his first concert in this city.

March 24, 1950

UNIQUE AND UNFORGETTABLE

¶ Arturo Toscanini directed in concert performance last Saturday afternoon the first half of Verdi's *Falstaff*. Next Saturday at the same hour—6:30 E.S.T.—the other half will be given. This reporter would like to add to the above bare announcement his feeling that those who miss hearing these performances (or their broadcast) will have passed over a unique and probably irreplaceable musical experience.

It is not that this opera does not here and there get given. It is simply that Verdi's great farce, for divers and complex reasons, almost never comes off in the theater. As instrumental music, as vocal music, and as pantomime, it is powerful like a bulldozer, elaborate like an electronic calculator, and yet simple and broad in its humor like a comic strip. It is the busiest opera in the world and the most exigent as to timing. It asks the singers to behave like clowns while singing with animation and precision. What they sing, moreover, is vocally difficult without being, in terms of audience effect, grateful. It is a conductor's opera, a virtuoso piece for the musical director. One might almost imagine it as having been especially designed for Mr. Toscanini.

The N. B. C. opera broadcasts in general are conceived as starring-machines for this conductor. Timing, the trajectory of an overall musical line comes first, orchestral refinement second, vocal charm last in their hierarchy of values. As correctives to a music world that more commonly cherishes these values in reverse order the N. B. C. operas have been tonic. They have also given us an opportunity to hear the most admired opera conductor of our century in the repertory that first brought him fame. Save for these broadcasts, Toscanini has not directed opera here in many years and seems determined not ever again to work in the American theater.

Falstaff, moreover, among all the works of standard repertory, is the one that profits most by the Toscanini treatment. No other conductor, in my experience, has ever made it sound so light and fast, filed its delicacies and its accents to so sharp an edge. He gives us, too, along with the music of it, an evocation of the stage, an essence of the theater, a concentration of comedy speeds and farce timings, a zest, an outline incomparable. His reading is a lesson to all who think that the theatrical circumstance profits by coarseness in texture or of appeal. Its steely elegance, like that of the score itself, is a far more powerful mover of audiences than any concession to vulgarity could possibly be.

The vocal execution on Saturday, though less brilliant, on the whole, than the orchestral, was clean and generally agreeable. This observation, I hasten to add, applies strictly to the center balcony seats of Studio 8-H. What the singers sounded like elsewhere in that tricky hall, or when heard through engineering adjustments, I cannot report. Listeners to these broadcasts have given highly divergent testimonies about vocal effectiveness.

April 3, 1950

GLORIOUS LOUDNESS

¶ Gustav Mahler's Eighth Symphony, as directed last night by Leopold Stokowski, was a glorious experience to one who had not heard it before. Its sculpture of vast tonal masses at the end of each of the two movements was handled by the conductor in so noble a manner that the sound achieved monumentality while remaining musical. The effect was unquestionably grand.

The whole work, indeed, has grandeur and humility. In its eighty minutes of execution time no touch of the meretricious mars its devotional concentration on the meaning of its texts. These are two, the Latin hymn *Veni Creator Spiritus* and the last scene (in German) from Goethe's *Faust*. The symphony holds together as a musical piece and expresses its author's deepest religious impulses, as well as his cultural convictions. A master workman, he gave to this work his utmost of seriousness and inspiration. It is a statue to his memory, if not his finest music.

Both as music and as a monument it is weakened by its melodic material, which is banal. Also by its harmony, which, though structurally adequate, is timid, unoriginal, unexpressive. The orchestral writing is ingenious, as always, though lacking somewhat in color for so long a piece; and the handling of the huge choral masses is both firm and delicate. The solo parts are lovely, too, as vocal writing. What the work lacks is melodic point, sharpness of outline. Weak thematic material, developed beyond its natural strength, becomes repetitive, loses communicative power. The last five minutes contain a real tune. The rest, for all the thought and skill involved in its composition, is pretty amorphous.

Some of this amorphousness comes from the composer's basic aesthetic assumption. This assumption, derived from the finale of Beethoven's Ninth Symphony, seems to be that it is possible to make an artistically perfect work of music that will combine in equal proportions the symphony and the oratorio (or cantata). No such work has yet been produced. Even the Beethoven movement has never been universally voted by musicians to be successful. I do not think Mahler's Eighth is successful, either. It is not, in my estimate of it, a pure crystal. It is ambitious and sincere, and it has character. But its grandeur lies in certain skillful handlings and in the conception. It does not permeate the piece, which is soft inside.

One is grateful to Mr. Stokowski and to his assembled forces for letting us hear it. Also for giving it to us with such great care for musical decorum. Such handsome loudnesses as took place in both perorations one does not encounter often.

April 7, 1950

KURT WEILL

¶ Kurt Weill, who died last Monday at the age of fifty, was a composer who will be missed. Nothing he touched came out banal. Everything he wrote became in one way or another historic. He was probably the most original single workman in the whole musical theater, internationally considered, during the last quarter century.

His originality consisted in an ability to handle all the forms of the musical theater with freedom, to make them expressive, to build structures with them that serve a story and sustain a play. He was not a natural melodist like Richard Rodgers or George Gershwin, though he turned out some memorable tunes. Nor was he a master of thematic development, though he could hold a long scene together impeccably. He was an architect, a master of musico-dramatic design, whose structures, built for function and solidity, constitute a repertory of models that have not only served well their original purpose but also had wide influence as examples of procedure.

Weill came to the light musical theater, for which most of his American works were conceived, from a classical training (he was the pupil of Humperdinck and of Busoni) and long experience of the artistic, the experimental theater. His literary collaborators were consistently writers of distinction. Georg Kaiser, Ivan Goll, Bertolt Brecht, Arnold Sundgaard, and Maxwell Anderson were among them. Brecht was the librettist of the epoch-marking works of his German period—*Der Jasager, Der Dreigroschenoper* and *Aufstieg und Fall der Stadt Mahagonny*. Also of a ballet with words, composed in Paris, *Les Sept Péchés Capitaux*, played in England as *Anna-Anna*.

These works have transformed the German opera. Their simplicity of style and flexibility of form have given, indeed, to present-day Germany its only progressive movement in music. Without them the work of Boris Blacher and Karl Orff would be inconceivable. Without their example also we would not have had in America Marc Blitzstein's powerful *The Cradle Will Rock* and *No for an Answer*. Whether Weill's American works will carry as far as his German ones I cannot say. They lack the mordant and touching humanity of Brecht's poetry. They also lack a certain acidity in the musical characterization that gave cutting edge to Weill's musical style when he worked in the German language.

Nevertheless, they are important to history. His last musical play, *Lost in the Stars*, for all that it lacks the melodic appeal of *Mahagonny* and even of *Lady in the Dark*, is a masterpiece of musical application to dramatic narrative; and its score, composed for twelve players, is Weill's finest work of orchestral craft. His so-called "folk-opera," *Down in the Valley*, is not without strength either. Easy to perform and dramatically perfect, it speaks an American musical dialect that Americans can accept. Its artfulness is so concealed that the whole comes off as naturally as a song by Stephen Foster, though it lasts a good half hour.

Weill was the last of our local light theater musicians to orchestrate his own scores and the last to have full mastery of composition. He could make music move in and out of a play with no effect of shock. He could write a ballet, a song, a complex finale with equal ease. (A successful Broadway composer once asked me, "What is a finale?")

These skills may turn up again in our light theater, but for
the present they are gone. Or they may be replaced by the
ability of Menotti, Blitzstein, and other classically trained
composers to hold public attention through constructed
tragic music dramas. Just at present the American musical
theater is rising in power. But its lighter wing has lost in
Kurt Weill a workman who might have bridged for us the
gap, as he did in Germany, between grand opera and the
singspiel. The loss to music and to the theater is real. Both
will go on, and so will Weill's influence. But his output of
new models—and every new work was a new model, a new
shape, a new solution of dramatic problems—will not continue. Music has lost a creative mind and a master's hand.

                                              April 9, 1950

FOR TEACHING AND FOR THE MIND

¶ The Composers' Forum gave us last Saturday
night in the McMillin Theater of Columbia University one
of its more entertaining contrasts. Music by Julia Smith
and Lou Harrison made up the program. The easy-going
jollity of the former set off perfectly the quiet poetry and
intense auditory expertness of the latter without placing
either at an unnecessary disadvantage.

Miss Smith had mobilized two pianists, three singers, two
conductors (including herself) and an orchestra of some
forty players. She produced with these forces extended selections from a fairy-tale opera, a five-piece twelve-tone piano suite, and a symphony on American folk airs. All were
marked by animation, clear expressive intent and a preoccupation with the school trade.

Mr. Harrison, with a quartet of string players, a solo cellist, a harpist, and three works of the most unassuming di-
mensions, produced memorable music. His Suite for Cello
and Harp is, I think, not really a suite, but rather a group
of four pieces united technically by their use of scales as

thematic material. The whole is delicate of sound, thoroughly alive rhythmically and melodically, evocative of some tranquil and vibrant scene. Few composers now alive can fascinate the ear, as Mr. Harrison does, with simple procedures. At once plain and sophisticated, his music reflects a concentration on music's basic elements that is as expressive, surprisingly, as it is intrinsically interesting.

His Suite for Strings, No. 2, consists of two movements in secundal diatonic counterpoint framing a chromatic duet for violin and viola. All three are canonic in structure. The whole work, lyrically conceived, is a meditation on Sebastian Bach's contrapuntal style-sources. It could not be more delightful to listen to, more musical, more graciously songful. Like the cello and harp suite, it communicates a beatitude as of Elysian Fields.

The evening's final delight (preceding the forum discussion) was a pair of Pastorals for strings that imitate the sound of a vielle, or medieval hurdy-gurdy. Sophisticated, picturesque, and exquisitely melodious, these pieces use Mr. Harrison's elaborate skill in composition toward the service of an utterly simple expressive purpose. And they, too, transport us to a dream world where all is music, really music, really interesting musically, really sensitive and elaborate and lovely and not about anything in the world but how beautiful the materials of music can be when handled with tenderness and with intelligence.

April 17, 1950

TOO MANY LANGUAGES

¶ The kind of program that vocalists, particularly the younger ones, feel obliged to offer in their recitals is a formula that has long seemed to this reviewer ill suited to advancing either musical or technical excellence. Its fault can be stated in three words—*too many languages*. Not long ago, speaking before a meeting of voice teachers, he reproached them with responsibility for its continued observance and asked why so stupid a violation of all sense, pedagogical and artistic, had ever become established in custom. They answered in unanimity, "We do not know, and we do not approve it." Nevertheless, every aspiring singer in our midst feels obliged to offer in recital an Italian, a German, a French, and an English group of songs.

Naturally, they sing all these languages badly, even, in many cases, English. Often, having merely learned their foreign songs phonetically, they have only an approximate idea of the texts' meaning. The communication of poetry under such circumstances is quite impossible. It is not easy, either, to sing agreeably when the full content of the composer's feelings, as embodied in verbal values, is not clear to the interpreter. Moreover, nobody demands this monkey-like behavior. The public does not like it; the press does not like it; and managements care only for what the audience and the press like. Singing teachers, who are responsible for the tradition and its preservation, all know it is opposed to good artistic standards. And yet they hesitate to do away with it. Several of them have suggested that since music schools in America require their vocal majors to sing in three languages besides English, if a degree is to be awarded, they themselves are the victims of a circumstance. But it is the singing teachers who determine, finally, degree requirements for singers. Surely they could demand revision of a faulty curriculum.

Such a curriculum is faulty because it is not a preparation for professional life. Few professional vocalists of the first class ever sing four languages in public. The best usually sing two, their own and one other. Knowing one foreign language gives depth and discrimination to an artist's handling of his own. Helen Traubel, by specializing in German repertory, has had a great career. Mary Garden did the same with French, Jan Peerce and Richard Tucker with Italian. A language means something in the mouths of these artists. They know its feel, its style, its nature, its relation to life and to music. A few singers have the gift of tongues; but for every Jennie Tourel in the world, there are a dozen Lotte Lehmanns, Pinzas, and Carusos, for whom a new language has to be approached slowly, circumspectly, once in a lifetime.

A young singer needs to know, for studio purposes, the Italian vowels, because they are pure. He needs also to sing (and translation will do) enough French, German, and Italian songs to acquire an acquaintance with these musical literatures. Then he should choose one for his own. He should adopt a country, speak its language, read its books, live among its people, eat its food. In this way he may learn to interpret its music with understanding. As he advances in professional life, travels, and reads, he may find it useful to pick up a smattering of other languages, including Spanish and Russian. But he does not have to sing them, and he should not sing them until he feels thoroughly at home with their sound and with their sense. An occasional compliment to local audiences will be enough exception to prove the value of this rule.

All this time he should be singing his own language, learning it, loving it, making its sounds behave, and making the farthest ticket-holder hear what he says. This is the way good singers work, and it is the right way. Any other is injurious and silly. Requiring young vocalists to sing four languages is like asking string players to be equally proficient on the violin, the viola, and the cello. Such acrobatics should be discouraged.

If any person reading this column knows any reason why the four-language formula should be further tolerated by teachers or by concert-goers, I hope he will correct my impatience. In my view, and the voice teachers met in convention did seem to agree with me, it is unmusical, unintelligent, inartistic, and pedagogically unsound.

April 23, 1950

JOAN OF ARC TO MUSIC

¶ Norman Dello Joio's lyric drama *The Triumph of Joan* was recently produced at Sarah Lawrence College. The music of the spectacle seems to me more vigorous than its dramatic composition. The latter contains no element of plot or character not familiar to contemporary audiences, and the tension of the narrative is low. The device of presenting this through memories recalled during the Maid's imprisonment gives the story a static quality, and the fact that all but one of the episodes (her acceptance as a military leader by the Dauphin) show her as unsuccessful in some immediate objective gives a depressive tone to the recital. The Maid's own meditations, moreover, which bind the remembered scenes together, consist largely of self-pity. The whole libretto lacks animation and lift.

The music is more inspired. This is at its most distinguished in the set-pieces. The coronation choruses, a lonesome soldier's song about a girl, Bishop Cauchon's prayer before the courtroom scene, the music accompanying Joan's march to the stake—all these have imagination, character, force. The recitative passages are vocally a bit wooden and instrumentally static. Their melismatic line and note-heavy harmonies do not easily move along. The purely instrumental passage are all delicious. They evoke the late medieval world with poignancy and grandeur. So does the choral writing. But the solo voice more often than not, and particularly when it is that of Joan herself, seems to deprive the composer of that boldness and freedom that are elsewhere his. The background of the story he has described with abundance of fancy. The saint, one suspects, he found a slight bore. Certainly her monotonous insistence, in this text, on how she is always right and everybody else is wrong might well provoke impatience.

The recitative line is derived from Gregorian chant. It moved diatonically for the most part and in skips of the minor third. Larger skips, which give such force to dramatic declamation, are few in number. The vocal line, as a result, is more atmospheric than communicative. The references to fourteenth-century musical styles that give to the ballet and to the church scenes power and picturesqueness have a weakening effect on the solo passages. Here they depersonalize the text, give it a ritual tone, retard its movement, diminish the possibilities of characterization. A spectacle that is full of fine music comes off, as a result, a bit heavily for audience comfort. Normally, recitative should speed the play and set-pieces hold it back where emotion needs time

for expansion. In *The Triumph of Joan* it is the set-pieces
that give whatever movement there is. The verbal text is
somewhat at fault in this matter, but I think the musical
text is too. Both harmonically and melodically it is a little
stiff in dealing with persons. The music of the soldier and
that of Cauchon are exceptions and welcome. The work, indeed, is full of handsome music; but as a theater piece it
lacks variety of pace.

May 11, 1950

A SPECIALTY OF OUR CITY

¶ Gershwin Night at the Stadium, complete with
Alexander Smallens and Oscar Levant, was attended last
night by some twenty-three thousand persons. This estimate
by the box-office people, who ought to know, is larger by
three thousand than the seating capacity of the place. Neigh-
boring rooftops were not untenanted either. Whether the
music's sound was also audible in the passing airplanes I cannot say. We heard theirs, as usual.

We also heard a great deal of lovely music. For George
Gershwin was a maker of tunes. There is life in them and
grace and a wonderful sweet tenderness. They are sewn together no matter how in the symphonic works and orchestrated by no matter whom. And still they speak and are
moving. They are music, our music, everybody's music.
Their annual performance, moreover, is one of the New
York's specialties.

Not that other cities do not have their annual Gershwin
Night, and often with Oscar Levant playing the *Rhapsody
in Blue* and the Piano Concerto. But the New York population (you can't call 23,000 people by any lesser noun) has
an especial love for this composer. He was one of them. And
Alexander Smallens, also a New Yorker, has an especial
knack for playing him.

No other conductor reads Gershwin with quite the ease

that Smallens does, or half the seriousness. The commercial leaders play this music without depth, and the symphonic conductors play it mostly without feeling. Smallens allows its melodic line to speak in the vernacular without vulgarity and without pomposity. He actually gives you real Gershwin and a real symphonic sound at the same time. The achievement is unique, delightful and utterly distinguished.

Nothing of the above applies to the Concerto in F, as played last night. Not that either straightforward Smallens or the impeccable Oscar was lacking in observance of the musical amenities. It is simply a piece so poorly conceived, with its overweening Tchaikovskian intent, and so weakly inspired, with its derivative themes and mechanical developments, that it rarely sails before the wind. It asks, moreover, on every orchestral page, for an oratorical rendering, though without offering matter for oratory. There is no choice but to give it the "wow" treatment, to simulate in performance the Tchaikovsky-like passions and climaxes that the composer has simulated in his composition.

So treated last night, the Concerto in F came out as a nervous piece and very loud. Levant produced huge sounds, and not at all ugly ones, from the pianoforte. Smallens drew massive sonorities, and occasionally quite ugly ones, from the orchestra. Every phrase, every turn, every grace-note was blown up to Holy Scripture authority and stentorian volume. The result was as portentous as a radio commercial, and about as convincing.

July 7, 1950

TASTE SURVEY

¶ The Indianapolis Symphony Orchestra has recently tabulated the results of a musical preference poll carried out last spring among season-ticket holders. The survey was conducted by Dr. Dennison Nash, of Washington University, St. Louis, Missouri, and seems to have observed all the devices of fairness required by the statistical profession. Answers were sought to the following questions:

1. What types of music does the Indianapolis audience prefer?

2. What specific composers?

3. Does the symphony audience approve of Dr. Sevitzky's [the conductor's] policy of fostering American music?

4. What is its attitude toward "modern" music?

5. Do men and women differ in their music tastes?

6. What types of music are preferred by listeners of different ages?

The answers to questions 1 and 2 will astonish no one. By dividing the symphonic repertory into five style-periods—classic (meaning before Beethoven), classic-romantic (meaning Beethoven), romantic (centering around Brahms and Tchaikovsky), modern (including Debussy, Sibelius and Gershwin) and extreme modern—the reult obtained was that symphony subscribers prefer the romantic style. This taste tends to diminish, however, after forty in favor of the classic-romantic style, which is that of Beethoven. Music written before Beethoven has its highest preference among the very young and the very old. Those in middle life care least for it. Ten composers are preferred by the whole audience in the following order—Beethoven, Tchaikovsky, Brahms, Bach, Mozart, Wagner, Debussy, Chopin, Sibelius, and Haydn.

American music and its performance are resoundingly encouraged by the poll. One-fourth of the audience would accept as much as half the playing-time from this category. Another fourth would limit American works to five per cent of the repertory. Forty-five per cent of the listeners would settle for a ten per cent Americanism in the programs, which has long been the proportion observed in Indianapolis. No particular American composer seems to be favored. It is American work in general that the audience enjoys, very much as Italian and French and Russian audiences have long been known to respond favorably to a musical diet rich in home-grown products.

This preference contradicts the conviction of many orchestral managements that American music is not popular. The truth is probably that it is not comparable with name soloists for attracting single-concert ticket purchasers to the box office, but that it is highly approved by season subscribers. Boston's experience corroborates this judgment. Its sold-out subscription houses have never raised any serious complaints against American music. Indeed, these have ever taken pride in the high interest and toleration they have been able to show toward the large amounts of American music long characteristic of Boston programs.

Modernism also comes in for an accolade. The Indianapolis audience (and this surprises even me) expresses a willingness to hear as much "extreme modern" music as it does of Beethoven, its favorite composer. Beethoven's present percentage of the playing time is probably around twelve. Thirty-one per cent of the subscribers would even accept as much as half the programs devoted to modern music.

Sex, you may be pleased to learn, plays no role in musical taste. Men and women at all ages, according to Dr. Nash's survey, appear to like exactly the same works, authors and styles.

Age, on the other hand, is a huge determinant. Those really receptive to modernism are almost all under forty and mostly under thirty. These ages want lots of modern music, including all the "extreme," or "dissonant" types; and they constitute an audience for this by no means negligible in numbers. Our orchestras should really in order to serve the whole public, play two series of programs, one for the elderly and another for those under forty. Their present efforts to please everybody at once derive from a paucity of rehearsal time, no doubt; but I am sure that somewhere behind them is an assumption that mature taste is the best taste and that it should dominate. The present survey has surely rendered culture a service in calling attention to the fact that those under forty have tastes of their own, that these are not the same as those of their elders and that there will be a long period after forty when they will be older persons themselves and can listen to all the Beethoven there is.

Another service of this survey (although a shocking one) is contained in a study of the influence of regular symphony-concert attendance on anybody's taste. For the first year romantic preferences run high, and so do those for modern composers. After one year of attendance, however, there is a sharp drop in both tastes and a strong move toward the

classic-romantic, or Beethoven-dominated repertory. After
that there is little change save for a slowly increasing interest in the classic, or pre-Beethoven, masters and a decreasing
toleration of the contemporary. This evolution runs parallel, of course, to the changes in taste that accompany maturity. The striking data for education are those that show the
active influence of regular orchestra-concert attendance on
any subscriber's taste to be limited to the first year. That
is the time when the whole educational benefit is operated.
Afterwards very little takes place. Dr. Nash concludes his
report with the statement that "an increasing length of concert attendance is associated with a narrower and narrower
preference range, i.e., a greater preference for fewer [and
fewer] composers."

September 17, 1950

GOLDEN THROAT

¶ Victoria de los Angeles, singing last night in Carnegie Hall, won the votes of a large audience with her very
first piece. By the last one, these had turned into a general
acclaim. Success was hers and by no narrow margin. Speaking purely as a musician, your reviewer finds himself wholly
in accord with that success. The voice is one of rare natural
beauty, the schooling impeccable, the artistry first class.
Miss de los Angeles is a real singer. Make no mistake about
it.

She is also a young singer. Her interpretations of German
lieder are still a little mannered. And she witholds her high
notes. She takes them commandingly but she diminishes
usually before they have given their full delight. Only a few
times during the evening did she omit to tease the searcher
after effects of obvious vocalism. Indeed, so careful was she
not to insist on bravura utterance that it is a little hard to
know just how high and how loud she can sing. A perfect
vowel projection, whether in pianissimo or in forte singing,

filled the hall at all times with vibrancy, beauty, warmth of
tone. Nothing was ever forced and nothing failed to carry.
She is a true lyric soprano, does not need to falcon.

Her most striking gifts are a natural cantilena, or sense of
melody, and a complete ease in florid passages. She tossed
these in the Handel aria as lightly and as accurately as a pianist might play them in a piece by Mozart or Chopin. Indeed, an unhesitating precision about pitches marked all
her work. She sang not only beautifully but true. Her
kind of ear and training are rare these days, and one could
not be more grateful to be reminded that they have not been
lost to music. To find them guiding a voice that is sweet,
young, and fresh is more than surprising. Here is vocal delight unique in our time. I must say that this delight, being
attained wholly through vowel vocalism, was not accompanied by much clarity of enunciation. At least, not in the
Italian and German works, plus one English piece, that
made up more than half her program. In Spanish she really
pronounced. Consonants clicked like castanets, and the
bright Spanish vowels glowed like copper and shining brass.
Perhaps she does not have the gift of tongues. But she does
relish her own. And whatever the tongue, she has a golden
throat.

October 25, 1950

MILHAUD COMPARED

¶ Dimitri Mitropoulos, conducting the Philharmonic-Symphony Orchestra, the Westminster Choir, seven
vocal soloists, and Madeleine Milhaud, who spoke, gave in
Carnegie Hall last night Darius Milhaud's music composed
for Paul Claudel's French translation of Choephoroi (The
Libation-Bearers) by Aeschylus.

The story of this work, recited, is plain, its music broadly
conceived. Its climax, a passage for speaking voice and
shouting chorus accompanied only by percussion, is as ter-

rifying on a platform as on a stage. Rarely, indeed, in any
presentation does the fury of Aeschylus communicate itself
so powerfully as in this French version.

The work invites comparison with Strauss's *Elektra*. The
Austrian composer's music-drama is all of a piece, violent
and sensual. Also, it is a musical structure throughout. Milhaud's tragedy is statuesque, monumental, objective, sculp-
tured in granite till the speaking begins. Here tonal music
ends; words and rhythms take over; and the dramatic impact becomes direct, immediate. Then there is music again,
and at the end a brief return to speech and percussion.
Whatever disunity may be felt by some spectators between
the differing dramatic tensions of the speech passages and
the singing passages is probably compensated by the composer's obvious determination to give you a Greek tragedy
with all the ritualistic tension and all the horror of mood
that the text implies. He has not written an opera, nor attempted one. He has brought an ancient work of poetry to
life. The achievement is as impressive as *The Libation-
Bearers* itself is. *Les Choéphores* probes the mind, plows
deep in the feelings, shakes foundations. It has the power
of great poetry. *Elektra,* for all its musical concentration,
does not quite, in your reporter's experience of it, have
that.

November 17, 1950

1951

ISRAEL IN AMERICA

¶ The Israel Philharmonic Orchestra, conducted by Serge Koussevitzky, played its second New York concert last Saturday night in Carnegie Hall. Its first had taken place last Monday night at the Hotel Waldorf-Astoria, following a $100-a-plate dinner. A second Carnegie Hall concert was conducted last night by Leonard Bernstein.

Mr. Koussevitzky's program, for reasons impenetrable by this reviewer, turned out to be a Russian program. One brief compliment to Israel itself preceded the Slavic devotions. that compliment was a slow movement, entitled *Psalm,* from the Symphony No. 1 by Ben-Haim, an Israel citizen of German birth formerly named Paul Frankenburger. This is a lyrical work, near-Eastern by its melodic allegiance to chants from the Hebrew liturgy but wholly West-European in its climactic structure. The central climax, indeed, of this sustained pastoral movement is an outpouring of song that carries high conviction. This listener would have preferred hearing the rest of the symphony to sitting through Prokofiev's Fifth, which followed it. Tchaikovsky's Fourth, which concluded the program, also told us more about Mr. Koussevitzky's hand with familiar repertory than about the musical temper of Israel.

The orchestra has a string body of unusual skill and power. Wind solos were played with grace, but nowhere in the wind ensemble was there brightness, brilliance, or any fullness of sound comparable to that of the strings. These played with the impeccable flexibility and with the unanimity of sound that mark the string playing of great orchestras. Volume, delicacy, finesse, and all the varieties of handsome tone are available to them. If the strings have any fault, that would lie in a tendency of the first violins to dominate all the other sections and to render thus some of the balances a little top-heavy.

Hearing Koussevitzky (or Bernstein, either) can be a pleasure, even when the pieces played have little to offer that is fresh to the ear. But bringing a whole orchestra from Tel-Aviv just to offer these artists in familiar repertory is surely carrying perfume to Paris. Has Israel no confidence in its own conductors? Or in its own music? Or in America's thirst for that which is new as well as of good report?

Israel is news, and Israel is popular. Its orchestra, moreover, has the major element of a fine orchestra. It must have also a musical orientation, as any region or country does. When a French or British or Italian orchestra is heard in New York, its programs and its playing reflect musical attitudes different from ours. That is its chief contribution. The Israel Philharmonic, as here presented, offers nothing of the kind. Even its admirable strings, for all their warmth and sweetness, are not very different from those of our own best orchestras. When we are given at the same time two of our own best conductors playing their own best pieces, we learn nothing about Israel save that its orchestra is a link in the international guest-conducting chain.

January 15, 1951

SUPERCILIOUS AND ARTY

¶ *Cav* and *Pag,* done over from scratch (and it was about time), drew a demonstrative audience to the Metropolitan Opera House last night. The conductor, Alberto Erede, did not play up much their Italianate vividness, their urgency. He seemed rather to be seeking in them grace and transparency, for all the world as if they were oratorios by Saint-Saëns.

Neither had the mounters and stagers of these new productions made much effort to keep that essential Italian-ness. Horace Armistead's set for *Cavalleria Rusticana* was a Sicilian village of today, and the singers all wore the kind of clothes modern Sicilians wear. But their gestures were straight out of Victorian English melodrama. Laundry on the line hit a trivial note. A statue of the Madonna, carried in an Easter procession, gave a false one. A large chorus walked into church and never came out again. There was a great deal of running around and crossing of bridges. Indeed, the whole tragic story came out slightly humorous, as if it were being observed by tourists. A supercilious note was present in the scenery, the costumes, and the staging; and as a result this ever so plain and touching drama wavered, from being poked fun at, between a tasteless joke and plain bathos.

Pagliacci, though more tasteful in conception, was even farther removed from Italian melodrama. It seemed to be taking place in the ruins of a recently bombed building, though the costumes were of no period recognizable to this reporter. Stylizations derived from contemporary ballet were also present in Max Leavitt's stage direction. The spectacle had color and fancy, but it was more an artistic evocation of *Pagliacci* than a direct rendering. If the music had not been there to reassure one that the piece, for all its universality of appeal, is utterly and completely Italian, one could have easily imagined it as taking place in the ruins of Berlin among the homeless members of some modern-dance troupe.

Modernizing operas like these is not a rewarding effort. They do not lend themselves to indirection, to added poetry, or to intellectual embellishment. All evening I was reminded of the French chef who in serving a New England boiled dinner had carved the beets like roses and turned turnips into lilies. *Cav* and *Pag* are spaghetti alla Napolitana. They can be done poorly or well. But their classical presentation cannot be altered to advantage.

January 18, 1951

FLAGSTAD AND REINER

¶ Standing applause and lengthy cheers (nineteen curtain calls) were the reward of Kirsten Flagstad last night after the first act of Wagner's *Tristran und Isolde* at the Metropolitan Opera House. Absent from that stage for ten years, she has returned with her vocal powers intact and her dramatic projection more imperious than ever. In a house that has long given the Wagner operas better, on the whole, than anything else, Miss Flagstad still set the place afire. Vocally vast and impeccable, and dramatically as convincing as this statuesque work allows, she held the attention and drew the gratitude of even so seasoned an anti-Wagnerian as this reporter. She also, and quite literally, held the center of the stage throughout the first act by working in a circle not much larger than twelve feet across, right in the middle down front.

This maneuver kept Blanche Thebom, her Brangaene, constantly up stage or off side. As a result, though she sang richly she could not match for volume the sounds that Miss Flagstad projected from downstage center. In the second act, however, she got that spot herself for a short moment and rang out handsomely. Ramon Vinay, as Tristan, came nearer being a match for the soprano.

Besides Miss Flagstad, the other star of the evening was Fritz Reiner. Transparency in the sound, flexibility and firmness in the beat, meaning and incandescence in the whole made the work what it really is, a symphonic poem with vocal *obbligato*. Mr. Reiner was respectful of that *obbligato* and gave it acoustical elbow room. But his orchestra, where all the real characterization and the continuity take place in this piece, was the source of musical line and substance. Save for the delights of the Flagstad voice, which are huge, the musical pleasure of the evening lay for this listener in an instrumental reading by Fritz Reiner that was no less impeccable than Flagstad's vocal one and far more intricate musically. That, after all, is the nature of the composition.

January 23, 1951

REACTIONARY CRITIC

¶ Eduard Hanslick, a Bohemian born in 1825 in Prague, came to Vienna in 1846 as a law student. He had already received a musical education, had met Schumann and Wagner, corresponded with Berlioz, and written music criticism. While preparing his doctorate in law, which he took in 1849, he continued to write music criticism, for most of which he was not paid. His first Viennese contribution was an analysis of Wagner's *Tannheuser*, published by the *Wiener Musikzeitung* in eleven installments. Hanslick was at this time a deep admirer of Wagner's genius and music. Till his death he continued to admire the genius; but from *Lohengrin* on, which he reviewed from the Vienna production of 1858, he did not approve the music.

Meanwhile, by easy stages, he had given up law (or rather the civil service career for which it had prepared him) and become a salaried reviewer of music in the daily press. From 1855 to 1864 he wrote for *Die Presse* and from 1864 to his retirement in 1895 for *Die Neue Freie Presse*. From 1861 he was Extraordinary Professor of the History and Aesthetics of Music at the University of Vienna. In the middle 1850's he had written a book on *Beauty in Music*. Thereafter, at the university and in print, he posed as world-expert and final authority on the subject. A classical education and a facile pen enabled him to defend his assumed position with ingenuity and wit. His determination to uphold the cause of classicism in music involved him in systematic denial of the artistic validity of Liszt, Berlioz, Wagner, Bruckner, Hugo Wolf, Verdi, and Richard Strauss. He barely tolerated Tchaikovsky and Dvořák, ignored wholly the rising movement in Russia and France. Henselt, Lachner, and Johann

Strauss he always mentioned benevolently. The dead—
Schumann, Schubert, Mendelssohn, Weber, Beethoven, Mozart, Handel, Bach—he treated with respect. The only living
composer of class that he deigned to defend was Brahms.
His banner Hanslick carried aloft as the banner of counter-
revolution till his own death in 1904.

Except for his early brochure on *Beauty in Music* Hanslick's work has not till now been available in English. Henry
Pleasants III, formerly music critic of the *Philadelphia Evening Bulletin*, has recently edited and translated admirably
a selection of Hanslick's reviews, complete with notes and
biographical preface, under the title of *Vienna's Golden
Years of Music: 1850–1900* (Simon and Schuster, N. Y.,
1950, 31 illustrations, 341 pp., $3.75). One is grateful for
even this brief acquaintance with the man Wagner pilloried
as Beckmesser in *Die Meistersinger*. One is pleased to learn
that he was not, as Wagner gave him to us, a bad composer,
a lecher, and a boor, but a skilled belles-lettrist and a master
reporter. One is charmed, too, by his literary culture, his
musical penetration and smooth easy man-of-the-world
ways. Reading him lightly, one might almost take him for
the perfect music critic, if perfection is conceivable in so
invidious a genre.

But no, three times no! Once because there was no real
warmth in the man. Twice because the truth was not in him.
And thrice because he never stuck his neck out.

To those who may think a twenty-five-year war with
Richard Wagner enough bravery to ask of any man, I
recall that Wagner did not live in Vienna and that Hanslick's readers, who did, were middle-aged, well-to-do, bourgeois. He wrote for a conservative paper. His readers asked
no better than to see a man of novel genius reduced to the
level of an incompetent entertainer. Critics writing all over
Europe on conservative papers—Chorley in London, Fé-
tis in Paris, not to speak of the German reviewers—had
given Wagner the same treatment; and in 1856 *The New
York Times* had denied to *Lohengrin* "a dozen bars that
could be called real melody." Anybody knows it is easier to
defend the public against novelty in art than it is to defend an original artist against the public's comfortable conservatism.

Actually there is not a point in Hanlick's attacks on Wagner that had not been made before. Berlioz, Meyerbeer, Rossini, and the young Bizet had long since put their finger on the inequalities in his talent. These were common knowledge in music circles. Time has not altered, moreover, their reality. Wagner's contemporaries, including Hanslick, denied him no excellence for which he is still cherished. Nor were even his closest friends, save a few, unaware of his imperfections. Even Hanslick's main theme about how for all its beauties this music is not "the music of the future," not a beginning but a glorious and dangerous dead end, that too was a familiar idea. That is what the famous Wagner "case" has always been about, and Hanslick did not invent it. As a matter of fact, his reviews spent far more space unmasking Wagner's literary weaknesses, which he was capable of doing quite well, than analyzing the musical structure which he could not always follow, even with a score. He knew that Wagner could orchestrate, paint tremendous musical landscape scenes, and prosodize in German; but he had not the musical technique to understand Wagner's complex chromatic harmony and asymetrical rhythm. So he complained about the "lack of melody," made fun of the librettos, and refuted the advertising. Compared with Nietzsche on Wagner, he was thoroughly superficial.

To protect himself against the possible charge of not patronizing home industry, Hanslick had sagaciously picked on Brahms as his "side" in the Brahms-Wagner war. He was sold this position by a surgeon named Billroth, who was a close friend of Brahms, and who, according to Dr. Max Graf, Hanslick's successor on the *Neue Freie Presse,* furnished the critic with analyses of Brahms's works. Hanslick cared little for Brahms; what he really liked was waltzes, light airs, and Offenbach. But Brahms was useful to him, and he to Brahms. The pair of them, if stories of the time and Bruckner's letters are to be believed, carried on a relentless intrigue, aided by two other critics who were also friends of Brahms, to prevent Bruckner's rise in popularity from endangering the carefully constructed celebrity of the older man. Brahms's ironic gesture of gratitude was the dedication to Hanslick of his *Love Waltzes.* To Billroth, who understood depth and complexity, he dedicated two of his grander quartets.

Hanslick could describe a performer to perfection—Liszt, von Bülow, Clara Schumann, Lilli Lehmann, Adelina Patti. He tells you what they looked like, the kind of sounds they made, the nature of their technique, and the character of their temperaments. His musical analysis of any composition was elementary and timid, reads like a quoted program note. Also he was a dirty fighter. He was a dirty fighter because his extraordinary intellectual and literary powers were used solely to convince people that he alone was right and all the living composers, except for a few minor melodists and for Brahms, were wrong. A mere reviewer, a belleslettrist, a reporter, and a professor of Music Appreciation (the first, I believe), he pitted himself in his own column against the creative forces of the age. Anywhere but in his own column, or surrounded by its glamour in a Viennese salon, he was just another irate customer complaining about modern music. In his column, and in private intrigues, he was formidable.

Having gone through my two provable indictments in reverse order, I am now back to the first, which is a matter of feeling. For me there is no warmth in the man, no juice, no passion for music. Sensuality, grace, some sparkle, a gift for ridicule, and a colossal vanity shine through his selected reviews. So does the insincerity of his pretended love for Brahms's music. He states it over and over, but he cannot make it glow. What comes through everything is an ever-so-careful conformism to the bourgeois tastes of his time, which, I am very sorry to say, are still the tastes of bourgeois Vienna at home and abroad. But he did not invent even these. He invented nothing but the style and attitude of the modern newspaper review. That, with all its false profundity and absurd pretensions to "sound" judgment, he will probably have to defend at everybody's Last Judgment. He was second-rate clean through, and he had no heart. Max Graf thinks highly of Hanslick's literary gift. "His essays and articles," says Dr. Graf in his excellent book, *Critic and Composer*, "have been published in twelve volumes, in which his intelligence, charm, clarity, and wit are preserved, like drugs and poisons in cut-glass vessels on the shelves of a pharmacy." "Venom from con-

tented rattlesnakes" was the late Percy Hammond's term for
similar critical contributions.

February 4, 1951

FROM THE HEART

¶ Leonard Bernstein, conducting the Philharmonic-
Symphony Orchestra last night in Carnegie Hall gave us
Charles Ives's Second Symphony, a work composed in
the late 1890s but never before performed in its entirety.
This is a five-movement rhapsodic meditation on American
hymns of the nineteenth century, American dance ditties,
and football songs. It is essentially a landscape piece with
people in it.

The first movement gives us the lush Connecticut valley
through a musical technique derived from the Bach chorale-
preludes. It is sustained, songful, organ-like, graciously contrapuntal, predominantly a piece for strings, with at the
end a quotation from "Columbia, the Gem of the Ocean"
to make the note of faith specific.

From here on, song and dance material dominate. There
is an ecstatic slow movement based on the hymns "Bringing in the Sheaves" and "Beulah Land." There are two animated movements involving dance music and the Yale
"Boola Boola" song, with a restatement in the last one of
the initial landscape material and an apotheosis in which
"Columbia, the Gem of the Ocean" sails out complete over a
busy texture containing dances and gay songs in contradictory keys. A Fourth of July picnic might well be the scene
here evoked. Orchestrally, harmonically, and melodically
the symphony is both noble and plain. It speaks of American life with love and humor and faith. It is unquestionably
an authentic work of art, both as structure and as communication.

February 23, 1951

SUCCESSFUL MODERNISM

¶ *Wozzeck*, the atonal opera that brought fame and financial security to its composer Alban Berg way back in the middle twenties, brought a full house to Carnegie Hall last night. Played and sung as a concert piece by the Philharmonic-Symphony Orchestra and a cast of admirable vocalists under the direction of Dimitri Mitropoulos, it attracted an audience of music lovers, opera lovers, atonality fans, and German literature devotees that should reduce to folly anybody's idea that modern music is not box-office. The occasion also disproved for all time, I imagine, any belief that anybody might have retained that Alban's Berg's music is in any way recondite.

The music of this opera and its plot, as told by the music, are easier to follow than *Madama Butterfly*. The tragic story about a soldier who kills his girl is plain and deeply touching. The music that points this up, blows it up, one might say, to epic pathos, is constantly on the job, alert, abundant, imaginative, and far easier to follow in its meaning than Wagner. The vocal line imitates, in large exaggeration, the cadences of speech. The orchestral composition gives in detail both the setting of every scene and its full emotional implications. Persons and locales that the composer disapproves are caricatured in broad strokes. Those for which he feels tenderness are caressed with a love no one could mistake. The whole is a theater piece that has never failed to move its hearers and that should certainly be in the repertory of our resident opera troupes.

There is charm in the music, moreover. For those unaccustomed to off-key harmonic textures it is a little surprising right off. But after fifteen minutes all sounds normal. The waltzes, the military references, the devotional music, the satire, the eerie landscapes, the scene of soldiers snoring, all the picturesque paraphernalia of it come forward in their off-center tonal garb even more sharply than if they were wrapped up in classroom chords and counterpoints. The dissonant interval-syntax actually serves the communication as no other idiom could do. It floodlights the meaning of everything until all that is left of the high dissonance content is a thin veil of dazzle, like that from a neon or fluorescent bulb. It does not get in the way. On the contrary, it becomes early in the opera an element of pleasure all the more welcome from its services to comprehensibility.

April 13, 1951

PRETENTIOUS AND UNCLEAR

¶ Busoni's *Arlecchino* (*The Harlequin*) was the novelty of last night's Philharmonic program. Though the Busoni comic opera is subtitled a "theatrical capriccio," your informant has long found himself resistant to the idea that there is either fun or funniness in this work. At this point his objections end. It is skillfully composed, intellectually and musically sophisticated to the last degree, a major effort of a major musician. Also, its execution, though a bit loud throughout, was a triumph of loving care on the part of Dimitri Mitropoulos, who conducted.

Reviewing this opera from a Berlin performance in 1946, your correspondent found that its music contained everything but "plain feeling." Having recently read it in score and last night heard it again, he remains of that opinion. It represents a hopeless effort to combine Italian animation with the heaviest sort of German satire and an equally impossible desire to eliminate schmalz from the German operatic style without renovating the late Romantic and early Modernist harmonic vocabulary of Germany, in which that schmalz is firmly embedded. The composer had, besides, no talent at all for writing tunes. The result is a mess all the more pitiful from its author's accomplished musi-

cianship, high motivation, and, let's say it, overweaning
ambition.

October 12, 1951

ESSENTIALLY FRIVOLOUS

¶ Jascha Heifetz, playing a violin recital last night
in Carnegie Hall, proved himself still a king among violin
operators. In the opinion of many this king can do no
wrong. Certainly the dictum holds if you define as "right"
whatever the king does. But if you admit in advance that
he might, just might be guilty of something, then you do
not have to look very far to find something for him to be
guilty of.

What Heifetz is guilty of (always supposing, just supposing, that he might be less than perfect) has always been the
same thing, a certain lightness of mind commonly known
as bad taste. Technically, he plays the violin better than
anybody else living. He makes unusually pretty sounds, too.
It was the appropriateness of the kind of sounds he used
last night to the pieces he used them on that could be called
in question as taste. So was the choice of pieces that he
played, since the Strauss Sonata and the Bruch C-minor
Concerto, entertaining as they are for demonstrating instrumental mastery, are not really serious repertory for a
serious artist of his fame to play in a New York recital. The
Schubert Sonatina No. 3 might have been, had he played it
more graciously, made one feel less than he did that one
had somehow got on the *Queen Mary* to go to Brooklyn.

The faults of taste that occur within an interpretation
by Heifetz, almost any interpretation, have to do with irregularities in the application of right-arm weight. His bow-
stroke is likely to be so emphatic that it produces, even on
an up-bow in a soft passage, accents that are no proper
part of the music's line. He makes crescendos, too, in the
middle of notes that have no rhetorical importance, simply,

one imagines, because he finds it interesting to vary the
tonal weight. As a result, his melodic line, for all its perfection of pitch and sweetness of sound, has no continuing
emotional tension and makes no sustained musical sense.
Not, at any rate, in the way that I understand emotional
tension and musical sense.

It is this teasing way of treating musical sounds and musical structures that led me long ago to consider Mr. Heifetz
as essentially a frivolous artist, in spite of his incomparable
mastery of violinistic operations. There is no weakness in
him; he can do anything he wants to do with the instrument. There is merely, for the listener, a vast banality about
what he seems to want, or at any rate to be satisfied with,
as musical communication. I am not inclined, even, to grant
him the word "communication." "Effects," rather, are what
he produces for me.

November 22, 1951

SPOKESMAN FOR THE MET

¶ During an intermission of the Metropolitan Opera broadcast of December 15 the General Manager of that
esteemed institution said, "Now you might say that only
by trying out these new operas, even if they are not too exciting, can an opera house hope to find the great work that
no doubt one day will appear. This frankly is a moot question."

Will you say that again, please, Mr. Bing? What is it you
consider a moot question? If I read you right (and I have
before me a copy of the manuscript you spoke from), you
consider that there are other methods of adding great works
to the opera repertory than by putting new operas into
production. I have never heard of any such method. Reading scores will, of course, enable your musical directors to
eliminate many works. But it cannot pick out the "great"
ones of any decade or epoch. That is done by the public.

And if there is any way the public can be led to consecrate with its favor the greatness of a *Carmen* or *Lohengrin* or *Aïda* or *Figaro* without some opera house having actually produced that work first, then I am sure we should all like to know what it is.

Perhaps Mr. Bing means that the Metropolitan does not need to give world premieres, that it can let the subsidized European houses do our try-outs for us. By skimming thus the cream off the world's production we might indeed procure a quite good contemporary repertory at small risk. But such a policy does not seem to be this manager's idea. In referring to Alban Berg's *Wozzeck,* a famous opera now thirty years old and consecrated by some quite impressive box-offices, he admits it to be an "extremely important opera" that "has been played in many European opera houses." But he also remarks that it has become part of the standard repertory in very few theaters.

Just a minute, Mr. Bing. You know perfectly well that it was removed from the German and Austrian theaters in the 1930s both for its political content and for its composer's religion. You also know that both its political content and its musical style place it out of bounds today everywhere behind the Iron Curtain. Also, that last summer's production in Salzburg, which you mention as selling less well than Verdi's *Otello* (hardly surprising) had to run against the opposition of the powerful Austrian clergy, determined to remove it from the repertory on theological grounds. You know, too, that Switzerland and Italy have seen the work revived since the war and that Paris will see the Vienna Opera Company's production next spring. Nobody ever suggested to you that *Wozzeck* would be a draw at the Metropolitan like *Cav* and *Pag*, though it would probably do as well in any season as *Parsifal*. It has merely been pointed out that if the Met is looking for twentieth-century works of unquestioned musical "importance" and tested appeal, *Wozzeck* is up near the top of the list. And if the Met is afraid of attempts at political or religious censorship, then I am ashamed of it.

Mr. Bing later in his speech denied acquaintance with any recommendable modern works and suggested "that anybody should send [him] a list of those new works performed in recent years that live to see a second season." I

should not care to offer such a list myself lest it be thought
I were proposing that the Met mount all the operas on it.
But just for fun I might mention Prokofiev's *The Love of
Three Oranges* from the City Center, Poulenc's *Les Ma-
melles de Tirésias* from the Paris Opéra-Comique, Milhaud's *Bolivar* from the Paris Opéra, Britten's *Peter Grimes*,
not so long ago of the Met itself. All these have seen second
seasons in one house, two of them even more. As for modern operas that have survived in the repertory of many
houses and even in some cases enjoyed runs in the commercial theater, there are Hindemith's *Mathis der Maler* and
the late operas by Richard Strauss, all of them current in
Germany and Switzerland these days, Menotti's *The Medium* and *The Consul,* worldwide successes both, and Gershwin's beloved *Porgy and Bess.*

Opera writing is, by actual count, not at all a dead art.
And neither, by actual count, is opera production. It may
be at the Met but not in the world picture. And when Mr.
Bing states it as "a highly regrettable fact that so few new
operas of real musical consequence are being offered" one
wonders what he means by "real musical consequence."
But one does not wonder long. He means and I think I read
his thoughts correctly, pure box-office. He "regrets" that
Beethoven "receives greater support" than Schönberg
from symphony audiences, though why he should regret it
I do not know. He ought to be happy that our symphony
audiences have access to Schönberg as well as to Beethoven. We opera audiences get no such heady diet.

But the slip about Beethoven is minor. Here is the evidence on which I accuse him of a box-office view of music.
He says: "No one in the world of the theater puts on any
show unless he is convinced that it will either be a 'hit success' or at least attract sufficient public acclaim to justify
the effort. I cannot see why this sound principle, which is
commonly accepted in the theater, should become a criminal offense when applied to opera."

Some member of the Metropolitan board should explain
to the General Manager that the Metropolitan Opera Association is not engaged in show business, that it is a non-
profit society vowed to the advancement of musical art
and of public taste, that this purpose has been recognized
by the State of New York as justifying an exemption from

real estate taxation and recently by the Federal government
as justifying exemption from the amusements tax. Gifts to
the Metropolitan, moreover, can be deducted from anybody's taxable income up to fifteen per cent. Such privileges
are not granted to the amusement trades.

It is not a "criminal offense" to play so conservative a
repertory as Mr. Bing has laid out for this season, and nobody ever said it was. It is merely a neglect of duty. I have
long found his program regrettable; and I found his radio
speech of two weeks back acceptable only for the frankness
of his admissions, shocking as they were. He admitted his
lack of faith both in the music of his own time and in the
public's aspirations regarding this. He does not believe, apparently, that good operas are being written now or are
likely to be written in the near future; and he considers that
it would be a waste of the Met's money to produce the contemporary stuff that *is* written. He does not think the Met
audience wants to hear new things anyway, says he did not
get one letter all last year asking for them.

All the same, he plans to take a flyer next season with
the new Stravinsky opera. "We shall then see what the public reaction will be," he added. Does this mean that he is
giving contemporary music just one chance to compete
with *Carmen*? Really, one has heard double-talk before
from Metropolitan spokesmen but nothing quite so cynical
as this.

December 30, 1951

1952

A GREAT TEMPERAMENT

¶ Guido Cantelli, conducting the Philharmonic-Symphony Orchestra last night in Carnegie Hall, risked everything, program-wise, and lost nothing. Indeed, if applause is the measure, his winnings were large. Even Monteverdi, which is far from a sure thing, payed off. On Beethoven, at the end of the concert, he really cashed in.

A young man making his first bow before a great orchestra risks a great deal by filling half his program with arrangements of music by seventeenth-century organists. He risks even more—all, in fact—by essaying Beethoven's Fifth Symphony, the hardest piece in the repertory with which to show originality or to compete with the interpretations of older men. Mr. Cantelli held his audience firmly, triumphantly in both halves. Here is obviously a great music-making temperament.

The four organ pieces by Frescobaldi, in Ghedini's instrumentation, were noble and rigid, evocative of a primitive instrument and of pre-Bach church services. The Monteverdi *Magnificat,* orchestrated also by Ghedini, seemed even more archaic in its contrapuntal textures, though its lengthy pedal-points (or long held notes against which other voices move) were really a modernism in 1610. They gave architecture to a piece, and poignant expressivity could take place against them. Equally a modernism then (and still surprising) is the intense emotional expression which this composer achieved. The emotional resources of the time both for composing and for receiving music must have been vast. Certainly Monteverdi's music, like that of Schütz in Germany, is vibrant with feelings more powerful than anything that preceded or followed it by nearly a century. And its rendering of verbal texts is heartbreakingly meaningful.

Mr. Cantelli, though a protégé of Toscanini, gave us no streamlined Beethoven. He gave us a young man's Beethoven, all passion and lyricism. His reading was not at all times orchestrally elegant. Once or twice roughnesses were heard that were certainly not his intention. But they mattered little beside the grace of his line, the warmth of his assertions. We are used to a colder violence in this piece and a more calculated showmanship. Mr. Cantelli was not occupied with either. He made it sing; he made it dance; he even made it rejoice. Let us be thankful for the presence among us of so pure a spirit.

January 4, 1952

DRAMATICALLY EXPRESSIVE

¶ Frank Martin is a Swiss composer whose work has long impressed your reviewer with its deep seriousness of aim and high skill. His oratorio *Golgotha*, heard last night in Carnegie Hall, added to these solid quantities a grandeur of dramatic expression rarely encountered in our century's compositions for massed choral and orchestral effectives. As sung by the Dessoff Choirs and conducted by Paul Boepple, it was wanting in the highest polish of execution. The musical sense of it was there, however, and the meaningful impact. It was an unusual experience and, to this listener, absorbing throughout.

Not quite throughout, perhaps. The beginning was a bit stodgy, as if the composer's thought had not yet found its ease. About half way through the first half of the Passion (for such is the oratorio's text and subject) your listener became aware that music was taking place which he had not heard before. From there to the end, its varied musical invention and expressive content seemed inexhaustible, unendingly powerful and fresh.

Sometimes he would listen libretto in hand. And Martin's

elegant prosodizing of the French text seemed to him the main matter. At other moments, following the concert with no attention for the verbal content, he was struck by how completely interesting every number was sheerly as music. The melodic lines, their harmonizations and contrapuntal additions, their rhythmic life and orchestral colorations, their vocal variety and invariable beauty all seemed to him infinitely satisfactory. The musical complexities, too, for Martin is a learned man, were welcome evidence of mastery, of fecund labors, of trouble taken toward the covering of a grand gamut.

Surely religious sincerity has gone into the making of this work too. Such fine pictorial vividness combined with delicate feelings and a sweet taste is not achieved by dramatic talent alone. One number, as a matter of fact, that which recounts the trial before Pontius Pilate, is a dramatic scene of the most exciting immediacy. That is no mere meditation on a sacred story. That is real theater with a real presence.

Here is the vein where I shall look in future for Martin's most forceful work. He is a skilled and serious-minded musician with a gift for the voice, for words, for specific meaning, and for (which is the real test) dramatic animation. Such composers are not plentiful these days. The opera, as well as the oratorio, can use another good one.

January 19, 1952

THE ABSTRACT COMPOSERS

¶ When John Cage came to New York some ten years ago out of California (by way of Chicago), he brought with him a sizable baggage of compositions. These were scored for divers groups of what are usually called "percussion instruments," orthodox and unorthodox.

Orthodox percussion instruments, let me explain, are those manufactured with musical intent, such as tom-

toms, temple bells, and the like. The unorthodox are those whose adoption by the music profession is not yet general. These include, in Mr. Cage's case, flower pots, automobile brake drums, electric buzzers, tubs of water, and many other sources of interesting and characteristic sounds. Cage's first New York concerts were given with ensembles of players using all these instruments and many more, himself conducting.

A few years later he simplified the execution of his music by devising an instrument on which it could be composed for one man. This instrument, an orthodox one with unorthodox attachments, was none other than the familiar grand pianoforte muted with screws, bits of rubber, copper pennies and the like to give a large gamut of pings, thuds, and other delicate aural stimuli. As my colleague Arthur Berger has pointed out, the Cage "prepared piano" is a conception not dissimilar to that of the one-man bands common in the jazz world. Nor has the Cage method of composition been radically altered for the solo circumstance.

This method is Cage's most original contribution to music. Designed specifically for making extended and shapely patterns out of non-tonal sounds, it is the most sophisticated method available in the Western world for composing with purely rhythmic elements and without the aid of tonal scales. To quote Lou Harrison, long an associate of Cage in percussive studies and rhythmic research, Cage has substituted "chronological" for "psychological" time as the continuing element of his music. Any composer who has ever worked with percussion has discovered that all our traditional composing methods deal with the psychological, or "expressive," relations among tones which have among themselves differing and *unavoidable,* acoustical relations. To make musical forms or constructions without these relations requires a substitute for them. Cage has substituted an arithmetical relation among the durations of sounds for the traditional arithmetical relation among their pitches. He has isolated rhythm as a musical element and given it an independence it did not have before.

In the last year or so he has added a further element to composition, which is chance. So secure does he feel in the solidity of his composition method that he has essayed to prove its worth under conditions the most hazardous. Last year we heard, in a concert of the New Music Society, a piece by Cage for twelve radio receiving-sets. The use of fortuitously chosen material in composition has long been familiar to the visual arts. The collage, the spatter, the blot, the accidental texture have been exploited by painters for forty years. From Duchamp and Picasso to the latest American abstractionists, the history is continuous. Music itself accepts a high part of hazard in execution, and perhaps it is from this fact that composers have not exploited its possibilities much in actual scoring.

Mozart did play around with composing machines, as well as with performing machines (like the mechanical organ, for which he wrote some very pretty music); but he did not go far with them. How far Cage will go with his Chinese dice-game (for this is the game of chance by which he at present chooses the next sound and its loudness) remains to be seen. One presumes that he will renounce it if and when it ceases to be valuable, as he, the composer, judges value. But let no one think his *Music of Changes* is wholly a matter of hazard. The sounds of it, many of them quite complex, are carefully chosen, invented by him. And their composition in time is no less carefully worked out. Chance is involved only in their succession. And that chance is regulated by a game of such complexity that the laws of probability make continued variation virtually inevitable.

Thus, in Cage's hands, the use of chance in composition gives a result not unlike that of a kaleidoscope. With a large gamut of sounds and a complex system for assembling them into patterns, all the patterns turn out to be interesting; an arabesque is achieved. In the hands of his pupils and protégés the result is not always so distinguished, simply because the musical materials employed are less carefully chosen. The method of their assembling, however, remains valid and will remain so until a better approach to rhythmic construction is discovered.

What kaleidoscopes and arabesques lack is urgency. They can hold the attention but they do not do it consistently. The most dependable device for holding attention is a "theme" or story, the clear attachment of art patterns to such common human bonds as sex and sentiment. How far an artist goes in this direction, or in the opposite, is up to him. "Abstraction" in art is nothing more than the avoidance of a *clear* and *necessary* attachment to subject matter. It is ever a salutary element in art, because it clears the mind of sex and sentiment. Only briefly, however. Because the human mind can always find ways of getting these back into any picture. And since the civilized mind likes to share its intensities of feeling, and since all the feelings provokable by abstract art are individual, abstract movements invariably end by attaching to themselves an intense feeling about the one thing that is consistent throughout their works, namely, a method of composition. The composition, or the method of composition, becomes the "subject," in the long run, of all abstract art.

This has happened to the music of Cage and his followers. Its admirers, who are many (and include your commentator), tend ever to defend it as a species rather than to attach themselves to any particular piece. This has happened before. Stravinsky's neoclassic production was long a similar cause. Whether it happened just this way in the 1890's to Debussy's impressionistic works I am not sure. We do know that something not dissimilar took place around Beethoven in Vienna, though the attendant polemics were not an attack upon intellectuality in music but rather upon an unusual degree of expressivity.

In any case, Cage and his associates, through their recent concerts at the Cherry Lane Theatre, have got the town to quarreling again. Many find the climate of the new downtown group invigorating. Others are bothered by the casual quality of their music. They find it hard to keep the mind on. This has always been one reaction to abstract art. I am sure that Cage's work *is* abstract, in any contemporary meaning of the term. I am also convinced that the workmanship is of the best. The fact that younger men are adopting its methods, as Cage long ago took on the influence of Cowell and Varèse, means that it has become something of a movement. Myself I find it only natural that music, usually, in our time, a good quarter century behind the visual arts, should have finally acquired its own "abstractionist" pressure group.

February 3, 1952

GOOD CHORUS FROM UPSTATE

¶ Singing under their regular director, Helen Hosmer, the Crane Chorus from the State University Teachers College at Potsdam, New York, proved themselves to be one of the great singing societies. Directed last night in Carnegie Hall during half their program by the celebrated Robert Shaw, they sounded not nearly so well. Guest conductors do not usually, as a matter of fact, bring out the best powers of choral groups.

I sometimes wonder whether Robert Shaw, who has such an inspiring hand with choral singers and who seems to feel music profoundly with his body, really hears it at all with his ears. Last night he forced the choral tone, obscured the diction, and got no harmony at all out of the orchestra. Yet all the while he was executing a pantomime of personal transports, as if the music were somehow being just too beautiful to bear. If he had really been listening, he must have known, as we all did out front, that nothing of the kind was going on.

Then Miss Hosmer conducted a group of some forty unaccompanied singers in the *Miserere* (Psalm 50) of Josquin des Près, and suddenly the voices were sweeter. This subtle music may have lacked the ultimate in expressivity under her delicate fingers, but Norman Dello Joio's work on the same text did not. Scored for large chorus, strings, brasses and percussion, this tender and powerful piece received from Miss Hosmer and her choir of 250 voices a performance in every way moving and beautiful.

During a large part of this psalm the orchestra plays antiphonally to the unaccompanied chorus. Its voice is like that of liturgical responses and its tunes and harmonies follow those of the singing body. When the orchestra plays with the choir its music has less character. But at all times its work is pleasingly composed. So is the choir's, too, though I was not entirely convinced about the appropriateness of an almost cheerfully energetic finale. None the less, this Psalm of David is a distinguished work and an expressive one. Said to be constructed in emulation of the des Près *Miserere* that preceded it, it seemed to me to be modeled, in spirit at least, much more after Monteverdi. This composer's passionate immediacy is surely closer to Dello Joio's than are the stylistic elaborations and mystical vibrancies of Josquin. In any case, the Psalm of David, though a very simple piece and not at all complex in texture, is constantly interesting because it is at once sensitive and straightforward.

February 4, 1952

HARMONIOUS POWERS

¶ Grant Johannesen's piano recital last night in Town Hall was, for this listener, an unusually satisfying experience. Seldom does one hear solo playing so clean, so elegant, so thoroughly competent, and at the same time so completely informed with all the qualities that are called "musical."

Grant Johannesen seems to be the rare artist who can both hear and play, understand and render. Listening to him, consequently, is ever a "musical" experience. It is also a distinguished experience, because there is no vulgarity in him and no weakness. For all the power of expression that is his, one encounters in a whole evening of his work no affectation, no clumsiness, no willful distortion. He renders straightforwardly music's emotional content, without exaggeration and without timidity. He also plays the written notes without fear, without self-assertion, without ugliness, and virtually without error.

An early and rather stiff Beethoven sonata (opus 10, No. 1), a set of graceful and slender pieces by Grieg, the great Schumann Fantasy, formless but full of wonderful thoughts, Aaron Copland's stylish and hieratic Piano Variations, a delicious (and rare) Impromptu by Chabrier, Stravinsky's night-clubish evocation of a Tango, even Albeniz's repetitive but technically impressive *Eritagna,* all came to life at his hands. This life was a matter of rhythm, of tonal beauty and of phraseological grace. It also had to do with emotional warmth and with the intellectual ability to plan a shape without destroying that warmth.

Mr. Johannesen worked all evening at the center of music's problems. Technically, expressively, and "musically," he skirted no edges. Talent, training, a mature mind, and mature feelings were everywhere evident in harmonious operation. I cannot tell you how rarely a music reviewer meets this harmony in the concert hall, or how satisfying is the encounter.

March 17, 1952

DON CARLO AND THE PICKETS

¶ Just for pleasure, and also to impress a visitor from Europe, your announcer dropped in last Monday night at the Metropolitan Opera for a performance of Verdi's *Don Carlo.* He had not seen or heard the production since it opened the house last season and inaugurated the managerial regime of Rudolf Bing; but he knew it for a distinguished one and thought it a good example of New York opera presentation at its best, all the more worth showing off since the work itself is not anywhere a common repertory item.

It was something of a surprise to learn that the performance was being picketed. Investigation revealed the following facts. The Archdiocesan Union of the Holy Name Society of New York, the American Society for the Preservation of Sacred, Patriotic, and Operatic Music, and the Children's Drama Guild have all made protests to the Metropolitan management. The latter group had already asked the Manhattan Supreme Court, back in 1950, for a declaratory judgment enjoining the Metropolitan Opera Association from disseminating subversive anti-religious propaganda. This suit is still awaiting action. A spokesman for the Holy Name Society has declared that he is informed that the script of the opera has been changed in such a way as "to have appear on the stage a character in the garb of a clergyman who points out Don Rodrigo to an assassin, directs the asassination, and then shields the assassin by taking him away from the scene."

This spokesman has been misinformed. The script calls for a man "dressed in the uniform of the Holy Office," and he is so represented at the Metropolitan. The uniform, moreover, is not historically exact but of fanciful design. It bears no resemblance to the clothing of a priest. And the Holy Office, or Inquisition, did not consist wholly of priests. It was a large organization employing many laymen as administrators, office workers, guards, and other functionaries, all of whom were distinguished by their uniform from members of the clergy. Verdi's stage direction has been scrupulously observed at the Metropolitan. And Franco Colombo, managing director of G. Ricordi and Co. has assured Mr. Bing by letter that he has "never heard that this opera has ever incurred any form of censorship on the part of the Catholic Church since the time of its first performance in Paris in 1867 or on occasion of any later performances, including those which have recently taken place in Italy, Austria, France, and Spain."

Further evidence of hasty judgment on the part of the picketers is provided by the fact that they first arrived at the Metropolitan on a night when *Die Fledermaus* was the opera. They had not even got their dates right. They seemed to be in some confusion, moreover, about their exact complaint. The signs carried by the picketers, who are about thirty in number, bore the following legends:

"The opera *Don Carlo* is a mockery of religion."

"The opera *Don Carlo* is anti-state and anti-religious."

"Stop Sovietizing operas."

"Moscow termites invade the 'Met.'"

"Don't support 'Met' Opera as long as they hire subversives."

"Who gets the money that the 'Met' loses?"

"Planned deficit financing is anti-American."

The main charges, therefore, are: That the "Met" has changed Verdi's script (which is not true); that this change (still not true) is the work of Stalinists within the organization; that these subversive characters should be fired; that they may well be tapping the till for the benefit of the Communist Party. All these charges are grave; and till evidence supporting them is offered, we must consider all attempts at "proof by picketing" as utterly irresponsible. There may be some commies around the Met; they turn up everywhere. But there is no evidence that they have made propaganda for their faith through the distorting of any opera text or opera presentation. As for the hint that the Met's annual deficit is a kickback to Communism, the idea is really the funniest I have encountered this season, especially if you stop to remember how completely the Metropolitan is controlled by political conservatives. One would have to look far for an institution more thoroughly in the hands of capitalists, their sons and daughters, their wives, their widows, and their lawyers.

March 31, 1952

RECITAL SONGS

¶ Singers' recital programs come up for attack about once a year from this reviewer. In past times he has complained vigorously against the multilingual convention which leads vocal debutants to expose their ignorances of German, French and Italian all in one evening, along with, more often than not, their lack of a cultivated English diction. He has also lamented the musical poverty of the English-language song repertory.

Not much can be done to change the multilingual convention as long as our music schools enforce it for degrees and credits. Young artists have to sing what they have studied. And what they have studied is the standard scholastic requirement of selections from German lieder, French art-songs, Italian airs and arias, and English verse settings.

Fine programs can be assembled from these sources. And if few singers are prepared to shine in so grand a galaxy, they can usually do pretty well in one of the groups. Also, their program's musical offering is far richer in such a lay-out than would be possible in a program devoted to English vocal literature alone. The only way out of the difficult situation is to specialize, to really sing well German lieder or French songs and to stick fairly close to that specialty.

For these two repertories are the great vocal repertories. Neither the English nor the Italian communicates so urgently. You have only to hear a whole evening of music from England's, or from Italy's, finest vocal period, which in both cases is the seventeenth century, to realize that for all that music's noble proportion and infinite grace of line, it does not work in depth like those fusions of music and poetry that are the particular glory of Germany's nineteenth-century and of France's early twentieth.

Not Dowland, not Purcell, not Handel nor Blow, not Cesti, Carissimi, nor even Monteverdi has the psychological power in short songs of Schubert, Schumann, Brahms, Wolf, Mahler, Fauré, Ravel, and Debussy. Neither were they able to extend their inspirations into long vocal forms without some cost to their expressive intensity. The Romantics and the moderns in Germany, Austria, and France have worked far closer to poetry's meaning than did their predecessors; and they have worked with poetry of greater complexity. The classical and pre-classical masters, though they often set the best poets of their time, never faced—such things were not there to be faced—the emotional elaboration and verbal subtleties of Goethe, Heine, Baudelaire, Verlaine, Mallarmé, Appolinaire, and Max Jacob.

The modern Italian and modern English vocal repertories do not come up to the French and German either. The poetic texts used are less substantial, the musical settings less detailed. The Italians have written in the last century and a half lots of fine arias for the theater. In English we have Sir Arthur Sullivan, also of the theater, and Stephen Foster, strictly for the home. The Russians have a handful of wonderful songs by Moussorgsky that are appropriate for recital use and some by Rachmaninoff that are far from negligible. Grieg wrote some in Norwegian, and Sibelius has composed well in both Finnish and Swedish. De Falla, in

Spanish, and Villa-Lobos, in Portuguese, have written charmingly for the solo voice; but their work is closer to folklore evocation than to those psychologically powerful fusions of music and poetry that stem from Schubert. It is all a little objective, impersonal, does best in any program's final group.

German and French songs of the last century and a half are to the song recital what Haydn, Mozart, Beethoven, Brahms, and Debussy are to the orchestral concert. They are the center of the repertory, its real weight and grandeur. All the rest is contributory. And only in France, in the work of Francis Poulenc and Henri Sauguet, is that great tradition being carried on today. The English, the American composer has not seized, not understood the fusing of music and poetry into an alloy stronger than either alone. He has realized, I think, the nature of lyric poetry. But he has underestimated the need, in this kind of expression, for a personal intensity, the kind that can come only from sincerity, emotional concentration, and self-containment.

The great composers of art songs have all identified themselves with the poet's feeling or with some aspect of it. They have got inside the poetry. The rewards of doing this are Franz Schubert's great and original contribution to music, and his 600 songs are a corpus of achievement now basic to the art. The composers who have not built on this foundation have built weakly. Their songs do not stand up under usage. It is a matter of regret to us all that the English-speaking composer has not achieved that inward-turned concentration that is the sine qua non of great song-writing since Schubert.

Consequently our recital singers are obliged, like those of many another country, to work mostly in foreign languages. I have heard rumors ever since I was a child that a few English and American composers were about to change all that. Certainly most of our composers have tried their hand at the recital song, many of them assiduously. But if the usable American repertory is any larger or more distinguished today than it was in the time of Edward Macdowell and George B. Nevin, I am unaware of the fact. Neither is Benjamin Britten, in England, one whit more significant as a song writer, for my money, than the late (and thoroughly charming) Liza Lehman.

It is pathetic to hear our artists, especially the younger ones, mouthing French and German that they scarcely understand. But it is even more painful to see them struggle with poorly conceived and amateurishly written English songs. There is nothing to be done about the matter. Only a great repertory of English songs can change it. And for that we must wait till our composers acquire the knack of working closer to poetry than they are accustomed to do just now. A good melody is not just a poem's new suit. It must be a new skin, inseparable.

April 27, 1952

COPLAND SONGS

¶ Aaron Copland's Twelve Poems of Emily Dickinson are Copland at his most characteristic and most reflective. The broken rhythms, the pandiatonic harmony, the subtle spacing of notes in a chord, the open piano writing, the melodic lines that seek wide skips, all color the work with this composer's personality. So do the seriousness and the poetic penetration with which the texts have been studied, and the frank search for charm (equally characteristic of Emily Dickinson) with which their thought has been expressed.

If this admirer of Copland has a reserve about the present song cycle, otherwise so appealing, that reserve comes from a certain ineptitude in the vocal writing. The range is extreme (a half-tone over two octaves) and the tessitura, or "lie" of the vocal line, is cruel. For a light voice the cruelty would come in the low notes, the Bs, B-flats, and the A. For Patricia Neway, whose low voice is warm, the cruelty comes at the top, from F sharp to B-flat.

This cruelty is less a result of the wide melodic skips, which are in themselves effective in a declamatory sense and strikingly expressive, as in the vowel sounds to which the high and the low-lying notes are set. Certain extensions of the short vowels also oblige the singer to deform these. And occasionally a lengthening out, syllable by syllable, of a word group that for comprehensibility requires being pronounced as if it were a single word ("the breaking of the day," for instance) makes it hard for the singer to communicate the sense of the poems.

These poems, more than a little arch sometimes in sentiment ("Dear March, come in!"), are nevertheless compact in phraseology and require time to understand. Spacing their ideas would have helped them more than stretching out their syllables does. Actually their sense is more picturesquely illustrated in the piano part (birds twittering, horses trotting, an organist improvising) than it is projected through their vocal declamation. The accompaniments are perfect, and they "sound." The vocal line, though full of expressive intentions, really comes off only part of the time. In three cases—*Nature, the gentlest mother, Heart, we will forget him* and *I've heard an organ talk sometimes* —the songs seem to me completely successful. In the rest, for all their tenderness and vibrancy, something experimental in the vocal writing, something not quite mastered in Copland's technique of handling words and singers, tones down their power to touch the heart, though this clearly is what they aim to do.

November 3, 1952

METROPOLITAN OPERA NOT YET A PART OF NEW YORK'S INTELLECTUAL LIFE

¶ Twelve years ago this commentator observed that the Philharmonic was "not a part of New York's intellectual life." Today that remark would not be true. It is still true, however, of the Metropolitan Opera.

By "New York's intellectual life" I mean everything that

inspires, even briefly, the interest of our powerful "intellectual audience." This audience is not wholly musical; nor does it represent any social class. It is made up of book-readers and book-writers, civic leaders and stenographers, artists of all kinds, and all the art consumers who have faith in the future. It is a critical audience, but a warm one; and it can make or break the prestige of any institution dealing in products of the mind.

Its dynamic character, its faith in tomorrow, is backed up by a better knowledge of the past than the non-intellectual audience has. You can't fool it by talking about "tradition," as you can often do with the less knowledgeable. It demands that the past be treated as a living thing and that today be considered as an honorable heir of the past and a gateway, the only gateway, to the future.

Typical of the intellectual operation I am describing is the recent performance at the Philharmonic concerts of Darius Milhaud's celebrated opera *Christopher Columbus*. This work has been in existence for over twenty years. It has been performed in Germany, France, and Belgium. It has never been a popular success, and it has never been agreed to be an artistic failure. It is a monumental work by a world-famous master, and New York also has a right to judge it. If recent judgments have not been wholly favorable, neither have they considered the Philharmonic to have done a foolish thing in giving it. Indeed, the Philharmonic's intellectual prestige has risen with the event.

The Metropolitan Opera production on Feb. 14 of the Stravinsky-Auden opera *The Rake's Progress* will certainly bring similar prestige to that establishment. But one event does not define a policy, and it is surely to be hoped that a policy of producing each season a certain number of contemporary and other works of intellectual distinction will one day put the Metropolitan into a higher intellectual neighborhood than it has dwelt in of late years. *Salome* and *Elektra*, as conducted there by Fritz Reiner, have been "musts" for the musical public that leads taste. And Alfred Lunt's staging of *Così Fan Tutte* enjoys attention from this audience. *La Forza del Destino*, for its scenery by Eugene Berman, and *Don Carlo*, for its scenery by Rolf Gerard and staging by Margaret Webster, have attracted similar interest; but musically neither work has inspired much public gratitude, though the singing in them has been excellent. The Met's other recent revivals, though necessary as re-furbishments, have added nothing remarkable to our musical or to our theater experience.

The City Center has given us in one calendar year a contemporary opera, *The Dybbuk,* and four famous works of this century—Wolf-Ferrari's *I Quattro Rusteghi,* Alban Berg's *Wozzeck,* Bartók's *Bluebeard's Castle* and Ravel's *L'Heure Espagnole.* Earlier, Prokofiev's *Love of Three Oranges* and Debussy's *Pelléas et Mélisande* made history for popular prices. As for the ballet companies, they all do new works constantly. Their relation to their own time is perfect, and a huge audience of young people is their reward.

Philharmonic spokesmen used to maintain, and Metropolitan spokesmen still do, that their institution cannot afford at present a policy of intellectual distinction but that if and when more money became available they would be delighted to spend some of it pleasing the intellectual minority. All such statements assume that a directorship which has for years abstained from any such effort has the taste and its subscribers the experience to take part in the life of their time by merely changing their minds. We have no evidence that this is true. At the Philharmonic it took a new conductor to make the change, and that change is not yet complete. But the change has brought into the house for the more advanced programs a public not previously served by the Philharmonic, and it seems not to have caused any grave defection among the subscribers.

Money does not produce intellectual distinction, nor does poverty prevent its exercise. Actually, in any given house one opera production costs about the same as another. The ones that make history are the ones that show choice, taste, and solid imagination. And it does seem to me that making history is the only criterion that we can accept in judging the activities of our cultural institutions.

November 16, 1952

CONTEMPORARY FESTIVAL
IN PITTSBURGH

¶ The First Pittsburgh International Music Festival took place the week of November 24–30. From the works heard by this reviewer, here are some of the impressions retained.

A Concerto, Opus 56, for piano, four hands unaccompanied, by Vincent Persichetti seemed to me extraordinarily expert in its piano writing. It is difficult; but it sounds, and its figurational ingenuity is vast. Musically the work is prolix and its expressivity diffuse; but the sound of it, moment by moment, is unusually brilliant. Its performance by the composer and Dorothea Persichetti was perfection, the ringing quality of their piano tone being especially noticeable beside the deadness of tone in the otherwise highly musical performances of Johana Harris, who played on the same program.

Quaderna Musicale di Annalibera (*"Annalibera's Musical Notebook"*) by Luigi Dallapiccola, most poetically played by Mrs. Harris, is a homage to childhood composed in the twelve-tone technique. It is a series of short pieces, ever songful and sweet, and might easily become a popular number on recital programs.

Arnold Schönberg's Trio for Violin, Viola, and Violoncello, Opus 45, composed for the Harvard Symposium on Music Criticism in 1947 and seldom performed since, is not much loved, even in twelve-tone circles. Myself I found it, as played by three members of the New Music String Quartet, delicious for sound. I do not pretend to know its emotional content, and I insist that persons who seek to recognize Schönberg's emotional content by sheer intuition are in general slated for disappointment. His microscopic examination of emotion precludes easy recognition, and the value of it comes far more from the surprising details re-

vealed than from any resemblance his study may bear to
any possible common-sense view or large-scale perspective
rendering of a similar subject.

Vaughan Williams's *Tudor Portraits,* five very long pieces
for chorus and orchestra on texts by the fifteenth-century
satirist John Skelton, is the least subtle work I have ever
heard by this composer. It must have been written for some
provincial English singing society, and a none too sophisticated one at that. It is brash and brassy, noisy, bustling, as if
the available executant forces were all vigor and no refinement. As a college glee-club-and-orchestra romp it might be
fun for five minutes. At a length of somewhere near forty I
found it bearable only by the beauty of Nell Rankin's lovely
singing in the solos. As a matter of fact, it was the only large
piece heard all week that seemed to me undistinguished.

Especially grateful to these ears was Roy Harris's Fifth
Symphony, composed in 1942. In one sense Harris's large
works are all the same work. He seems to approach a single
problem of expression in varying ways rather than to use a
perfected and personal instrument of expression for depicting a variety of subjects. His central problem of expression
is by now familiar to us all, and the solution offered in his
Third Symphony has become America's most popular (and
most exportable) single expression in symphonic form. That
offered in the Fifth, though less compact, seems to me to
have a greater intrinsic beauty. Whether its expressive force
is as great I cannot say. Only time and the box office can
tell that.

What it does have is Harris's two best advantages handsomely embodied, his extended thematic line and his skill in
treating the orchestra as an antiphony of strings and brass.
His tendency to write as if the work he is writing has already
been judged a masterpiece (at least by himself) even before
it has been composed is not one of Mr. Harris's most winning
traits. But I must say that it bothered me less in his Fifth
Symphony than it has ever done before in an orchestral
piece. And I strongly suspect that this circumstance was
produced by Harris's having composed and orchestrated the
piece with a high degree of perfectly real mastery. In the
American repertory it is a far from negligible work.

December 7, 1952

1953

MUSICALLY ENCHANTING

¶ *The Rake's Progress* brought yesterday afternoon to the Metropolitan Opera House the brillance of a great premiere. The cast, headed by Hilde Gueden, Eugene Conley, and Mack Harrell, sang impeccably. The orchestral accompaniments, after forty hours of rehearsal under Fritz Reiner, were perfect. The scenery of Horace Armistead was adequate, the stage direction of George Balanchine brilliantly unobtrusive. As for the opera itself, it has a fine libretto by W. H. Auden and Chester Kallman; and its music by Igor Stravinsky is enchanting.

The subject is a young man's downfall through money, drink, gambling, sex, and speculation. He ends up in bedlam, imagining himself Adonis in the arms of Venus, but really being rocked to sleep by his hometown sweetheart. He is abetted in self-destruction, I may add, by a Mephistophelian servant named Nick Shadow. The story is thus a morality play touched up with Goethe's *Faust*. Setting it in eighteenth-century England has allowed the authors to lean on the prestige of Hogarth's engravings of the same title and also to stylize their poetic language. Very pretty is that language, too. Few composers in our time have been served by an English libretto so high-class all through.

Dealing with a poem made all out of references to a period of literature, it was appropriate (indeed inevitable) that the composer should derive his inspiration from the same period in music. Mr. Stravinsky has clearly used as his model the operas of Mozart and Pergolesi, adding touches of thematic material and devices of musical syntax from classical composers as closely related to the Mozart tradition as Bach, Gluck, and Donizetti. There is even here and there a memory of Beethoven's *Fidelio*. But *The Rake's Progress* is no eclectic score. Its style is powerfully Stravinskian. I should say that it sounds throughout more like Stravinsky than any other single piece we have heard from this master in twenty or more years, since *Oedipus Rex* and the Symphony of Psalms, to be exact.

Its difference from those earlier vocal works lies in the greater freedom, variety, and expressive power of the vocal line. The opera is full of fine airs, set-pieces, and recitatives, all handsomely designed to show off both the human voice and the English text. Its similarities lie in the harmonic texture, a dissonant diatonic idiom of almost arbitrary simplicity, and in the complexity of the musical metrics. Stravinsky's inspiration, let us remember, has always been rhythm, dancing, gesture. Song is secondary with him. And although the present work is chock-full of good tunes, many of them more or less familiar, it is the rhythmic structure of the instrumental accompaniments—elaborate, subtle and tense—that gives to the whole work its electric potential. This tension, characteristic of all Stravinsky's music, is in his stronger works the most powerful musical individuality of our time. Its permeating pressure in *The Rake's Progress* is grounds for suspicion that this work is probably among his finest.

If so, it will stay in the repertory. If not, it will still have delighted us all with its musical fancy. Certainly there is no weakness in the poem or in the possibilities of its dramatic mounting that would tend to make the work, like *Les Noces* and *The Rite of Spring,* fall out of the theater into the concert hall. If there were any such weakness, it would lie, I think, in the passages having to do with the Bearded Lady, a character drawn from female impersonation and not easy to make convincing. All the rest works perfectly, in my opinion, and should continue to do so for quite a time. In the Metropolitan's admirable production, the artists will probably (unless the cast begins to shift) little by little add characterization to a spectacle that so far has been drilled primarily for musical excellence. *The Rake* is a fine opera in an extraordinarily perfect musical production. It is no tearjerker nor much of a melodrama. It is simply a quite good poem on a moralistic theme, and the music is enchanting.

February 15, 1953

GERMANY'S FUNERAL SONG

¶ Bruno Walter, conducting the Philharmonic-Symphony Orchestra last night, gave a burningly clear and moving performance of Gustav Mahler's *Das Lied von der Erde*. The excellent soloists were Elena Nikolaidi and Set Svanholm.

This *Song of the Earth* is really six songs, plus a short orchestral interlude, set alternately for tenor and alto voice to German translations of Chinese poems. The sadness of wine, of the seasons, and of growing older is their theme. And if a certain self-pity is not absent from the composer's treatment, neither is the objective enjoyment of nature. The amplitude of the work's expressive content comes, indeed, from the placement of a personal sadness in a landscape that sets it off by every device of contrast.

This sumptuous orchestral landscape is no attempt to reconstruct an authentic China. It is rather a wish, a yearning toward a China picturesque and exotic in detail but filled to the brim with Germanic pathos. The permanence of the East is there only as décor for the decline of the West. And make no mistake about it; Mahler's sadness at the approach of his fiftieth year was no private vanity. He thought of himself as the end of German music, just as Brahms had done. Brahms in spite of Wagner, Mahler in spite of Strauss, and later, Alban Berg in spite of Schönberg and Webern, all considered their music to be the closing off of a great epoch.

All were right in the sense that German music was experiencing in their time a sumptuous and deliquescent decay. It had lost all sense of form, all reserve, all ethical distinctions among the sources of emotion; and the aging giant had no strength to revive him. He could only die in grandeur. And each of these introspectives, bound to pessimism by clarity of mind as well as by temperament, wished

that the whole great fireworks could expire with him in one
final bursting.

It did not happen that way. German music still goes on,
running weaker and thinner, but alive. It is all a very sad
story; and Mahler was right to be sad. But he did leave, in
The Song of the Earth, at least one lovely burst, an opulent and ornate poetic address to the musical decline of the
great tradition of which he was so proud to be a part. All
this somehow came through last night in the reading of
it, tender, eloquent, and grand, by Bruno Walter and the
two soloists.

February 20, 1953

GLORIOUS ORGAN PLAYING

¶ French organ playing has been one of the musical glories of our century; and Jeanne Demessieux, who
played an organ recital last night in the Central Presbyterian Church, is clearly a light in that glory. All evening
long your reviewer, who has known most of the great
organ playing of our time, from that of Widor and Bonnet
and Vierne through Dupré to Messiaen, could only think of
those masters as company for this extraordinary musician
and virtuoso.

Miss Demessieux's program contained from the Baroque
period (which is the organ's classical period) a Bach overture from a cantata and a Handel concerto. From Romantic
times came the Liszt Fantasy on *Ad Nos, Ad Salutarem.*
Two works by the organist herself and a movement from
Marcel Dupré's *Symphonie-Passion* brought us into the
modern world. And for dessert the artist improvised on a
theme presented her on the spot. None of the works was a
hackneyed piece. Indeed, the Liszt Fantasy is so little played
that many organists have never heard it at all. It is a won-
drous work all the same, abundant of musical invention,
brilliant in technical display, richly imaginative as to har-

mony, and utterly grand in its moments of apotheosis, diabolic and celestial. When one remembers that the great Romantics wrote so little for the organ, and for the most part without any boldness, this work stands almost as a solitary beacon in the deep fog that surrounded this noble instrument throughout the nineteenth century.

Miss Demessieux's work as a composer appeared, from the two selections offered (a chorale-prelude on *Ubi Caritas* and a Study in Thirds) to be skillful and musically sophisticated. It was not possible to gather from them any characteristic profile of individuality. Neither was anything of the kind manifest in her improvisation beyond perhaps an assurance of taste, intelligence, and technical skill of the highest order. She improvised, as is the French custom, in the Baroque forms, including a dazzling Toccata. Since the theme composed for her by Seth Bingham did not lend itself easily to fugal treatment, she omitted the customary fugal finale and finished her series of improvisations quietly with a poetic variation based on thematic alterations.

Notable throughout the evening were the soloist's elaborate and subtle treatment of registration and her powerful rhythm. No less subtle and no less powerful were her phraseology and her acoustical articulation. Accustomed, no doubt, to compensating for the acoustical lags and other echoing characteristics of France's vast cruciform churches, all stone and glass, she employed to great advantage in the smaller but similarly reverberant walls of the Central Presbyterian a staccato touch for all rapid passage work involving bright or loud registration. This device kept the brilliance clean; and its contrast with the more sustained utterance of broader themes gave a welcome variety, a contrapuntal dimension. We are not used here to so dry an articulation, to so striking a clarity in organ playing. I must say that the fine brightness of the registration possibilities in the organ she was playing on aided the artist, as a good French organ also does, to avoid the muddy noises that so often pass for serious organ execution.

Last night there was no mud anywhere, only music making of the most crystalline and dazzling clarity. Every piece had style, beauty, gesture, the grand line. And perhaps the grandest line of all, the richest color and the most dramatic form were those of Liszt's magniloquent Fantasy. I wonder why organists play this work so rarely. Is it too hard to learn? Surely not. Miss Demessieux swept through it, as she did everything else, from memory.

March 23, 1953

LOUD AND GRAND

¶ Beethoven's Missa Solemnis is a work which this reviewer has long preferred reading or thinking about to actually hearing. The grandeur of its conception cannot be questioned, but much of its detail is weak and does not carry. Nor does a great deal of the choral writing really "sound"; it is too loud and too high too much of the time. Orchestrally also the work has little to offer of charm or variety. The scoring lacks color, as does also the harmony, which is limited almost entirely to its architectural function. The work is of an extraordinary plainness, in spite of its length and seeming complexity. Its glory lies in its straightforwardness, its insistence, its triumphal assertion, as if the whole Mass were one dauntless, relentless Hallelujah.

Naturally the execution by mere musicians of so grand a concept is limited by human possibilities. And Mr. Toscanini resolved none of the work's well known practical difficulties save only that of giving us whole and straight its noble simplicity of mood. The N. B. C. Orchestra did not play throughout with an agreeable sound, nor did the Robert Shaw Chorale so sing. The soloists were lovely, especially the soprano Lois Marshall; but the conductor left them little leeway for singing other than at the top of their power all the time.

The whole reading seemed to me weighted on the loud side, and there derived from this loudness a certain monotony. Excitement there was, yes, a tension of rhythmic insistence and a tension of strain. Also that fullness of affirmation that is the glory of Beethoven. A not dissimilar affirmation on the interpreter's level, of course, is the glory of Toscanini, just turned eighty-six. For these gifts let us be thankful. All the same, I do repeat, every time I hear the Missa Solemnis, that there seems to be no satisfactory way of making this work sound less like a tempest over the Atlantic and more like a piece of music comparable in intrinsic interest to any of the same composer's symphonies.

March 30, 1953

SINGING ENGLISH

¶ The increasing use of English on our operatic stages has begun to make evident the inefficiencies of many an opera singer's diction in that language. Also the fine verbal projection of certain others, of Mack Harrell's, for instance. Several times lately, in reviewing such occasions, this reporter has mentioned the tendency, encouraged by many vocal studios, to mute, to neutralize all unstressed English vowels into a sound such as might be represented in spelling by the letters *uh*. This sound exists in many modern languages; and it has a sign in the international phonetic alphabet, which is a lower-case e printed upside down. It is also recognized by all students of pronunciation that English vowels, unless they bear the stress accent of a word or word-group, tend toward neutral sound. The first and last syllables of *potato* and *tomato* are partially neutralized vowels; but they remain o's never the less, especially in speech destined for large-hall projection. The last syllable of *sofa,* on the other hand, is completely worn down to the neutral state of uh; and no speaker can say it otherwise without seeming affected.

Several letters from phonetic students have seemed to invite discussion of these matters, and almost all of them have assumed as axiomatic that musical declamation should imitate as closely as possible the customs of spoken speech.

I find the assumption hasty, if only in view of the fact that conversational speech and shouted speech do not observe the same vowel qualities. Nowadays that public speaking is done more and more through electrical amplification, it tends more and more also toward the conversational tone. But the great orators and the great actors, when working without a microphone, still project their phrases through vowel observances that at a lower level of loudness would be considered frank distortion.

Singing requires even greater distortion of speech customs, since tonal resonance must be preserved at all times. It is most curious, once you think about it, that while no one would ever mistake a British actor's speech for that of an American, and vice versa, there is practically no difference at all in the way that British and American artists articulate their common language in song. This means that some dominant consideration wipes out in their singing all localisms of speech. What is that consideration? It is the essential difference between speech and song, the simple fact that singing permits an extension of the vowel sounds that is outside the conventions of speech.

It is unfortunate that most of the phonetic studies available in print deal only with speech. They are all right so far as they go; but they do not, as a rule, deal at all with the tonal problem that is cardinal to musical declamation. They are like qualitative analysis in chemistry. The next step will have to be a quantitative analysis of English vowels and diphthongs. Because our vowels are not equally extensible. Those of *pit, pat, pet* and *put* allow of hardly any holding time at all. Whereas the *o* of *home* can be sustained to the farthest limit of breath, though the identical *o* in *pope* resists extension.

All these matters need study. And for singers a great refinement in vowel intonations is needed if the unaccented ones are not to be hastened pellmell into that limbo of similarity where popular radio and movie artists tend to throw them. Singing is by its nature conservative in this regard, because neutralized vowels are neither beautiful nor sonorous. And composers can be ever so cruel in asking for extension of these weak sounds. The word *garden* is correctly spoken as *gahdn,* but it cannot be sung that way if the second syllable has a long note. A vowel must be invented for it by each singer, a sound at once becoming to his voice and not too absurdly inappropriate to the speech-sound of the word. *Jerusalem* is another tricky word, at least the first syllable of it. Jee and Jay are clearly absurd, though I've heard both in New York City. On the whole, American artists prefer *Jeh,* though the British have long maintained that only *Juh* is correct.

Gradations of vowel color are necessary even for long accented syllables, because vocal beauty demands some darkening of the bright *ay*'s and *ee*'s, some brightening of the dark *oh* and *ou,* especially if the notes involved are high or loud. Further gradations are needed for the vocalization of unaccented vowels. The *er* of *river* in "Swanee River" comes out best, for instance, if sung as something very like the French sound *eu.* The *y* in *melody,* though it may seem to ask for an *ee* sound, admits tempering in some cases. The word *little* is a headache all round, and so is *bottle.* The last syllable of *Saviour* is clearly neither *yrrr* nor *yaw;* as in *river,* something approaching the French *eu* is probably the best solution.

A cultivated singing-speech does not fear to exaggerate, to color, to alter English vowel sounds (as these are used in speech) for clarity, for resonance, for carrying power. What it must avoid like sin, for it is one linguistically, is the undue neutralization of vowels, which can endanger clarity, resonance, and carrying power. Studios teach the correct declamation of Italian, German, and French. Some teach good singing English, too. Many do not. And many English-speaking singers sing a corrupt and vulgar English. This fault should be corrected in the studios. Indeed, it *must* be corrected if English-language opera is to be successful. The music public will accept an occasional folksy touch, but by and large it wants a classical style in its musical executions. And declamation, diction, are a part of musical execution. They are in need right here and now of serious attention.

April 12, 1953

GREAT MAN IN DECLINE

¶ Sergei Prokofiev's last symphony, No. 7, composed only last year, was the novelty nugget of last night's concert of the Philadelphia Orchestra in Carnegie Hall. Eugene Ormandy conducted it with perfect clarity; and since the work itself is both simple and frank, there need be little hesitation about anyone's attitude toward it. That of the audience, as expressed in applause, was warm. The piece seems to have been designed, indeed, for appealing easily. How long this charm will last leaves many a reserve in this listener's mind, since it failed for him to survive through even the first hearing.

In his judgment the work shows the influence of the composer's long illness. He would not care to credit any of its faults to government pressure, because Prokofiev has long composed better music under identical pressures. I must admit, however, that it bears a striking resemblance to what the Party leaders say they want. It is flowing, facile, open, and filled with reminiscences, both melodic and harmonic, of the kind of tune and sentiment that all of us associate with films manufactured for wide distribution.

It is not impossible that the symphony may have been derived or assembled from a film accompaniment, though I know no evidence to prove this. It is ever so loosely built; and its melodic content, though broad and songful, is quite without dignity. It is both casual and, artistically considered, corrupt. It does not sound in any way like Prokofiev, who, though he had a streak in him of vulgarity, a very little one, was also a distinguished musical mind. The commonplaceness in this work is not that of basic music materials nor of universal human communications. It is the banality of commercial art and commercialized sentiments. It is sticky and sweet and, in its lighter moments, just plain silly. Were it not so signed, I should not believe that Prokofiev wrote it. And surely the Prokofiev that did is not the same

Prokofiev that the music world has so long loved for his vast vitality, his pungent skill and acid sarcasms, his insistent and delirious powers of sustaining an ecstasy. Even more than from the news of his death we shall miss him terribly now.

April 22, 1953

A POWERFUL WORK

¶ Elliott Carter's String Quartet is a sumptuous and elaborate structure that lasted forty-five minutes without losing at any point its hold on this listener's attention. The piece is complex of texture, delicious in sound, richly expressive, and in every way grand. Its specific charm is the way in which it sounds less like a classical string quartet than like four intricately integrated solos all going on at the same time. Each instrument plays music which is at any given moment melodically and rhythmically complete. It could be played alone. But it also serves as contrasted thematic matter against which three other seemingly independent parts all stand out as if in relief. As in fugal writing, the tunes, rhythms, figurations, and placements as regards pitch are mutually contrasted and mutually contributory. Their relation to one another lies in their studied differences.

They are all in the same key; but often, by the use of double-stops, each instrument makes its own harmony. They also swap their tunes and counter-tunes about, too, as in the fugal style. Only toward the very end do they actually cooperate in the production of a communal, a blended harmony. And this passage seemed less interesting than the rest of the piece, simply because the rhythmic contrasts of the work's contrapuntal texture were no longer present to animate its flow—again a phenomenon not uncommon in fugal writing.

The work is not a fugue; it is a free composition deriving equally from the improvisational toccata-style and the constructed sonata. It is a summation of many composing methods, though its source lies in neoclassicism. Richness and variety are its glory, freedom and mastery its most impressive message on first hearing. It is difficult to play; it was beautifully played by the Walden String Quartet of the Unversity of Illinois. It is an original and powerful piece, and the audience loved it.

May 5, 1953

HENRI SAUGUET

¶ The music of Henri Sauguet, as presented in the Museum of Modern Art under the auspices of the International Society for Contemporary Music and of the Juilliard School, came to many as a surprise as well as a delight. The warmth and the spontaneity with which New York responded both to the music and to the person of the composer was a match, indeed, for the same warmth and the spontaneity that are his music's most powerful qualities. And the rarity of these qualities in contemporary music makes them all the more welcome in a time when music lovers have grown used to hearing from composers every imaginable idiom save the language of the heart.

Sauguet has been speaking his heart in music for nigh on to thirty years, and he has long been loved in Europe for doing so. But America has had little chance to love his work. His operas, of which there are four, have not been produced here, presumably because our troupes are not staffed for producing French opera. And his ballets, of which there are upwards of twenty, have mostly been composed for organizations that do not visit our shores. Even his chamber music and his songs, which constitute a large repertory, have scarcely been touched; and when isolated works of any kind have been given, they have usually passed almost unperceived. It took a whole concert of Sauguet's work to make clear that it is the expression of a remarkable personality, one of the strongest musical personalities, in fact, now alive and working.

Perhaps the time has not been ripe till now for America to love and understand a music at once so elegant and so humane, so void of insistence and so deeply felt. We have had to work our way through all the fashionable forms of stridency to arrive at the point of being able to hear again that which is not strident and to exhaust our delight in violence, frigidity, and the obsessions of abnormal psychology before we could notice again the dignity of the more nourishing sentiments, the ones we live on. Perhaps also a few vested interests have discouraged up to now any venturings of the contemporary music societies into paths not clearly marked as leading to the further success of already successful movements.

The quickest musicians to take up Sauget may well be the recital vocalists. His production of songs has been large and ever distinctive. Admirably composed for singing and perfectly prosodized, these comprise settings of some of the finest French lyric poetry by Paul Eluard, by Georges Hugnet, by Max Jacob, by Mallarmé, Laforgue, and Baudelaire, as well as French translations of Rilke and of Schiller. These are French songs in the tradition of Poulenc and Fauré, the lyrical tradition, rather than the more declamatory vein of Debussy and Berlioz. They have not Poulenc's bounce nor Ravel's irony; they simply have a lovely tenderness and a tragedy all their own. Like all fine songs, they are a distilled poetic essence, different each from each yet all full of the composer's own flavor.

It is surprising that a composer so gifted for the theater and so versed in the dramatic forms should indulge so little in rhythmic surprise or weighty emphasis. It is Sauguet's sharp sense of character differences and of distinctions among the sentiments that make violence no temptation to him. Everything in his music is made up out of contrasts and oppositions; but these elements are composed into a harmony, not set at war. The result is a vibrant equilibrium rather than a tension. Sauguet does not purge the emotions; he feeds them, makes them flower, give off perfume. The drama in his stage works is as intimate as in his chamber music, just as his chamber music is capable of evoking vast scenes and lofty laments worthy of the opera.

This primacy of expression makes him a romantic; and the consistent shapeliness of his work unmasks him as a neo-Romantic. He is, indeed, one of the founding fathers of the musical movement so denominated, as he was the close friend and frequent theatrical collaborator of Christian Bérard, its leader in painting. Whether this movement has run its course or scarcely begun, I shall not argue here, though my faith is in the latter outcome. But whatever the future may decide, Henri Sauguet has already brought us a sweetness, a beauty, a sincerity, and a savor that contemporary music has long lacked and that are dew and strawberries to us just now.

May 9, 1953

CHORAL CONFERENCE

¶ *The American Composer and Choral Music* was the subject of a two-day conference held last Monday and Tuesday at Harvard University.

The ceremonies included also two evening concerts held in Harvard's thoroughly ugly, nearly a century old, and acoustically perfect Sanders Theater. The second of these was a choral concert conducted by Harold C. Schmidt, of Stanford University, director of this year's Summer School Chorus, and by myself. This group numbered about forty works by Randall Thompson.

Randall Thompson's *Last Words of David* is notable for its ending, a softly floating Alleluia. Elliott Carter's *Musicians Wrestle Everywhere* partly displays and partly conceals its fanciful Emily Dickinson text in a deliciously complex contrapuntal texture modeled, if I guess rightly, after the madrigals of Orlandus Lassus. It is a gay and busy piece, at once airy and compact in sound, and marked by the very great precision of workmanship that is characteristic of Carter. Irving Fine's *Have You Seen the White Lily Grow* and *O Do Not Wanton With Those Eyes* have all the tender poetry and very unusual melodic grace that are Fine's especial gifts. The first of these in particular struck me as one of the really lovely contemporary works in madrigal style.

Contradicting the musical distinction of these selected works, the forum discussions of the two-day meeting had returned again and again to the American composer's lack of interest in writing for chorus and his poor mastery of the medium. It had been pointed out frequently that American choral works have been, on the whole, neither inspired nor expert, as compared to those that have come out of Europe in our century. Debussy, Ravel, Roussel, Stravinsky, Milhaud, Honegger, Poulenc, Malipiero, Hindemith, Orff, Blacher, Frank Martin, Holst, Vaughan Williams, Walton, and Britten have all composed as pungently for grouped voices as for grouped instruments. But our American choral work seems, on the whole, to compare less well with our country's contributions to orchestral and to chamber music.

The choral conductors present were all for changing this situation by a program of commissioning choral works and of collaborating technically with composers. The composers showed small enthusiasm for the prospect, harped continually on the musical and textual limits of the choral medium, on its compromising associations with musical amateurism, and its hopeless involvement with all that is most basic in American life. Far too basic, indeed, for much freedom of feeling about them are religion and patriotism as subject-matter for art nowadays. And far too basic also for comfort in artistic execution is all that close ambience of the church, the school, and the home that binds the choral circumstance to respectability, to impersonality, and to emotional common denominators.

No artist is opposed to these firm foundations. Nor are they here, as they have long been in Europe, in any grave danger of collapse. We accept, approve, take them for granted, build our lives on them. But as artists, we try to get away from their power over us. This is why, I think, the American composer has rarely embraced choral composition with any warmth. And it is the reason why choral singing in America, for all its wide practice and frequent high standards of execution, remains after three centuries of undiminished vigor more striking as a sociological phenomenon than as a musical gold mine.

At the same time, educators, conductors, and choral singers are yearning for a contemporary American repertory comparable to the European. How to get it out of our composers was the subject of a symposium lasting nearly two hours. Nobody seemed to think that money could not be found, if necessary, for commissioning works. What everybody wanted to know was how to choose the composers, how to inspire them and how to cooperate with them on the technical level. The composers tried to tell them. Nevertheless, to the end the composers remained coy, engaged themselves to no program. And the educators remained determined. I suspect that that determination, backed up by commission money and here and there by an understanding of the composer's essentially childlike mentality, may end by creating an American choral repertory and a tradition, a style. This, at least, plus the excellent performance of some pleasing choral works, was as near to a hopeful note as the Harvard Summer School Conference on *The American Composer and Choral Music* could find to end on.

August 16, 1953

IN SPITE OF CONDUCTING

¶ William Lincer, playing viola solo last night in the Philharmonic's opening concert of the season at Carnegie Hall, was a delight for his dark tone and the grace of his phraseology. If he did not project dramatically the solo part of Berlioz's *Harold in Italy* as one sometimes hears it done and did not attempt to make a concerto out of a work that is nothing of the kind, that reluctance was welcome, too. It enabled one to hear the piece as what it is, an orchestral landscape "featuring," as show business would put it, the viola.

Dimitri Mitropoulos, conducting, was less discreet. He did not cover the viola with noise when it was playing. But he crowded it, when it was not, with sudden loudnesses and brassy balances. Indeed, our Philharmonic's celebrated conductor overplayed his brasses most of the evening. And in the *Symphonie Konzertante* of Karl Stamitz, which "featured" seven other of the orchestra's first-desk musicians, he pushed his soloists for time as well as for volume.

The conductor's personal excitement, bordering on hysteria, was least under control in the Schumann Third, or *Rhenish* Symphony. Here the rhythm was often unclear, the counterpoints lost, the shape of the lovely work distorted by a nervous passion. If its reading nowhere lacked eloquence, it was everywhere lacking in elegance, in sweetness, in proportion, and in that spontaneity that is the heaven-sent grace, the unique gift of Robert Schumann.

Actually, when the conductor, in moments of calm, conducted straightforwardly and with a minimum of motion, his orchestra followed with a maximum of beauty and with the authority of style that is our Philharmonic's way. But for the most part he did everything to the orchestra but conduct it. He whipped it up as if it were a cake, kneaded it like bread, shuffled and riffled an imaginary deck of cards, wound up a clock, shook a recalcitrant umbrella, rubbed something on a washboard and wrung it out. Really, there were very few moments when a film taken of the conductor alone, without sound, would have given any clue to the fact that he was directing a musical composition.

October 9, 1953

SCIENTISTS GET CURIOUS

¶ The scientific schools, long a fortress of pure reason and practicality, have lately been encouraging in their students a curiosity about the arts. The Massachusetts Institute of Technology and other technical training centers have introduced music to the elective parts of their curricula with notable success. Even on the philosophic plane the scientific world, classically disciplined to a positivisitic attitude, has begun to wonder if perhaps there is not something to be learned from the more spontaneous working methods of the musician, the painter, the poet.

Last week at a convention held in this city the Engineering College Research Council of the American Society for Engineering Education devoted a whole morning to "creativeness." The painter John Ferren, the novelist Ralph Bates, and the present writer, as composer, were asked to explain "creativeness" and answer questions about it. The assignment was a tough one, partly because artists and scientists do not use the same vocabulary, and also because the very word "creativeness" assumes a good deal.

For scientists it seems to imply that something has been invented out of nothing, or at least that some object or principle has been arrived at without its discoverer having followed the deductive procedures. For artists it implies nothing at all about method; it means originality rather, the bringing into existence of something different from everything else. This difference may be vast or very small, but it must be there. If it is, something has been created. If not, we have merely a copy.

Copies are legitimate, of course. The world lives on them. Their production and distribution are a province of engineering, as witness the printing press and the gramophone. But music recognizes two kinds of copies, the multiple and the unique. Multiple copies, all pretty much alike, are an industrial product. Single copies made by hand are an art product. A painter's copy of another painter's picture has a personal expression in spite of all attempts to keep it out. And an executant musician's rendering of a composition is as individual an achievement as what a builder erects from an architect's design. This duet of design and execution, thoroughly familiar to engineers, is characteristic of music. Painting is a one-man job and does not, in its high-art aspects, envisage reproduction. Poetry is a one-man job which envisages (or hopes for) multiple reproduction by print. Music, like architecture, envisages from the beginning collaboration. It is a design for execution.

Now considering the design as "creative" and its execution merely an "interpretation" is customary among musicians. But it applies better to the execution of scores from the past than to contemporary music. Co-operation between the living composer and his executants is an essential part of musical creation, of bringing a work into real existence. Because music's real existence is auditory; it is sound, not notes on a page. Actually, music and architecture, music and engineering, are similar in their dependence on execution. Who am I to say that the executant's contribution to my work is not a "creative" act? It is certainly part of one.

What scientists want to know, of course, is how a composer arrives at his design. Well, sometimes an expressive, a communicable idea is arrived at by reasoning. Sometimes it bursts up from the unconscious. And its organization into a piece of music comes in the same two ways. Often a practical workman will write it all down quite rapidly, as if he were taking dictation. At other times it comes more slowly. And if he hits a snag he has to reason his way around it. The simplest parallel I know for what a composer does is what anybody does when he writes a letter. He wants or needs to make a communication. He thinks about it a little. He writes it. Then he reads it back to find out whether he has said what he meant to say and, most important of all, whether he is willing to mean what he has actually said.

Music, all art for that matter, depends on meaning. The prestige of non-Euclidean geometry has all through this century caused artists to insist that their work at its best and most "advanced" is theoretical, an abstraction comparable to the higher equations. At the same time they have hoped that within twenty years its acceptance as communication would make them loved and famous. Actually music does not work like that. The most novel modern music has always had a public that understood and accepted it. The battle has been one of obtaining access for it to the existing mechanisms of distribution. All music is about something, just as all music that can stand up under concert usage has a sound technical structure. There is no abstract music. There is only expressive music. This expression may depict an inner or an outer reality. But it always depicts something. And unless both the reality depicted and its manner of depiction have an essential uniqueness, a personality strongly different from that of all other existing artifacts, there is no work of art. "Creation" has not taken place.

Science deals with a unified universe governed by laws universally applicable. Art deals with a multiple universe in which no two apples or carburetors or love affairs are alike. Revealing the common properties of apples and carburetors and love affairs is the business of science. To individualize them is the province of art. As to what is "creative" and what not, I suppose that the defining of all that is the critic's job. But critics can be terribly presumptuous. Who is to say that Stravinsky is more creative than Einstein? As Gertrude Stein used to say, there is the "human mind" and there is "human nature." There is also the visible or knowable universe. The human mind, like the rest of the knowable universe, follows patterns. That is its strength. Human nature, which is essentially unknowable, is at its most interesting when least predictable. And art, poetry, music are similarly most powerful when from work to work, school to school, age to age, and decade to decade they show the widest imaginable diversity from their own standard patterns of style, of subject-matter, of communicative effect.

October 18, 1953

CHUNKY AND PALATABLE

¶ Thomas Scherman, conducting the Little Orchestra Society's first concert of the season last night in Town Hall, gave us three chunky and highly palatable works, two of them contemporary. The other, Pergolesi's *Stabat Mater,* is a characteristic eighteenth-century piece whose popularity I have never quite understood. Gracefully written and melodious enough, this setting of the liturgical hymn for soprano, alto and orchestra has long been a favorite with audiences. Myself, I have never been able to keep my mind on it; and I had the same trouble last night,

ℳusic Reviewed

though Ann Ayers and Sandra Warfield seemed to be singing ever so nicely.

Paul Creston's Second Symphony, which Mr. Scherman conducted lovingly, is an easy-to-listen-to work, melodious and orchestrally rich. A certain self-indulgence on the harmonic plane makes for lushness, and constant use of ostinato figures in the structure gives a semblance of emotional intensity. All the same, though the work is seriously conceived and skillfully scored, it did not impress me on last night's hearing of it (my third in eight years) as quite firstclass. It is a work that stands some rehearing, and it has dignity. But I do not find its expressive content very personal. And its ending up with a wholly objective dance number denies the validity of the meditative mood in all the rest of it. That dance does not come out of the symphony's premise.

Stravinsky's comic opera *Mavra*, which closed the evening, is a delicious piece of musical fooling and of real dramatico-sentimental expression under all the fooling. Playing it for low farce, as was done (although in evening clothes and with no scenery) is, I think, a mistake. The characterization needs to be taken seriously, leaving all comic comment to the orchestra and to the music's own exuberance. Perhaps a puppet show would be the work's ideal presentation. Either that or a wholly stylized choreography that would evoke the pathos of puppets. Its irony, a doubletake, gets lost in comic-strip clowning.

The singers sang it straight, and Mr. Scherman played the music straight. That was as it should be. Only the acting, far too easy-going for so intense a work, a piece at once bitter, biting, hilarious, and tender, was out of key. That and also an explainer who addressed us at the beginning through a microphone, reading a script that recounted the plot (though program-notes were provided, and the opera was sung in English anyway) and told us what to think of the music, for all the world like a radio announcer. I never figured out what he was supposed to serve for. Maybe he had been left over from an earlier children's concert. Especially pleasing on the other hand, was the singing of Ann Ayers and of John Druary in this difficult and ever-so-Russian florid-aria skit on a *Charley's Aunt* theme out of Pushkin.

October 20, 1953

INTERPRETATION

¶ What does a composer of music need from his interpreters? What are the living composer's rights about the interpretation of his work? And what are an interpreter's obligations? All these matters have been disputed for centuries, because music is a collaborative art like architecture or engineering. A piece of music on a page is only an idea. Its real existence is in performance.

By performance I mean live performance. The transmission or recording of live performance has great value, like photography or print. But unlike print, it does not replace the original. Even when adjustments are made to compensate for accidents of performance and for the inefficiencies of recording, the result is still an imitation. A recording is not even a performance; it has to be itself performed on a machine operated by a live man or woman or child. And don't think such performances do not vary enormously in sound quality, in their volume patterns, even in speed. A recording played or a live performance broadcast under an engineer's control (plus the receiver's control) is an interpretation of an interpretation, a performance of a performance.

But let us get back to performance itself, as this takes place with live musicians and no microphones. And let us further suppose that the composer of the work has been present at rehearsals. Is the performance merely a rendering of the composer's plan? Or do the executants add something valuable of their own? The answer is that they do. Even if they try to do nothing but reflect the composer's thought and feeling, that effort at neutrality gives its own emotional tone, its own expressivity. It is a style like any other and comparable to what happens when you read aloud a piece of literature as if it were a contract. (Over-expressivity in performing Stravinsky can be like reading a contract as if it were literature.)

The truth is, of course, that a musical score is not a contract. It is much more like a cooking recipe, an indication (in many details quite precise and in others wholly approximate) that presupposes familiarity with traditional techniques and current tastes. For musical notation is highly inexact at best. It is a text that requires in the most literal sense "interpretation." And even when the author of it is present to guide that interpretation into the channels of his own desire, he must work through live people, accept their inefficiencies and take advantage of their particular temperaments in order to arrive at a result that will have life in it.

As a matter of fact, the composer in such a case is the interpreter of his own work. And the performance that he gives or guides is as much that of an experienced performing artist as it is that of an author. For it is a mistake to think the composer always knows what he wants. At certain points in the piece he knows precisely, has a vivid auditory image of a particular sound or a particular expressive effect. At others he is mostly aware of what he does not want.

If a piece of music depicts some scene or other exterior view, such as landscape or hell-fire or dancing, its score is likely to contain many indications of what is and is not wanted; and its tempo requirements can be quite exact. Even many years after its first performance this kind of music tends to preserve a standard interpretation. The landscapes of Debussy and Ravel, the ballets of Stravinsky do not vary enormously from performance to performance in tempo or in tonal balance. The symphonies of Sibelius, on the other hand, which are roughly contemporary with these, have no standard reading, cannot have, indeed, because their theme is not objective. They are depictions of the composer's emotional life.

The music of introspection, the music of the heart, requires of its interpreter that which is specific to the heart, spontaneity. If the music of Schumann or Schubert or Brahms or Fauré or Richard Wagner, for that matter, and certainly that of Arnold Schönberg is to be read convincingly, it must be read also with conviction. The composer can and should make an effort to get over to his interpreter how he wants the music to sound and to feel. But the artist must then take the music for his own, adopt it, feel it, and perform it as if it were an expression of his own deepest needs. If he does not treat it so, it will not communicate. If he overtreats it so, it will also not communicate; the interpretation will seem false. But in performing the music of anxiety and relief, of private tensions and their resolution —the music, in other words, of pure feeling—there is no substitute for feeling.

The music of the last three centuries, our practicable repertory back through Monteverdi and Schütz, includes depictions of both outer and inner realities. Both require in-objective reading, while the others demand subjectivity. The terpretation. But the depictions of outer reality require an musical depictions of outer reality are likely to be quite precisely scored also and to acquire early in their life-course a standard reading which is the correct one. The depictions of the inner world are of necessity less precisely set down, since spontaneity of expression is essential to their existence. Such music varies vastly in tempo, in rhythmic flow, in rhetorical emphasis from one interpreter to another, from one age or country to another. And no reading is ever definitive. The symphonies of Beethoven, for example, exist in the mind only. Their reality is a memory of many versions, not of one.

Interpreters vary, too. Some are better with objective music, and some specialize in the introspective. The great ones imagine themselves as masters of both, just as great composers do. But it is not true in either case. What is true is that all music requires interpretation. Even when a composer conducts his own music, his reading is not quite definitive. It is merely one version, perhaps the most authoritative and perhaps not, depending on how skillful a performer he is and how precise his original idea was. In all cases it is a privileged communication. The professional performer must consult it if he can and consult the composer if he can. But the best final result obtains, even in objective music and in the theater, when the interpreter, in full knowledge and in full acceptance of responsibility, takes over the show and plays Hamlet not as if he himself were Shakespeare, but as if he were Hamlet.

October 25, 1953

BIGGER THAN BASEBALL

¶ Among all of America's leisure activities, the most widely indulged, believe it or not, is the art of music. I am not talking about radio music, the universal background of home life, or the various forms of transmitted music that are the steady accompaniment to public eating and drinking, to bus-riding, automobile trips, and shopping. "Canned" music has become an auditory decor so constantly present in American life that virtually nobody can escape from it.

But music in this sense cannot be called a leisure activity any more than sleeping in a bed or wearing shoes can. An activity is something one is active about. Well, the latest bulletin of the National Music Council, a very serious documentary publication, reports over the signature of Mrs. Helen M. Thompson, executive secretary of the American Symphony Orchestra League, that thirty million people in this country are "actively interested in concert music." This does not mean jazz or popular ditties, or hillbilly dance-bands, or shows and films employing music, or hymn singing, or wedding marches. It means the classical music of the last three centuries, including the one we live in. And thirty million people are one-fifth of our population.

The statement is even more difficult to believe when one realizes that only half that number, fifteen million, watched major league baseball games last year, that only thirteen million ordinarily engage in hunting, and that a mere five million, according to the same report, play golf. Considering classical music as a spectator sport, its total cost in a recent year, says Mrs. Thompson, was $45,000,000, compared to the following gross revenues of organized sports:

Baseball $40,000,000	Professional foot-	
Horse and dog	ball	9,000,000
tracks 38,000,000		

In addition to the $45,000,000 paid at the gate for public

performances of classical music, which represents 30,000,-
000 separate paid admissions, last year's sales of classical
recordings totaled $60,000,000. This amounts to 24 per
cent of all record sales. And among the ten best sellers
were two full-length classical symphonies.

Let me give you some more details about our professional
music life. America has eighty opera companies operating
in nineteen states. We have 150 music periodicals, 750 music
critics, 1,196 writers on musical subjects. We have 938 symphony orchestras, all or in part professionally staffed. One
of our large booking organizations reports that last year
three times as many concerts were given in the United States
as in all the rest of the world put together. Music in general
—its teaching, performance, manufacture of equipment,
and distribution—has for some years now ranked sixth
among America's industries in volume of business, being
somewhat smaller than food or motor cars but a much
bigger affair than steel.

As for music on the non-professional level, let us begin
by noting the existence, again according to the National
Music Council, of 20,000,000 music students. More than
one-tenth of our population is taking lessons of some kind
toward the acquisition of musical skill. Seventy-five lay organizations comprising over 600,000 members aid in disseminating international standards of workmanship. Fifteen
thousand school orchestras actually perform symphonic
repertory. For adults who enjoy playing string quartets and
the like there is a society of more than 3,000 members called
Amateur Chamber Music Players. They have a national
directory, too, where they are graded A, B, C, D for skill,
and they can phone one another anywhere, just like Al-
coholics Anonymous. As for choruses, choirs, glee clubs,
and singing societies, they number surely upward of a million. There are very few citizens among those able to carry
a tune at all whose lives have not at one time been permanently enriched by participation in this most rewarding of
all forms of musical exercise.

Now with a large part of our nation involved in some way
with music, nobody has to worry right now about the state
of the art. It is in every way a going concern. But it might
help to understand how deeply music is honeycombed into
American life if I sketch, even superficially, music's organi-

zation. For with the possible exception of medicine, music is
the most highly organized activity in the Western world. Religion has its sects, literature its language barriers. Sports
have different rules in different countries. Love and war,
as we know, have no rules at all. But the symphony orchestra is a machine so standardized that any conductor, any
player, any piece in its repertory can be replaced overnight
by a conductor, player, or composition from any other orchestra in the world of similar skill-category. And the skill-
categories are only about three. All this without language
difficulties. The instruments used, the manner of sounding
them, and the compositions performed do not differ in any
notable way from Tel-Aviv to Valparaiso.

And since the symphony orchestra is the kingpin of our
whole musical system, the conservatories of music from Tel-
Aviv to Valparaiso and from Cape Town to Murmansk, by
way of Seattle and Tokyo, are devoted to the production of
players, conductors, and composers who will be ready at a
moment's notice to step into any symphonic operation.
Also, since a standardized art needs a standardized public,
our schools, colleges, and universities have set themselves
the task of teaching to future orchestral subscribers an accepted history of music (with orchestral composition at the
top), a standard method of musical analysis (for the understanding of orchestral music), and a standard hierarchy of
values for the admiration of orchestral works.

Contributory to this effort of our educational system is
a network of music clubs, laymen's auxiliary aid societies,
technical guilds, and trade groups. National associations of
music teachers, of instrument manufacturers, of piano tun-
ers, of flute players, societies for the pooling of copyrights
and the collection of royalties, groups opposed to the performance of contemporary music, others who agitate for it,
a managers' association, a union of soloists (in addition to
the great Musicians' Union itself), a half dozen sororities
devoted to general do-gooding, musical therapists, music
publishers, collectors of recorded music, youth organizations of music lovers world-wide in membership, statisti-
cians devoted to the collecting and pooling of information
about how symphony orchestras are financed—everybody,
literally everybody connected with the music world belongs
to something, has a part in its complex organization.

This organization has no hierarchy or center. It is not a professional clan, a business monopoly, or an exercise in amateur philanthropy, though it is something of all these. It is basically a vast network of spontaneous co-operation that happens to work efficiently because the modern world loves music and because musicians themselves are, among all workers in the intellectual branches, the most given to effective organization. Their talent for this is probably associated with their private feeling of consecration. In this they are like the clergy, which is also good at organizing everybody. In any case, the music world is a maze of power-lines in which the professional, the amateur, the educator, the student, the man of business, and the woman of society are equally involved.

Some years ago the late Louis Kirstein, at that time president of Filene's department store in Boston, received a visit from some trustees of the Boston Symphony Orchestra. The orchestra needed $75,000 quickly; could Mr. Kirstein help? Mr. Kirstein, aware of the suburban business which the concerts brought to his store every Friday afternoon, though he himself rarely attended, recognized his responsibility, gave $25,000 and telephoned two other retail merchants, who gave the same. The orchestra's emergency was closed.

Another case of business tie-up came to attention recently in the decision of the General Electric Company to build a subsidiary plant in Louisville.

The cultural advantages of that city, of which the symphony orchestra is one, had determined its being chosen. Culture works as follows in the decentralization of industry. You cannot establish a branch factory without moving executives and technicians. And your executives and technicians cannot move their families without their wives' consent. And their wives will not consent unless the city proposed can offer educational advantages in the form of (and prized in this order) good schools, a near-by college, a symphony orchestra, a public library, and an art museum.

Mayor Charles Farnsley of Louisville demonstrated some years ago in a doctoral thesis that municipal prosperity follows from city to city a curve parallel to the availability in these cities of (in this order) music, theater, and art. In those cities department store business is good, restaurant business is good, hotel business is good; and there is a traffic problem, infallible index of prosperity.

It has long been known from history that culture follows commerce. Today it is clear also that commerce follows culture. And it is also clear to any one who deals with the world of classical, or "serious," music that music is purely a cultural and educational manifestation and forms no part of the entertainment trades, of show business. On the contrary, it is esteemed beneficial like religion; and people give money to it. Musical exercise is well known to be good for the body, the feelings, and the mind. A further presumption that it can also lift up the soul, though rarely stated, is ever present in the American view of life.

To occupy the young, to ennoble adulthood, to train the hand, elevate the mind, lift up the spirits, and at the same time make business boom—all these are what America expects out of music and, surprisingly enough, gets. No country before us, not Germany nor Austria nor Italy nor the England of Tudor times, ever quite so gleefully turned itself over to the tonal art. What will come of it all there is no way of knowing. But for this century at least, music is our hobby and our habit; and the chiefest, after breadwinning, among all our avowable preoccupations.

October 25, 1953

KAPELL

¶ The pianist William Kapell, who died in an airplane accident near San Francisco on Oct. 29, was a fine artist. So were Grace Moore, soprano, Ginette Neveu and Jacques Thibaud, violinists, who have died in similar fashion in recent years. Every time an airplane falls persons distinguished in professional, political, business, or military life are among the dead. Because it is exactly such persons to whom the speed of air travel offers an irresistible convenience. A musician who moves about the globe in this way can play twice to three times as many engagements a season as the one who is earthbound. Also it is known that aviation fatalities per passenger-mile traveled are far fewer than those due to the deadly automobile. Still, the number of famous names that appears in the aviation accident lists is impressive. And still the advantages, economic and artistic, that come from being able to move quickly from one date to another will keep a large number of our most valued musicians among the inveterate air travelers.

Among musicians of his generation William Kapell, just thirty-one on Sept. 20, was one of the great ones. His career, like that of Ginette Neveu, was at the point where he was no longer considered just a young genius but was recognized by his colleagues as a mature artist. At nineteen he was winning big prizes. At twenty he began his career as a touring recitalist and a much-in-demand orchestral soloist. But for a decade his repertory had remained heavily weighted with the easy-to-put-over works of Rachmaninoff, Tchaikovsky, and Khatchaturian. It was only in the last two years that he had gained real access to the grand repertory of the piano, to the concertos of Mozart and Beethoven and Brahms and Chopin and to the suites of Bach and Debussy, and that he had been genuinely successful with that repertory.

Kapell had fought hard for this access and for this success. He had fought with his management and with the press. And he had wrestled with the repertory itself, not only alone but also with the counsel and the detailed cooperation of musicians who knew that repertory. He had studied, labored, consulted, digested, ripened. Kapell had become a grown man and a mature artist, a master. He could play great music with authority; his readings of it were at once sound and individual. He had a piano technique of the first class, a powerful mind, a consecration and a working ability such as are granted to few, and the highest aspirations toward artistic achievement.

Kapell was conquering the world. In one decade he had won a world-wide audience. At the beginning of a second he was recognized as a master to be taken seriously in the great repertory. He was already laying plans (and operating, too) toward the renewal of this repertory through the application of his great technical and interpretative powers to

contemporary piano music and through devoted co-operation with contemporary composers. And his conquests were
not easy. Few artists have ever battled so manfully with
management or so unhesitatingly sassed the press. He was
afraid of nobody, because his heart was pure.

It is not germane that as a man he was a good son and
brother, a good husband and father, and a loyal friend,
though he was all these. What is important to music is that
he was a musician and a fighter. He did not fight for himself or for just any music. He fought to play well and to
play the best music. Also to take part in the creative life of
his time. And he was winning, would have gone on winning, for he had a star.

He had also an unlucky star, else he would not have been
taken from us. And our loss, music's loss, is irreparable.
Other men of comparable genius and sincerity may arise;
but none will ever take his place, because that place was
unique. Kapell had built it to fit his own great talents. And
built it so that his talents could serve the whole world of
music in their own particular and powerful way. Past services
will remain and be of use to others. But Kapell himself, that
huge life-force, is dead; and his continuing musical presence
will not be with us any more. Since he was buried last Monday it has been a week of mourning for musicians.

November 8, 1953

RICH RESOURCES

¶ The Philharmonic Chamber Ensemble, which
opened its third annual series of concerts on Saturday night
at the Y. M. H. A., is the richest among all our chamber
music groups in instrumental resources. Drawing its players
from the whole Philharmonic-Symphony Orchestra, and organized as a co-operative society, this group offers regularly
in its programs works for a great variety of instrumental
combinations; and the great expertness of the players per-

mits them also to offer works of unusual stylistic and technical difficulty.

The star number of last Saturday's program was Arnold Schönberg's early *Kammer-Symphonie,* Opus 9, for fifteen solo instruments, conducted by Dimitri Mitropoulos. Rarely performed at all, on account of its great technical difficulty, this deeply passionate and eloquent piece is at once a monument of late Romanticism and a picture window turned toward twentieth-century chromatic experiment. It is a powerful work that seems to invite (like its predecessor *Verklärte Nacht*) choreography by Antony Tudor.

No less expert and stylish (in the best sense) was the performance of Beethoven's Quintet for Woodwinds and Piano, with Aba Bogin at the keyboard. Mozart's Duo for Violin and Viola (No. 2, in B-flat Major) came off less well. The string players of the Philharmonic, many of them at least, seem less accustomed to the refinements of chamber music execution than the wind players are, used, these latter, to the constant playing of solo passages. Nevertheless Leon Temerson and Bernard Andreasson, accompanied by Mr. Bogin, gave a delicious and even brilliant performance of Manuel Rosenthal's *Sonatine* for Two Violins and Piano. This lively work, composed in 1923 at the age of nineteen, is musically inspired by Milhaud and Poulenc, rather than by Ravel, who was Rosenthal's teacher. It is an outgoing work, frank, vigorous and entertaining. Thirty years later, one can still find it valid. It is not only skillful but, for all its youthful enthusiasms, strongly personal.

Milton Babbitt's Woodwind Quartet, an Alma Morgenthau-Locust Valley Festival commission which received its first performance on this occasion, is also a strongly personal work. Music composed in the twelve-tone-row syntax has long tended in its finer examples toward a supercharged emotional expression and in its more commonplace ones toward a sterile academicism. It is Mr. Babbitt's distinction to have produced in a twelve-tone technique derived, like that of the contemporary Parisian school, from Webern rather than from Schönberg or Berg, music of an airy elegance wholly his own. It is not crabbed like the French stuff, nor does it seek pathos at any point. It is lacy, good-humored, disinvolved, water-clear. At its least concentrated it goes a bit abstract. At its most intense it has a studied relaxation that is very American, very Princetonian, and utterly distinguished.

November 23, 1953

IRRESISTIBLE

¶ The program that Nathan Milstein played last night in Carnegie Hall, accompanied at the piano by the impeccable Arthur Balsam, was a serious one. Three great chunks of uncompromising music for the violin made up its first three quarters—a Vitali chaconne, a Bach unaccompanied sonata and the Beethoven "Kreutzer." Even the final plate of tidbits offered pieces by Schumann and Brahms. And nothing is more serious than Paganini, especially when it is a set of variations of the utmost difficulty composed on a theme from one of the Caprices by Mr. Milstein himself and executed with the utmost brilliance.

Everything seemed, indeed, to be executed with brilliance, even the severest of the classical selections. For it is the gift of this artist to make music shine. His tone is bright, his rhythm is alive and compelling. His music-making glows not with a surface lustre but with an inner light and a warmth all its own, an animal warmth. Soul is not his specialty; nor are tears. For emotional satisfaction he gives us a clean reading of the text and a boyish humility before the great masters. He gives us too a boyish delight in fine technical workmanship, in controlled muscular activity exercised to his powers' limit.

And that limit is a far one, for nobody plays the violin more expertly. But along with the expertness there is a love of the violin and of playing it well that are irresistible. Mr. Milstein is no great or original interpreter. Nor is he any authoritative spokesman for the masters of musical thought. There is no vulgarity in him, but neither is there any deep penetration or especial sensitivity. There is simply a personal vibrancy that makes his work at all times completely alive.

In the "Kreutzer" Sonata of Beethoven the dramatized emphases and strong accents were almost over-live, but they were not rough or ugly. They were simply an interpretation and a legitimate one. And they were matched by fine delicacies and many a full-singing line. Fullness of sound at all the levels of softness and loudness is one of this artist's grander gifts. It gives his playing an equalized surface tension, a power of complete projection, that holds the attention in a way that the work of few artists is capable of doing. And so his exact interpretative conception of a piece is never a very important matter.

It is by sheer efficiency and charm, by modesty, enthusiasm, and an utter loyalty to what he is doing that Milstein makes his mark. After twenty and more years on the concert stage he is still the perfect pupil, reasonable, master of his trade, devoted to the sound of his instrument, and not afraid of it. Neither is he afraid of the great classics nor of approaching them with passion and with common sense. The latter quality, of course, is as rare among musicians of any age as is technical mastery. The combination is irresistible.

December 15, 1953

1954

REMEMBERING MAHLER

¶ A very great pleasure was yesterday afternoon's Philharmonic concert, with Bruno Walter conducting. The program was two symphonies, a Haydn and a Mahler, both evidently beloved of the conductor. And the orchestra played perfectly, sweetly, beautifully. One didn't have to worry about what one thought of the symphonies as musical scripts. It was enough that they were being played, understood, rendered into loveliness.

Mr. Walter's reading of the Haydn G-major commonly known as No. 88 was robust, straightforward, an ultimate in rightness and ease. The kind of sophistication that avoids super-refinement is the ultimate sophistication in the reading of this work. And this kind of sophistication is Walter's gift with the German classics. He can make them seem as natural as breathing. And he can make the Philharmonic, which can do everything, sound as if playing a classical symphony were the most natural thing in the world. All the care for beauty and exactitude that goes into such a reading is great workmanship, of course, on his part and on that of the orchestral players. But the result is not any awareness of workmanship at all; it merely brings a piece to life, makes it real. At least that was your reviewer's experience yesterday.

The experience was no less intense in Mahler's First Symphony than in the Haydn. The Mahler is a young man's work, written at thirty, ambitious as to length, abundant in musical ideas. Most of these ideas are orchestral, the ingenuities of a conductor. Expressively the symphony is a patchwork of contrasts. It begins as a pastoral scene with bird calls and hunting horns but turns military by the end of the first movement. The second is a waltz, something be-

tween a real country waltz and the urban kind. One might call it suburban if the term were not derogatory. In any case, it bounces along with good spirits and also turns military at the end.

The third movement, the most original of the four, is a joke about a funeral march, beginning with a solo passage for one bass viol and going on to a ravishing orchestral imitation of the Hungarian night-club style before returning to the funeral, at which point it adds a French children's ditty, *Frère Jacques,* to its comical allusions. The last movement starts apocalyptically, imitates a Viennese sentimental song, adds trumpets, and ends with a brassy coda. Everywhere the tunes are good and the orchestral treatments picturesque. There is a young man's fascination with rhetorical structure elements—with introductions, transitions, and perorations. It is charmingly immodest and delightful for the outrageousness of its satire. I think it is the loving hand beneath it all that gives the work its reality. Mahler loved writing music and loved dramatizing the relation between the composer and his material. This drama, I think, is his music's most intense expression and its most original.

The vigor with which this drama came forth yesterday was Mr. Walter's contribution. Among all living conductors he has the freshest remembrance, I suspect, of exactly how Mahler's music felt in Mahler's time. Certainly it all felt fresh at that time, and certainly the First Symphony felt like a striking and somewhat scandalous piece by a young conductor of genius. Walter did not underline the scandalousness; he leant rather on its sweetness. And by doing so he made it seem youthful and aspiring, which it also is. He could have given it the portentous treatment. Some do. Instead, he read it as if remembering his youth, which was not far, after all, from Mahler's, only a decade and a half.

January 25, 1954

COMPOSER AND CRITIC

¶ Music in the twentieth century is the subject of a congress to be held in Rome this spring from April 4 through 15. Composers, critics, and interpreters from everywhere will be present as the guests of the inviting organizations, which are the European Culture Center (Geneva, Switzerland), the Commiteee for Cultural Freedom (Paris and New York), and the Italian State Radio. Twelve composers, including the Americans Ben Weber and Lou Harrison, have been commissioned to write works which will compete for three large cash prizes (plus other benefits). There will be lots of twentieth-century music performed by the visiting soloists and conductors. And there will be forum discussions of subjects especially interesting to composers, critics, and interpreters.

This writer has been asked to lead a discussion entitled *The Composer and the Critic.* The choice was an obvious one, I suppose, since he has long been active in both roles. But that very fact may have led him to lack consistency. When another composer's music is unfavorably reviewed, for example, he knows that, just or unjust, the reviewer has done his best. But when his own or that of one of his close colleagues receives such a review he tries to convince himself, just as any other artist does in that circumstance, that the reviewer is ignorant, stupid, and very probably in the pay of some enemy.

The truth is, at least in America, that music critics do not take graft. They are not even offered it on any scale that might be tempting. Neither do they fight very vigorously against the survival of new techniques, new talents, new aesthetic positions. They inform the public as well as they can about these; that is what they are hired for. They cover the musicial front, report on it as knowingly and as sympathetically as they are individually capable of doing.

Actually critics, composers, and performing artists have at

least one motivation in common, namely the advancement of music, which is the art they live by. They are also busy advancing their own careers. Now any workman in the arts is entitled to consider his own career important. Every career is, as a matter of fact. The music of this our time, indeed, is simply the music composed by the present writer and his colleagues, nothing else. And this goes for music criticism in our time too. All living musicians—and no critic is respected by his readers unless he has some skill in the technique of music and some responsibility to it as an art— all living musicians, I say, are part of one great band (or conspiracy, if you will) vowed to the defense of the musical faith and to its propagation.

Their methods of going about this differ widely, and they are always treading on one another's toes. Treading on the toes of composers and performers is, indeed, considered by many as the main business of critics. This is not so. Their main business, really their only business, is explaining the creative or executant artist to the public. Explaining the public to the artist is management's business and that of older artists. Defending the public against the artist is nobody's business, not the impresario's nor the politicians, nor the clergy's, still less that of the critic, whose living depends on the survival of the art he speaks for. Civic and religious leaders are permitted in free countries to alert the public to the danger of circulating seditious or immoral ideas; but their power to stop such circulation is based in really free countries wholly on an agreement among the adult population about what actions are to be considered seditious or immoral. Critics have a different role; they are commentators, not censors. And artists are producers, not traitors or charlatans. Neither is the public a fool.

A newspaper man once advised me, "Never underestimate the public's intelligence; never overestimate its information." The moral of this for the critic is that he does his duty best by his readers when he describes and explains to the public what the artist is doing. If he adds a paragraph of personal opinion, that is his privilege as a musician. It is also his duty as a reporter, since the confessing of his personal prejudices and predilections helps the reader to discount them. But the description of music is his business, as the performance of music is the performer's business and the designing of it for possible execution the composer's. Consuming it is the public's business and, to this end, judging it. We all judge it. That is a human right granted even to the reviewer. But if the reviewer is not to be mistaken by artists and managements for just a cog in their publicity machine, neither should he set himself up as a Bureau of Standards. We still live in a Republic of Art, thank God. And I, as a member of that republic, as a plain consumer, want access to all the music there is. I also want all the description and information about it I can get, as a consumer's guide. I even enjoy knowing, as a consumer's guide, who likes it and who doesn't. But as an artist, I do not enjoy being disapproved or misinterpreted.

A climate of receptivity is what the artist most desires. It is also a thing that even the most experienced reviewer cannot always offer. Individuality and originality are the bedrock of musical achievement, not ease of learning or technique, which anybody can have. And individuality, originality are no end shocking. The reviewer sometimes takes the shock of them harder than the public. At other times he acts as a buffer, transmits the shock gently to his public. At still other times he serves for nothing at all.

Haydn, Mozart, and Beethoven came to maturity as artists without benefit of the press and without any hindrance from it either. The artist can perfectly well do without criticism, prefers to, in fact. But he loves praise, flourishes on it. And his publisher, his manager help him to live by publicizing the praise that he receives. So any artist tends to consider that praising him is the critic's business, or at the very least giving him lots of space. The critic, on the other hand, is an essayist who knows that he can write a more interesting article about something he knows than he can do about a work or personality that he has only recently encountered. There is the further fact, too, that a vigorous attack is more entertaining than any defense. (As William Blake said, "Damn braces; bless relaxes.") And so any critic, faced with the even faintly unfamiliar, will tend, like any knight-errant, to attack it, or at the very least to dismiss it with a snort.

To the critic every producing composer is a challenge. To the composer every critic is a danger. All this makes tonic the musical air. But there are fools in both camps. The composing fool thinks the press is out to get him, does not realize that he is merely grist for its mill and that as long as he gives it grist the mill will grind for him. The reviewing fool thinks he can make his fame by praising successful performers and dead composers, not knowing at all that critical championships have always been won and are only won still in bouts with a living composer.

The audience for all this is one audience, for the same people read about music that listen to it. Toscanini's public, Stravinsky's public, and Olin Downes's public are drawn from the same pool of music consumers. And all three men are workers before that public and are not, except as individual consumers, members of it. What they have in common is membership in the professional world of music. Their quarrels about music are family quarrels. A critic is therefore a musician who offers to the public as his contribution to the art an inside view of loves and hatreds and mechanics and methodological warfares that were never intended to be exposed, but of which the public exposure is considered to be good for business. Your critic seldom kisses, but he always tells.

February 14, 1954

CRITIC AND PERFORMER

¶ Reviewing performances of familiar music takes up the largest part of a critic's week. It is also the easiest part. Reviewing new pieces is the hardest and the most important, for that is where criticism touches history. The history of music, we know, is the history of its composition, not of its performance. But musical performance, by mere abundance, occupies the foreground of the contemporary scene. Consequently the reviewer is largely occupied with reporting it.

He is usually, moreover, fairly well prepared to report on it, because his musical education has surely given him some experience of a musical instrument. Rare is the reviewer who is not able to identify himself with a man at a pianoforte. Others play a stringed instrument. Many have a vocal history. And if they know before they start reviewing music something of performing techniques, they also, through going to concerts, become soon familiar with the repertory and with current standards of interpretation. It is not hard to spot an ugly tone, an off-pitch phrase, a messy jumble of notes, a lovely sound, a transparent texture, an authoritative personality. One critic can make a mistake, hear wrong; but the ensemble of the press in any musical center rarely misjudges gravely a performing artist.

Misjudgments in this field occur most frequently with regard to advanced styles of interpretation. Reviewers tend to accept the customary approach to any piece as an inherent characteristic of that piece. A radical change based on the most advanced musicological research they not infrequently mistake for clumsiness. They imagine a norm of interpretation to exist for any works or school of work and consider the artist to have failed who deviates from that norm. The opposite is true, however. No such norm exists; there are merely habits imitated from successful artists. The true version of a work is not to be found in the most admired contemporary interpretation but rather in its printed notes and in such historical information as is available about what these notes meant to the composer and to other musicians of his time. Styles of interpretation change about every quarter of a century, and the great interpreters are the ones who change them, not those who copy yesterday's changes.

It is this constant restudy of the classics that gives life to our musical tradition. Attempts to discourage such restudy whenever it does not originate in Vienna, which it seldom does, are characteristic of that large segment of our music world that stems from Vienna. Berlin was never so reactionary and Paris never so powerful. Our musical press in America owes some of its finest qualities (its consecration, for instance) to the influence of Vienna, but also its tendency to reject without examination any restudy of the great classical and Romantic repertories.

But if our musical press lacks (and sometimes willfully) an intellectual background for the judging of new interpretations, interpreters themselves have for the most part no clear conception at all of the reviewer's assignment. They think every review is written to them, is a personal communication. It is no such thing, of course. It is not a free lesson offered the artist; it is a description *for the public* of how the artist works. And if it involves, as it must, some analysis of technical faults and virtues, that analysis has as its only purpose answering the question, "How did he get that way?"

I admit a tendency among reviewers to give vocal lessons in public, and I deplore it. No critic ever complains that a pianist used too little arm weight or that a violinist's bow lacked control from the forefinger. They do not correct the soloist's fingering of octaves or the conductor's beat. But they do say that Miss So-and-So failed to "support her tones." This phrase does not describe an auditory effect but a state of muscular control. Bad pitch, gasping breath, false notes, wavering tone, these things can be heard; and it is legitimate to mention them. It is not legitimate to tell an artist in public how to correct them. Our business is to describe the symptom, not to diagnose its cause or prescribe a cure.

Another common fault of the reviewer, and one which causes the greatest bitterness among artists, is carelessness of statement. The reviewer all too frequently fails to meet the performer on the performer's own level of workmanship. When an artist has devoted large sums of money and years of his life to acquiring a skill, however imperfect the result may be, the reviewer owes him the courtesy, the proof of integrity, of exercising a comparable care in his report to the public about the artist's work. He does not have to be right; nobody does. But if he wishes the public to believe him and musicians to respect him, he must arrive at his opinion by fair methods; and he must state it in clear English.

The reviewer gets tired toward the season's end of hearing music, all too often the same music, and of sitting through third-class performances. The music world is incredibly full of third-class artists, many of them in first-class posts. It takes some self-control to keep one's patience with them. But they are doing their best; and they have a great deal to lose, even the most famous ones, from a review which lowers their dignity. And the kind that lowers their dignity most is the kind that is badly written.

An artist's privilege is to make music as beautifully as he can, and a critic's privilege is to write about the artists as truly as he can. This involves some thought and some care. Also some humility. The artist works best when his ego is big, when he feels confident. The reviewer works best when his ego is small, when he feels respect for the artist's integrity, however minor may be his interest in the artist's work. The poorest performance does not justify a poorly written review or any assumption of the right to grant or withhold degrees. Writing a review is not giving an examination; it is taking one. The subject is whatever musical occasion one has attended. One has, as in any examination, a limited time in which to produce an essay on some theme suggested by the occasion, preferably one which permits the reviewer to include in his essay a clear report and a fair estimate. It has been my experience that the public is invariably grateful for an informative and well written review and that the artist rarely resents it. It is my conviction that he has every reason, however, to resent from the reviewer inaccurate reporting and slovenly writing.

February 21, 1954

CASALS AND THE MATTERHORN

¶ Switzerland contains forty-three big climbs, thirty-nine of which start from Zermatt. The most celebrated of these are the Monte Rossa and the Matterhorn. To this diamond necklace of summits which surround the village, itself as charmingly intimate, and about as inaccessible, as Aspen, Colorado, has lately been added that gem and pinnacle of music-making in our time, Pablo Casals. For three weeks, from August 18 to September 8, the great cellist presided over a summer academy, small but ever so distinguished, and gave for the first time in many years public master-classes in the interpretation of cello literature. He says that he cannot remember exactly when he gave his last course of the kind at the École Normale de Musique in Paris but that surely it was not later than the 1920's. I remember his course on the Bach suites, given there in 1922; but I do not know whether it was the last.

In any case he has been giving such classes again; and this season their subject was the cello works of Beethoven. The Zermatt Summer Academy of Music, let me add, bears little resemblance to its famous elder brother the Prades Festival. The latter is a recording deal, and its concerts are largely concerned with showing the master cellist in musical association with some of our younger pianists, violinists, and conductors. It does not cater to cellists or attract them much, save for a few former Casals pupils who turn up now and then for a private lesson.

Zermatt, on the other hand, is chiefly for cellists. A string quartet in residence (the Vegh) illustrated this year a course in quartet playing. A trio (Arpad Gerecz, Madeline Foley, and Karl Engel) did the same for a course in the Beethoven trios given by Paul Grümmer, who also gave, under Casals, a cello class. Sandor Vegh (of the quartet) handled the Beethoven violin sonatas and played them with Engel. Vocal coaching, not limited to the works of Beethoven, was offered by Hans Willi Haeusslein. Mieczyslaw Horszowski played a recital of Beethoven piano sonatas but did not teach. He also played (but perfectly) with Casals in two private concerts, limited to the students of the Academy and a few invited guests, all five of the Beethoven sonatas for cello and piano, including the horn sonata, opus 17, which has been played as a cello piece for over a century and which was probably familiar to Beethoven in this form. Casals's own class included sixteen cellists, four pianists who came as members of cello-and-piano teams, two pianists who came independently to study the Beethoven cello-and-piano works (twenty-two working students in all), and nine auditors.

This listener climbed the steep mountain valley (by car and electric train) to hear the master play with Horszowski Beethoven's chief cello works. (The three sets of variations were omitted.) And the experience was both memorable and revelatory. He discovered for himself that Casals is not only a fine musician, which everybody knows, but also a great technician of the cello still, a fact which has

been little played up in the Prades publicity and a fact of
cardinal importance to music today. Because, though there
are fifty, at least, living musicians of the cello literature who
are comparably enlightened about it, there is none other, to
my knowledge, who knows so well the limitations and possibilities of the cello as an instrument of music and who can
demonstrate them so convincingly in their application to the
cello's classical repertory. If this is true, as I believe it to be,
then the cellists of the world should remain in contact for
as long as Casals himself remains in the world, with their
instrument's chief present source of artistry and excellence.

There is no doubt that the cello's present period of technical expansion derives from the playing of Pablo Casals.
Anybody in the cello world will tell you that. And, though
many of the devices involving the so-called "thumb positions" (for playing high passages, for instance) were invented by the nineteenth-century Belgian virtuoso Franz
Popper, their application to music-making in a first-class
musical way was made by Pablo Casals alone more than
forty years ago. His technique has always excited musicians
profoundly because of his musical penetration. And his musicianship has always stirred them because of his technical
superiority. He has viewed music through the technician's
lens and studied technical problems through the microscope
of musical analysis. As a result he makes Beethoven sound
better than it ever did before, and he makes the cello sound
better too. He has done this for many years; he still does
it. And if other cellists are doing it more and more of late,
that is because he is the father of them all.

His technical mastery (and musical too, for with him
they cannot be separated; in that way his mind is as Spanish
as a bull-fighter's)—his mastery in general, let us say, has
always been remarkable for three qualities. These are, still
are, his ability to play on pitch, his ability to move his left
hand up and down the finger-board without sliding, and the
studied character of his vibrato. The first two are technical
skills; the other is a matter of musical analysis. All apply to
the left hand. It was easily observable the other day in Zermatt that for simple harmony notes that were not part of
the thematic discourse he used no vibrato at all. But as soon
as melody spoke vibrato began. If a melody note diminished
in volume, his vibrato diminished in speed and width, com-

ing completely to rest just before the end of the note. For a crescendo on the bass strings he used a very wide vibrato, produced by means of it a tone of great power. At other times, especially playing without vibrato, his tone was so soft that only its penetrating and stringy character seemed to give it any presence at all.

Great presence it had, nevertheless; and this presence all came from the right arm, from the bow. The evenness of his bow from heel to tip, moving very slowly and playing ever so softly, betrayed a muscular control that few cellists of any age have at their command. In fact, the bow was so wholly under his command, at all times in optimum contact with the strings and moving at exactly the necessary speed, that not once in either of the sessions did the cello's tone whistle, grunt, growl, or scratch. Neither did it weep, I may add, though tears on the cello are a matter of deliberate musical taste rather than of technical abandon. If Casals does not indulge in them, that is because his expression has ever been impersonal, objective, a little distant. His Catalan reserve has no place for self-pity, for what the Spaniards call *patetismo*.

His personal expressivity nowadays is toward a straightforward vigor in vigorous passages, a healthy muscular vigor quite void of emotional urgency, toward a meditative quality in all those misterioso passages that were so dear to Beethoven, and in the songful ones toward an intense sweetness that is less an outpouring than it is an evocation of the memory of song. At the peak of his senescent years, for he is only seventy-two, it was with Beethoven's last cello sonata that the Casals qualities of sensitivity, of sadness, and of resignation seemed most perfectly paired. One understood both in the work and in its performance, the meaning of the poet's phrase "all passion spent." And the whole presence of both was the more vibrant since every other vigor had remained intact.

Vibrancy in resignation is what makes of Casals today a sort of musical saint. But the miracle that he performs, and a true saint must do miracles, is to make familiar music flower and a familiar instrument sing. For doing this he has, like any saint, both inspiration and method. And if the result seems at times almost supernatural, that effect comes from an interpenetration of ends and means so complete that we wonder however it could have been achieved. One can name the elements of it, but not explain their fusion.

Cellists have a great deal to gain from studying that result and consulting the author of it. As does any other musician, too. But let no one ever forget that when Casals plays the classical masters he is also playing the cello, an older and possibly more miraculous creation than any piece ever written for it. I suspect, indeed, that the instrument itself, even more than Bach or Beethoven, is his true love. There is something almost marital about Casals's matter-of-fact command, as if the way he plays the cello were the true way finally found, the way it always should have been played, the way it finally now can be played, and surely the way it will henceforth always demand to be made to sound.

September 14, 1954

INDEX

Index

About the Author

A Personal Statement

BY VIRGIL THOMSON

I was born in Kansas City, Missouri, grew up there and went to war from there. That was the other war. Then I was educated some more in Boston and Paris. In composition I was chiefly the pupil of Nadia Boulanger. While I was still young I taught music at Harvard and played the organ at King's Chapel, Boston. Then I returned to Paris and lived there for many years, until after the Germans came, in fact. From 1940 to 1954 I was Music Critic of the New York *Herald Tribune*. I still live in New York.

My best known works are the operas *Four Saints in Three Acts* and *The Mother of Us All* (both to texts by Gertrude Stein), *The Plough That Broke the Plains* and *The River* (films by Pare Lorentz), and *Louisiana Story* (film by Robert Flaherty), though there are also symphonies, concertos, Masses, string quartets and many other works in many forms. I have made over a hundred musical portraits too, all of them drawn from life, the sitter posing for me as he would for an artist. I have appeared as guest-conductor with every major orchestra in the United States and many others both here and abroad. I am the author of five books: *The State of Music* (1939; now available in Vintage Books), *The Musical Scene* (1945), *The Art of Judging Music* (1948), *Music Right and Left* (1951), and *Virgil Thomson* (1966).

A free catalogue of VINTAGE BOOKS *will be sent at your request. Write to* Vintage Books, 457 Madison Avenue, New York, New York 10022.

VINTAGE BELLES-LETTRES

A free catalogue of VINTAGE BOOKS *will be sent at your request. Write to* Vintage Books, 457 Madison Avenue, New York, New York 10022.

VINTAGE FICTION, POETRY, AND PLAYS

A free catalogue of VINTAGE BOOKS *will be sent at your request. Write to* Vintage Books, 457 Madison Avenue, New York, New York 10022.

VINTAGE POLITICAL SCIENCE
AND SOCIAL CRITICISM

A free catalogue of VINTAGE BOOKS *will be sent at your request. Write to* Vintage Books, 457 Madison Avenue, New York, New York 10022.

VINTAGE BIOGRAPHY AND AUTOBIOGRAPHY

A free catalogue of VINTAGE BOOKS *will be sent at your request. Write to* Vintage Books, 457 Madison Avenue, New York, New York 10022.